SPEAKING OF THE SELF

SPEAKING OF THE SELF

Gender, Performance, and Autobiography in South Asia

ANSHU MALHOTRA & SIOBHAN LAMBERT-HURLEY, EDITORS

Duke University Press   Durham and London   2015

© 2015 DUKE UNIVERSITY PRESS
All rights reserved

Designed by Courtney Leigh Baker
Typeset in Minion Pro by Westchester Publishing Services
Library of Congress Cataloging-in-Publication Data
Speaking of the self : gender, performance, and autobiography in South Asia / Anshu Malhotra and Siobhan Lambert-Hurley, editors.
pages cm
Includes bibliographical references and index.
ISBN 978-0-8223-5983-8 (hardcover)
ISBN 978-0-8223-5991-3 (pbk.)
ISBN 978-0-8223-7497-8 (e-book)
1. Autobiography—Women authors. 2. Self—South Asia. 3. Women—South Asia—Biography—History and criticism. I. Malhotra, Anshu. editor. II. Lambert-Hurley, Siobhan, editor.
CT25.S618 2015
920.00954—dc23
2015015085

COVER ART: *Jahanara*, attributed to Lalchand, c. 1631–33. © British Library Board. Add. Or.3129.f.25v.

FOR AVRIL

CONTENTS

Acknowledgments [ix]

INTRODUCTION
Gender, Performance, and Autobiography in South Asia [1]
ANSHU MALHOTRA AND SIOBHAN LAMBERT-HURLEY

PART I. NEGOTIATING AUTOBIOGRAPHY
Between Assertion and Subversion

....

1. A PASSION FOR READING
The Role of Early Twentieth-Century Urdu Novels in the Construction of an Individual Female Identity in 1930s Hyderabad [33]
SYLVIA VATUK

2. PENTIMENTO
The Self beneath the Surface [56]
RITU MENON

3. INTERRUPTED STORIES
The Self-Narratives of Nazr Sajjad Hyder [72]
ASIYA ALAM

4. KAILASHBASHINI DEBI'S JANAIKA GRIHABADHUR DIARY
A Woman "Constructing" Her "Self" in
Nineteenth-Century Bengal? [95]
SHUBHRA RAY

PART II. FORMS AND MODES OF SELF-FASHIONING

5. BETRAYAL, ANGER, AND LOSS
Women Write the Partition in Pakistan [121]
UMA CHAKRAVARTI

6. TAWA'IF AS POET AND PATRON
Rethinking Women's Self-Representation [141]
SHWETA SACHDEVA JHA

7. MASCULINE MODES OF FEMALE SUBJECTIVITY
The Case of Jahanara Begam [165]
AFSHAN BOKHARI

PART III. DESTABILIZING THE NORMATIVE
The Heterogeneous Self

8. PERFORMING A PERSONA
Reading Piro's *Kafis* [205]
ANSHU MALHOTRA

9. THE HEART OF A GOPI
Raihana Tyabji's Bhakti Devotionalism as Self-Representation [230]
SIOBHAN LAMBERT-HURLEY

10. PERFORMING GENDER AND FAITH
IN INDIAN THEATER AUTOBIOGRAPHIES [255]
KATHRYN HANSEN

Select Bibliography [281]   Contributors [301]   Index [305]

ACKNOWLEDGMENTS

This edited collection on gender, performance, and autobiography in South Asia has evolved through ongoing discussions at several workshops and conferences connected with the international research network Women's Autobiography in Islamic Societies (http://www.waiis.org). We are extremely grateful to the Arts and Humanities Research Council in the United Kingdom for funding this project so munificently over two years (2010–11). During that time, the editors organized two academic events that especially facilitated this collection: a panel entitled "Speaking of the Self? Women and Self-Representation in South Asia" at the European Conference on Modern South Asian Studies at Bonn University in Germany in July 2010, and the workshop "Women's Autobiography in Islamic Societies: Context and Construction" at the India International Centre in New Delhi, India, in December 2010. The latter also received the generous support of Delhi University and the Centre for the Study of International Governance at Loughborough University. Our thanks to a number of other scholars who participated in these events, but did not ultimately prepare papers for this volume, for their extremely useful contributions. The Department of Politics, History and International Relations at Loughborough University (where Siobhan Lambert-Hurley has been based) also hosted Anshu Malhotra as a visiting scholar in May 2011, during which time we researched and planned the volume's introduction. A later draft was then presented at the conference "Unveiling the Self: Women's Life Narratives in the Middle East and South Asia," hosted by the inspirational Professor Farzaneh Milani at the University of Virginia at Charlottesville in the United States in October 2012. Special thanks to Evelyn Hiscock for literally holding the baby—four-month-old Tess Lambert-Hurley—while we presented our work on that occasion. Finally, we would like to recognize our editor, Miriam Angress, our anonymous readers, and many others at Duke University Press for their many suggestions, able assistance, and kind support through the publication process.

We wish to recognize that earlier editions of two chapters in this volume were published previously. Anshu Malhotra's "Performing a Persona: Reading Piro's *Kafis*" is a revised and shortened version of "Telling Her Tale? Unravelling a Life in Conflict in *Peero's Ik Sau Saṭh Kāfiaṅ (One Hundred and Sixty Kafis)*," *Indian Economic and Social History Review* 46.4 (2009): 541–78. Siobhan Lambert-Hurley's "The Heart of a Gopi: Raihana Tyabji's Bhakti Devotionalism as Self-Representation" first appeared in *Modern Asian Studies* 48.3 (May 2014): 569–95.

This book is dedicated to our mutual doctoral supervisor, Dr. Avril A. Powell. Many will know her for the passion and generosity that she has brought to her area of study during her long career first at Loughborough University and then at the School of Oriental and African Studies at the University of London. It was during an event in 2008 to celebrate her retirement that we first schemed to work together on this project. The book is thus a tribute to the superlative training and incredible kindness that we received at Avril's hands, as well as our own friendship, which has flourished over the many years since we were graduate students together at SOAS in the mid-1990s.

INTRODUCTION

Gender, Performance, and Autobiography in South Asia

ANSHU MALHOTRA AND SIOBHAN LAMBERT-HURLEY

For many, autobiography is their only path to the past. Autobiography offers a way in which individuals can interweave their personal stories and remembrances with a public account of those major historical events that have social and political meaning within a given society. But how do autobiographies differ in their form, content, and purpose depending on their place or time? Do men and women write differently in given political, social, and cultural circumstances? And how far may the autobiographical genre be understood as a type of performance?

This book's aim is to begin answering these questions by theorizing the relationship between gender, history, and the self. It does so by looking at life histories and beyond to take a more complex approach to the history of women and their conceptualization of the self in South Asia. In particular, it explores how notions of "performance" and "performativity" might be especially useful in opening up the autobiographical genre. For a genre that is inherently confessional—an artifice insofar as it is about self-fashioning—the idea of performance teases out the choices made in terms of forms and narrative strategies employed, and the audiences addressed. In other words, if we look at autobiographical practice as a "self in performance," we begin to appreciate the historical, social, and cultural milieu in which the self was imbricated, and what enabled gendered subjectivity and speech. Linking this discussion then is a new set of questions significant to the theory, methodology, and practice of women's history more broadly: what genres of self-representation do women employ in precolonial, colonial, and postcolonial contexts? Were there common motivations, lingual and stylistic choices, preferences of genres, or issues that took center stage among women? Or do their disparate cultural matrices resist such a reading? And what happens when gender identity itself is not stable?

The chapters themselves examine the writings and experiences of a wide range of "women"—among them, a Mughal princess, a famous courtesan from Hyderabad, an ascetic from a minor sect in Punjab, a Bengali housewife, a singer from Bombay's Bohra community, an Urdu novelist from north India, an educationalist from Hyderabad, several Indian and Pakistani novelists, and even female impersonators in colonial Indian theater. This book thus moves away from the crevices created for women's subjectivity by the nationalist and reformist agendas to focus on historical circumstances and characters that have hitherto not received due attention. The list, however, is naturally selective. In part, it reflects the contributors' own research interests—but, as this is a book that focuses primarily (though not entirely) on the written life, these subjects are, in turn, limited by the requirement of literacy, a marker that remained woefully low in South Asia until very recently and, indeed, still does in certain sectors.[1] Significantly, some wrote in contexts of performative traditions; others performed selves under the aegis of specific sectarian affiliations with particular audiences in mind. Through the study of particular genres, language, and cultural codes, we seek to unravel (wo)men's attempts at engagement with and fabrication of the self that lie embedded in their personal narratives. As such, the chapters reach out to women (and men) from different walks of life, from different places and times, but all explore dimensions of expressing the gendered self through various modes of self-fashioning and representation—from poetry, autobiography, and novels to architecture and religious treatises. Let us explore these variant forms and histories of autobiography to begin.

Autobiography and Its Histories

For there to be a history of autobiography, there needs to be a beginning. And, more often than not, that beginning is Jean-Jacques Rousseau's *Confessions*, completed at the French Enlightenment's height by one of its denizens in 1770. Of course, as theorists recognize, there had been life writing before that time—who could forget St. Augustine's own *Confessions* (c. 400)? Or the memoirists of the Italian Renaissance: Petrarch, Cellini, Cardano. Rousseau though represented something different and specific. As Jill Ker Conway summarizes, he kept the "inner story of the hero's emotional life and conflicts," but "without St. Augustine's sense of sin": "the trajectory of his life moves not toward God but toward worldly fame and success."[2] As the "atomistic individual," Rousseau set a pattern to be reproduced again and again throughout the nineteenth century and beyond. Hence, Roy Pascal, in his influential *Design and Truth in Autobiography*, could write in 1960 that a distinction needed to be made between the "memoir or reminiscence" that came before Rousseau and the "true autobiography" that came after.[3] Even as scholars continue to debate how autobiography may be distinguished from other literary forms—biography, the novel, history— so "definitive" definitions continue to reflect Rousseauian origins.[4] Consider Philippe Lejeune's "pronouncement" in his influential *L'autobiographie en France* (1971): "We call autobiography the retrospective narrative in prose that someone makes of his own existence when he puts the principal accent upon his life, especially upon the story of his own personality."[5] His subsequent work and that of other theorists may have "eroded" his definition, and yet it continues to be reproduced.[6]

But is this narrative of autobiography's origins anything more than a historical construction? A "fallacy," to borrow Dwight Reynolds's provocative descriptor, promulgated by Western literary critics from the mid-twentieth century? Before this time, Reynolds argues, European scholars were often willing to consider autobiography as a literary genre that—comparable to biography and the novel—invited comparison across temporal and geographical boundaries. Then, abruptly, perhaps in response to the end of empire or out of fear for a new cultural relativism, autobiography began to be treated as the "exclusive creation of the modern West."[7] The clearest articulation of this stance came from Georges Gusdorf in a 1956 article: "It would seem that autobiography is not to be found outside our cultural area; one would say that it expresses a concern peculiar to Western man, a concern that had been of good use in his systematic conquest of the universe and that he had communicated to men of other cultures; but those men will thereby have been annexed by a sort of intellectual colonizing to a mentality that was not their own."[8] Thus, as Pascal too recognized, other "civilizations" may have produced autobiographies "in modern times"—a notable example from South Asia being Gandhi's *An Autobiography, or, The Story of My Experiments with Truth* (1925–28)—but, in doing so, they had "taken over" a European practice. Even as Pascal recognized the existence of the Mughal emperor Babur's often intimate sixteenth-century memoir, he proclaimed: "There remains no doubt that autobiography is essentially European."[9] In relation to South Asia, perhaps he was relying on the judgment of S. P. Saksena, who had asserted a few years before in his important book *Indian Autobiographies* (1949) that "self-portrayal" was of "recent origin in this country" and "essentially the result of English education."[10] Even today, modern autobiography continues to be seen in South Asia as a legacy of the colonial period.[11]

These presumptions then, as Reynolds asserts, have continued to underline autobiography studies until far too recently—and perhaps, in some quarters, still continue to do so.[12] The effect is that, where non-Western autobiographies have been addressed, they have often been cast as "exceptions" to the rule—however many of them there may be—and measured against an ideal type seemingly typified by Rousseau. We may consider, as an illustrative example, Marvin Zonis's rather bleak pronouncement on autobiography in the Middle East: "Those works from the region that achieve the 'true potential of the genre' are few in number, limiting the utility of autobiography for illuminating Middle Eastern conceptions of the self."[13] In a South Asian context, Stephen Dale similarly notes of the aforementioned Babur that he "wrote autobiographically but did not produce a fully realized life of the 18th-century type": while he conveys a "vivid and plausible individuality," he is "not often introspective."[14] Inherent to both of these judgments is an assumption that autobiographical revelation—measured against the theoretical bar of definitions evolved almost exclusively in a European context—is a means to understanding cultural notions of self. "The almost inevitable result," according to Reynolds, "is that other, particularly non-Western, forms of autobiography are discounted as immature and underdeveloped, as pale shadows of the 'real' or 'true' autobiography known only in the modern West, and therefore as literary productions clearly not born of the same sense of individual identity."[15] We return to this discussion of individuality and identity in the following section.

What is relevant here is that all these debates have had an important impact on nomenclature. Having read to this point, many readers may question how appropriate it is for this book to use the term *autobiography* in its title when it is so bound up in historical terms with the life narratives of the "atomistic Western male hero."[16] Indeed, many postmodern and postcolonial theorists have discarded the term on the basis that, as Smith and Watson summarize, "its politics is one of exclusion."[17] Not only does it fail to recognize the breadth of autobiographical practice around the globe and at different times—something this book aims to do—but, as we have seen, it also privileges a specifically "Western" notion of self, thus marginalizing other cultural forms of self and self-representation.[18] Smith and Watson, in their authoritative reader on "autobiography," consequently favor the terms *life writing* and *life narrative* on the basis that they are more "inclusive of the heterogeneity of self-referential practices" and thus offer a means by which "a new, globalized history of the field might be imagined."[19] And yet scholars of South Asia have favored other terms: *life history* or, if concerned that the former would indicate some sort of truth-claim, *life story*.[20] The limited scholarship in South Asian languages similarly adopts conjunctive terms denoting one's own life writing or story: the Persianized *khud navisht* in Urdu, *atma jiboni* and *atma carita* in Bengali, or *atma katha* in Hindi, and other vernaculars.[21] Autobiography is sometimes used,[22] but, as Arnold and Blackburn argue in the introduction to their important *Telling Lives in India*, its association with text means that it is understood "to privilege print over orality and to ignore the often fragmentary or allusive nature of many life-historical forms."[23] For similar reasons, other South Asian scholars, particularly of women's history, have preferred the term *personal narratives* on the basis that it includes not just "the more formal, full-length, structured autobiography," but also diaries, letters, interviews, poems, stories, essays, and other "portraits from memory."[24]

Contributors to this book also consider a wide range of source materials, and thus the chapters employ and interrogate many of the terms discussed here. Indeed, it is the aim of this book's part I to uncover the ways in which South Asian women have negotiated the autobiographical genre—so manipulated or disrupted the forms that had come to be accepted as standard or even proper by the late nineteenth century. Sylvia Vatuk, to begin, examines how a Muslim woman from Hyderabad, Zakira Begam (1922–2003), negotiated with available reformist models when writing in a family magazine in the early 1950s about her childhood in the 1920s and 1930s. Specifically, Vatuk argues that Zakira Begam used fictional characters in Urdu novels—some of whom she identified as "worthy of emulation" and others whom she "disdained and resolved to avoid imitating"—as a means of articulating the adult self that she wanted to be. Like Zakira Begam, Nazr Sajjad Hyder (1892–1967), the focus of Asiya Alam's chapter, published her life story in serial form in Urdu journals, but in two phases: first as a diary from 1942, and then, after Partition, as a memoir accompanied by letters from 1950. In Alam's words, the narrative thus represents a "kaleidoscope of genres" that is especially distinguished by its recovery of "everyday life." Ritu Menon, on the other hand, examines the autobiographies of well-known Indian novelist Nayantara Sahgal (b. 1927) as a "monument to a buried self" that deviated from accepted social and gender scripts for women in 1950s India. The final chapter in this section, by Shubhra Ray, takes the case of a relatively lesser-known Bengali autobiography, *Janaika Grihabadhur Diary* [The diary of a housewife], initially composed, as the title indicates, in diary form between 1847 and 1873, though published as a whole only in 1952. Against a background of reformist politics, Ray shows how the author, Kailashbashini Debi (c. 1829–1895), used her diary to express a self that, while aware of cultural constraints, challenged the way in which the "new woman" was being constructed.

Part II of this book also focuses explicitly on the question of form. It does so by examining the different modes employed by South Asian women—whether princesses, prostitutes, or Partition writers—to express a sense of female subjectivity from the Mughal period to the near present. In the first chapter, Uma Chakravarti examines three novels written by Pakistani women on the Partition of the Indian subcontinent in 1947 that she understands to be "deeply autobiographical in sentiment." In particular, she makes the point that the novel form allows the female authors to "speak for a larger feminine self beyond personal experience," thus amalgamating the individual self with history at South Asia's "most intensely violent moment." Shweta Sachdeva Jha's chapter, on the other hand, examines how Maha Laqa Bai "Chanda" (c. 1757–c. 1824), a famous *tawa'if*, or courtesan, at the Hyderabad court, asserted her celebrity through various acts of self-fashioning—from building tanks and mosques to writing Urdu poetry that she then produced and circulated as a collection, or *divan*—which together, she asserts, may be read as "autobiography." Similarly, Afshan Bokhari explores the "dual personas" of the Mughal princess Jahanara Begam (1614–1681) as a daughter of the emperor and a self-proclaimed spiritual authority of the Sufi Qadiriyah order by examining her articulations of self in an autobiographical Sufi treatise, *Risalah-i-Sahibiyah*, and, intriguingly, sacred architecture, specifically mosque design.

The focus of part III is on destabilizing some of the categories that may otherwise be taken for granted when considering delineations of the self, notably religion and even gender itself. But the overlapping nature of this book's three parts is perhaps most evident in that the three chapters located here also reflect very consciously on the question of genre. Anshu Malhotra's essay examines how Piro, a Muslim prostitute in mid-nineteenth-century Punjab, used the poetic form of the *kafi*, a rhyming verse with simple meters, to narrate the "scandal" of her "conversion" to the establishment of a "Sikh" guru Gulabdas, particularly through reference to "fables and parables." Malhotra thus concludes that "emulation, allusion, and allegory" offered means by which individuals in premodern societies could not only order and make sense of their life experiences, but also mold a self. That other narrative forms, like Bhakti devotionalism, could offer a means of self-representation even in the modern period is explored in Siobhan Lambert-Hurley's chapter. Here, the spiritual writings of a nominally Muslim devotee of Krishna, Raihana Tyabji (1901–1975), are explored for their self-representation, Lambert-Hurley ultimately concluding that, in the tradition of Islamic life writing, the "miraculous" narrated should be understood as a "form of autobiography, if only the autobiography of the imagination." The Indian theater autobiographies from late colonial India discussed by Kathryn Hansen are perhaps less controversial in terms of form, but, in narrating the experiences of male actors who performed as women on the stage, they too complicate autobiography's identification with the "male hero." As Hansen concludes, far from being "made mute through subordination," her autobiographical subjects, Jayshankar Sundari (1889–1975) and Fida Husain (1899–2001), spoke in voices that were "often bold, daring, and feisty."

As editors then, we take a conscious decision to reclaim the term *autobiography*—or, perhaps more correctly, its wide-ranging derivative, *autobiographical*—to apply to a diversity of forms, subjects, and expressions from the Mughal period to the regional courts of the eighteenth century, from the high colonial period into Independence. Some may critique this inclusive approach for bringing too much under autobiography's umbrella: for collapsing the differences between genres and thus not drawing a sufficiently clear line between autobiography and its others. But, as Paul de Man asks, is not a major problem with autobiographical theory that it seeks to do just that: "to define and to treat autobiography as if it were a literary genre *among others*."[25] Any historian in the field will know that autobiography in reality, if not theory, is a hybrid and elastic form that absorbs and intersects with other genres.[26] Hence, de Man concludes that autobiography is best characterized not as "a genre or a mode," but instead as "a figure of reading or of understanding that occurs, to some degree, in all texts."[27] Developing this approach, we reject autobiography's politics of exclusion by which South Asian forms may be judged against a Western ideal by assuming an expanded, if simplified, definition replete with global and temporal resonances. What implications this inclusivity has for our understanding of self-representation, gender, and voice is explored further in the following section.

Self-Representation, Gender, and Voice

It is somewhat of an axiom that South Asian societies privilege the social and communal over the individual. Yet what scholars of this region have made clear is that self-representation has been practiced in different ways and for varied purposes throughout South Asian history: from early Pali and Sanskrit narratives of the Buddha through to celebrated autobiographies by Indian nationalists and beyond.[28] In order to construct life histories, historians have employed sometimes disparate and fragmentary sources. A useful example is the piecing together of the mystic poet Kabir's biography/hagiography through the use of "autobiographical" verses available in three different recensions.[29] Anthropologists, on the other hand, have used oral and folk traditions in order to understand the significance of life legends for storytelling.[30] Others, including literary specialists, have examined the specificities of a cultural milieu in an attempt to understand why an autobiographical narrative—like the eighteenth-century Mughal poet Mir Muhammad Taqi's *Zikr-i-Mir* analyzed by C. M. Naim—was constructed in a particular way.[31] As Naim shows, Mir's self-image, personal agendas, and social expectations all played a part in shaping the tone and content of his autobiography. Life histories can thus offer a means, as Arnold and Blackburn assert, of countering an idea of India essentially made up of "castes, religious communities, and kinship networks": where "a sense of selfhood, of personal identity and agency, is muted and subsumed within large social and cultural domains."[32]

At the same time a sharp distinction between the self and society needs to be qualified. What seems to define South Asian autobiography right into the twentieth century and perhaps beyond is the active dialogue between the "life of the individual" and the "lives of others"—or, put more simply, the "self-in-society."[33] It would, however, be wrong to assume that social and cultural norms always act as constraints that stifle individual expression. As Farhat Hasan has demonstrated in his reading of the early seventeenth-century autobiography *Ardhakathanaka* (Half a Tale), of a Srimal Jain merchant Banarsidas, that society was tolerant of and gave space to individual preference, agency, and autonomy. Though Banarsidas often reinforced social norms in reflecting on his life, he still made it a point to record his disagreements and resistances against social and familial values and expectations.[34] Indeed the idea of a "sovereign self," unified and autonomous, is increasingly perceived as a myth in the West where it originated, and where postmodernism and a variety of Black American and feminist critiques have put an end to the idea, instead looking at selves in "relational" terms. Besides the modern state's technologies of power that circumscribe individual lives, there is recognition that cultural norms exert their influence on people.[35] The difference is, as Hansen has argued recently, that in the West the move has been from looking at the self as sovereign to seeing it increasingly in relation to others; whereas in South Asia, instead of seeing the self as "fragmented" with weak individuality, the assertion is that all selves construct themselves in relational terms.[36]

What is perhaps curious about this observation is that it is one more often applied to autobiographies written by women, wherever they may come from. Gender specialists have raised their own set of theoretical questions in relation to autobiography—among them, can women even write about their experiences in a genre shaped by misogynistic conventions that "denigrate the feminine"?[37] Others have focused on how women's autobiographies may be distinguished from those of men in terms of structure and content, offering what Smith and Watson summarize as a "difference" theory of women's autobiography.[38] Accordingly, women's autobiographies are said to be more personal than political, focusing on the relationships of the domestic realm, rather than charting the accomplishments of a public life or career. They are also characterized as more fragmentary than linear, rejecting the coherent construction of self that distinguished the Rousseauian model in favor of a more disjointed telling of one's past. Women's narratives, we are told, are characterized by "understatements, avoidance of the first person point of view, rare mention of personal accomplishments and disguised statements of personal power."[39] What this adds up to, as suggested already, is a narrative that is more collective than individual: less about the carefully crafted public self and more about the self-in-society. In seeking to understand why, the suggestion is that women, like minorities and those in colonized societies, have not had the "privilege" of thinking of themselves as individuals in the way that a "white man" has the "luxury of forgetting his skin color and sex."[40] When women's writing does not follow the given "feminine" script, we also tend to see their self-construction as "masculine"—in other words, the reader's expectations of a text color its reception. Haimabati Sen, in Indrani Sen's reading of her autobiography, casts herself in a "male-type" role, in her detached tone, rational and scientific attitude, and eye for empirical detail, and also presumably because she shares the particulars of her professional life of a medical practitioner.[41]

In this book Vatuk takes up this question to understand the specificities of autobiography when written by women, emphasizing that when women speak, they often do so not only for themselves, but also for women generally, a point further examined below. It may be briefly noted that Sharmila Rege speaks of collective representation of pain and suffering in the context of dalit women's autobiographies, calling them "testimonios," witnesses to a community's oppression (the term *testimonio* emerged in the context of Latin American individuals' narratives of the exploitation of the indigenous communities). Acutely aware that the representation of pain should not become a spectacle, Rege emphasizes the significance of the collective voice as against what she refers to as bourgeois individualism, exploring the possibilities of an emancipatory dalit feminism in politics and pedagogical structures.[42] The politics of self-representation is thus, inevitably, about power. Appropriately then, what scholarship on South Asia specifically has shown is the importance of autobiography as a genre to marginalized groups such as women, religious converts, and dalits as a means to "talk back."[43]

An expression of a collective voice can be discerned in the manner in which biographies can be autobiographical; that is, sometimes an imperceptible fusion or extension of the self and the other can take place in the writing of the auto/biography. The link between biography and history, on the other hand, is a well-established one, for instance in the Islamic world, where biography, as elsewhere, is structured by history. As Judith Tucker has argued about Arab biographers, those individuals were always located within time, and so individual life served to illuminate its age.[44] In colonial India, as men took to writing "autobiographies," they seldom wrote of their personal, intimate lives. This could be because the idea of a private life was not fully formed,[45] or because a self was not seen worthy to be written about, or because it was considered too egoistical to focus on the self (the trope of self-abnegation apparently not being exclusive to women though they may resort to it more frequently).[46] And so men wrote of their times, perceived to be out of joint. Documenting earlier times in a period of rapid mutations became a motivation to write, discussed by Venkatachalapathy through showing the persistent usage of the trope of "those days/these days," in the redolent Tamil expression *antha kulam/intha kulam*.[47] However, the biographical as a ruse for the autobiographical, or the autobiographical incorporating the biographical, seems more often deployed by women in many parts of the world.[48]

Marilyn Booth, studying biography and gender politics in a modernizing Egypt of the late nineteenth century, comments on the manner in which women used and changed the exemplary biography tradition of the Islamic world. Speaking particularly of the "obituary biography," she shows how women inserted the autobiographical in its composition, and so the authorial "I" represented both an individual and a collective identity.[49] As Booth put it, a text cannot be read in isolation from its "pre-texts" and "con-texts," pointing to what may prompt and promote women's autobiographical initiative. A similar point is made by Vijaya Ramaswamy in her reading of the multiple narratives of Neelambakai Ammaiyar's life, a woman deeply involved in the promotion of Tamil language in the early twentieth-century Madras. It is in Ammaiyar's biographical sketches of women—white feminists as well as those from the Tamil society—that Ramaswamy finds a distinctly autobiographical "sub-text."[50]

In a subtle mixing of genres, Bharati Ray has recently written an auto/biography of five generations of women in her family, starting from her maternal great-grandmother, continuing through her grandmother and mother, to her, and mentioning her daughters.[51] Ray, self-consciously feminist in her endeavor, both follows certain norms, for instance in omitting intimate details of the women's lives, including her own, and breaks new ground. The latter is visible in the pride she displays in her extraordinary achievements in public and professional life. One can even argue that the first three generations act as a foil to brighten her illustrious career, their biographies laying the ground for her autobiography. Mythily Sivaraman's effort to piece together the life of her maternal grandmother, Subbalakshmi, also grew out of her own feminist stirrings.[52] Constructing the fragile life of Subbalakshmi (she appears so both in her projected persona, and in the scanty and tenuous contents of her archive, "the blue tin trunk") was possible through careful preservation of its contents by her daughter and Mythily's mother, Pankajam.[53] The collective and determined enterprise to write Subbalakshmi's story is obvious. Chakravarti, in this book, as noted earlier, uses three Pakistani women's novels on the Partition of India to elaborate on the multiple conjunctions in the lives of the women of the Indian subcontinent. Chakravarti not only shows how the novels were autobiographical but also weaves into her essay her own autobiographical interest in histories of violence and their impact on women's everyday lives. From her essay one can in fact surmise that the novelists' voice was the cathartic release of the congealed emotions of a generation or more of women affected by that tragedy.

But, to return to the question of autobiographical voice, can South Asian women actually "talk back"? Can they even speak? Gayatri Spivak famously asserted that the South Asian woman, so completely strangled by patriarchal modes of thought and discussion, had no real voice.[54] Certainly it has proved difficult for scholars to get at women's voices in light of the premium placed in South Asian culture on keeping women away from public gaze. These challenges have encouraged some anthropologists to undertake the project of deciphering women's songs, poetry, and folktales, while others have employed ethnographic methods to extract life stories in oral form.[55] Historians, on the other hand, have remained more focused on text, seeking to uncover written autobiographical narratives—a body of materials that is necessarily restricted by literacy and education, but still is perhaps not as limited as was once thought.[56] Hence, as probably indicated already, it is an underlying assumption of this collection that the challenges involved in recovering women's voice should not indicate a lack of voice. On the contrary, if women had the temerity to negotiate with their own cultures in order to speak, so do we have a duty, as scholars, to uncover and understand the cultural context in which their speech was created. As the essays in this collection demonstrate, women's voices and thus their self-representation may be convoluted, elusive, paradoxical, and metaphorical—or, to borrow the lovely word applied by Booth to Egyptian women's autobiographical writings, "diaphanous"[57]—*but they are still there*. South Asian women have always found ways, as we assert with our title, of speaking of the self.

A question remains, though, of the self of which they speak: is it necessarily a gendered self? Did the authors discussed here think of themselves as "women writers" at all? The last question is especially pertinent being that the authors discussed in Hansen's chapter are not, in fact, biologically women at all, even though they were known by female personas. In this context, we may question our role as editors in grouping these texts together: are we simply perpetuating the assumptions of nineteenth-century observers who categorized such writings as "women's texts"? Clearly there is not one answer here: some of the authors discussed in this collection thought of themselves consciously as women writing, while others were more aware of other roles and identities. And, whatever their intention in writing, the audiences by which they were read may have interpreted them as something different, particularly within the context of reformist and nationalist agendas. Nevertheless, we would assert that, even where these authors were not necessarily *writing* as women, they were—with the partial exception of Hansen's actors—still *living* as women, and thus the constraints of life within a specifically South Asian patriarchal society put constraints on their ways of writing as well, even if these choices were not conscious. Hence, in the end, we come to the conclusion that the authors discussed in this collection do fit together in that they all speak of a gendered self that is definably South Asian. The use of *gender*, rather than *women*, in the book's title is thus purposeful in that it reflects these underlying assumptions, while also acting as a strategy against the marginalization of women's history within the academy.

Still, it is fundamental to feminist writing to grant women agency, even as they may employ tropes of modesty in their autobiographical writings that deny their own importance or autonomy. In writing about autobiographies constructed within the long tradition of Islamic life stories, Barbara Metcalf makes the point that authors employ a "convention of passivity" according to which nothing that happens to them—including the very act of writing itself—is attributable to their own initiative.[58] A parallel may be drawn here with many of the writings discussed in this collection in that they too are, to quote Vatuk's analysis, "particularly deferential and apologetic"—and thus perhaps even definably "feminine" within their cultural context, though deference could be, as noted, formulaic and conventional. But, as in Metcalf's case, modesty should not be confused with a lack of agency, nor self-effacement with a lack of self. Rather, Smith and Watson make the point that it is the very way in which people operate *within* constraints—changing existing narratives or "writing back" to scripted cultural stories—that can suggest "a strategy for *gaining agency*."[59] Hence, Margot Badran goes so far as to claim that, for the Egyptian nationalist and feminist Huda Shaarawi (1879–1947), the very act of writing a memoir—of revealing her "private life, family life, inner feelings and thoughts" in a society in which these matters were "sacrosanct"—was a "feminist act."[60] Similarly, Farzaneh Milani interprets the "literary misfit" of women's autobiographical writing in Iran as the "ultimate form of unveiling"—and thus, in Smith and Watson's understanding, the very definition of agency in that it is disruptive to "existing social and political formations."[61] Thus we wish to understand agency as more than resistance to patriarchal formations. While employing strategies and tactics to maneuver patriarchies is significant, it is also important to recognize how choices are made within the constraints placed on individual lives by cultures they are situated in. Women's agency therefore is polysemic, and we have to uncover ways of locating and focusing on it.[62] One of the ways in which agency can be grasped is to understand the heterogeneity of the self; that is, one can be a different person at separate times, underlining the salience of a performing self, a concept we explore in the next section.

Gender, Performance, and Memory

Within the folktale tradition in India, scholars have drawn attention to a genre they refer to as "women's tales," insofar as women are its primary raconteurs and characters.[63] Categorizing these stories as those that revolve around the "innocent persecuted heroine," Stuart Blackburn sees them as narrating life histories where the template of the denouement is about truth telling—when the suffering heroine is finally restored to her rightful place in family/society.[64] This occurs mostly when amnesia dissolves and memory returns. Such tales have a wide currency and are popular all over India.[65] Although not autobiographical, being cultural stories of generic characters, they throw up questions that are central to some of the issues about life writing that are discussed in this section. These relate to questions of memory—remembering, forgetting, and misremembering; and of the voice of the marginalized, mostly women of disparate classes and statuses—how do those who do not normally have a voice in society speak? Do they follow coded patterns of self-revelation, as in women's tales above, or do they invent selves in new and unexpected ways? Also noteworthy is that storytelling (autobiographical narration included) is performative, requiring a performer and an audience, every fresh rendition of a tale, whether "on stage or page" different from any already performed or yet to be performed.[66]

The term *performance* is used in this introduction for the various semantic and conceptual openings it makes for us. Though not relating to the actual performances of life narratives in theater, it is to the metaphorical and figurative aspects of life writing—that can be no less theatrical—that we refer.[67] The autobiographical "text" is never a transparent rendering of a life, nor is it a straightforward documentation of it. Deeply implicated in the politics of remembering and what is to be remembered, memory and what is to be memorialized, the autobiographical is intrinsically interpretive and performative. The subjectivity that the life writer wishes to create in the narration of a life is performative, both in the process of selection employed to create the text, and in the audience for whom it is practiced, which may include the self. The distancing between the self as a subject and an object—in Paul de Man's words that between the author "of" the text and the author "in" the text, a necessary aspect of the autobiographical practice—allows the self to be gazed at as in a drama.[68] De Man speaks of prosopopeia as the trope of autobiography, drawing attention to the author's simultaneous presence and absence in the text.[69] As Sidonie Smith writes, "Whatever that occasion or that audience, the autobiographical speaker becomes the performative subject."[70] In other words, self-referential materials are produced to relate "a" story about the self, not "the" story: a degree of design and its particular articulation is inherent in the genre. Naim's reading of Mir's autobiography, referred to above, uncovers intentionality as an aspect of autobiographical writing. Mir wished to present himself as a person of Saiyyad lineage and hoped to elevate his father to the level of a Sufi master.[71] Hansen's masterly analysis of four Parsi theater actors and playwrights, two of the actors discussed in this book, shows their investment in creating particular self-representations. Jayshankar Sundari's feminine stage persona and his desire to present himself as a modern bourgeois subject seeking ideal heteronormative companionate marriage especially stands out, even as he attempts to smoothe the conflict over his ambivalent gendered self and sexuality.[72]

The autobiographical narrative may be invested in perpetuating a specific image or a particular understanding of the self, among other rhetorical uses of such practice, for consumption among intimates or a larger public. The intersubjectivity of such a narration—the relation between the narrator and the assumed audience—accounts for the assumption of a specific subjectivity, in a particular context, at a given time. If autobiographical practice is not transparent—akin to a mirror that refracts rather than reflects—then the issue of its reception becomes salient. Not only may the narrator imagine a specific audience when authoring an autobiographical tale; the putative audience is likely to impact and shape the telling itself—its manner, tone, or form. Sensitive issues related to the impact of self-revelation on the self and others are tied up with this question.[73] Vatuk, in her reading of the memoir of Zakira Begam written in the 1950s, stresses this author-audience interaction. The memoir she reads began its life as a girls' journal circulated within the immediate family circle, her *khandan*, pushing its author to adopt certain specific modes of self-presentation, among them self-deprecation, as noted earlier.[74] However, despite this conventional modesty suitable to her gender, Zakira did go on to write at length about herself, acting out the painful memories of her upbringing whose onerous burden she wished her family to be acquainted with. Thus in two ways—in her deferential tone and in her recall of a wronged childhood—the family audience influenced her writing. At another level, Zakira's later commentary on her text to the researcher, a parallel retelling, allowed her to perform her life all over again, but for a different audience, and perhaps to different effect.

We may underscore this point about the performativity of the autobiographical oeuvre implicated in perpetuating specific agendas, particularly through the essays on the premodern period in this book. As noted, Bokhari, in writing of the unmarried Mughal princess Jahanara, uses both her Sufi treatise and her munificent architectural patronage to show how the princess produced her "dual persona." She was simultaneously an imperial patron and a pious Sufi. In stretching the given norms of class and gender behavior within the Timurid imperial codes, Jahanara endeavored, as she performed, to give expression to herself and identity. Her stage was the Mughal imperium, where she set out to "light the lamp" of her piety, evocatively described by Bokhari. Sachdeva Jha also reads the multiple "autobiographical acts" of the courtesan Maha Laqa Bai Chanda—as a patron, a poet, and a builder—to show how she (re)invented herself. As a sophisticated performer of poetic *mujra* as of selfhood, Chanda insinuated herself in the power politics of the rich courtly world of Hyderabad in the late eighteenth and early nineteenth centuries. Sachdeva Jha uses deconstruction theory to make the important point that the autobiographical utterance resides in the act of reading/interpreting, including various self-representational acts. Similarly, Malhotra in her essay on the Muslim prostitute Piro, who went to live in a Sikh guru's establishment, enunciates the justificatory rhetoric of a self-fashioned saga. This autobiographical fragment was what may be called a "conversion narrative," where events move toward "the" transformative moment, and most things of note are referenced to its valence. In this narrative Piro gave no clue to the motive for her unusual step but used its theatrical mode to perform piety, loyalty, and allegiance to her new sect and its guru, even as she manoeuvred for acceptability within it.

Self-referential narratives, however, are not performative only in terms of the conscious or unconscious messages or images they carry. All autobiographical practice is based on memory, inherently selective and interpretive, and therefore performative in what/how it congeals or enacts, conceals, and reveals. Moreover, cultural codes often determine who remembers and what is remembered. Peter Burke has written of the "schema" that is frequently present in the organization of community and individual memories.[75] Indeed, even dreams people dream may be choreographed to cultural demands and expectations,[76] or form an important aspect of people's lives, pushing them in given directions.[77] The making of cultural heroes or villains, the saintly, the godly, and the demonic, are embedded within this complex matrix of remembrances and memory. David Shulman, for instance, speaks of the dominance of the astrological or predictive forms of writing heroic tales in India, the unfolding of the saga as one already foretold, in a culture that believed that heroes are born for godly purposes and follow life patterns laid out for them.[78] Similarly one may draw attention to the genealogical and bardic tradition of remembering in India, the genealogists, bards, and astrologers crucial to the task of remembering and performing their feats of memory or prediction on public platforms.[79]

The mythic as a model of remembering and organizing memories—both communal and individual—is particularly potent in South Asia. We may model our lives on values passed through characters of mythologies, and so reenact them, or we may mythologize people we revere. Sometimes we may live double lives, an exterior ordinary self, forming a carapace that shields an interior magical or a moral one. The topos of an exterior/interior duality was a common one in Indian Bhakti and Sufi literatures. Externals, including bodily comportment and rituals, were seen as unnecessary worldly accoutrements, while one may find God in the inner recesses of a being—in the heart/liver (*ur, hridya, man, jigar*) continuum.[80] This interiority must be seen as different from the Western post-Enlightenment psychological development of bourgeois subjectivity, which stressed inner character development.[81] However, in the case of Raihana Tyabji studied here by Lambert-Hurley, the inner world may have been constructed in both senses: as an interior pure/ethical self, and one where a person inhabited her private world. Raihana, a Sulaymani Bohra Muslim, in her mystical *The Heart of a Gopi*, portrayed her innermost being as that of a "gopi" Sharmila. While outwardly living the life of a Muslim and a staunch Gandhian, it was in the mold of the Vaishnava Krishna Bhakti model of a gopi's erotic love of Krishna that Raihana fashioned herself. In other words, in her "inner" life she performed a role that Indian culture was familiar with. The more difficult question to answer in Raihana's case is whether she affected this character because her cultural memory gave her a model to follow or because expressing her emotions and sexuality in these terms made it more acceptable?

On the other hand, Fida Husain, a stalwart of the Parsi theater, who throughout his career staged lives of Hindu gods and saints, seemed to blur the boundaries between his performative self and his constructed yogic one. Can one speculate that the purity demanded of him to perform saintly characters, particularly the fifteenth-century Gujarati saint Narsi Mehta, translated into Husain cleansing his somatic being? Hansen draws attention to his ambiguity about his Muslim background, as she does to his strict "oral and anal" regimentation, an ingredient of his disciplined self-construction. In her essay Malhotra too shows the willful impersonation of the abducted Sita by the Muslim Piro, making her guru assume the role of Rama rescuing her from her Muslim (demonic) captors. In these narratives of religious crossovers and performed personas, mythological memory becomes the central node around which a self is fabricated.

Another way of seeing these above-discussed case studies relates to the Indic tradition that emphasizes right remembering as essential to be fully integrated with oneself. A. K. Ramanujan indicates the significance of the remembrancer in many Indian literatures, a trigger for the flow of memory, as the ring in the famous tale of Shakuntala. He also makes the point that amnesia and misremembering in this cosmos lead to alienation from the self and its intimates.[82] Although Ramanujan does not discuss the issue of a specific memory as the "right" one, or the only possible one of an event, it is important to underscore that the autobiographic impulse is often imbricated in ensuring the "right" projection of the self, the issue of image discussed above. To put it another way, the image one may be performing is the one that at some level we may feel most integrated with or we may feel is an integral part of who we are. This may well have been the case with Raihana, Husain, and Piro. Such an understanding leaves open the possibility of multiple identities/selves we carry and nurture, shattering the idea of a unified, coherent self. However, at the same time it creates the space to underscore that we may strongly relate to a certain aspect of ourselves at a given time.

Memory, as the use of oral sources has alerted historians, is notoriously unstable, sometimes telescoping time, and at others coagulating events in a given format.[83] Personal narratives have to be read with this caveat. The acts of remembrance that create autobiographical narratives are selective, as noted above, and also variable over time. Asiya Alam's chapter in this book brings out this shifting, whimsical quality of memory and remembrance through showing the different narrations of her life by Nazr Sajjad Hyder over a substantial period of her life. Alam discusses her diary (*roz namcha*) that appeared in a serialized format in the journal *Tahzib-e Niswan*; her serialized account of past days (*ayyam-i-guzashta*) in the journal *Ismat*; her letters that accompanied many of her *Ismat* entries; and finally her daughter Qurratulain Hyder's collection of her mother's autobiographical narrations in a book (*Guzashta Barson ki Baraf*), heavily edited and prefaced with her own literary and contemporary feminist concerns. The mutable nature of Nazr's articulation, as Alam shows, was impelled by her changing circumstances and experiences, both personal and political. Her later accounts that commemorated familial life were her personal way of countering the fissures of Partition and its discontinuities. Beside Alam's, some other essays in this book are also sensitive to the variable and multiple versions of an individual story. Scholars have commented on the role of editors and other mediators who help reproduce earlier autobiographical texts (a number of women's nineteenth-century texts in India were made available to the public in the twentieth century through such intervention) and that they have their own reasons to do so.[84] It is like the use of oral sources by scholars, these sources become available necessarily mediated through them. The dialogic quality of such narratives needs to be recognized, not the erasure of the mediator, or a search for a (false) "authenticity" of a text, as Alessandro Portelli has underscored by insisting on seeing the "hybridized" and "mongrelized" quality of such discourses.[85] That memory is socially produced, both individual and collective, needs to be understood, even as we focus on individual life in that of a community.[86]

Inner Lives and Performative Selves

The modern notion of our "inner" psychological individual selves, of who we "really" are, also becomes important as we move into more contemporary times. This develops in tandem with the older idea of character building and introspection, of utilizing difficulties and obstacles in life to "learn lessons" in order to strengthen our inner beings. In the West this latter idea is as old as Augustine's *Confessions*, when his stealing of pears from a neighbor's orchard made him learn a lesson for life.[87] In the early modern period it was Montaigne's retreat to his *arriereboutique*, "the back room of his mind," where he led his readers, that the invention of our psychological beings might be pegged, though its full realization perhaps occurred two centuries or more later, especially with Freud.[88] Interestingly, the early modern in Europe was a period marked by a struggle between being "sincere," attributed to Reformation's insistence on confronting one's God, and "prudence," according to the performative and dissimulating needs of courtly life captured in Baldassare Castiglione's *The Courtier*.[89] However, the conflict between sincerity and artifice, that is, between the revelation of the "inner-most" self and particular projections of the self, lies at the heart of the autobiographical practice and reception everywhere.

In the Indian context, colonialism and its disciplining of Indian habits, be they related to time or customs, may be compared to dissimulation for those Indians who necessarily entered the public sphere. This was the polluting world of interacting with the colonial state, the world of *chakri*, to atone for which many urban Bengalis trooped to the simple, and presumably cleansing, discourses of the guru Ramakrishna.[90] Did such daily transactions and transgressions—the double life of an inner and outer world—make a sense of the self more keen? It certainly led to a feeling of being witness to a unique phase of history, as noted earlier.[91] Participation in the national movement and the accompanying imprisonment at the hands of the colonial power afforded many Indian men, including Gandhi and Nehru, with the opportunity for self-reflection, as it did for building steely characters.[92]

What can be said about the inner selves of the modernizing Indian women? Partha Chatterjee sees change between the first woman autobiographer of Bengal, Rassundari Debi (1809–1900), who assigned Providence an important role in her acquiring the magical ability to read, and Prasannamayi Debi (1857–1939), who came to distinguish between an "inner" and an "outer" world.[93] Whereas Chatterjee speaks of the inner/outer distinction in the context of the patriarchal nationalist program that sought sovereignty over the former domain by taming women, the analogy may be stretched to include the inner life of an individual subject as an autonomous self. Chatterjee's analysis, which indicates a seamless "resolution" of "women's question" as one left the cogitations of the early and mid-nineteenth century behind, has been critiqued by feminist historians, who have stressed the conflict in the domestic domain, emphasizing the impossibility of resolution therein.[94] They have nevertheless shown the obsessive focus on issues of the everyday, domesticity, and making women the bearers of customs and rituals. It is in this locus of the domestic as a conflicted zone, and in the contradictory demands that a modernizing patriarchy made of women, that one may find women's nascent voice articulating a self.

The moot question however remains whether women, adjusting lives to roles men laid out for them, claimed a relatively sovereign inner self. Did they too have a core self that was noncolonized by men? This question is likely to yield varying answers as embattled women juggled a known way of life with often persistent efforts of their husbands to transform them into their mold of modernity, or even when they became willing helpmates in this transformation. For some women the existence of their older devotional worlds, as that of Vaishnava Bhakti for Rassundari, left aspects of their lives where neither the colonial state nor their own men could intrude.[95] Tanika Sarkar, for example, points out the fleeting appearance of Rassundari's husband in her autobiography. For others, the knowledge of being colonized by their men, or that their ability to think for themselves was considered a rebellion—a "treason against men"—as with Kashibai Kanitkar, does indicate interior spaces all their own.[96] But few had the resources or the capability to make their rebellious lives true to their inner calling, and when they did, its consequences were perilous and isolating, as with Pandita Ramabai.[97] However, in Shubhra Ray's reading of the diary of Kailashbashini Debi, Kailashbashini emerges as someone inherently aware of herself being special. For Ray, Kailashbashini's diary does not fit into Chatterjee's reading of women who learned to adhere to the rituals of domesticity of the Bengali inner world. It was also not amenable to being read as a memoir that merely captured the changing social world of the *bhadralok*, the sociological interest in Bengali customs and rituals of the later editors of these writings. In her pleasure of the extraordinary, of travel, of being cared for by her husband, Kailashbashini displayed her sense of the self, at a time when the norms of what such a memoir was expected to be were still not worked out.

Ritu Menon, the biographer of Nayantara Sahgal—a niece of Nehru and the daughter of Vijaylakshmi Pandit—reads two of her autobiographical works to reflect on this conflict between the inner and the projected self. In many ways Sahgal's first autobiographical work, *Prison and Chocolate Cake* (1954), may be compared to the kinds of memoirs men wrote—their lives a reference point from where to observe momentous changes taking place around them, particularly relating to colonialism and nationalism.[98] Sahgal too, in this work offered a "ringside" view of history, recollecting her connections to the foremost families of modern India. However, in her second autobiographical work, *From Fear Set Free* (1962), Menon sees the conflict between her inner self, straining to emerge, and the outward "women's script" of marriage and domesticity, suppressing the claims of the inner being. In Sahgal's inability to integrate the inner with the external, Menon sees Sahgal's "polite exercise" in writing "a monument to a buried self." We are undoubtedly at a postmodern moment of splintered and multiple selves, assigned and performing different roles. However, the ray of optimism for Menon comes from the fact that Sahgal persisted in writing, fiction and nonfiction, doggedly refusing to bury the burgeoning self.

The issue of performativity is significant also from the point of view of studying the "ego documents" of those who literally perform for a livelihood/ in a profession. The question of how to decipher what they perform in their various narratives, however, is more complex. In her essay, referred to earlier, Hansen centrally broaches the issue of gender impersonation when speaking of Sundari's and Husain's autobiographies, both of whom enacted women characters at certain times in their careers. Judith Butler's concept of "gender performativity," in the sense in which a subject is decided *by* gender, and not by a willful taking *on* of gender, points to the regulatory regimes that produce normative, heterosexual behavior.[99] The destabilizing of given gender norms in staged masquerades illuminates the power of *verfremdungseffekt*—"making the familiar strange so that we can understand it as neither natural, nor inevitable, and therefore something that can be challenged and changed."[100] For us what Butler's discussion on reiterative regulatory regimes does is to focus on the issue of how the marginalized may rupture the coherence of their culturally defined roles. Here we wish to reiterate how through autobiographical practice the marginalized assume "center stage," overwriting the normative codes of behavior. The term *overwriting* is developed to emphasize the act of destabilizing the normative, and reinscribing social rules. Literally actors, what Husain, but especially Sundari, did by staging parodies of gendered identities was to undermine the definitiveness of such identities, "denaturalizing" the ostensible natural, "the always and the already."[101] In the role model that Sundari became for women, and in the passion that some men nurtured for "her," Sundari allowed for the changeableness of our apparently enduring selves. The act of performing could thus transcend the limits of the proscenium, opening varied potentialities of the self. Smith, while discussing Butler and the manner in which agency may be garnered, notes that for Butler, the performance of a unified, coherent self is bound to be a failure because the "autobiographical subject is amnesiac, incoherent, heterogeneous, interactive."[102] In the ruptures between who we are, and what we are expected to be, lies the potential for grasping an agential self.

The theatrical metaphor of "staging" identities remains salient when considering some other performers. We wish to underline that those in performing professions are liable to be more sensitive than others to the multiplicities of identities within us, thus more successful in fabricating selves that undermine given norms while configuring new roles. Many of our autobiographers in this book were linked to performing professions. Maha Laqa Bai as discussed by Sachdeva Jha, or Piro of Malhotra's essay were courtesans. Lambert-Hurley shows Raihana as an adept singer, performing and recording her songs. Princess Jahanara, Bokhari's muse, was indubitably used to performing on an imperial stage. At a general level what these various performers had was the skill to articulate their personas. This skill may or may not have nullified the marginality of their specific circumstances. However, what it did give them was the ability to reimagine and re-present themselves in varied ways. Their extraordinary situation—liminality in social intercourse with the skilled ability for vocalizing selves—made them inimitable performers of their own identities.

One last issue needs to be taken up when we speak of the performing self/selves. How do we relate the autobiographical to truth claims? Multitudinous selves and the contingent nature of performances, bound to questions of space and temporality, undoubtedly dilute the relationship between the two. Philippe Lejeune in his "autobiographical pact" speaks about the contract between the author and the reader, "a contract of identity sealed by a proper name," an assurance, in other words, that a person exists in history.[103] But is that enough to render the autobiographical "truthful"? The relationship between fiction and the autobiographical nonfiction is notoriously unsteady, and the demand of authenticity cannot be met by autobiographical practice steeped in performativity. Both the scholars and the practitioners of the autobiography and the memoir are conscious of the thin line separating fiction from an autobiographical work. While Milani, the scholar of Iranian women's autobiographies, insists on a fundamental distinction between the two—no other genre of literature claims this correspondence between the writing and the writer, she notes—she nonetheless concedes that the self at the center of all autobiographical narratives is a fictive structure. "Self-representation is an extension of fantasy rather than a platform of Truth," she writes.[104] Paul de Man, on the other hand, argues that the distinction between autobiography and fiction is "undecidable," looking at the autobiographical discourse as one conflicted between mortality and restoration, giving a face and "defacement."[105]

Are we then to negate any association of "truth" and the autobiographical? Conway, while introducing black slave narratives, notes that many were produced under fictitious names and with the help, and sometimes tweaking, of their white facilitators.[106] Did such editorial or pseudonymous interventions take away the "truth" of unbearable suffering, or that of the triumph of the will? A similar question may be posed in relation to many dalit autobiographical accounts in India. But it is just not pain, suffering, and humiliation that are at the core of the issue, we may be "artful" or "truthful," in equal or awry measure, about other facets of our life. While we may all be performers—whether assiduously working toward a self-fashioning or unwittingly projecting a personality—we are in the business of representing ourselves the way we can, or wish to. This may not be "the" truth, but certainly it is "our" truth, or at least some version of it, unless we deliberately choose to misrepresent. And our version of the truth, of course, may be fiction to you, unless we can use a remembrancer to set off the flow of right memory, or concoct a potion to induce amnesia in you . . .

IN THIS WIDE-RANGING INTRODUCTION we have tried to grapple with contemporary global understandings of autobiography, and the manner in which personal self-representational narratives have been a part of South Asian culture. We have attempted to recuperate the term *autobiography* for the varied ways in which a self is represented, fashioned, and articulated. Aware of the changes that modernity may have introduced to life writing as a textual practice, we have used autobiography for a range of autobiographical materials and ego documents. Equally we have sought to focus on how women's autobiographical oeuvre may be different or similar to that of men in South Asia. Our emphasis on a relational self as against the idea of an autonomous sovereign self is important in the context of men as of women, though we have emphasized women's greater recourse to it, as to self-deprecatory intonation. Women's auto/biographical practice has shown their investment in relational selves, though there will always be many exceptions, particularly as we move toward the contemporary times. However, we have wished to iterate that women through different times spoke for themselves, though this could come through in coded or allegorical expression or in more individualistic, self-reflexive ways. We have also hoped to show the performative nature of storytelling, whether presented as a life story or served in poetic, or novelistic, fictional mode. The nature of memory and its selective use, so intrinsically a part of the autobiographical practice, make it a genre of design and fabrication, and so of performance. Nevertheless, we do not wish to sever it from truth claims, for both the nature of truth, illusive and elusive, and of life writing is complex, as it is conflicted. That the oeuvre of autobiography has lent voice to the marginalized underlines the need to take it with the seriousness it deserves. We hope the essays that follow will highlight the autobiographical as a genre both personal and political, illuminating people and their times.

NOTES

1. According to the 2011 census, India boasts a functional literacy rate of 74.04 percent, up from just 12 percent at Independence in 1947. This figure, however, hides gender, regional, and social disparities. Female literacy remains lower at 65.46 percent, though this represents a marked increase from just 18.4 percent in 1971 and 0.9 percent in 1901. "Census of India," accessed January 8, 2013, http://www.censusindia.gov.in/; *Towards Equality: Report of the Committee on the Status of Women in India* (Delhi: Ministry of Education and Social Welfare, 1974), 94.
2. Jill Ker Conway, *When Memory Speaks: Exploring the Art of Autobiography* (New York: Vintage, 1998), 8.
3. Roy Pascal, *Design and Truth in Autobiography* (Cambridge, MA: Harvard University Press, 1960), 5, 26–31.
4. Summarizing these debates is Sidonie Smith and Julia Watson's *Reading Autobiography: A Guide for Interpreting Life Narratives*, 2nd ed. (Minneapolis: University of Minnesota Press, 2010), chap. 1.
5. Philippe Lejeune, *L'autobiographie en France* (Paris: Colin, 1971), 14. This translation is from *The Culture of Autobiography: Constructions of Self-Representation*, ed. Robert Folkenflik (Stanford, CA: Stanford University Press, 1993), 13.
6. Lejeune, *L'autobiographie*, 14. For another example, see Smith and Watson, *Reading Autobiography*, 1.
7. Dwight F. Reynolds, ed., *Interpreting the Self: Autobiography in the Arabic Literary Tradition* (Berkeley: University of California Press, 2001), 17.
8. Georges Gusdorf, "Conditions and Limits of Autobiography," in *Autobiography: Essays Theoretical and Critical*, ed. and trans. James Olney (Princeton, NJ: Princeton University Press, 1980), 29.
9. Pascal, *Design*, 22.
10. S. P. Saksena, *Indian Autobiographies* (Calcutta: Oxford University Press, 1949), v, vii.
11. A. R. Venkatachalapathy, "Making a Modern Self in Colonial Tamil Nadu," in *Biography as History: Indian Perspectives*, ed. Vijaya Ramaswamy and Yogesh Sharma (Hyderabad: Orient Blackswan, 2009), 30–52.
12. Reynolds, *Interpreting*, 19.
13. Marvin Zonis, "Autobiography and Biography in the Middle East: A Plea for Psychopolitical Studies," in *Middle Eastern Lives: The Practices of Biography and Self-Narrative*, ed. Martin Kramer (Syracuse, NY: Syracuse University Press, 1991), 61.
14. Stephen Frederic Dale, "Steppe Humanism: The Autobiographical Writings of Zahir al-Din Muhammad Babur, 1483–1530," *International Journal of Middle East Studies* 22 (1990): 39.

15 Reynolds, *Interpreting*, 19.
16 Conway, *When Memory Speaks*, 3.
17 Smith and Watson, *Reading Autobiography*, 3.
18 For a development of this idea, see Julie Rak, *Negotiated Memory: Doukhobor Autobiographical Discourse* (Vancouver: University of British Columbia Press, 2004), ix.
19 Smith and Watson, *Reading Autobiography*, 4–5.
20 David Arnold and Stuart Blackburn, eds., *Telling Lives in India: Biography, Autobiography and Life History* (Ranikhet: Permanent Black, 2004), 9. In defence of the latter position, see J. L. Peacock and D. C. Holland, "The Narrated Self: Life Stories in Process," *Ethos* 21 (1993), 367–83.
21 See, as example, Wahhaj al-Din Alvi, *Urdu Khud Navisht* (New Delhi: Maktaba Jamia, 1989). For a discussion of *atma carit* or *atmacharit*, see Sudipto Kaviraj, "The Invention of Private Life: A Reading of Sibnath Sastri's Autobiography," in Arnold and Blackburn, *Telling Lives*, 84–85. Kaviraj discusses the term *carit* as encompassing the character—*charitra*—of a person as well as the recounting of that story. *Carit* in early Pali and Sanskrit meant both history and legend. See "Introduction: Life Histories in India," in Arnold and Blackburn, *Telling Lives*, 7–9.
22 See, as an example, Udaya Kumar, "Autobiography as a Way of Writing History: Personal Narratives from Kerala and the Inhabitation of Modernity" in *History in the Vernacular*, ed. Raziuddin Aquil and Partha Chatterjee (Delhi: Permanent Black, 2008), 418–48.
23 Arnold and Blackburn, *Telling Lives*, 9.
24 Malavika Karlekar, *Voices from Within: Early Personal Narratives of Bengali Women* (Delhi: Oxford University Press, 1993), 12; Aparna Basu and Malavika Karlekar, eds., *In So Many Words: Women's Life Experiences from Western and Eastern India* (London: Routledge, 2008), viii.
25 Paul de Man, "Autobiography as De-facement," *Modern Language Notes* 94:5 (December 1979), 919, emphasis added.
26 On this conflict between autobiography in theory and reality, see Siobhan Lambert-Hurley, "Life/History/Archive: Identifying Autobiographical Writing by Muslim Women in South Asia," *Journal of Women's History* 25.2 (summer 2013), 61–84.
27 de Man, "Autobiography as De-facement," 921.
28 For a useful overview of "life histories in India," see David Arnold and Stuart Blackburn, "Introduction: Life Histories in India," in their *Telling Lives*, 6–9.
29 Charlotte Vaudeville, ed., *A Weaver Named Kabir: Selected Verses with a Detailed Biographical and Historical Introduction* (Delhi: Oxford University Press, 2005).
30 See, as an example, Stuart Blackburn, "Life Histories as Narrative Strategy: Prophecy, Song, and Truth-Telling in Tamil Tales and Legends," in Arnold and Blackburn, *Telling Lives*, 203–26.
31 C. M. Naim, introduction to *Zikr-i-Mir: The Autobiography of the Eighteenth Century Mughal Poet: Mir Muhammad Taqi "Mir*," ed. C. M. Naim (Delhi: Oxford University Press, 1999), 1–21.

32 David Arnold and Stuart Blackburn, "Introduction: Life Histories in India," in Arnold and Blackburn, *Telling Lives*, 5.
33 Arnold and Blackburn, "Introduction," 20–21.
34 Farhat Hasan, "Presenting the Self: Norms and Emotions in Ardhakathanaka," in Ramaswamy and Sharma, *Biography as History*, 105–22.
35 Roy Porter, ed., *Rewriting the Self: Histories from the Renaissance to the Present* (London: Routledge, 1997).
36 Kathryn Hansen, *Stages of Life: Indian Theatre Autobiographies* (Ranikhet: Permanent Black, 2011), 299–314.
37 Conway, *When Memory Speaks*, 3–4.
38 Sidonie Smith and Julia Watson, "Introduction: Situating Subjectivity in Women's Autobiographical Practices" in *Women, Autobiography, Theory: A Reader*, ed. Sidonie Smith and Julia Watson (Madison: University of Wisconsin Press, 1998), 18.
39 Gwen Etter-Lewis quoted in Joan Sangster, "Telling Our Stories: Feminist Debates and the Use of Oral History," in Robert Perks and Alistair Thomson, eds., *The Oral History Reader* (London: Routledge, 1998), 89.
40 Susan Stanford Friedman, "Women's Autobiographical Selves: Theory and Practice," in Sidonie Smith and Julia Watson, *Women, Autobiography, Theory*, 75.
41 Indrani Sen, "Resisting Patriarchy: Complexities and Conflicts in the Memoir of Haimabati Sen," *Economic and Political Weekly* 47.12 (March 24, 2012), 55–62. Sen does point to the contradictions in Haimabati's self-portrayal, of her slipping into the role of a dutiful wife.
42 Sharmila Rege, *Writing Caste/Writing Gender: Narrating Dalit Women's Testimonios* (New Delhi: Zubaan, 2006), 9–91. On Dalit women's autobiographies, also see Raj Kumar, *Dalit Personal Narratives: Reading Caste, Nation and Identity* (New Delhi: Orient Blackswan, 2010)—especially chapter 6: "Beyond the Margin: Dalit Women's Autobiographies."
43 For a theoretical discussion of how autobiography may be used by those "excluded from official discourse" to "embody subjectivity" or "talk back," see Sidonie Smith, *Subjectivity, Identity, and the Body: Women's Autobiographical Practices in the Twentieth Century* (Bloomington: Indiana University Press, 1993). For South Asian examples, see Uma Chakravarti, *Rewriting History: The Life and Times of Pandita Ramabai* (Delhi: Kali for Women, 1998); Tanika Sarkar, *Words to Win: The Making of Amar Jiban; A Modern Autobiography* (Delhi: Kali for Women, 1999); Kumar, *Dalit Personal Narratives*.
44 Judith Tucker, "Biography as History: The Exemplary Life of Khayr al-Din al-Ramli," in *Auto/Biography and the Construction of Identity and Community in the Middle East*, ed. Mary Ann Fay (New York: Palgrave, 2001), 9–17.
45 Kaviraj, "Invention," 83–115.
46 Kumar, "Autobiography."
47 Venkatachalapathy, "Making a Modern Self."
48 The point about women speaking for collective others has been made in contexts of other cultures as well; for example, Hanadi Al-Samman emphasizes how Arab women in diaspora often write of a collective "we," including in their authorial "I,"

"mothers and others," making for a "mosaic autobiography." For her, autobiographies and autobiographical fiction are genres used to resist erasure, a point also made in the context of women's and dalits' autobiographies in South Asia. Hanadi Al-Samman, "Mosaic Autobiography," in her *Anxiety of Erasure: Trauma, Authorship and the Diaspora in Arab Women's Writing* (Syracuse, NY: Syracuse University Press, 2013). We thank the author for sharing this chapter with us.

49 Marilyn Booth, *May Her Likes Be Multiplied: Biography and Gender Politics in Egypt* (Berkeley: University of California Press, 2001).
50 Vijaya Ramaswamy, "Muffled Narratives: The Life and Times of Neelambakai Ammaiyar," in Ramaswamy and Sharma, *Biography as History*, 123–51.
51 Bharati Ray, *Daughters: A Story of Five Generations* (New Delhi: Penguin, 2011).
52 Mythily Sivaraman, *Fragments of a Life: A Family Archive* (New Delhi: Zubaan, 2006), xi–xxi.
53 Uma Chakravarti underscores the fragility of Subbalakshmi's life and her archive. See her afterword, "The Blue Tin Trunk," in Sivaraman, Fragments, 186–207. Chakravarti's own commitment to air Subbalakshmi's story also comes through in her film *A Quiet Little Entry*.
54 Gayatri Spivak, "Subaltern Studies: Deconstructing Historiography," in *Subaltern Studies: Writings on South Asian History and Society IV*, ed. Ranajit Guha (Delhi: Oxford University Press, 1985), 330–63.
55 See, as examples, Gloria Raheja and Ann Gold, *Listen to the Heron's Words: Reimagining Gender and Kinship in North India* (Berkeley: University of California Press, 1994); Josiane Racine Viramma and Jean-Luc Racine, *Viramma: Life of an Untouchable* (London: Verso, 1997).
56 See, as examples, Sylvia Vatuk, "*Hamara Daur-i Hayat*: An Indian Muslim Woman Writes Her Life," in Arnold and Blackburn, *Telling Lives*, 144–74; Basu and Karlekar, *In So Many Words*. On the breadth of source material available for a study of autobiographical writing by South Asian Muslim women specifically, see Lambert-Hurley, "Life/History/Archive."
57 Marilyn Booth, "Subjectivities on the Nile, 1890s to the 1920s: Intellectual Openings in Egypt and Gendered Representations of the Self," paper given at the conference "Women's Autobiography in Islamic Societies: Context and Construction," India International Centre, Delhi, December 16–18, 2010.
58 Barbara D. Metcalf, "What Happened in Mecca: Mumtaz Mufti's 'Labbaik,'" in Folkenflik, *Culture of Autobiography*, 149–67, quotation p. 157.
59 Smith and Watson, *Reading Autobiography*, 235.
60 Margot Badran, in the preface to *Harem Years: The Memoirs of an Egyptian Feminist*, ed. and trans. Margot Badran (London: Virago, 1986), 1.
61 Farzaneh Milani, *Words, Not Swords: Iran Women Writers and the Freedom of Movement* (Syracuse, NY: Syracuse University Press, 2011), xix; Smith and Watson, *Reading Autobiography*, 235.
62 On the wider connotations of agency, see Anshu Malhotra, "Miracles for the Marginal? Gender and Agency in a Nineteenth-Century Autobiographical Fragment," *Journal of Women's History* 25.2 (summer 2013), 15–35.

63 A. K. Ramanujan, "Towards a Counter-System: Women's Tales," in *The Collected Essays of A. K. Ramanujan*, ed. Vinay Dharwadker (Delhi: Oxford University Press, 1999), 429–47.
64 Stuart Blackburn, "Life Histories as Narrative Strategy: Prophecy, Song, and Truth-Telling in Tamil Tales and Legends," in Arnold and Blackburn, *Telling Lives*, 203–26.
65 Both Ramanujan and Blackburn give examples from Kannada and Tamil literature respectively of the heroine telling a doll her story. The doll motif is similar to the tale of "sister Viro" that is recounted in North India when women observe married women's fast of *Karva Chauth*.
66 We borrow the expression *on stage or page* from Sherrill Grace, "Theatre and the Autobiographical Pact: An Introduction," in Sherrill Grace and Jerry Wasserman, eds., *Theatre and Autobiography: Writing and Performing Lives in Theory and Practice* (Vancouver: Talonbooks, 2006), 13.
67 In some Western countries the performance of autobiographical narratives in theater has become common and has been theorized. See Grace and Wasserman, *Theatre and Autobiography*; Deirdre Heddon, *Autobiography and Performance* (Basingstoke: Palgrave Macmillan, 2008).
68 de Man, "Autobiography as De-facement," 923.
69 de Man, "Autobiography as De-facement," 926.
70 Sidonie Smith, "Performativity, Autobiographical Practice, Resistance," in Smith and Watson, *Women, Autobiography, Theory*, 108.
71 Naim, *Zikr-i-Mir*, 11–12.
72 Hansen, *Stages of Life*, 321.
73 In repressive societies, for instance, an autobiographer has not only to be careful about what and how much to reveal, in order to avoid self-revelation becoming self-destruction, but also to be constantly aware of a secondary audience of censors, and so deploy self-censorship to ensure self-preservation. These points came across in Azadeh Moaveni's paper "After the Fact: Hedging, Self-Censorship, and the Prospect of Return in Iranian Memoir" in the conference "Unveiling the Self: Life Narratives of Muslim Women in the Middle East and South Asia," held October 29–30, 2012, Department of Middle Eastern and South Asian Languages and Cultures. Also see Farzaneh Milani, *Veiling and Words: The Emerging Voices of Iranian Women Writers* (Syracuse, NY: Syracuse University Press, 1992), 201–28.
74 Vatuk, "Hamara Daur-i-Hayat."
75 Peter Burke, "History as Social Memory," in his *Varieties of Cultural History* (Cambridge: Polity, 1997), 43–59.
76 Peter Burke, "The Cultural History of Dreams," in his *Varieties of Cultural History*, 23–42.
77 Tucker, "Biography as History."
78 David Shulman, "Cowherd or King? The Sanskrit Biography of Ananda Ranga Pillai," in Arnold and Blackburn, *Telling Lives*, 175–202.
79 On orality and memory, see Rustom Bharucha, *Rajasthan: An Oral History; Conversations with Komal Kothari* (New Delhi: Penguin India, 2003).

80. Kabir, the foremost of Indian Bhakti saints, often spoke about looking inside the heart for God. J. S. Hawley and M. Juergensmeyer, eds., *Songs of the Saints of India* (Delhi: Oxford University Press, 2008), 52. Similarly, within the Islamic Sufi tradition the emotion of love was situated in the heart and god/liness in the *ruh*, spirit. Scott Kugle, *Sufis and Saints' Bodies: Mysticism, Corporeality, and Sacred Power in Islam* (Delhi: Munshiram Manoharlal, 2009).
81. On "archetypal life scripts" see Conway, "Memory Plots," in her *When Memory Speaks*, 3–18.
82. A. K. Ramanujan, "The Ring of Memory: Remembering and Forgetting in Indian Literatures," in Molly Daniels-Ramanujan and Keith Harrison, eds., *A. K. Ramanujan: Uncollected Poems and Prose* (New Delhi: Oxford University Press, 2001), 83–100.
83. Urvashi Butalia, *The Other Side of Silence: Voices from the Partition of India* (New Delhi: Penguin, 1998).
84. Linda H. Peterson, "Institutionalizing Women's Autobiography: Nineteenth-Century Editors and the Shaping of an Autobiographical Tradition," in Folkenflik, *The Culture of Autobiography*, 80–103.
85. Alessandro Portelli, *The Death of Luigi Trastulli and Other Stories: Form and Meaning in Oral History* (Albany: State University of New York Press, 1991), 76.
86. Perks and Thomson, *Oral History Reader*, 4.
87. Conway, *When Memory Speaks*, 7–8.
88. Smith and Watson, *Reading Autobiography*, 47.
89. John Martin, "Inventing Sincerity, Refashioning Prudence: The Discovery of the Individual in Renaissance Europe," in *The Renaissance in Europe*, ed. Keith Whitlock (New Haven, CT: Yale University Press, 2000), 11–30. In this context the paradoxical use of "self-fashioning" for this period by Stephen Greenblatt is revealing: it points to the ability of the men of this age as never before to write their destinies, as at the same time this self-fashioning also makes them puppets in the hands of power structures including the growing monarchical power. See his *Renaissance Self-Fashioning: From More to Shakespeare* (Chicago: University of Chicago Press, 1980).
90. Sumit Sarkar, "Kaliyuga, Chakri and Bhakti: Ramakrishna and His Times," *Economic and Political Weekly* 27.29 (July 1992), 1543–66.
91. Kumar, "Autobiography," 418–48.
92. David Arnold, "The Self and the Cell: Indian Prison Narratives as Life Histories," in Arnold and Blackburn, *Telling Lives*, 29–53.
93. Partha Chatterjee, "Women and the Nation," in his *The Nation and Its Fragments: Colonial and Postcolonial Histories* (Princeton, NJ: Princeton University Press, 1993), 135–57.
94. Partha Chatterjee, "The Nationalist Resolution of Women's Question," in Kumkum Sangari and Sudesh Vaid, eds., *Recasting Women: Essays in Colonial History* (New Delhi: Kali for Women, 1989), 233–53. For a critique of Chatterjee, see Tanika Sarkar, "Hindu Wife, Hindu Nation: Domesticity and Nationalism in Nineteenth-Century Bengal," in her *Hindu Wife, Hindu Nation: Community, Religion and Cultural Nationalism* (Delhi: Permanent Black, 2005), 23–52.

95 Tanika Sarkar, "A Book of Her Own. A Life of Her Own: Autobiography of a Nineteenth-Century Woman," in Kumkum Sangari and Uma Chakravarti, eds., *From Myths to Markets: Essays on Gender* (New Delhi: Manohar, 2001), 85–124.

96 Meera Kosambi, *Feminist Vision or "Treason against Men"? Kashibai Kanitkar and the Engendering of Marathi Literature* (Ranikhet: Permanent Black, 2008), 3, 21.

97 Uma Chakravarti, *Rewriting History*.

98 Kumar, "Autobiography"; Kaviraj, "Invention."

99 Judith Butler, *Bodies That Matter: On the Discursive Limits of "Sex"* (New York: Routledge, 1993), x. Also see Butler's *Gender Trouble: Feminism and the Subversion of Identity* (New York: Routledge, 1990). While for Butler gender performativity refers to the repetitious acts that "naturalize"—the repeated stylization of the body—we use "performativity" in this introduction in the sense of a cultural act, a performance.

100 Heddon, *Autobiography and Performance*, 1.

101 For a discussion of Butler's concept of performativity, see Samuel A. Chambers and Terrell Carver, *Judith Butler and Political Theory: Troubling Politics* (London: Routledge, 2008), 34–50.

102 Smith, "Performativity," 110.

103 Smith and Watson, *Reading Autobiography*, 11. Also see Heddon, *Autobiography and Performance*, 8–9.

104 Milani, *Veiling and Words*, 203–4.

105 de Man, "Autobiography as De-facement."

106 Conway, *When Memory Speaks*, 43, 47–48.

PART I. NEGOTIATING AUTOBIOGRAPHY

Between Assertion and Subversion

1. A PASSION FOR READING

The Role of Early Twentieth-Century Urdu Novels in the Construction of an Individual Female Identity in 1930s Hyderabad

SYLVIA VATUK

This chapter explores the role of popular Urdu-language fiction in the development of a young Muslim girl's sense of self, as she grew up in the 1920s and 1930s in the city of Hyderabad in southern India. Zakira Ghouse was born in Hyderabad in 1921 and raised in a large extended family household, part of a close-knit religious and scholarly lineage—a *khāndān*—of illustrious ancestry but relatively modest means.[1] In the 1950s she wrote an account of the first twelve or so years of her life, which she titled *Hamārā Daur-i Hayāt* [My life course—subsequently *HDH*].[2] In one full chapter and parts of two others from this sixteen-part unpublished memoir,[3] Zakira Begam describes at length her love of books and the passion for reading that consumed not only her childhood but much of her later life, until her death in early 2003. In the sections of the memoir that I will discuss here she recalls for her readers the plots and characters in the Urdu novels about Muslim family life that she devoured in her early years.[4] She tells us how she first learned to read, who her early teachers were, and how—influenced by her mother's love of Urdu literature—she became an avid reader of children's books and very soon thereafter of adult novels as well, to such an extent that her preoccupation with reading became almost an obsession.

Many of the kinds of books that Zakira Begam particularly enjoyed were not readily available in her religiously conservative home, in part because the men of her extended family considered them unsuitable for unmarried girls. Zakira Begam notes the barriers she and her girl cousins encountered when trying to get access to books and describes the various stratagems they employed to overcome them. Whenever one of them did get her hands on a book, they would pass it around from one to another and back again, and each would read it over and over. Zakira Begam outlines the plots of several of the novels that she read and particularly enjoyed in her preteen years and identifies those female characters whose personalities and behavior, as depicted therein, made the greatest and most lasting impression on her.

My discussion of those sections of Zakira Begam's memoir that deal with her passion for reading—and specifically her interest in novels depicting women's lives and the complex dynamics of the Indian Muslim family—is meant to contribute to arguments made by a number of scholars about the important role that the reading of popular fiction plays in the construction and development of female selfhood.[5] In the generally didactic Urdu-language fiction that she was exposed to in her early years Zakira Begam encountered many female characters, some of whom she was expected to admire and emulate. Other female characters were more negative, providing examples of behavior that a good Muslim woman should be careful to avoid. Becoming absorbed in these fictional worlds helped Zakira Begam—as it did other young girls of her time and place—to construct a sense of the kind of person she wanted to be and what she wanted to do with her life when she grew up. It also aided her in coming to terms with certain ongoing distressing family issues for which she could find no solution in the real world of the home.

The Memoir as a Text

I will not go into great detail about the text itself, having already written about it quite extensively elsewhere.[6] In the late 1980s Zakira Begam and I worked together for a few years, on and off, as I tried to reconstruct—for my own research purposes—the history of her khāndān and the role of women within it. At one point, she showed the memoir to me and allowed me to make a photocopy. But I had great difficulty deciphering her handwriting, so she kindly offered to read it aloud to me while I recorded it on tape. As she went along she commented spontaneously from time to time on what she had written so many years before. She also responded to my questions about words or passages that I did not understand and people with whose names I was unfamiliar.[7] The result is a multilayered text. At one level it is a straightforward autobiographical account, a self-portrait of a young Muslim girl's life in 1920s and early 1930s Hyderabad, but one painted, not at the time, but more than twenty-five years afterward, by the adult woman whom that girl eventually became. This later, deliberate reconstruction of selected incidents and events—and the emotions remembered to have been associated with them—represents the second layer of the text. A third is provided by the autobiographer's elaboration of and commentary on that text, as it was offered to a foreign woman anthropologist who had an imperfect grasp of her language but a strong desire to know more than the author had felt was necessary—or, perhaps, desirable—to put down on paper thirty-five years before.

Members of Zakira Begam's own extended family were the sole audience for the original text; I alone had heard her commentary on it. But the potential for the memoir reaching a much broader audience arose when, sometime in the 1990s, I proposed polishing the very literal translation that I had been using for research purposes and editing it for publication. Zakira Begam was already a published author of articles and stories in Urdu magazines, and had even published a scholarly book in English that was based on her MLitt thesis.[8] But, as far as I knew, she had never considered publishing her memoir, whether because of its very personal nature or because she was concerned about how other members of the family might react to having private family matters exposed to public scrutiny. When, somewhat to my surprise, she welcomed my proposal, I began to work on the translation.[9] Unfortunately, however, because of the pressure of other commitments, I was not able to complete it before Zakira Begam passed away, and she never had the satisfaction of seeing her work in print.

The proposed English version of the memoir would add a fourth layer to the work.[10] The process of translation would inevitably introduce changes in meaning; cuts would also be necessary in order to eliminate redundant passages. And in order to protect the privacy of individuals mentioned in the text and avoid giving offense to their—and Zakira Begam's own—descendants, additional passages would have to be eliminated before the memoir could be published. The result would be a very different narrative from the one that she penned more than sixty years ago.

Autobiographical "Truth" In Zakira Begam's Memoir

As many postmodernist critics of autobiographical writings have noted, the content of works of this kind cannot be taken at face value, as direct, "truthful" recreations of what "actually" happened in the past.[11] Even at the time an event is happening, each participant has a different understanding of what is going on and what it means. Even over a short time, our memories of past events lose their stability. The issue is not simply one of the inability of the human mind to preserve the details of events that happened long ago but also that over the course of many years—in this case, two and a half decades—the author of a memoir comes to occupy a new personal and social position and in the process has unavoidably developed a different point of view on the events she is trying to describe than that which she had at the time they occurred. This affects the way that she represents those events in writing, however conscientiously she strives for "accuracy," "objectivity," and "truthfulness." Furthermore, when she picks up her pen to construct a narrative of her life, an author inevitably has particular motives, conscious or not, for embarking on the very enterprise of writing a memoir at all, for structuring it in a certain way and for deciding how to represent herself and the other characters in her story.

In this connection, Sidonie Smith speaks of "autobiographical storytelling" as a "performative act." There are many stories, she says, that a person could tell about her life and a myriad of different possible occasions and settings in which to tell them, each of which may call for a very different narrative and mode of narrativity.[12] Another key determining variable for the form and content of such a narrative performance is the identity of her intended audience. Every writer of an autobiographical work has to consider the possibility that family members or others may react badly to what she has written about herself, about them, or about events at which they were present and may remember differently from the way she has represented them. This is a particular concern for one who intends to *publish* her life story. But it is a consideration too for an author who is writing only for her own close relatives—as in this case—or even for her eyes alone, since she cannot ensure that others may not later discover its existence and be distressed by its contents. Therefore, most autobiographers find themselves either indulging in a certain amount of self-censorship or simply deciding to let the chips fall where they may, knowing that some of their most intimate relationships may be ruptured as a result.

Zakira Begam clearly took the former course, consciously trying to avoid offending any of the individuals mentioned in her memoir. She treated deceased relatives with particular discretion and respect. There is much about her family situation that she did not mention or that she alluded to only indirectly. In some cases this was because there was no need to tell her readers something of which they were already fully aware. But her silences were often motivated by a reluctance to reveal private information or recount embarrassing incidents involving someone close to herself or deserving—because of age or kinship relationship—of special deference.

Inevitably, however, her desire to avoid offense sometimes conflicted with her need to "tell the truth," as she saw it, of what she had experienced in her youth—and how she had felt about it. One way she tried to resolve this dilemma was by adopting an apologetic tone, assuring her readers that she did not intend to hurt anyone's feelings or to alienate their affections and begging them to forgive her if she had inadvertently done so. In such contexts she often quoted lines from the works of well-known Urdu poets: appealing for one's readers' indulgence by assuming a humble and remorseful demeanor was clearly not a strategy of her own devising but a familiar convention learned from within the literary culture in which she had been brought up.

A Home Education

Zakira Begam's extended family placed a high value on religious learning and scholarship. For generations children of both sexes had been taught to read and write, though not in *maktabs* or *madrasas*: these traditional Islamic schools were considered necessary and appropriate only for children whose elders were insufficiently knowledgeable to teach them themselves. In scholarly khāndāns like her own, parents, grandparents, and other relatives customarily taught children of both sexes at home, though tutors from outside of the family were sometimes engaged to provide older boys with more advanced instruction.[13]

According to Islamic traditions, children began their formal education after the ceremony of *bismillah*, at the age of four years, four months, and four days, which for Zakira Begam fell on February 3, 1926. Shortly thereafter her paternal grandfather retired from his position in the Nizam of Hyderabad's administration and moved with his wife to Madras, where the khāndān had been based for over one hundred years and where he had been born and raised. Zakira Begam's immediate family soon found it necessary to follow them to Madras, as her grandfather had fallen seriously ill shortly after his arrival. Therefore, an uncle who lived in Madras became her first teacher. Describing the architecture of the khāndān compound where they were staying,[14] she says that one could go from one house to the other through connecting inside passages, a design feature that enabled the strictly secluded women of the family to freely visit their relatives in other houses without having to go out of doors and risk being seen by unrelated persons. Zakira Begam took this route to her uncle's house for her first Qur'an lessons. When she arrived, "there [he] would be, sitting on a mat on the verandah, engrossed in his educational activities" (*HDH*, part 5).[15]

Within a few months, however, her grandfather died and the family returned to Hyderabad with his widow, who then took over the supervision of Zakira Begam's education. A year later, Zakira Begam and her mother went to spend several months in the town of Bidar, where her maternal grandfather, also a Hyderabad government employee, was posted. Now she came under the tutelage of her *maternal* grandmother. She compares the teaching techniques of the two grandmothers as follows:

> The Qur'an was usually taught by having the child recite it in unison [with the teacher].... Because children are impatient to get through it quickly, [my paternal grandmother] used to follow this method. She was a soft-spoken and gentle person and tried, as far as possible, not to be harsh with the children, even when it was for their own good. [My late maternal grandmother] followed an entirely different system. She was a believer in firmness.... She would give lessons that were as short as possible but had to be memorized well. So in Bidar... the lessons were short but one would have to remember everything from the previous several days. Since I didn't have a very good memory, I was dealt with strictly. I don't remember very clearly, but I have a feeling that, in the educational context, she didn't consider spanking to be wrong![16] Anyhow, her firm attitude, however reasonable it may have been, was rather difficult for a child to bear. So I was scared of being taught by her and always wanted to put off beginning my lesson. I can still recall her angry face when, despite being told a number of times, I still couldn't read correctly! (*HDH*, part 5)

Once Zakira Begam had mastered the Arabic script, her mother began teaching her to read Urdu. An avid reader herself, she passed on her enthusiasm for books to all of her children. "My mother was very much interested in Urdu literature. It was her fervent love of reading that made me want to learn to read when I was a child.... She gave excellent guidance and in such a manner that in a very short time her children attained a high standard of expertise in the language" (*HDH*, part 5).

Once the British consolidated their control over the region and began to introduce Western-style schools, many elite Muslims of Madras enthusiastically took advantage of the opportunity to educate their sons in English in preparation for employment in the colonial administration. But the men of this khāndān were, from the outset, implacably opposed to this new form of knowledge that was rapidly supplanting their centuries-old traditions of Islamic learning. This attitude had begun to weaken somewhat by the time Zakira Begam was born, and several boys and young men of her parents' generation—including her own father—had attended Western-style schools. But the idea of sending girls to school had not yet gained acceptance.[17] There was, however, one girl in the household whose parents had taken the revolutionary step of enrolling her in the English-medium Nampally Zenana School, established in 1887 for upper-class Hyderabadi girls. It had careful arrangements to enable the pupils to observe strict seclusion. Zakira Begam wanted badly to be allowed to attend school with her cousin and would get very upset when the school carriage came in the morning to pick her up.

It was not until she was twelve years old that her dreams were realized. One day, upon returning from a visit to her maternal grandparents, she was surprised and overjoyed to be greeted with the news that, in her absence, her father had made arrangements to admit her to school. But after attending the school for one year, during which she was somewhat embarrassed to be in the same class with girls much younger than she and struggled to keep up with lessons in an unfamiliar language, her father arranged a transfer to an Urdu-medium girls' school. Within a few years she obtained a high school diploma and later studied privately for her BA, MA, and MLitt degrees.

Zakira Begam had for many years harbored an ambition to become a medical doctor. For various reasons she was never able to realize this ambition; the emotional distress caused by her inability to achieve her early goals is alluded to in a final chapter of the memoir. However, other academic and professional attainments brought her considerable satisfaction and enabled her to finally come to terms with having had to abandon her youthful dreams. Her crowning achievement came when, in her midseventies, she completed a doctoral dissertation on the educational and literary accomplishments of the women of her ancestral khāndān, on the basis of which, in 1994, she was awarded a PhD in Urdu from the University of Madras.[18]

A Life in Books

....

In her early years Zakira Begam read books and magazines meant for children, but she soon moved on to more adult fare. At first a slightly older girl cousin would read books aloud to her, but by the age of seven or eight she was able to read by herself and before long began devouring the works of all the prominent Urdu writers of her time and earlier, such as Nazir Ahmad, Rashid-ul Khairi, 'Abdul Halim Sharar, and women writers such as Muhammadi Begam, Nazr-i Sajjad Haidar, Walida Afzal 'Ali, and others. She writes:

> I had a strange obsession with reading. I didn't care about the time or the place. In those days there was no electricity [in our house]. . . . There was a lantern in my room, but when Mother got annoyed with my incessant reading she would turn it off. [On moonlit nights] I would lie there for a while, holding my breath. When I saw that she had fallen asleep, I would take my book into the moonlight and continue reading, getting back into bed only after I had finished it. (*HDH*, part 5)
>
> Father used to sleep in the adjoining room, so there was also the fear that, if he should find me reading in the dark, he would be angry. So I had to take precautions. Sometimes he left the door of his room ajar; if I heard him getting up I would hide the book.

THE SEARCH FOR READING MATTER

Zakira Begam goes on to describe the difficulties she encountered in her continual search for books to read. Generally speaking, she says, the women and girls in the family were cooperative about sharing the books that they owned or had been able to borrow from others. And some mothers, her own among them, were fairly liberal in allowing their daughters to read what they liked. But many of the men, ambivalent at best about the girls' desire to expand their knowledge of the wider world through reading, tried to keep what they considered "unsuitable" fare out of their hands. As members of a scholarly family with a proud tradition of female literacy, they expected their daughters to learn to read and write. But they did not want them exposed to influences—whether direct or through reading—that might lead them to neglect or abandon their domestic roles, come out of seclusion, or deviate in other ways from accepted standards of feminine modesty. Their fears, of course, echoed those of prominent Muslim reformers who had been warning for decades of such dangers.[19]

THE LENDING LIBRARY

Most of Zakira Begam's male relatives had civil service jobs in the Nizam's administration, but her father had not been able to secure a position of that kind. Therefore, to support his family, he started a modest business venture, a small lending library housed in rented quarters not far from their home. The existence of the library did not, however, make it easier for his daughter to acquire reading matter: neither she nor the other young girls of the household were allowed to go there. Nor could they prevail on him to bring books home for them to read. She gained entry to the library only once, when she went with some family members to watch a parade from its windows. "Looking at the packed shelves of the library I felt a strange longing: 'to think that here, all around, are spread great treasures of knowledge and literature, but those who wish to benefit from them are deprived of the privilege!'" (*HDH*, part 6).

TRICKS AND STRATEGIES

Sometimes her father would bring books home from the library for his own and his brothers' enjoyment. The girls did not really share the men's literary tastes—which ran heavily to detective stories and the like. But even though they didn't enjoy them very much and sometimes found the plots difficult to follow, in their desperation for something to read they were willing to try. One day, after reading aloud from her memoir the convoluted story of an orphaned childhood and a case of mistaken identity that provided the main plot for one of these books, Zakira Begam told me, "When my father left for the library in the morning, he would put the book [that he had been reading] under a window [in his room]. As soon as he was gone, my cousin and I would go and get the book.... We knew that he normally came back at four o'clock, but sometimes he would come earlier than this. We would read standing in the window, so that when we saw him coming, we could immediately put the book back where he had left it" (*HDH*, part 5).

The girls sometimes resorted to less than admirable methods to obtain the reading matter they desired. On one occasion she wanted very much to read one of the historical novels of Sadiq Hasan. "Someone had brought one of Sadiq Hasan's books to be bound by the bookbinder who occupied that big room in Uncle Mazhar's house. He had erected a screen to divide the room down the middle, behind which he kept the books and all of the materials for his [part-time] bookbinding business" (*HDH*, part 6).

Zakira Begam asked the bookbinder to let her read the book before he returned it to its owner. But he refused.

> As he was getting ready to leave one morning for his office, I pleaded with him to give it to me, but he would not. Sister Sufiya was with me—she advised me to wait, whispering that, once he left, we could figure out a way to get hold of the book. When he was out of sight she showed me that there was a gap between the screen and the floor, large enough for us to crawl through to reach the back part of the room. I don't remember whether she or I or both of us crawled under the partition and found the book.... He didn't notice right away that it was missing, so I was able to read it. Sister Zakiya also wanted to read it, and I promised that when I finished I would send it over to her maternal grandfather's house, where they were living at the time. But before I could do so, the owner of the

book came to our house. He had found out that I had the book and asked me to give it back. So I was unable to keep my promise to Sister Zakiya, for which I was very sorry. (*HDH*, part 6)

One book that many considered inappropriate for young female readers was *Begamāt-ke Ānsū* [The ladies' tears] by Hasan Nizami. Zakira Begam had heard of it but hadn't been able to obtain a copy. One day, while visiting the home of relatives, she saw it lying somewhere in their house, picked it up, and began reading. "I spent almost the whole day reading that book, which presents a heartbreaking picture of the calamity that befell the ladies in the fort during the Mutiny [of 1857]. We had to return home in the evening, but I hadn't been able to finish it by that time and wanted to take it home. Sister Humaira asked [our hostess] daughter if we could borrow it. But Auntie didn't approve of girls reading that kind of book, so she refused, saying 'Wait until Humaira comes here with her bridegroom—then she can take it!'" (*HDH*, part 7).

MEDICAL ASPIRATIONS

I have mentioned that Zakira Begam had developed at a young age a desire to study medicine and become a doctor. In those days there were no Western-style doctors, male or female, in her khāndān. She had often heard family stories about the ancestress who had learned the rudiments of Unani medicine by listening in from behind a curtain while her father—a skilled *hakim*—was teaching her brothers. She became so knowledgeable, it was said, that family members often called on her to treat common illnesses.

The idea that she should become a doctor apparently seized Zakira Begam's imagination quite early on in life. She was then about five years old, staying in Madras with her parents and grandparents and learning from her uncle how to recite the Qur'an.

'Abdullah Sahib had just been born, and because of that his mother . . . was ill. And one day, while I was having my lesson with my uncle, a doctor came to the house [to treat her]. This is one of the earliest memories imprinted upon my mind (*HDH*, part 5).

When the doctor visited, a screen was put up between him and the patient. . . . The woman would be in bed, the doctor would be on a chair on the other side, and there would be a screen in the middle. I recall that being done on that occasion.

In Hyderabad a Christian nurse-midwife used to come to the house whenever a baby was born, and she provided another living role model for

Zakira Begam's career aspirations. But there was at least one literary character as well, a woman doctor named Surayya in the novel *Gūdar kā La'l* [A ruby in rags].[20] "I was very much impressed by... this fictional Surayya, [who], after overcoming innumerable difficulties,... became a doctor.... Her character was an ideal one.... I wished that I might acquire all of the skills, arts, and knowledge that Surayya had and adopt all of her good qualities.... So, from that time on I began to think about becoming a doctor!" (*HDH*, part 6).

For a while, after reading this book, she began using the name *Surayya* for herself. But she had little success persuading others to call her by the new name and soon reverted to the old one, consoling herself with the realization that the name *Zakira* had a certain unique attractiveness that she had not fully appreciated before.

EXEMPLARY WOMEN

Much of the literature that Zakira Begam *was* allowed to read was specifically meant for women and was didactic and reformist in intent. It encouraged women's education (so as to make them better housewives and mothers) and attacked the "wasteful" and "non-Islamic" rituals customarily associated with Muslim weddings and other life-cycle ceremonies. Incidentally, these rituals and customs were largely the preserve of women and provided their chief opportunities to meet and socialize with women from other households and enjoy a respite from their everyday domestic preoccupations.[21]

The ideal woman in these novels was knowledgeable and enlightened, capable of running a modern household and raising modern sons while retaining the traditional feminine virtues of modesty, patience, self-abnegation, gentility, and religiosity. Negative female characters were either ignorant, petty, and intriguing or highly Westernized and alienated from their own religion and culture. Not surprisingly, Zakira Begam identified, as she was meant to do, with the virtuous female heroines.

Mirāt-ul Urūs [The bride's mirror] by Nazir Ahmad was a book of this kind which she greatly enjoyed.[22] It is about two sisters, Akbari and Asghari, married to two brothers. Akbari is "illiterate, ill-tempered, and absolutely without any talent.... Asghari, on the other hand, is literate, sweet-tempered and multitalented."[23] Though younger than her sister, she takes charge of the joint household almost immediately upon her marriage, straightens out the family's financial affairs, and manages over time to teach Akbari how to run a household efficiently and become an exemplary wife and mother.

Another book that Zakira Begam enjoyed is the novel *Jauhar-i Qadāmat* by Rashid-ul Khairi.[24] As in *Mirāt-ul Urūs*, there are two sisters, Zahida and Shahida, one of whom is admirable, the other despicable. "Zahida was the product of orthodox culture, and Shahida . . . was a typical daughter of modern society. The way they were described made one feel dislike and repulsion for the character of Shahida, while the character of Zahida seemed to shine like a star" (*HDH*, part 6).

'Azim Beg Chughtai, a very prolific prose writer of the period, was another author whose books and short stories Zakira Begam read with enthusiasm. One of his memorable characters was a woman named Bi-Khatun in a story entitled "Ālū kā Bhartā" [Spicy mashed potatoes]. The male protagonist, as Zakira Begam described him to me, is a cruel man who mistreats his wife and demeans her by bringing "street women" into the house and demanding that she cook and serve them his favorite potato dish. She is such an ideal wife that she obeys her husband without ever complaining. Zakira Begam writes: "She was so faithful to her husband that she tried to make him happy in every possible way. Eventually he was so deeply affected by her devotion that he threw the other women out of the house and returned to her." (*HDH*, part 6)

Another of Chughtai's characters, Shahida, from the novel *Angūthī* [The ring], also held great appeal for Zakira Begam, but for a different reason: Zakira Begam was enthralled by her cheerfulness and her lively personality.

> She was a favorite of mine . . . lively . . . cheerful, bright and bold, brimming with life. Her personality seemed an ideal one. I used to think, "Oh, if only there were one such talkative and cheerful person living among us!"
>
> She muses in her memoir: "I don't know why it is that in our khāndān such liveliness is in very short supply. In our family, life is viewed with such sober and serious eyes that one can hardly find a single jolly, talkative woman among us. I liked this character intensely and wished with all my heart that I could mould my personality upon hers." (*HDH*, part 6)

THE ISSUE OF POLYGYNY

The writer Rashid-ul Khairi was a champion of women's rights, well known for his opposition to various social practices then prevalent among Indian Muslims that he felt caused special hardship to women, such as polygyny and child marriage.[25] In her memoir Zakira Begam characterizes him as someone who "favored the oppressed class of women." After reading me this passage she remarked that he "wrote what I felt strongly about, so I liked him." Zakira Begam felt especially strongly about polygyny. It was rare in her khāndān but had occurred in her own immediate family. Her parents were first cousins; their marriage had been contracted when her mother was in her early teens. The union was not a very happy one, and sometime after Zakira's birth her father contracted a second marriage with an unrelated woman who eventually bore him two daughters. He also had four children (three daughters and a son) by Zakira Begam's mother. He did not bring his new wife into the family home but kept her in a separate domestic establishment. Thus, not only his time and attention, but also his meager income, had to be shared between two households. The situation caused Zakira Begam's mother considerable economic and emotional distress; it is not surprising that her unhappiness was communicated to her children.

It is doubtless for this reason that novels about polygynous marriages especially appealed to Zakira Begam. She particularly enjoyed those novels in which two women married to the same man live harmoniously in one house or live separately but have adapted comfortably to the challenges of sharing a husband. Perhaps she wished—though she does not explicitly say so—for some such resolution of her own family's situation.

The three-volume novel *Gūdar kā La'l*, mentioned above, was particularly meaningful in this regard. One of its several plot lines involves a young man, Yusuf Raza, who is locked in an incompatible and therefore unhappy union with his mother's brother's daughter, Maqbul. Whereas Yusuf is a well-educated lawyer, "modern" in outlook, Maqbul is illiterate, lazy, argumentative, neglectful of her religious duties, a poor housekeeper, an indifferent wife, and a careless mother. The couple's relationship deteriorates drastically as time goes on. He tries to make her improve her behavior, but she ignores him. As Asiya Alam has observed, the conflictual relationship between husband and wife as portrayed in this novel "point[s] to a larger problem at the center of modernity in the *ashraf* community in India" at that time,[26] where the growing discrepancy in education between husbands and wives presented new challenges of adjustment and compromise.[27]

Eventually Yusuf takes a second wife, an educated woman of excellent character, Mehr Jabin. She proves not only to be a perfect match for him but also manages over the course of many pages to win the affection of Maqbul, who in the beginning was understandably very hostile to her. She also succeeds in mending the antagonistic relationship between her husband and Maqbul, both of whom eventually see the error of their previous ways and reconcile with one another. By the end of the novel, Mehr Jabin has created a harmonious ménage à trois in the family home. Zakira Begam cites this ending as having been one of her favorite parts of the novel: "The way she bore the bad and hurtful behavior of her cowife, Maqbul . . . and despite this was good to her and succeeded in making her into an exemplary wife. The part where Yusuf comes back from London, sees the two wives together and is amazed at Maqbul's change of heart, made a great impression on me" (*HDH*, part 6).

Another book on the same theme that deeply affected Zakira Begam is *Raushnak Begam* [Lady Raushnak], the work of a lesser-known woman writer, Mahmuda Begam.[28] "I read this book numerous times and each time felt a desire to read it again. Brother Habib used to tease me a lot in those days. . . . Do you know what he used to do? The moment he realized that I had custody of *Raushnak Begam*, he would immediately snatch it from me, and I would be left rubbing my hand. . . . I would then be on the lookout for an opportunity to go into his mother's room [and get it again]. . . . Now, after so many years, it may not be inappropriate to admit . . . that I repeatedly stole that book. . . . And then, out of fear of Brother Habib, I would try to hide, sitting in a corner somewhere to read it [out of his sight]" (*HDH*, part 6).

The plot of *Raushnak Begam*—as Zakira narrated it to me at length, from memory, in 1989—involves a rich young man, Humayun Far, and his wife, Raushan Ara (Raushnak Begam). She is his cousin, the daughter of his father's brother, adopted as a child by her father, who now plans to send him to England to study. For this reason, even though both are still very young, he insists that the two marry before Humayun departs. But the girl's mother, an illiterate and scheming woman, had wanted her to marry one of her own nephews instead. Therefore, after Humayun goes to London, she tries to drive a wedge between the pair by writing a letter to him, in which she claims that his wife doesn't care for him and urges him to send her a "divorce letter." Upon receiving this news, he falls seriously ill and is nursed back to health by an English woman friend, Mary. He does not divorce Raushan Ara, but, feeling that his marriage to her is effectively over, he decides to marry Mary. He stays in England, and they have two children. Later he goes to India for a visit and learns to his surprise that his aunt/adoptive mother had deceived him. Raushan Ara is actually a very virtuous and devoted wife and has been waiting patiently all these years for him to return. The two reunite, and he eventually tells her of his second marriage. She magnanimously accepts his explanation and even agrees to allow him to hide from Mary the very fact of her existence. Mary conveniently dies, and Humayun Far brings his children from England to be raised in India by Raushnak Begam. Zakira Begam writes that one of her favorite chapters was the one in which Humayun Far and his wife discuss this issue of his having two wives.

Conclusion

One of the issues that was raised in the early days of scholarly theorizing about the "newly discovered" genre of women's autobiographical writings is whether there are identifiable gender differences in the way men and women, respectively, narrate their lives. In one of the first edited volumes devoted to critical readings of (American and British) women's autobiographies, Estelle Jelinek suggested that men and women do indeed approach the autobiographical project in different ways. Men, she says, focus on their professional careers, while women write about house, family, and their relationships to others. Men "aggrandize" themselves, casting themselves into "heroic molds," while women are more understated and self-effacing, feeling the need to "sift through their lives for explanation and understanding." Men present life trajectories that progress in a coherent, linear fashion, while women's texts are disconnected and fragmentary, just as the patterns of their daily lives tend to be.[29]

Jelinek's sharp dichotomies are clearly too oversimplified to be neatly applied over the enormous corpus of autobiographies that we now have at our disposal, produced by writers of both sexes and in countless different cultures. Some of Jelinek's insights into women's ways of writing seem, at least at first glance, to have some utility for understanding particular aspects of the form and content of Zakira Begam's memoir. She does write mainly about domestic matters—but cannot this be largely accounted for by the fact that she is writing about her childhood, which is by definition a time when both sexes, in all cultures, are living at home with members of their immediate family, and particularly so in her case? On the other hand, as Walsh has observed, childhood is a period of life that in most autobiographies by Indians—at least, those written in English—tends to be given short shrift.[30] But the texts that Walsh examined were almost entirely male authored. So it is possible that the fact that Zakira Begam chose to write about *this* period of her life, rather than some other, is related in some way to her female identity. We can only speculate about whether, if she had ever embarked on a full account of her life, she—like so many male autobiographers—would have left out or drastically minimized the amount of space allotted to those first twelve years.

I have indicated here—and have elaborated in more detail elsewhere[31]—that in her memoir Zakira Begam clearly avoids the practice of self-aggrandizement that Jelinek considers to be characteristically masculine. She is, indeed, exaggeratedly self-effacing, humble, and—in portions of the memoir not discussed here—very self-critical and frank about what she perceives to be her many failings and faults of character. However, this manner of self-representation cannot be properly interpreted without taking account of the cultural and literary context within which she composed her memoir. Urdu literary conventions, whether in poetry or prose, demand that men too, when writing about themselves, should avoid explicit self-promotion and assume a modest demeanor, leaving the reverse impression to be read between the lines, if at all. Hansen points out that there are similar autobiographical conventions in other non-Western cultures that have nothing to do with the gender of the author: "Reticence or embarrassment may be narratorial positions with their own intentionality.... The impulse to profess the insignificance of the self... is a common thread, related to widely held cultural norms of deference.... Sentiments of modesty and humility in the autobiographical text may have more to do with the narrator's good breeding than ... [his or her] selfhood."[32] Given this cultural context, would one be justified in assuming that Zakira Begam's manner of representing herself in her memoir arises simply out of the fact that she is a woman?

Finally there is the question of whether the choice of a linear versus a discontinuous life trajectory bears any relationship to the author's gender. Zakira Begam does not relate the events of her childhood in a linear fashion. The initial chapters, outlining her family's genealogy, are ordered chronologically. But the rest are organized by topic: education, domestic milieu, festivities, hobbies, and so on. Nor is there much sense of linearity within each topic. The narrative jumps back and forth in time, and the author repeats herself and periodically goes off into lengthy digressions and interjects anecdotes at every step. But is this mode of structuring a life peculiarly "feminine," or does it simply show that the author is following a familiar cultural template—in this case from the Islamic Indo-Persian biographical tradition, where lives are usually presented topically and through anecdotes, rather than in a strictly chronological form.[33]

Sheila Rowbotham's ideas on the subject of the formation of the female self provides a perhaps more useful framework for understanding how Zakira Begam's sense of self developed during her early years. Rowbotham asserts that a woman, unlike a man, is always aware that she is not simply a unique individual, but is a member of a group, a group of *women*, as that gender is defined by the dominant male culture within which she lives. Consequently she develops a *dual* selfhood.[34] This is well illustrated in the way that Zakira Begam keeps shifting discursively from speaking of herself as an individual to speaking about womanhood—or girlhood—in general. She writes frequently about experiences that came about not following from any personal qualities or circumstances of her own but simply by virtue of the fact that she belonged to that male-defined category of "female person." For example, descriptions of her own personal difficulties acquiring desired reading material repeatedly slide into descriptions of how "men" restrict the freedom of *all* young girls to read what they wish. In my view it is this consciousness of being female and consequently constrained and limited in one's movement and activities—more than the structural features that Jelinek posits as diagnostic of an author's gender—that makes it possible to characterize Zakira Begam's memoir as a distinctively feminine one.

The dynamics of Zakira Begam's intensely involved relationship to the printed word during her childhood is hardly something unique to her, either as an individual or as a representative of a particular social/cultural category: early twentieth-century Indian Muslim preadolescent girls. Literate young women in all times and places imbue the literary characters—especially the female ones—in the stories and novels they read with personal meaning. As Rachel M. Brownstein has so cogently observed, young women readers "like to read about heroines in fiction so as to rehearse possible lives and to imagine a woman's life as important—because they want to be attractive and powerful and significant, someone whose life is worth writing about, whose world revolves around her and makes being the way she is make sense. The reader can see the heroine of a novel and be her, too, as she wishes she could simultaneously be and critically see herself."[35]

Notwithstanding the fact that she was raised in a very different cultural background, certain passages in Zakira Begam's memoir closely echo these remarks. She speaks repeatedly of yearning to become someone of importance when she grows up, to accomplish things that will make others look on her with admiration rather than—as she felt everyone did in those days—ignoring her, looking down on her or dismissing her as inept and unattractive. And she tells how she continually sought out—as do Brownstein's American young women—female literary characters who represented exemplars of the kind of person she aspired to be.

Janice Radway examines from a somewhat different perspective questions of the meaning of reading as an activity and of romance novels in particular as a preferred literary genre for middle-class housewives in the United States. Her findings echo Brownstein's idea that women see themselves in the novels they read, but they also raise other issues about the true nature of the emotional and psychological satisfaction her interview subjects derived from the almost formulaic novels that some described themselves as "addicted to." Radway characterizes the activity of reading for these women as both "combative and compensatory." She maintains that it provides "a space of privacy" within which they are able to focus, for a change, on themselves, "refus[ing] momentarily their self-abnegating social role" as nurturing wives and mothers. Furthermore, from their chosen genre of romance novels they obtain forms of "gratification [that are] ordinarily ruled out by the way the culture structures their lives."[36]

The women Radway interviewed were, of course, adult married women rather than preteen girls and, like the readers discussed by Brownstein, belonged to a very different culture from that of 1920s Hyderabad. But the theme of resistance to patriarchy in her analysis provides a significant link between the two. Indeed, both Radway's and Brownstein's observations resonate to a surprising degree with Zakira Begam's reflections on her almost obsessive desire to read certain kinds of popular novels over and over again and on her identification with and strong aspirations to emulate—though more consciously than Radway's adult romance readers appear to have done—their heroines.

In order to fully understand Zakira Begam's compelling desire to identify in the fiction she read female characters worthy of imitating in her own life, one must also take into account another aspect of the cultural context of her childhood. Even before she learned to read she was accustomed to listening on a regular basis to the stories that her mother, aunts, and grandmothers related to the children in the household about the Prophet Muhammad and his companions and about other heroes and heroines of Islamic and Indian history. Children were explicitly instructed to take the more admirable among these individuals as behavioral exemplars, for storytelling in this society was not only a form of entertainment but an educational tool. Later they began reading for themselves books that similarly related the lives and praiseworthy deeds of important religious and historical personages, and it was expected that they would be guided through that reading to become good daughters, wives, and mothers, good Muslims, and worthy citizens. One such book, written in the mid-nineteenth century by one of their ancestors, a renowned religious scholar and Islamic judge in the Carnatic court, dealt with the exemplary lives of women of the Prophet's family. According to Zakira Begam, some men of the family even believed that this book was the only one that young girls of their khāndān ought to be allowed to read![37] Given this background, it is not surprising that when Zakira Begam began to read popular fiction she would approach it in the same way that she had been taught to approach the oral stories she had heard and the classical literature she had earlier imbibed when learning to read Urdu and Persian.

But even aside from the influence of this particular cultural and religious literary tradition, I would argue that the appeal and the meaningfulness of reading as an activity and the strong tendency to identify vicariously with exemplary fictional heroines, while certainly fairly universal cross-culturally, are especially heightened for girls whose real-life social circles are highly circumscribed by culture or by circumstance. Manisha Roy makes a similar point about the major role that the reading of novels played in the socialization of upper-class Bengali Hindu young women in Calcutta in the post-Independence years. Roy's chief focus is on the impact of *romantic* fiction and poetry—genres that Zakira Begam avoids discussing directly—on a girl's fantasy life. She shows how it contributes to forming a girl's expectations for married life and creates aspirations for a loving and intimate relationship with the unknown husband-to-be that are, unfortunately, rarely realized in practice. In Roy's words, "Literature . . . , although it reflects reality, also exaggerates it and often exaggerates only those aspects of life that are beautiful and unattainable. Many thrive on reading such literature, which makes them aware of feelings they may not feel able to articulate."[38]

Girls like Zakira Begam and others of her generation and social position who were raised in late colonial India in very religiously and socially conservative Muslim households, where the seclusion of women was strictly observed, had even more limited opportunities than did Roy's upper-class Bengali Hindu girls to meet outsiders or to closely observe and partake of modes of interaction practiced within families that were outside of their immediate kinship networks. They had fewer opportunities to become personally acquainted with the values and lifestyles of people of different religious and cultural backgrounds, and it was, therefore, not easy for them to find real-life role models other than those with whom they interacted every day in their own homes. Fictional characters would have played an even more important role—in terms of contributing to a developing sense of self and helping them to deal psychologically with troubling issues in their own lives—than they would for girls of the same age living in well-to-do, cosmopolitan Bengali families. The contrast is even starker when we compare Zakira Begam's milieu with that characteristic of many cultures outside of South Asia, where young girls are permitted, are indeed expected, to move within wide social and geographical arenas and to regularly engage in interaction with a varied assortment of unrelated peers, schoolmates, teachers, neighbors, and family friends and associates. In any event, the role that the reading of fiction played in the development of Zakira Begam's selfhood cannot be overstated. It would be no exaggeration to say that the passion for reading that overcame her at an early age and never left her throughout her long life is what made her the vital, accomplished, and widely admired woman that she eventually became.

NOTES

1 Her full given name was Zakira Amat-ul Wahid. She began writing in her late teens under the name "Zakira bint [daughter of] Fazlullah Ahmad" but later adopted the surname of her husband, Muhammad Ghouse. When I knew her in the 1980s and 1990s her younger relatives, friends, and acquaintances usually appended to her name the respectful title *begam*, literally "lady" or "noblewoman." I will use that mode of reference for her here, as I did in her life. From 1801 to 1855 key male ancestors had held high positions in the courts of successive Nawabs of the Carnatic in Madras (now Chennai). For more about the family see my "Household Form and Formation: Variability and Social Change among South Indian Muslims," in *Society from the Inside Out: Anthropological Perspectives on the South Asian Household*, ed. J. N. Gray and D. J. Mearns (New Delhi: Sage, 1989), 107–39; "The Cultural Construction of Shared Identity: A South Indian Muslim Family History," in *Person, Myth and Society in South Asian Islam*, ed. P. Werbner, special issue of *Social Analysis* 28 (1990), 114–31; "Schooling for What? The Cultural and Social Context of Women's Education in a South Indian Muslim Family," in *Women, Education and Family Structure in India*, ed. C. C. Mukhopadhyay and S. Seymour (Boulder, CO: Westview, 1994), 135–64; "Identity and Difference or Equality and Inequality in South Asian Muslim Society," in *Caste Today*, ed. C. Fuller (New Delhi: Oxford University Press, 1996), 227–62; "Family Biographies as Sources for an Historical Anthropology of Muslim Women's Lives in Nineteenth-Century South India," in *The Resources of History: Tradition, Narration and Nation in South Asia*, ed. J. Assayag (Paris: École française d'Extrême Orient, 1999), 153–72; "Older Women, Past and Present, in an Indian Muslim Family," in *Thinking Social Science in India: Essays in Honour of Alice Thorner*, ed. S. Patel, J. Bagchi, and K. Raj (New Delhi: Sage, 2002), 247–63.

2 I have described and analyzed this memoir in some detail elsewhere; see my "*Hamara Daur-i Hayat*: An Indian Muslim Woman Writes Her Life," in *Telling Lives in India: Biography, Autobiography and the Life History*, ed. D. Arnold and S. Blackburn (Delhi: Permanent Black, 2004), 144–74. I have also drawn on it for a more general profile of the author and her life in "Dr. Zakira Ghouse: A Memoir," in *Muslim Portraits: Everyday Lives in India*, ed. Mukulika Banerjee (New Delhi: Yoda Press, 2008), 109–27.

3 The memoir was written for a family women's magazine *Mushir-un Niswān* [The woman's advisor], which she and a girl cousin began producing in 1935 (after the period covered by the memoir), when she was fourteen years old. The magazine was modeled on popular Urdu women's magazines that were widely read by literate Muslim women all over India when Zakira Begam was growing up. See Gail Minault, "Urdu Women's Magazines in the Early Twentieth Century," *Manushi* 48 (1988): 2–9; "Women's Magazines in Urdu as Sources for Muslim Social History," *Indian Journal of Gender Studies* 5 (1998): 201–13; *Secluded Scholars: Women's Education and Muslim Social Reform in Colonial India* (Delhi: Oxford University Press, 1998), 105–57.

4 Minault, *Secluded Scholars*, 31–55. For synopses and discussion of some of these novels, see Shaista Akhtar Banu Suhrawardy, *A Critical Survey of the Development of the Urdu Novel and Short Story* (London: Longmans, Green, 1945). See also Ralph Russell, *The Pursuit of Urdu Literature* (London: Zed, 1992).
5 See, for example, Janice Radway, *Reading the Romance: Women, Patriarchy, and Popular Literature* (Chapel Hill: University of North Carolina Press, 1984); Rachel M. Brownstein, *Becoming a Heroine: Reading about Women in Novels* (New York: Viking, 1982).
6 Vatuk, "*Hamara Daur-i Hayat.*"
7 An initial rough English translation of the transcribed tapes (undertaken by Dr. Yasmin Zaim) fills approximately four hundred double-spaced typed pages. The memoir itself accounts for about two-thirds of the total.
8 *Baquir Agah's Contribution to Arabic, Persian and Urdu Literatures*, MLitt thesis, Madras University (1973). She wrote this thesis in Urdu; her husband helped her to translate it into English for submission to the university. She later had the Urdu version published as *Maulānā Bāqir Āgā Velūrī: Shakhsyat aur Fan* [Maulana Baqir Aga of Vellore: Personality and accomplishments] (Madras: Tamilnadu Urdu Publications, 1995). Her other published book is a biography of Abdul Haq, author of a well-known Urdu-English dictionary and other linguistic and literary works, for whom her father was a research assistant for a time in the 1930s: *Hayāt-i Haq: 'Abdul Haq kī Zindagī kī Cand Jhalkiyan* [Abdul Haq: Some glimpses of his life] (Madras: Model Art Press, 1975).
9 I am grateful to C. M. Naim for his generous assistance during the initial stages of the project.
10 Work on an edited translation is still ongoing, with the encouragement and valuable assistance of one of Zakira Begam's daughters, Rafeth Yasmin, and a son, Muhammad Javed.
11 See, for example, Diane Wood Middlebrook, "Postmodernism and the Biographer," in *Revealing Lives: Autobiography, Biography, and Gender*, ed. S. G. Bell and M. Yalom (Albany: State University of New York Press, 1990), 155–66; Elinor Ochs and Lisa Capps, "Narrating the Self," *Annual Review of Anthropology* 25 (1996): 19–43.
12 Sidonie Smith, "Performativity, Autobiographical Practice, Resistance," in *Women, Autobiography, Theory: A Reader*, ed. S. Smith and J. Watson (Madison: University of Wisconsin Press, 1998), 108–9.
13 This was in contrast to the practice followed in some other families, where boys were sent to school and even encouraged to pursue advanced studies, while their sisters remained illiterate. If girls expressed an interest in learning to read—and particularly in learning to write—they were often forcibly prevented from doing so, on the grounds that it would distract them from their domestic responsibilities and possibly tempt them to engage in illicit correspondence with members of the opposite sex (see, for example, C. M. Naim, "How Bibi Ashraf Learned to Read and Write," *Annual of Urdu Studies* 6 (1987), 99–115; and Tanika Sarkar, *Words to Win: The Making of Amar Jiban; A Modern Autobiography* (Delhi: Kali for Women, 1999).

14 Recall Antoinette Burton's discussion of the centrality of "house and home" in Indian women's memoirs (*Dwelling in the Archive: Women Writing House, Home and History in Late Colonial India* (New York: Oxford University Press, 2003).
15 At the end of each quotation from the memoir I have indicated the section from which it was taken. Quotations from Zakira Begam's comments to me as she read aloud from the text are printed in italics.
16 The use of physical punishment by teachers—whether family members, hired tutors, or schoolteachers—was not unusual. This passage is very reminiscent of Abida Sultaan of Bhopal's account of learning to read the Qur'an under the tutelage of her paternal grandmother around the same period (Abida Sultaan, *Memoirs of a Rebel Princess* [Karachi: Oxford University Press, 2004], 16-19). Judith Walsh gives several similar examples from a selection of (mostly male) Indian autobiographies written in English (*Growing Up in British India: Indian Autobiographers on Childhood and Education under the Raj* [New York: Holmes and Meier, 1983]).
17 See Vatuk, "Schooling for What?"
18 *Khawātīn-i Khānwāda-i Badr-ud Daula kī Adabī, Tālimī aur Mazhabī Khidmāt* [The literary, educational and religious contributions of the women of the family of Badr-ud Daula], PhD diss., Madras University, 1994.
19 Faisal Fatehali Devji, "Gender and the Politics of Space: The Movement for Women's Reform in Muslim India, 1857–1900," *South Asia* 14 (1991): 141–53.
20 Walida-i Afzal Ali [Akbari Begam], *Gūdar kā La'l* [A ruby in rags] (Lucknow: Nasim Book Depot, 1967). The book was originally published around 1911–12 in installments in a women's magazine. For a synopsis and critique see Suhrawardy, *Critical Survey*, 141–46.
21 Barbara D. Metcalf, *Perfecting Women: Maulana Ashraf 'Ali Thanawi's Bihishti Zewar* (Berkeley: University of California Press, 1991).
22 Nazir Ahmad, *Mirāt-ul Urūs* [The bride's mirror] (Karachi: Sultan Husain, 1963). It was originally published in 1869.
23 C. M. Naim, "Prize-Winning *Adab*: A Study of Five Urdu Books Written in Response to the Allahabad Government Gazette Notification," in *Moral Conduct and Authority: The Place of Adab in South Asian Islam*, ed. B. D. Metcalf (Berkeley: University of California Press, 1984), 302.
24 Rashid-ul Khairi, *Jauhar-i Qadāmat* (Karachi: 'Allamah Rashid-ul Khairi Akaidami, 1971). For a synopsis, see Suhrawardy, *Critical Survey*, 110–12. See also Gail Minault, "*Ismat*: Rashid ul-Khairi's Novels and Urdu Literary Journalism for Women," in *Urdu and Muslim South Asia*, ed. C. Shackle (London: School of Oriental and African Studies, 1989), 129–36.
25 See Minault, *Secluded Scholars*, 129–48.
26 The term *āshraf* refers to Muslim families of "respectability" and good breeding, often distinguished from the Muslim masses on the basis of their claims of foreign, rather than Hindu convert, ancestry. See David Lelyveld, *Aligarh's First Generation: Muslim Solidarity in British India* (Princeton, NJ: Princeton University Press, 1978), 35–101, for a discussion of the values, lifestyles, and culture of this class in the second half of the nineteenth and early twentieth centuries.

27 Asiya Alam, "Polygyny, Family and *Sharafat*: Discourses amongst North Indian Muslims, circa 1870–1918," *Modern Asian Studies* 45 (2011), 631–68.
28 I have not been able to locate a copy of the book, but see the synopsis in Suhrawardy, *Critical Survey*, 148–50.
29 Estelle C. Jelinek, Introduction, *Women's Autobiography: Essays in Criticism* (New York: Twayne, 1980), 1–20.
30 Judith E. Walsh, *Growing Up in British India*, 13.
31 In my *"Hamara Daur-i Hayat,"* 151–52.
32 Kathryn Hansen, *Stages of Life: Indian Theatre Autobiographies* (Ranikhet: Permanent Black, 2011), 305–6.
33 See, for example, Hamilton A. R. Gibb, "Islamic Biographical Literature," in *Historians of the Middle East*, ed. B. Lewis (London: Oxford University Press, 1962), 54–58; Ann K. Lambton, "Persian Biographical Literature," in *Historians of the Middle East*, ed. B. Lewis (London: Oxford University Press, 1962), 141–51.
34 Sheila Rowbotham, *Woman's Consciousness, Man's World* (London: Penguin, 1973).
35 Brownstein, *Becoming a Heroine*, xxiv.
36 Janice Radway, *Reading the Romance*, 210–11.
37 Muhammad Sibghatullah, *Riyāz-un Niswān: Misāil-i Fiqh Shāfa'i* [Devotional training for women: Issues in Shafa'i jurisprudence] (Hyderabad: Matbu'a Ibrahīmiya Mashīn Parais, 1937–38). This book was originally published in Urdu—or Hindavi, as it was called in south India at that time—in 1809.
38 Manisha Roy, *Bengali Women* (Chicago: University of Chicago Press, 1972), 11. See also 32–58. On how more contemporary Indian young women read romance novels, see Jyoti Puri, "Reading Romance Novels in Post-colonial India," *Gender and Society* 11.4 (1997): 434–52.

2. PENTIMENTO

The Self beneath the Surface

RITU MENON

I begin with Virginia Woolf's assertion that "very few women yet have written truthful autobiographies" (meaning thereby that concealment with them is reflexive)—and yet it is a fact that, in India at least, many women first came to writing through autobiography. In a crucial sense, writing her autobiography was a woman's way of narrating her own story, of recognizing the importance of doing so, of knowing deep down, in a fundamental way, that "to be storyless" was, as Carolyn Heilbrun says, her ultimate anonymity.[1] Some of the earliest autobiographies (in Bengali) date from the mid-nineteenth century onward and were written without fanfare or artifice, sincere attempts at recording lives and times when both mobility and education were hard to come by for women. Often moving and poignant, they are also valuable as unselfconscious social history, offering a glimpse into cultural mores, codes of behavior, and gender relations. Yet, the genre itself is complicated, fraught with contradictory pressures. It hovers, as Sabir Khan points out, between reportage, retrospection, and revision.[2] It slips between truth and memory; between revelation and concealment; it comes to us loaded with affect, raises questions of "veracity and the fictive, of privacy, of partiality, of mediation."[3] It is, moreover, not simply a narrative, but an act of narrativization, "a two-fold transformation of lived life: the figuration into memory of experiences and sensations, and then the transmutation of that memory into a coherent narrative."[4] It is even, perhaps, via the autobiographical act, an attempt to reinvent a life and thus "possess it more fully."[5] A feminist reading of autobiographies must necessarily attend to yet another factor—the split between the personal and political selves, the separation of private and public, and often, between private and secret.

How then, and where then, should I situate myself when attempting to write about two autobiographical texts by the well-known novelist Nayantara Sahgal, whose own biography I am researching? How am I to reconcile not only all the contradictions and complications inherent in reading such texts, but accommodate what I know of her life from other sources, including letters, interviews, and conversations with her—information and material that the general reader is unlikely to have—with what she herself has chosen to represent, reconstruct, recall, and retell? I cannot pretend that I have in any way resolved this predicament or arrived at a clearer understanding of my relationship both to the author or to her autobiographies, but let me attempt a tentative narration of the unfolding as it occurred.

The Past Recalled

Nayantara Sahgal belongs to one of India's most distinguished political families, the Nehrus, and is also one of the most eminent Indian writers in English today. She has been a journalist, political commentator, essayist, biographer, and novelist, and perhaps the only woman writer in English to have consistently reflected the political life of India in her novels. From her first novel, *A Time to Be Happy*, published in 1958, to her latest, *Lesser Breeds* (2003), she has followed the evolution of democracy and politics in the country, from its promise of equality and freedom from want to its present crisis of credibility. In all, she has written nine novels, among them the well-known *Storm in Chandigarh* (1969), *The Day in Shadow* (1972), *A Situation in New Delhi* (1977), *Rich Like Us* (1985), and *Mistaken Identity* (1988). But it was her memoir of growing up during the freedom movement, *Prison and Chocolate Cake*, published in 1954, that brought her early fame; and it is her two autobiographical works, *Prison* and *From Fear Set Free* (1962) that are the subject of this paper.

Growing up in Allahabad in the 1930s and 1940s as the daughter of Vijaya Lakshmi and Ranjit Sitaram Pandit, and niece of Jawaharlal Nehru, politics was Sahgal's daily diet, and prison, her parents' second home. "My family plunged into civil disobedience," she says; "here it was that national and family history met.... The connection became rooted, emotional, permanent."[6] "Normal" family life for Nayantara was an extended experience of separation and personal sacrifice, in pursuit of independence and freedom from colonial rule. Arbitrary arrest, unjust fines, unprovoked violence, and the response to them by her family made for an early exposure to—and lasting impact of—two fundamental tenets of Indian resistance: nonviolence and satyagraha. Nehru— whom she calls her third parent—and Gandhi's political ideology remained the barometer by which Sahgal gauged the practice of Indian democracy post- Independence, their idealism and integrity to political principle the lodestar that guided her own commitment to India and the political developments of the day. Her novels of the 1970s and 1980s, as well as her political columns, reflect her anxiety at the abandonment of a particular, Nehruvian political and social project for India, and at the consequent debasement of its political culture.

Prison and Chocolate Cake, Nayantara's first book, was written in the winter of 1952–53, when the author was twenty-five years old and the mother of two children. Married at twenty-one to Gautam Sahgal, the son of a prominent Punjabi family of professionals, she lived with her husband in Bombay, where Gautam was employed with the Swiss pharmaceutical company Ciba-Geigy. Tara Pandit (as she had been known) could hardly have chosen a partner whose background and temperament were so completely at variance with her own, but their attraction to each other had been immediate and electric, and they made an extremely striking couple. Introduced to each other by Tara's aunt, Fori Nehru (married to Nehru's cousin, B. K. Nehru, and who stayed with the Sahgals when she first came out to India from Hungary), they met at the Delhi Gymkhana Club in December 1947, very soon after Tara's return from the United States.

Although Gautam belonged to a well-known West Punjab family and the Sahgals had considerable property in East Punjab as well as Lahore, the news of Tara's engagement to him was greeted with some concern. Letters flew between Mrs. Pandit and her brother, between her and Fori Nehru, and between her and her brother-in-law in Bombay.[7] The haste with which Tara announced her intention to marry Gautam, a mere two months after meeting him, prompted even her beloved Mamu into cautioning her. Nehru's misgivings about his young niece's whirlwind romance were expressed in characteristically mild tones: he thought she should do something with her education, work perhaps, there were so many ways in which she could make herself useful, and there was time enough for marriage.[8] She was only twenty, after all, and her education was just beginning. At the very least, she should take some time off to think it over. Tara herself was acutely aware of the mismatch.

The Partition became for me more than a troubling event. Because of it I had met a young man employed in a British firm, an Indian whose India had been as different from mine as any man I could have met, whose home in Lahore had had the best of linen, glass and wine that his father's frequent trips to Europe could provide, in contrast to mine, which in support of the Swadeshi movement used only Indian-made goods. What was more, this was an Indian to whom Gandhi was just a name, and freedom for his country an event that had deprived him of his home and a part of his inheritance. I worried about the differences between us, and soon learned that hesitation was not a part of Gautam's make-up. He tackled problems with a figurative lawn-mower. After a while they no longer existed. Everything eventually became smooth lawn. For me, life resembled a rock garden full of unaccountable small crevices and obstructions. How could I enter his world or he mine? We would make a new one, said Gautam. He envisaged no problems. He concentrated on the particular, and the particular issue soon became marriage.[9]

Gregarious and ambitious, Gautam Sahgal rose rapidly up the corporate ladder in Bombay, and the family enjoyed all the comforts and privileges of his success: a beautiful home, two precious children, a social circle that consisted of the city's business and political elite, and the adventure of being young in a newly independent country where everything was possible.

Bombay's social life glittered with the city's corporate smart set and its old business elite, a circle in which Gautam felt completely at ease, and at home. Unlike his first employer, Bird and Company, Ciba-Geigy was Swiss and noncolonial, eager to enter the huge market for pharmaceuticals that India promised; the management trusted Gautam to do his best. He responded with characteristic vigor. The Sahgals entertained with gusto, and along with Gautam's business contacts, assorted diplomats, and her mother's acquaintances, Nayantara frequently met the industrialist Jeh Tata and his wife, Thelly; the painter Jehangir Sabavala and his wife, Shireen; Raj and Romesh Thapar, journalist and later publisher of *Seminar*; Peter Jayasinghe of Asia Publishing House and his wife, Lily; the journalist Frank Moraes and cartoonist R. K. Laxman, brother of the writer R. K. Narayan. Through Premi Wagle, the writer Santha Rama Rau's sister, she was introduced to a circle of lunchtime women friends who were much more varied than her evening company, but despite an extremely full and busy social and family life, she never really took to the city.

The change for Nayantara was dramatic. "Bombay was very cosmopolitan and westernized, a complete change from Allahabad. I had never been there except to visit Masi [her aunt, Krishna Hutteesingh] during vacations. It was my first experience of what people call normal life, for which I had no preparation. I had no idea that people could go to the office from nine to five, come back, go to the Club. . . . The routine, the whole ambience, was foreign to me."[10]

An unfamiliar domesticity, together with the unaccustomed idleness of the upper middle classes, now encircled Nayantara. The urge to do something beyond the domestic, to partake actively in some way in the life of the country, made itself felt in her life as early as two years after her marriage. In 1951 she wrote to her uncle, Jawaharlal Nehru, confiding in him her frustrations at being just wife and mother, as well as her difficulties, and seeking his advice. Should she join the Congress? Engage in social work? Or, given her circumstances, just write? Nehru replied immediately and sympathetically, encouraging her to do something worthwhile outside the home. "One cannot ignore the domestic sphere," he said, "but a wider activity gives more meaning to life." He refrained from telling her what to do, however, remarking only that there were several ways of doing something socially useful. Should she decide to write, her writing should have some purpose. "In the final analysis," he wrote, "one writes from one's experience of life. The richer the experience the better the writing."[11]

But biology intervened; Nayantara's second child, her son Ranjit, was born nine months after she wrote to Nehru, and it was only a full year later that she had the time and leisure to pick up her pen.

Prison and Chocolate Cake became that work written from experience, her attempt at capturing the "special magic" of growing up during India's struggle for freedom, as part of a family whose men and women had committed their lives to it. "I knew history would record the struggle," she has said, but her purpose was altogether different. She wanted to present the "texture of a time, the froth and bubble of a mood or a moment,"[12] the everyday reality of that struggle and what it meant as she experienced it, to offer a ringside view of history in the making.

There may not be too many opening sentences in a memoir or autobiography as immediately arresting as the following: "Some things will always remain a mystery to me. How did Mummie and Papu have the courage to send us to America in 1943? . . . Few went as we did, at our age, from a peaceful country on a troop ship at the height of war."[13] "We" were Nayantara, then sixteen, and her older sister, Chandralekha, nineteen, headed for the United States and Wellesley College in Massachusetts, on an ocean journey that would take several weeks. The year was 1943, and India was part of Britain's war effort, while at the same time resisting British imperialism and demanding that they quit India. It would have taken an extraordinary set of circumstances for any parent to dispatch two teenaged girls, unchaperoned, to a country several thousand miles away, while a war was in progress. And the circumstances were indeed extraordinary. On August 8, 1942, the All India Congress Committee passed its Quit India Resolution in Bombay, and on August 9, Gandhi, Azad, Patel, Nehru, Sarojini Naidu, and other members of the Congress Working Committee were arrested and taken by a special train to Poona.[14] The AICC office at Swaraj Bhawan was sealed yet again by the police, and because it was only a matter of time before she and Indira and Feroze Gandhi were also arrested, Vijaya Lakshmi Pandit set about organizing Anand Bhawan (where the family now lived) in preparation for her absence. This included disposing of pamphlets and incriminating documents before the police got hold of them, sending valuables to friends' homes for safekeeping, and finding refuge for two young friends, fugitives from the police.[15]

Lekha herself had been imprisoned for participating in the Quit India protests of 1942, and other family elders were liable to be picked up at any time. The political situation was likely to worsen very quickly, and so, at Mme. Chiang Kai-shek's suggestion, Nayantara and Lekha were sent to Wellesley and, in 1945, their younger sister, Rita, sent to the Putney School in Vermont.[16]

All this is recounted, sometimes humorously, at other times, poignantly in *Prison and Chocolate Cake*, interleaved with vignettes of family life at Anand Bhawan, with experiences of changing schools again and again as the uncertainty of their parents' presence at home grew, and the sisters learned to come to terms with the fact that Vijay Lakshmi and Ranjit Pandit were more likely to be in jail than out of it. The heartbreak of separation had to be borne without tears, with stoicism and a steely resolve to continue the fight. When Chandralekha at one point wistfully wondered to Nehru whether life would ever be normal for them, "'Normal?' Mamu repeated, savoring the word as though it was as foreign to his vocabulary as it was to his life. 'The fact is that we live in an upside-down world, darling, and it's no use expecting life to be easy. It is not a simple matter adjusting to such a world, especially for those who are sensitive. It is not normal for most of us to spend our lives in prison cut off from our families and dear ones. It certainly should not be normal for intelligent human beings to spend all their time and energy killing each other off, as they are doing all over the world. It isn't normal either for some people to starve and others to get indigestion through overeating. All this is very abnormal and wrong, but it is happening.'"[17]

The bleakness of those days in a sprawling house, stripped of valuables, even carpets and furniture, would be temporarily banished whenever Padmaja Naidu, beloved friend of the family, alighted like an exotic bird to keep the children company. Brilliantly plumed in glowing silks and flowers in her hair, Padmasi (as she was called) dispelled the gloom with warmth and cheer and wit. Delicious tidbits like the girls being laughed at when they wore khadi frocks and little Gandhian topis when out for a walk, or a nervous Indira Nehru offering "potato-Cripps" to Sir Stafford Cripps when he came to visit, are part of a happy recall of times when all the adults were in residence and Anand Bhawan buzzed with political activity, with streams of people, great and humble, passing through, staying, discussing and deciding strategy.[18]

As a welcome counterpoint to that upside-down world is the excitement of New York, the pleasure of an uninterrupted four years in an invigorating academic environment at Wellesley opening up new intellectual vistas, and hugely enjoyable vacations on the East and West Coasts of America or in Mexico, and in the homes of luminaries like Pearl Buck and her husband; the powerful singer Paul Robeson and his wife, Essie; the Henry Luces, the photographer Dorothy Norman, whose apartment in New York was Nayantara's second home—and a host of others.

Prison and Chocolate Cake was published in 1954 in New York. A network of friends and acquaintances in places that mattered enabled the smooth passage of the manuscript of *Prison and Chocolate Cake* from Nayantara's typewriter to her editor, Herbert Weinstock, at the publishing house of Alfred A. Knopf. Her mother showed it to a friend, Govind Biharilal, who in turn showed it to *his* friend, the literary agent Sarah Neumeyer, and she sold it to Knopf. The book was well received and happily reviewed for a variety of reasons. The author was a young, well-connected writer, writing about a contemporary political situation in a country that had captured the world's imagination for its nonviolent resistance to colonial rule. She presented an insider's view of India's freedom movement with all the freshness and idealism of a twenty-five-year-old, and she wrote a limpid prose. Contrary to what might have been expected, hers was no picture of exotic India, or of beleaguered womanhood, comforting to those who looked for conformity, rather, a warm and human account of an unusual family that lived in and shaped its country's fortunes at a historic moment. It became a literary and commercial success, marking out a space for itself as a political memoir with a difference.

The Present Recounted

....

From Fear Set Free, the second volume of Nayantara Sahgal's autobiography, was written in Bombay and published in 1962 by W. W. Norton in the United States, and by Victor Gollancz in the UK. Knopf, who had published *Prison and*

Chocolate Cake in 1954, declined *From Fear Set Free*, saying it did not strike the right note for them, that they were not confident about its marketability, even though they had met with considerable success with *Prison*. Weinstock, by then Knopf's publisher, wrote to Nayantara to say that gross sales of the book in the United States, not long after it was published, were seven thousand copies in hardback. "This is not a bestseller," he said, "but it is a very handsome sale in what has been a very poor publishing season."[19] However, the left-wing British publisher Victor Gollancz, who had published *Prison and Chocolate Cake*, was more than happy to take *From Fear Set Free*, and not only because he was a great supporter of Indian independence. At the time, Gollancz's stable of authors included the South African Nadine Gordimer, whose two collections of short stories, *The Soft Voice of the Serpent* and *Occasion for Loving*, were published in the late 1950s; Kingsley Amis; A. J. Cronin; Daphne du Maurier; Dorothy Sayers; Ivy Compton-Burnett; Colin Wilson; and a galaxy of other major writers. The only other Indian on his list, however, was the philosopher J. Krishnamurthi. Nayantara was one of Gollancz's acquisitions from America, which he had begun visiting professionally during the 1950s.[20]

Beginning with her return to India from the United States in 1947, after her graduation from Wellesley College, *From Fear Set Free* deals with the early years of Nayantara's marriage to Gautam Sahgal, the birth of her three children—Nonika and Ranjit were followed by Gita, born in 1956—and the first few years of her life in Bombay. Interspersed with anecdotal accounts of family reunions and amusing but sharply observant comments on Bombay society are glimpses of how the country was making its transition to independent governance. The first post-Independence elections were held in 1952, and Pandit Nehru undertook a nationwide tour to alert the electorate about the importance of voting, of exercising their franchise for the first time ever. Around the same time Vinoba Bhave started out on the first leg of his Bhoodan movement, spurred by his visit to Telengana in 1951 and his encounter with its desperately poor landless farmers. It was here that one man in the audience pledged one hundred of his two hundred acres to anyone in need; Vinoba's tour of Telengana that year netted fifteen thousand acres for the landless peasantry. Slowly other states followed suit.

The linguistic division of states in the 1950s was another change that began in the South, with Telugu speakers in the Madras Presidency demanding a state of their own—Andhra Pradesh. Bombay province followed suit, with the two dominant languages, Marathi and Gujarati, agitating for separate state status with Bombay as their capital. The first of the language riots and stormy sloganeering erupted on the streets, but Bombay remained in Maharashtra, while a new capital was mooted for Gujarat.

In 1963, Nayantara Sahgal embarked on a book tour of the United States for *From Fear Set Free*, which consisted of eighteen speaking engagements at various public and educational institutions across the country, and though she enjoyed it, she said she didn't care to repeat it. (Writing in her Chandigarh diary later that year she remarked wryly, "Lecture tour decidedly helpful in preparing one to face almost anything. Everybody ought to go on a lecture tour which, if it doesn't drive one mad, has character-building possibilities. Grateful my tour over and character built.")[21] The book itself received mixed reviews, some decidedly tepid; one in fact called it "a glamourised version of a housewife's diary," an assessment with which Nayantara herself agreed reluctantly. In a letter to her close friend, civil servant E. N. Mangat Rai, she wrote: *"From Fear Set Free* has irritated me profoundly, the fact that I allowed it to be published at all without a struggle. Originally, it was very political and the publisher—Knopf—said no one would be interested in that kind of book from me. They wanted something lighter, more 'readable.' They are very fond of using words like 'heart-warming,' and 'charming'—both of which make me a little ill. Anyway, the whole thing was rehashed in a lighter vein and it became all about nothing in particular."[22]

Left to herself, she said, she would have dwelt on India's prickly relationship with the United States of John Foster Dulles, would have introduced much more of the political context in the country, of the business and social environment they lived in. The irony is that, despite the rehashing at its request, Knopf declined its publication, and they ceased to be Nayantara's publisher after this experience.

Although Nayantara has written that "the process leading to freedom had so closely affected my family and my upbringing that it seemed to me an event almost of personal significance,"[23] the difference in tone and texture between *Prison and Chocolate Cake* and *From Fear Set Free* is marked; it marked, as well, a shift, albeit temporary, in her preoccupations. *Prison* was focused almost exclusively on the struggle for freedom in which the intertwined histories of the nationalist movement and family involvement came together seamlessly in a narrative that was, at once, charming autobiography and incipient national biography. This was what made it unusual and interesting as a maiden venture.

Between Past and Present
....

Eight years separated the publication of *Prison and Chocolate Cake* and *From Fear Set Free*, during which time Nayantara wrote and published her first novel, *A Time to Be Happy*, in 1958. She appeared to have settled into a writing groove, finding in it an activity that allowed her to create an intimate space, a space of the mind, that she could inhabit or retreat into almost like a refuge. It became a daily discipline. "I write the way some women go into the kitchen and cook," she told me. "If I wrote something I liked or was working satisfactorily on a book, I felt I'd eaten and slept. It was nourishment."[24] More crucially, however, it enabled her to reconnect, through recall, with a life she had known and cherished, a life of political commitment dedicated to a noble, uplifting cause. The nourishment for her was intellectual, of course, but it was also emotional and psychological. For her circumstances, as hinted in her letter to her uncle, had undergone a sea change.

By the mid-1950s, the "electricity" that had sparked between Nayantara and Gautam had lost its powerful charge, and suppressed strains in the marriage were beginning to surface. Nayantara felt confined and dissatisfied in her role as corporate wife, had few close friends in Bombay, and missed the deep and direct engagement with the country's political life that had been bread and butter for all her growing years. Gautam, meanwhile, young, dynamic, and upwardly mobile in the world of business and profit, sensed neither his wife's loneliness nor her discontent—nor, crucially, her growing apart from him, perhaps because his own intense involvement with her never flagged. Nayantara acknowledged in a letter that: "I always felt he gave me much more than I gave him. He surrounded me with a storm of feeling, a never-ending passion along with tenderness. He repeatedly told me, and made me feel, and I did feel, that I was his whole world. Even the children, the first two, had no place in his life because it was me he wanted. No one could be sweeter or more considerate than Gautam. No one could be more ruthless, either. . . . He could not bear the thought that I did not belong wholly to him, and there was an integrity about our physical relationship, a wholeness and reality about it that I could not doubt. . . . He knows, and I know, that this is true."[25]

Restless and dissatisfied, Nayantara began to feel she couldn't continue with her marriage. As always, when beset by doubt and confusion, she turned to her uncle for advice. Nehru suggested that she and Gautam go to Nagpur, where he was attending the January 1959 All India Congress Committee session, and discuss the problem in as open and accommodating a way as possible. In Nagpur he suggested that Tara spend some time with him, Mamu, in Delhi, then go to her mother in London in order to think matters over. She took his advice, did go to Delhi, and after a month returned, "nearly whole," to Bombay. Although she and Gautam, two wounded birds, tried hard to make a fresh start, they had been badly shaken by what had happened to their relationship. Nayantara recalled years of "inquisition with periods of normalcy, of a slow divorce from myself. Ten years was perhaps the limits of what the mind could take in this respect because that was when the explosion came. Even during this period I sometimes tried to tell Gautam how dissatisfied I was with our relationship, how I felt I was carrying a burden alone—not only of our marriage, but of our children, of everything big and small that had to do with a household. We were not building anything together. There was no meeting of our minds."[26]

Afraid and increasingly vulnerable in the face of Gautam's violent mood swings, Nayantara decided to act on Nehru's suggestion and visit her mother in London, give herself a chance to think about her marriage, away from her own home. London decided Nayantara. In several letters to Gautam she sought some kind of response from him to her genuine misgivings about their relationship, some acknowledgment or reassurance that he understood her unhappiness with the life they were leading. He evaded the issue; but she returned to Bombay with the decision to make her marriage work.[27]

Personal/Political

....

Not a ripple disturbs the smooth surface of *From Fear Set Free*, written *after* Nayantara's return from London, and dedicated to Gautam. Her interlude in England is recalled as a series of lighthearted anecdotes about the vagaries of household staff, of rediscovering friends she had made when she and Gautam visited London in 1955, and Mrs. Pandit's verve and élan as high commissioner after the controversial Krishna Menon, whom she succeeded. It betrays nothing of the emotional turmoil Nayantara was experiencing at the time, or her anxiety about her marriage and her children. The month she spent in Delhi is mentioned only toward the very end of the book and only obliquely, with a telling reference to a conversation with her uncle, Pandit Nehru: what quality, she asked him, did he consider most important for a successful marriage? "It is important always to leave the way open to talk," he replied; "as long as two people can talk there is a way back to understanding."[28] And so Nayantara left neither her home nor her marriage.

When she came back from London, Gautam was unexpectedly gentle and considerate, promising to give her the space she required for herself, to doubt her less, trust her more. He wanted to give the marriage another chance, he said. But for Nayantara there began now a long period of an emotional freeze. "I longed to have a proper conversation with somebody, just someone to talk to," she told me in 2008, but couldn't. Didn't dare, is how she put it, and her life was lived on two different planes: the conventional one of domesticity in her role as mother and wife of a successful corporate husband, within the well-defined norms of acceptable behavior; and an inner world of feeling, thinking, and growing discontent, which remained a closely guarded secret. "*From Fear Set Free* never said a word about anything that was really happening in my life then, nothing about the difficulties, emotional and otherwise, that I was up against at the time."[29] Sahgal's admission strikes a chord with Woolf's assertion about "truthful autobiographies," reinforcing the point that, for many women, although it may be possible to reveal the "private" in their autobiographical writing, the "secret" might well continue to remain concealed.

The Nehrus and Pandits were not simply a family of rebels against empire, but a family of rebels against empire who also wrote—and in a subtle way, wrote back. "There was no such thing as an Indian point of view," Nayantara has said, "we were always being interpreted by others.... As people under occupation one of the main ways you were suppressed is that you were not allowed to express yourself politically.... Even the fiction and non-fiction written at the time was through the lens of the Raj. It became a way for me to have my say about what really happened. A political way of writing was for me a very fundamental thing because one had been denied freedom of speech. There was very real censorship then... a degrading and humiliating experience to have one's mouth shut.... To write politically was the only way for me to proceed."[30] Nayantara's foray into writing, then, was not so much an exercise in self-expression or a young woman's dabbling in the realm of the literary. Rather, it was the medium she chose in order to fulfill a clear purpose: communicating an idea of India in an idiom inflected with an Indian accent, presenting a perspective that was a counter to prevailing and received wisdoms, presenting moreover, an account of alternative politics.

And yet her two memoirs cannot be read in the same register. Where *Prison and Chocolate Cake* is wholeheartedly about the tumult and exhilaration of political action and an intense personal commitment to it, *From Fear Set Free* is about concealment, with the tension of uncertainty replaced by the mundane detail of daily or, what Nayantara called, "normal" life. It was written in 1959, after she had made a conscious decision to bury her past so that her marriage could continue peacefully. The writing became a "polite exercise," reflecting nothing of what was going on; it became part of her attempt to bring the curtain down on everything that had happened earlier. Superficially, it was a continuation of her life as it had ended in *Prison and Chocolate Cake*, but of course, it was a very different life. "Before marriage and after marriage, a woman's life changes," she said, by way of explanation; "a woman's life is very different from a man's."[31]

Although this provides a clue to the differing tone and temper of *Prison and Chocolate Cake* and *From Fear Set Free*, I believe it tells only part of the story. In *Prison and Chocolate Cake* the author's personal and political selves are a harmonious whole, there is no disjunction between the life she and her family led, and the politics they believed in and practiced, and her recounting of it. Although she might later have described it as "naïve," and wondered how it could have "come out sounding like this (that is, upbeat) when it was about emotional strain and tragedy, about financial pressures, the repeated hardships of jail sentences,"[32] and the uncertainty about how it would affect the family, she never doubted the integrity of the endeavor or of her own place in it.

From Fear Set Free, on the other hand, sees a split in this personal/political persona, where both personal *and* political are concealed, the former as a conscious, deliberately exercised choice, the latter, because she was no longer connected to the historic and heroic in the same way.[33] She was far removed from it, in fact. Tara Pandit had become Nayantara Sahgal. Although her family connections obviously exposed her to the political life of the country—her mother was a diplomat, she contested elections, became governor of Maharashtra while Nayantara lived in Bombay, and so on—her own circumstances at the time militated against anything more than a superficial involvement in it.

Pentimento

As her biographer I had obviously begun by reading all of Nayantara's published work, a substantial oeuvre over five decades covering almost every genre, including her political columns, written between 1967 and 1975. At the same time I had also begun a series of long interviews with her, read files of correspondence, especially a few thousand letters written to E. N. Mangat Rai during the most difficult time in her marriage, and spoken to her children and other members of her family. As I continued my research it became increasingly clear that I would have to "read" her autobiographies differently, read them as a kind of pentimento.[34] I would need to read them as personal/political, naturally, and possibly also as intended by her (at least, *Prison and Chocolate Cake*) but for any closer understanding of them, I needed to acknowledge not only the public and private, but perhaps also the private and secret.

Yet this rereading would not have been possible without the supplementary material and resources that were made available, or if, like any lay reader, I had only her two published texts as my source. Nor would it have been as rewarding without the questing feminist interrogation of that defining fact of many writing women's lives—marriage and domesticity. Carolyn Heilbrun has claimed, boldly, that for women writers, marriage represents a kind of closure, the end of the romantic road, and of the possibility of anything other than a domestic routine. She quotes Mary Mitford, who, when asked if she would not have liked to have been married, said, "No, I never wanted a full, normal life."[35] Most marriages, especially first marriages, continues Heilbrun, are bad bargains for women writers; all good marriages are remarriages. "Only those who remarry," she says, "are married," echoing Stanley Cavell's conviction that it is in remarriage that we "must look for its conversations, for its qualities of friendship, above all for its equality and the equality of the man's and woman's quests."[36]

All our earlier qualifications regarding autobiographies apart, it would be unrealistic to expect such writing by a woman in her late twenties and early thirties to be a "complete" or even substantial account of her life. Nor, really, am I preoccupied with whether or how much Nayantara Sahgal revealed or concealed in her two texts, how "true" she is to her experiences, how "authentic" is her representation, or how "reliable" her recall. The self is seldom represented as unvarying, stable, and consistent over time; representations of it will change as the autobiographer or memoirist's contingent reality and circumstances change—indeed, as her life is lived. I see no serious contradiction between the self that Nayantara foregrounded in her autobiographies and what she revealed to me in her interviews close to fifty years later. Concealment, or what is also called self-censorship, is a spontaneous and understandable reflex when the issue is as intimate as marriage or when relationships are being renegotiated. It took Nayantara more than thirty years after her divorce in 1967 to publish a selection of letters between her and E. N. Mangat Rai (whom she later married), in which, for the first time, we get a glimpse of the strains and stresses in her marriage. To have made this public earlier might well have entailed permanent closure of a relationship she still cherished with Gautam; when the correspondence was eventually published in 1994, she said her decision to do so was impelled by the need to "set the record straight."

However, I would like to suggest an alternative, supplementary reading of her autobiographies, without supplanting or discounting any of my observations made earlier. Nayantara Sahgal's married life began to fall apart when she tried to deviate from a male-designed social and gender script for women, and very specifically, from her husband's script for her—and for them as a couple. Ostensibly, and certainly as far as Gautam was concerned, she had everything a woman could want—a husband who idolized her, the comfort and security of his success, a future of assured privilege. What could be ailing her? But as we know, chiefly from her letters, by her midtwenties she had begun to want to create another script for her life, perhaps even to create another self. In the eight years that elapsed between *Prison and Chocolate Cake* and *From Fear Set Free* she simultaneously found and suppressed an emerging self, an alter ego who held the promise of freedom, but who also threatened to rock the marital boat. The terrible poignancy of her decision, in 1959, to reconcile herself to an arid marriage, to bring the curtain down, as she said on everything that might provoke another violent outbreak of jealousy, signified a deliberate and willed silencing. *From Fear Set Free* reads like a "polite exercise" because, at a superficial level, it is a monument to a buried self; as an autobiographical text, therefore, it could go no further. But we must read it as a testament to Nayantara's determination to continue writing, and through her writing to create "another possibility of female destiny,"[37] both for herself and for her female characters. It is in her fiction, in the novels she wrote after *From Fear Set Free*, that we see a more composite self articulated; it is in them, written through what has been called "a curtained autobiographical practice," that we see a less-troubled reconciliation than what she had been able to achieve in her own life, till then.

NOTES

1 Carolyn G. Heilbrun, *Writing a Woman's Life* (New York: Ballantine, 1988), 12. The quotation from Virginia Woolf also comes from this source.
2 Sabir Khan, "The Enunciation of Space in Autobiography: Two South Asian Accounts," in 87th ACSA Annual Meeting Proceedings, n.d., 360.
3 Ann Snitow and Rachel Blau Du Plessis, *The Feminist Memoir Project: Voices from Women's Liberation* (New York: Three Rivers Press, 1998), 23.
4 Sabir Khan, "Enunciation," 360.
5 Tanika Sarkar, *Words to Win: The Making of* Amar Jiban*; A Modern Autobiography* (Delhi: Kali for Women, 1999), 3.
6 Nayantara Sahgal, interview with the author, Dehradun, March 15, 2009.
7 Nayantara Sahgal, interview with the author, Dehradun, August 3, 2008.
8 Nayantara Sahgal, interview with the author, Delhi, November 12, 2009.
9 Nayantara Sahgal, *From Fear Set Free* (New York: W. W. Norton, 1962), 34–35.
10 Nayantara Sahgal, interview with the author, Dehradun, August 3, 2008.
11 Jawaharlal Nehru to Nayantara Sahgal, unpublished letter dated February 2, 1951.
12 Nayantara Sahgal, *Prison and Chocolate Cake* (Delhi: HarperCollins, 2007), xv.
13 Sahgal, *Prison and Chocolate Cake*, 3.
14 From Zakaria Rafiq, *100 Glorious Years: Indian National Congress, 1885–1985* (Bombay: Reception Committee, Congress Centenary Session, 1985), 325–30.
15 Vijaya Lakshmi Pandit, *The Scope of Happiness: A Personal Memoir* (New York: Crown, 1979), 161–63.

16 Recounted in Sahgal, *Prison and Chocolate Cake*.
17 Sahgal, *Prison and Chocolate Cake*, 139.
18 Sahgal, *Prison and Chocolate Cake*, 139.
19 Herbert Weinstock to Nayantara Sahgal, unpublished letter dated October 1954.
20 Sheila Hodges, *Gollancz: The Story of a Publishing House 1928–1978* (London: Victor Gollancz, 1978).
21 A diary that the author kept while on vacation in Chandigarh in December 1963. Published in Nayantara Sahgal and E. N. Mangat Rai, *Relationship: Extracts from a Correspondence* (Delhi: HarperCollins, 2008), 295.
22 Nayantara Sahgal to E. N. Mangat Rai, unpublished letter dated September 7, 1964.
23 Nayantara Sahgal, *From Fear Set Free*, 9.
24 Nayantara Sahgal, interview with the author, Dehradun, March 15, 2009.
25 Nayantara Sahgal to E. N. Mangat Rai, unpublished letter dated October 31, 1964.
26 Nayantara Sahgal to E. N. Mangat Rai, letter dated September 14, 1964, published in *Relationship*.
27 There is a discrepancy here between what I was told by Nayantara Sahgal verbally, and what she wrote in a letter to E. N. Mangat Rai, in 1964, in which she says she had made up her mind in London that she and Gautam would have to part. The fact that she returned and that their marriage continued only highlights a common predicament for women in troubled marriages—you can't stay but don't want to leave. Or vice versa—you don't want to stay but can't leave.
28 Sahgal, *From Fear Set Free*, 237.
29 Nayantara Sahgal, interview with the author, Dehradun, March 15, 2009.
30 Nayantara Sahgal, interview with the author, Delhi, May 5, 2008.
31 Nayantara Sahgal, interview with the author, Dehradun, August 3, 2008.
32 Sahgal, *Prison and Chocolate Cake*, 13.
33 Although Nayantara said it was "rehashed" at Knopf's insistence, the fact remains that, when they declined publication, she did not amend her narrative in any way for Gollancz, who would have welcomed the political content.
34 That technique in painting whereby there are visible traces of earlier painting beneath the paint on a canvas.
35 Heilbrun, *Writing a Woman's Life*, 76.
36 Heilbrun, *Writing a Woman's Life*, 95.
37 Heilbrun, *Writing a Woman's Life*, 95.

3. INTERRUPTED STORIES

Self-Narratives of Nazr Sajjad Hyder

ASIYA ALAM

This chapter takes the diary and memoir of Nazr Sajjad Hyder (1892–1967) as the subject of its investigation. Born to an elite Shi'ite family in Punjab, Nazr Sajjad Hyder (Nazr from here) belonged to the class of Muslims that found employment in the colonial government and were supporters and beneficiaries of Sayyid Ahmed Khan's ideas and the Aligarh movement. In her life she wrote novels; contributed columns and journalistic pieces to Urdu women's magazines like *Tahzib-e Niswan*, *Khatoon*, and *Ismat*; and was actively involved in several reformist efforts directed particularly at the expansion of women's education. In the second half of the twentieth century, her daughter, Qurratulain Hyder, also acquired renown as a writer.

Nazr's diary and memoir were serialized over a period of twenty-one years from 1942 to 1963 in the Urdu magazines *Tahzib-e Niswan* and *Ismat*. Urdu women's magazines provided one of the most accessible print forums for Muslim women to express their ideas and publicly converse with other members of society in early twentieth-century India. The development of a vibrant print culture in all Indian languages including Urdu provided alternate forms of narration in a public sphere already animated by traditional modes of oral performance.[1] Along with several genres of writing such as short stories, polemical articles, and instructional columns, self-narratives such as the diary, or a *roz-namcha* (daybook) as it was called, also featured in the pages of Urdu women's magazines.² Scholars need to integrate these earlier narratives of diary, memoir, or even self-reflective essays published in Urdu women's magazines more fully in South Asian historiography.³ What was the structure and format of these narratives when they were published? What kind of self-fashioning emerges from these accounts, and what is left out? What can they reveal to us about a society and its changing conditions? This chapter attempts to answer these queries through a close analysis of Nazr's serialization of her diary and memoir in *Tahzib-e Niswan* and *Ismat*. Instead of reading Nazr's autobiography as a single document, I argue in this chapter that it must be viewed through a lens of multiplicity where it is composed of different styles of self-narration and is closely related to the contexts of its production. Narrative and historical context are constituted mutually here and form an interdependent archive to reveal a space where remembrance and memory can be discerned and historicized.

Modes of Self-Narration: Diary, Memoir, Letter
....

The writing of Nazr's self in public has taken place through multiple genres including diary, memoir, and letter. Nazr started to serialize her self-writing in 1942 in *Tahzib-e Niswan* under the heading of "roz-namcha" (diary), stopped in 1944, and then continued it as a memoir in *Ismat* in 1950. In order to understand the difference between the genre of diary and memoir both in the abstract and in its particular relation to Nazr's voice, it is crucial to discuss here the context and construction of the two narratives in Nazr's own life. Nazr started serializing her diary in *Tahzib-e Niswan* on the suggestion of its editor Imtiaz Ali. The diary of Hijab Imtiaz Ali, his wife, was serialized in *Tahzib-e Niswan* from 1941 to 1942 under the title of *Lail-o Nihar* [Day and night]. Nazr writes that Imtiaz Ali encouraged her to also publish her diary in *Tahzib-e Niswan*, saying this would make "*Tahzibi* sisters very happy."⁴ Thus beginning its public life in August 1942, the diary was subtitled "Copy of an Old Diary from Some Places" and had been written by Nazr several years before in the early twentieth century. The narrative conventions of a diary dictate that one record on a regular basis the daily activities of a particular day. Nazr's diary in *Tahzib-e Niswan* illustrates the experiences and events of a particular date and begins on January 8, 1908, with the sentence, "today was the most tragic day of my life," describing her grief at the death of her mother Mustafai Begam.⁵ With this striking note, Nazr's *Tahzib-e Niswan* diary goes on to describe events from a decade of her life from January 8, 1908, to April 15, 1919. In these ten years, her diary provides glimpses of her marriage in 1912, the establishment of a girl's school in Dehradun in 1914, the death of her children, and the stressful impact of the First World War on her familial life.

In contrast to the diary format of the *Tahzib-e Niswan* narrative, the text of *Ismat*, starting in 1950, has no chronology of dates, and the episodes and experiences recounted in it are not matched systematically to any particular day. Although Nazr's memoir in *Ismat* continued to be called roz-namcha for a while, in 1952, two years after resuming her self-narrative, she changed the description to *Ayyam-e Guzashta* [Past days] stating, "my friend Raziq-ul Khairi's objection is correct. The pattern and continuity of a diary is completely absent in these articles. I, therefore, change the title and now this won't be a diary but a true story of bygone days."[6] In order to fully understand this transition in Nazr's writing from a diary format to an explicitly historical one focusing on her past life, we need to explore events outside the text, which were often beyond Nazr's individual control and shaped the larger structural arc of her writing.

Nazr's *Tahzib-e Niswan* diary was serialized every week until May 8, 1943, when the sudden death of her husband, Sajjad Hyder Yildirum, forced her to discontinue writing. A note by her daughter, Qurratulain Hyder, to Imtiaz Ali, informing him of her father's death was published in the journal.[7] Addressing its readers, Ali wrote that "all parts of Mrs. Nazr Sajjad Hyder's diary that were available in the office have been published, and even though I along with several other *Tahzibi* sisters would be unhappy at its incomplete publication, considering the trauma that Mrs. Nazr Sajjad Hyder just endured, one can't request her to send any more columns."[8] He further noted that Nazr "not only had an esteemed position as a writer but was also at the forefront of women's movement when Muslim women of Hindustan had woken from the deep slumber to pass through a social revolution." He therefore believed that the future would value Nazr's autobiography more than the present, and it was his "heartfelt desire that it be completed and published in book form."[9] After her period of mourning, Nazr next sent only one diary entry in 1944 and then a few irregularly in 1945 and 1946.

Despite these interruptions borne out of personal tragedy, Nazr wished to actively contribute her writing to *Tahzib-e Niswan*. But destiny decreed something else for the serialization of Nazr's diary in the Lahore weekly of Imtiaz Ali. Following the Partition of the subcontinent, Tahzib-e Niswan endured arduously until the 1950s but Nazr's personal copy of her diary suffered a different fate. Her diary, along with several other books, was destroyed in the goods train that was to bring her belongings from Dehradun in India to Sialkot in Pakistan.

When Nazr started writing in *Ismat* in March 1950, she had fled from rioting in Lucknow, India, and was living in an ordinary flat in Karachi, Pakistan.

Unlike *Tahzib-e Niswan*, *Ismat* survived Partition but resumed in Karachi and not Delhi. Several of the employees who worked at its Delhi office either were killed or disappeared. The arrangement for the publication of *Ismat* was started in November 1947 in Karachi when one of the employees arrived with great difficulty with some written copies of the October editions along with a few tattered registers. As a result of the mass migration of Partition, the journal also suffered heavy financial losses when it lost readers owing to changes of address.[10] Hundreds of copies of the journal were returned to the Karachi office with a note that the addressee no longer lived at the mentioned address. Announcements in the journal routinely asked readers to report changes of address so that money and journals were not wasted on old defunct addresses.

Against a background of these arduous conditions, the first memoir entry of Nazr in *Ismat* started with a preface note, which said that: "today after four years when our world has been destroyed and it is the third year of 1947's great revolution, I have again picked up the pen for the diary. It is the demand of hundreds of sisters and women that I finish this. My health has deteriorated; reading and writing is difficult; I'm far from country and displaced from home."[11] She further noted that *Tahzib-e Niswan*, in which her diary was earlier serialized, was "today like its founders not in this world anymore, and only its memory remained."[12] Nevertheless she said that she had decided to send some writing every month to *Ismat* based on whatever she could remember of her old diary. Raziq-ul Khairi had persuaded Nazr into writing when he asked her to complete the unfinished diary of *Tahzib-e Niswan*. It is evident here that Nazr's *Ismat* narrative is not a completion of her old diary, but a beginning of a new narrative drawn from memories of people who had departed. It is constructed as an act of remembrance, its memoir structure allowing her not only to commemorate the past, but to also defy the present. It preserved what was disrupted and lost for her—along with many other men and women during Partition—and thus served as a symbolic resistance to the displacement and violence of Partition. Compared to the *Tahzib-e Niswan* diary, the *Ismat* memoir illustrates in much greater detail her past family life, with descriptions of family gatherings in their everyday settings involving meals, socialization, and activities of recreation and leisure, particularly music.

While diary and memoir constitute the major narrative genres of Nazr's life writing, they were not the only forms of self-expression that we encounter in publication. One of the unusual features of her diary and memoir writings from 1944 in *Tahzib-e Niswan* to 1963 in *Ismat* is that they were sometimes accompanied by a short letter to the editor explaining her current state of mind and health. In content, these letters were unconnected to the main diary or memoir and were published separately in the journal before the major column of roz-namcha or ayyam-e guzashta. These letters were usually written to explain her irregularity in writing and the resulting gaps in the weekly or monthly serialization of the narrative. I would argue that the letters constitute a parallel form of self-writing to the main diary or memoir, and elaborate for us the conditions of her writing. For instance, in her letter to Ali along with the first diary entry sent after Yildirum's death, she wrote that she had finally "gathered courage and had started writing again."[13] Referring to her last diary column, she mournfully wished that her life "had come to a close with the diary" and that she "would not have remained alive to write the last chapter of this tragic life."[14] Nazr stopped again in April 1945 for three months, and when she resumed, she apologized to Ali for not sending the copy of her diary and wrote in the letter that she had come to Delhi to meet one of her aunts who had been extremely ill. Citing the Second World War, she said that her aunt's son had been at war for two years, which had caused the aunt's health to deteriorate and made her life miserable.[15]

The letters especially appeared with increasing frequency in *Ismat* from the mid-1950s. Most apologized to the readers for her absence from the magazine and often cited severe health problems, including prolonged periods of hospitalization. These letters reveal to us the final decade of Nazr's life and the extent to which illness, old age, and a sense of impending death plagued and disrupted her health and happiness. In November 1955, explaining her absence for three months, Nazr wrote that her illness, especially high blood pressure, had separated her from the world and complained that while "reading and writing were already prohibited, doctors now even prevent me from talking."[16] Two years later, she again regretted the pause in her writing and informed *Ismat* readers that she had been hospitalized for a month, enjoining them to pray for her health.[17] The persistence of her illness caused Nazr to reflect more on its causes and its impact on her well-being. Attributing her condition to her past, she wrote in 1958: "Several of my fellow sisters know that I suffered severe traumas one after another. Mother died in youth when she was thirty-five. My father at the time of his death was fifty years old. My smaller siblings who loved me dearly also departed from me forever. Then the snatching of four out of six children; and the most apocalyptic for me was the sudden departure of Sajjad *saheb* in a few minutes. Despite a lot of treatment, the effect of these events was that the pain of hypertension kept on increasing."[18]

In later years, the letters were not even accompanied by the memoir but published separately.[19] Not all focused on her health, and she sometimes also reported that her absence was because of travel. In 1961, she visited London along with her daughter, Qurratulain Hyder, and thus wrote a letter informing Raziq-ul Khairi that she was traveling and would be unable to write from Britain.[20]

Taken together, the diary, the memoir, and the letters reveal to us the different modes of self-narration practiced by Nazr. Nazr's *Ismat* memoir ended in 1963, and she passed away in 1967. But, remarkably, the production of her self-narrative did not cease. Forty years after her death, Qurratulain Hyder collected some of Nazr's entries from *Tahzib-e Niswan* and almost all of those from *Ismat* in a book entitled *Guzashta Barson ki Baraf* [The snows of past years; hereafter GBKB], published in 2007. In her introduction, she critiques the ignorance of women writers by the Urdu critical canon and views the publication of her mother's diary and memoir as a corrective to dominant frameworks in the canon. Along with information about Nazr's family background, she presents a broad overview of colonialism in India and the movement for women's education among Muslims, especially the role of Urdu journalism. In particular, she laments greatly the decline in Urdu readership in the younger generation, hinting that the marginalization of Urdu women writers especially in the public sphere is also due to the larger crisis about the gradual disappearance of Urdu culture. This concern with forgetting of tradition and history from memory unites GBKB with Qurratulain's other works of writing. For Qurratulain Hyder, the activity of writing amounts to a search for the lost and the forgotten, transforming her fiction and her autobiography into grand historical narratives.[21] In fact, at the end of the text's introduction, she muses that "actually only some of all writing and literature which has been composed from the earliest times to the present lasts for a long time. Most fade away very quickly."[22]

In editing Nazr's diary and memoir, Qurratulain Hyder brings her own sensibility of a fiction writer to the text. She borrows the title of the book from an old French ballad by François Villon written in 1461, which rues the passing away of French queens and other famous women.[23] Like a collection of short stories, each entry has a different title suited to its content, which is absent in the original magazine text. The book, however, lacks almost fifty pages from the *Tahzib-e Niswan* diary and several pages of *Ismat* memoir and also leaves out Nazr's letters that were published in the magazine. Most importantly, some entries have been modified in the book from their version in the magazine.[24] I would therefore argue that GBKB is another production of Nazr's self-narrative not framed and shaped entirely by Nazr and distinct from both the *Tahzib-e Niswan* diary and the *Ismat* memoir.

We can now see how the different genres of Nazr's self-narration, including the diary, memoir, and letters, were inextricably linked to the context of their production and publication. Spanning several years, the ruptures in her life narrative reveal intimate personal tragedy like her husband's death along with spectacular political upheavals such as the Partition. Having commented on the structure, construction, and context of Nazr's narratives, we may now turn our attention to its rich contents.

Nazr's Narrative as a History of Everyday Life

Most of Nazr's diary and memoir is devoted to depictions of what historians refer to as "everyday life."[25] As a topic of investigation, the history of everyday life is distinguished much more by its methodology than by the categories of research. Developed largely as a dissident microhistorical approach in West German historical studies in the 1970s and the 1980s (*Alltagsgeschichte*), it attempted to evolve a perspective that did not rely exclusively on earlier methods of social history involving macrohistorical investigation of social structures and large-scale processes.[26] Influenced by ethnographic analysis and anthropology, it wished to enter "the inner world of popular experience in the workplace, the family and household, the neighborhood, the school—in short, all those contexts normally assigned to the cultural domain."[27]

Central to our investigation is the importance of gender relations and their changes within the framework of the history of everyday life. Dorothee Wierling has argued that "if women were 'hidden' in the unexplored tissue of everyday life within the framework of traditional historiography, it became possible to discover them for history concomitant with the discovery of everyday life."[28] The space of everyday life can reveal specifically how men and women interact with each other and what strategies and negotiations they engage in to subvert structures of hierarchy in different social, political, and cultural settings.

The diary and memoir of Nazr reveal the everyday life of *sharif* Muslims around two major themes/tropes. The first is the interpersonal relationships involving significant milestones of birth, marriage, and death, as well as daily and casual encounters of friends and family at social gatherings. The second is the presence of movement in their lives involving travel, job transfers from one town to another, and leisure activity such as "spending the season."[29]

Attachment and Sorrow

....

As mentioned earlier, Nazr's diary begins on January 8, 1908, with the death of her mother Mustafai Begam. Stunned by witnessing his wife's death, Nazr's father had fainted by the bedside. Describing her mother's final journey for the funeral, Nazr writes that it felt "nothing less than doomsday for me," where "elders as well as young people were taking away forever the lady of the house."[30] Following this note on her mother's death, the next detail in the *Tahzib-e Niswan* diary is an account of her marriage, dated May 1912. Nazr experienced the marriage ceremony with mixed emotions owing to her own lack of interest and also her mother's absence. While the elder women of the house were preparing for celebrations, she felt that "the one who would have been most happy and most engaged in marital arrangements was absent from the world. I sat alone in the corner and wept in memory of her." Moreover, she felt little acquaintance with the man to whom she was to be married and thus had "a strange feeling in her heart that evening."[31] She sat on a sofa with her younger sister and several other women when Yildirum entered the room and greeted everybody. Her face was not veiled, and she had covered it only with a handkerchief. For the rest of the day, she grieved over the separation from her widowed father and loved ones, made still more unbearable by the summer heat. After her marriage in Kohat, she left for Mussoorie via Dehradun, establishing friendly relations with Yildirum on the two-day train journey.[32] In Mussoorie, she met her sister-in-law and her family. Her time there was spent happily with them, and her morning engagements usually involved writing letters to her family or reading the newspaper.[33]

Details of Nazr's early married life reveal important complexities around the custom of *purdah*, or gender segregation. Although Yildirum was opposed to purdah and Nazr herself did not observe it much in her life, she practiced it in the early days after her marriage as evidence of the modesty expected of a new bride. Sometimes, especially when meeting the elders of Yildirum's family, she would ask him how she should greet them and if she should cover her face. Yildirum usually discouraged veiling, claiming that the custom did not exist in their family.[34] By 1912, the critiques of purdah had created an ambiguous and fluid situation within families, and consequently there were women who did not observe purdah some of the time and some who observed it all the time. One of Nazr's nieces, Waheeda Begam, for instance, observed strict purdah even from Yildirum, and therefore organizing meals and visiting other families with her was a complex and constant negotiation.[35] Nazr found this difficult, for she often had to choose between Yildirum and her niece when she wished that she could spend time together with both of them.³⁶ When Nazr had meals or tea with Yildirum, her niece had to eat alone, and when Nazr had food with her niece, Yildirum had to eat separately. When Nazr tried to convince her niece to relax her purdah, she refused. When invited for dinners, there were segregated arrangements for meals and socialization. This made Yildirum uncomfortable because he wanted Nazr to meet his friends and felt that the two cloistered in purdah appeared very *dehati* (rural).³⁷ From Yildirum's response, we can say that the critique of purdah and gender segregation in colonial India represented, for some of its advocates, "urban modernity." Even though practices of gender segregation were more strict in sharif Muslim families living in urban spaces than those in the countryside, for men like Yildirum, socializing and mixing of men and women emerged to be a symbol of urbane sophistication, which distinguished modern urban residents from the ways of villagers in rural country.

The first marriage anniversary of Nazr was marked by pain and grief. A year after her marriage, she gave birth to a girl, who survived for just over two months before passing away on the evening of Nazr's wedding anniversary. After the death of her first child, her second child, Syed Jawad Hyder, a healthy son born in July 1914, was struck with cholera and died in 1916. Within a few days, her second son, then two months, also died of cholera.³⁸ Subsequently, her sixteen-year-old brother, Mustafa Baqr, too became victim of this disease and passed away in the summer of 1918. Nazr recounts how the onset and fatal impact of the illness on Mustafa Baqr was quick and catastrophic. He was rushed to the hospital on the night of May 29 with symptoms of vomiting and fever and died the following day.³⁹ The death of her brother had a lingering impact on Nazr, with his memory haunting her in life and being reflected in her work.⁴⁰ Her third son, born in 1920, was named Mustafa Hyder in memory of Mustafa Baqr and palliated some of the grief of Nazr and her sister, Sarvat Ara.

As a personal tragedy, the death of Nazr's children is very crucial for an understanding of parenting and familial relations. For most parents, the death of a child in infancy or early childhood was a constant fear, and childhood deaths due to illness or epidemics like cholera were not uncommon. Struggles to keep a child healthy and alive in beginning years worried parents regardless of class or heritage and shaped cultures of cure, prevention, and child-rearing.⁴¹ Women were involved in the care of the sick, and women's journals witnessed on a regular basis columns on disease and care.⁴²

For Nazr, tragedy struck again when her maternal aunt, Murtazai Begam, who had treated Nazr as her own after the premature death of her mother, also passed away soon after the death of her children. Nazr writes that "with this news, the world started to appear dark to me."[43] These years were made especially difficult by the absence of her father, Nazr-ul Baqr, to whom she was extremely attached. In 1914, Nazr-ul Baqr was sent off to France in the British cantonment to fight in the First World War. He left smaller siblings of Nazr in the care of his sister Akbari Begam and Nazr's uncle Mir Fazl Ali. Unfortunately, a few days after his departure, Mir Fazl Ali died suddenly of a heart attack.[44] For Nazr, the effects of health epidemics like cholera combined with the uncertainties of the First World War made the four years following her marriage some of the roughest in her life. Families whose men were affiliated with the British Indian Army and were drafted in various wars of the British often survived under great tension in their absence. In the years that Nazr-ul Baqr was away, Mustafa Hyder refused to wear any new clothes on festivals. Pale and weakened by war stresses, a gaunt Nazr-ul Baqr finally returned after four years in 1918.[45]

One of the distinct features that emerges from Nazr's description of her family is her intimate attachment to her networks of relatives and friends. This is of special significance in Nazr's life because the death of her mother at an early age brought her extremely close to her aunt; her siblings Sarvat Ara and Mustafa Hyder; and her father, Nazr ul Baqr. The health and death of each of these and her subsequent grief is described in vivid detail in her *Ismat* memoir. Nazr-ul Baqr suffered from heart conditions, and in the years prior to his death, doctors often advised him to move away from heat and reside somewhere cooler like Nazr's home in Dehradun. When Yildirum was employed as the university registrar at Aligarh Muslim University from 1920 to 1928, Nazr sometimes lived in Dehradun attending to her father's health, while Yildirum stayed back in Aligarh. In the final days of his life, Nazr-ul Baqr and Nazr corresponded with each other through daily letters. When Nazr-ul Baqr died in the winter of 1928, Nazr was so overwhelmed with grief and poor health that she did not attend her father's funeral or any of the death rituals.[46] The situation was made worse when, exactly forty-three days after Nazr-ul Baqr's death, Nazr's paternal aunt, Akbari Begam, also died.[47]

Besides her father, Nazr was also deeply fond of her sister, Sarvat Ara. Despite her suffering from ill health for a long time, the death of Sarvat Ara was an unexpected and sudden event for Nazr, and she initially mistook it for one of the fainting spells that plagued Sarvat Ara often. When the doctor who had been treating Sarvat Ara for almost twelve years arrived to examine her and informed Nazr about her death, Nazr fainted, and the injection that he had brought to revive Sarvat Ara was given to Nazr instead.[48] Describing the hours following

Sarvat Ara's death, Nazr writes: "the house was haunted by the loneliness of death. From the verandah, the voice of Maqsood reading the Qur'an reached one's ears. Following the usual routine, trains passed the house. The graveyard was visible through the window's mirror where no one had yet gone to dig the grave of my sister."[49]

Nazr's description of the death of her children, brother, father, and sister turns her narrative into a characteristically emotional and affective one. Her life account is defined in no small measure by its sorrows and a focus on deaths and suggests a life shaped by obligation to elders and a deep affection for her siblings. Outside her relationships, her individuality was constituted by her intense commitment to social questions of her day.

Reform and Activism

While personal tragedies inform significant sections of Nazr's narrative, her personality also had a feisty characteristic, which revealed itself in her campaigns for social reform. A predominant theme in Nazr's narrative, and particularly her *Tahzib-e Niswan* diary, involves her efforts for women's education. Of special significance to women's education and gender reform were purdah parties, events in which women invited only women to their quarters for discussion, socialization, and recreation. Purdah parties were occasions for women to gossip, arrange marriages, and establish *anjumans* or associations devoted to women's education. In Dehradun, Nazr mobilized women to form the Anjuman Hami-e Talim-e Niswan (Association for the Support of Women's Education). The first meeting of the anjuman was held at her house and was attended by approximately fifty women. A donation of four *annas* by each woman was to be contributed every month and around thirty rupees were collected in the first few days. On the eighth day after the establishment of the anjuman, a second meeting was held and was attended by eighty women. Within a few days, a full campaign was started for women's education, and strength of attendance at these meetings increased markedly. These meetings started at noon after the *zohr* prayer and continued till *asr* prayer, when they ended with tea. Within a month, Nazr was able to raise enough money to start a school. The school also received added donations of sitting boards, pens, ink, copies, mats, and drinking pots from other women who attended these home meetings.[50] A Muslim *ustani* or a female teacher was hired for ten rupees a month to teach the Qur'an and Urdu, while a Christian woman taught English and mathematics for twenty rupees a month. The school started with twenty-five girls, and a wealthy member of the anjuman offered one of her homes to be used without rent for the school building.[51] The school was inaugurated with the reading of a few verses of the Qur'an by one of its girl students. Nazr described the inauguration of the school as the "happiest day of her two-and-a-half-year-old new life."[52] Nazr's elation over women's education continued well after the establishment of her primary school. Within a few months, there was enough money for the school to be shifted to a more spacious building combined with the possibility of an increase in class level. After acquiring a bigger location, Nazr, along with her anjuman friends, immediately cleaned it and made arrangements for the building's repair and furnishing. There was also an addition of an ustani to the school.[53] In March 1914, Syed Mumtaz Ali visited the school and commended Nazr for her efforts. He gifted books to the students and chatted with the teachers and students for a long time.[54]

Nazr's efforts for women's education extended beyond Dehradun to the towns of Aligarh and Lucknow as well. In January 1914, Nazr received a letter from Begam Sheikh Abdullah from Aligarh informing her about the establishment of a girls' school in Aligarh and inviting her for the ceremony. The school was inaugurated with a speech by Sultan Jahan Begam of Bhopal and was attended by women from various parts of the country including Bombay, Hyderabad, and Punjab.[55] Begam Sheikh Abdullah requested Nazr to increase the numbers of attendees by bringing other women. Expressing her joy at this request, Nazr noted that "as long as I could remember, I had been dreaming of the establishment of a *qaumi* (community) girls' school in Aligarh."[56] Nazr's fascination with a qaumi school suggests her own concern to particularly improve the lives of Muslim women and also the extent to which movements of social reform were interwoven with communitarian consciousness. Nazr, in fact, also campaigned to raise funds for the establishment of a Muslim university in Aligarh.[57]

The Hyder family also lived in Lucknow after 1914, when Yildirum took the job of political secretary of Ali Muhammad Khan, a leader of the Muslim League. In Lucknow, Nazr kept herself busy at Syed Karamat Husain Girls School.[58] She formed an association called Talim-e Niswan [Women's education] devoted to raising money for the school, which deeply impressed Syed Karamat Husain. A library with a few books and women's journals was also started in the school on the suggestion of Nazr.[59]

Throughout her life, Nazr wrote numerous essays and short stories on issues of gender and learning in women's magazines, and her account of her involvement in the cause of women's education is not surprising. The publication of her reformist efforts several years later in 1942 in the *Tahzib-e Niswan* diary served to reiterate the magazine's commitment to women's education and to narrating the lives of its most vocal advocates.

Leisure and Entertainment

One of the most important differences between Nazr's diary in *Tahzib-e Niswan* and her memoir in *Ismat* is that her diary focused more on her reformist activities. Her diary was more engaged with important tasks that had been accomplished, especially the establishment of various associations for reform or the school in Dehradun. On the other hand, Nazr's *Ismat* narrative acquires its memoir structure through substantial illustration of reminiscences of family events, particularly gatherings and dinners with her close friends and relatives. It is a vivid record of celebration with loved ones who had departed from her life. The contents of Nazr's *Ismat* narrative thus constitute the memoir form of its writing. Nazr's memoir beginning in *Ismat* contains cherished memories of festive family occasions from the past.

The most frequent locations for family gatherings were hill stations like Dehradun, Abbottabad, Shimla, and Mussoorie in the cooler areas of northern India during the summer season, a practice often called "spending the season." Spending the season was probably one of the most exclusive and privileged lifestyles of wealthy Indians, which distinguished them from those of lesser means. Weather and changing seasons influenced not only clothing and eating habits but also lifestyles of leisure, work, and relaxation. Practiced in imitation of the British, who shifted the colonial administration to Shimla each summer, sharif Muslims who could afford a home in the hills spent the summer in cooler regions shielded from the heat of the plains. One occasion of spending the season, which Nazr reminisces about at length, is the summer spent in Abbottabad at Sarvat Ara's home. Nazr's paternal aunt Akbari Begam, her sister, her brother-in-law, Afzal Ali, her father, Nazr-ul Baqr, and her paternal uncles Thahoor Ali and Ghazanfar had all come to Abbottabad and stayed together enjoying the town's pleasant weather, rains, and hilly terrain in their private garden adorned with fruit trees and flowering plants. Stylistically, Nazr's description of these gatherings at Abbottabad is highly evocative, communicating her love of natural surroundings and comfortable homes: "The view of the dining room was indescribable. Surrounded by rooms on three sides, its door and windows were all open. On one side was an airy verandah on which hung flower creepers whose fragrance reached indoors. In front of the verandah were bushes of roses and jasmine. A home in the hills always provides breathtaking vistas, but words cannot capture the attraction of a house surrounded by a garden full of fruits and flowers."[60]

An important feature of these social occasions was the opportunity for photography, a technology that had started to captivate elite Indians in early twentieth century.[61] Yildirum suggested that arrangements be made for a family photograph to memorialize the occasion. Both women and men dressed themselves up especially for the occasion. Nazr changed into another sari, explaining her decision that "she always liked dark colors for photographs."[62] Following the photography session, family members relished on tea and snacks in an ambience of cheerful conversation.[63]

Besides chitchat and good food, these gatherings in the Hyder family often involved music, especially the recitation of *ghazals* and the singing of *qawwalis*. Both ghazals and qawwalis are crucial cultural components in Muslim culture, and educated Muslims were especially expected to have at least memorized Urdu poetry and love couplets, which were then recited depending on the occasion.[64] Nazr writes that for both her and Yildirum, "the food for the soul was music, followed by books."[65] On one occasion during Ramzan, when one is supposed to pray all night, she instead played harmonium and sitar with her friends until half past four in the morning.[66] She reminisced that her sister, Sarvat Ara, also sang very well and "that nature had endowed her with a musical voice."[67]

The everyday social life of *ashraf* Muslims, both while spending the season and in their towns of residence, witnessed regular parties and dinner or tea invitations from friends and family. It was these social interactions in different towns among women that often maintained networks of reform. On February 17, 1923, Nazr and Yildirum were visiting Bombay and were invited to a tea party at Atiya Fyzee's house.[68] Nazr was particularly impressed by Atiya Fyzee's husband, Rahmeen Fyzee, with whom she discussed issues of women's rights and their education. She talked to him for almost two hours, during which Atiya Fyzee entertained them as well as other guests.[69]

A Life of Mobility

In addition to an active and vibrant social life, the second feature that predominates Nazr's *Ismat* memoir is ceaseless movement from one town to another either for travel or owing to Yildirum's job transfers. It was not unusual for Indians employed in the colonial government to be transferred to different cities throughout the country. In his professional career, Yildirum worked in several towns and cities of the country, including Mussoorie, Dehradun,

Aligarh, Sultanpur, Ghazipur, Etawah, and even the Andaman Islands. The Hyders' residence in the Andaman Islands reveals a radically different dynamic in terms of racial hierarchy in the politics of imperialism. Located at the extreme social and economic margins of colonial society, the Andaman Islands became settlements for Indian convicts and criminals who had been sentenced, usually on murder charges, to inhabit these islands for long periods of time.[70] At the Andaman Islands, Yildirum was given a large and spacious house with one side facing the sea, serviced by eight servants, all of whom were convicts. Nazr mentions that the caretaker for her children had been charged with the murder of four people, but nevertheless attended the children and took them out for boating and long walks. Not surprisingly, when they returned late to the house, she felt scared.[71]

During their stay at Andaman Islands, the Hyders enjoyed picnics and outings at natural spots such as gardens, forests, riversides, and beaches. Sometimes Nazr and the children accompanied Yildirum on his official tours and met other residents. There was much in terms of entertainment and leisure, particularly picnics and sporting events, for British and Indian families stationed at the islands, and several of them enjoyed the social life and natural landscape of the islands.[72]

After the Andaman Islands, Yildirum was transferred to Ghazipur and then to Etawah. It was at Ghazipur that Nazr developed her love of music and learned to play the sitar and harmonium. Another pastime at Ghazipur was the hours spent on a steamer that operated between the banks of the Ganges River. The steamer comprised two cabins and a small restaurant, and whenever guests visited the Hyder family in Ghazipur, they were taken for a ride on the steamer.[73]

It is crucial to note that in all the transitions that came with Yildirum's transfers in employment, it was always Nazr who independently searched the town for a house and made the necessary arrangements to shift locations. Raised with little training in nondomestic tasks, Nazr nevertheless mastered the requirements of estate management. Therefore, it was not just the demand for gender desegregation and women's education that enabled social change, but also the practical conditions emerging out of colonial employment that compelled many women of elite backgrounds to negotiate business outside the home.

Also related to the theme of movement is the experience of travel among modern Muslims. After the death of her father, Yildirum persuaded Nazr and Sarvat Ara to accompany him to Iran and Iraq. In the colonial period, several educated Muslims visited foreign lands, especially the Middle East, and recorded their experiences in travelogues.[74] Travelogues like other narratives were also serialized in Urdu women's journals, where they educated the readership about distant lands and unfamiliar cultures.[75] Turkey in particular had a special resonance for Yildirim as he had visited it before his marriage and continued to advocate Turkish-style reform agendas for Muslims in India.

The Hyders traveled to Iraq on a luxurious ship on which they met people from many different countries. Among many comforts, the ship housed a ballroom, which Nazr and Sarvat Ara visited regularly to observe and comment on others, but never to dance.[76] The ship arrived at the port of Basra, from where they took a train to Baghdad. In Baghdad, they stayed briefly in a hotel and then moved to live with friends. During one such stay, Nazr and Sarvat Ara commented on the household, revealing the priority of cleanliness and display in the discourse of reform.[77] Specifically, Nazr noticed that the house was rather ordinary, that the bed was not arranged, that children were in their dirty clothes, that chewed scraps of sugarcane lay in the courtyard, and that there were flies humming over the food and tea offered to them. Especially disappointed after their comfortable stay at other homes, Sarvat Ara wanted to stay instead in a hotel.[78] In order to persuade her sister to move, Nazr employed a discourse of class, manners, and education. Housekeeping was a central tenet of Muslim sharif reform, and reformers often argued that a woman who failed to maintain a clean and well-ordered house had failed to reap the full benefits of education.[79] Expressing this sentiment, Nazr says that "every house has differences in society and manners" and that disorderliness and poor taste could be found not just in ordinary but also in wealthier households. "Stupid women are present in every class," she continued, "so what can one say about the uneducated when we see inefficiency and laziness even in college and university graduates who have servants at their disposal and still can't keep their homes clean." Bringing a regional emphasis to her point, she added, "leave aside Uttar Pradesh, consider the households of Bombay and Bengal, where education long ago made an intervention and they are well-mannered and urbane. Even there, one can find houses that are not clean."[80] Arguments such as these were not uncommon in the ideology of reform, and they connected taste and cleanliness to education, revealing class hierarchy and transforming the display of the home into a matter of pride.[81]

These sentiments also emphasize Nazr's own attention to the home and its surroundings. Material conditions of home and the memories associated with it are often significant in writings of women. Antoinette Burton has demonstrated how women writers like Janaki Majumdar, Cornelia Sorabji, and Attia Hosain made use of their memories of home to claim a place in history and how home is an "archive from which a variety of counterhistories of colonial modernity can be discerned."[82] The numerous descriptions of residing in homes, whether it be family gatherings or household arrangement in Nazr's account, testify to the significance of house and home as tropes in memory and history. Nazr for instance gave considerable space in writing about setting up her home and tending to the gardens. For her, gardening and home décor were interests of tastes and aesthetics to which she enjoyed giving attention. In her memoirs, there are several illustrations of spacious homes and beautiful gardens. When the Hyder family transferred to Ghazipur, Nazr changed homes twice to acquire more space for living and gardening. The first home had two bedrooms, a dining room, a huge sitting area, and a verandah. In front of the house was a "big garden of roses, jasmine, and *bela* flowers, whose fragrance perfumed the air all the time."[83] She also planted ten to twelve different kinds of vegetables in her garden and says that "there was hardly any ground visible in this home; it was surrounded only by flowers."[84] Her second home at Ghazipur had nine rooms, and she not only built a garden with rose and jasmine plants but also sowed sweet peas all around so that the house was scented with fragrance.[85] Nazr writes that "of the necessities of life, if there is anything that makes me happy, it is a good home," and that "from childhood, I was interested in gardening and did more work than the appointed gardener."[86] One of the most admirable qualities for Nazr was a well-arranged home accompanied by graceful hospitality of the host. In her numerous encounters with both close friends and distant acquaintances, she never ceased to mention décor and design of the house if it impressed her, along with congeniality of the host especially in serving meals. Both these qualities, in women particularly, were larger manifestations of *adab* or manners that were integral to the norms of *sharafat*. The sharif ideal of domesticity transformed the household into a site of consumption, a comfortable space for tasteful furnishings, and an interior that reflected experiences of leisure and intimacy.

Conclusion

Having explored Nazr's experiences under major themes prevalent in her diary and memoir, we can say a few things about her self-identity from these writings. In the theoretical interventions on autobiography, Joan Scott calls for historicizing experience where "it is not the individuals who have experience but subjects who are constituted through experience."[87] From this understanding, our attempt should not be to find ways in which Nazr's writing corroborates assumptions about Muslim women but to comprehend how these narratives construct and reveal a self that resisted, negotiated, and adapted with dictates and norms of society.

First, the self fashioned in this narrative is constituted by its intimate relationships. This is illustrated best by the amount of space given to the death of family members. Indeed, as we know from one of her letters, Nazr attributed her ailments in old age to these tragedies. It is not just the sorrows of attachment that shape her writing self, but also the joys of togetherness and celebration manifested in accounts of family gatherings. Does this mean that Nazr's writings reveal a self less driven by individual ego and unique to women, especially in South Asia? Such a view of the self as part of the larger network of social relationships may affect the kinds of narratives women construct, but it doesn't do justice to Nazr's own audacity in revealing her whole emotional life to the public. If self-effacement is the culturally acceptable and expected norm for women in South Asia, then the "unveiling" of her intimate feelings, her "private" life not just to women who made up the reading public but also to men illustrates her defiance of the social order. The act of publishing her life, I argue, is an extension of her effort in making women more visible as speaking and acting members of society instead of mute and passive beings. In its spirit, the publication of Nazr's self-narratives thus is consistent with the resistance she demonstrated in social reform. She mentions, for instance, that she received intense condemnation and harsh words for proposing a Muslim Ladies Conference, but that she "never lost courage and, after persuading a few like-minded women, managed to establish the Muslim Ladies Conference."[88]

While Nazr openly wrote about her feelings and advocated her reformist concerns forcefully, at the same time, there are also absences in her narrative that illustrate her precarious position as a woman autobiographer in the late colonial period. Throughout her writings, there is a striking silence about her sexual experiences, and there is absolutely no discussion on issues of sexuality. In keeping this intimate detail strictly private and closed from public view, Nazr followed the social norms of modesty and shame associated with women. It is significant to note here that we cannot simply know from her silence whether this shrouding of sexuality was coercive or her own chosen persona necessary for her public life as a female writer and a reformer. What it illustrates is that even women who defined their own position publicly against a patriarchal society did not completely disavow its customs and conventions but lived a life of negotiation between their individuality and their social heritage.

Considering the extensive space given to her social and emotional life, care also needs to be taken in assuming that Nazr was not interested in politics or that life writings of women lack political content. Several important figures such as Jahan Ara Shahnawaz, Begam Aiziz Rasul, and Shaista Suhrawardy Ikramullah rise to contradict this view.[89] In her old age, Nazr, in fact, lamented that while there were several young women with professional degrees in her family, they had little interest in books, reading, and concerns of politics and society, whereas educated women of her generation invested themselves wholeheartedly in improving lives of other men and women.[90] Several years before this observation, Nazr had encouraged Muslim women to participate in the Indian nationalist movement.[91]

We now know the construction and context of Nazr's self-narrative, its multiple genres of expression, the self that it fashions, and the distinct interpersonal snapshot that it provides of an elite group in society undergoing large-scale changes of modernization and urbanization. More importantly, class is a central feature in Nazr's narrative and her description of her travels, homes, and family gatherings suggests the emergence of an educated and privileged upper middle-class of Muslims in late colonial India, with its own unique cultural codes of conduct and beliefs, informed by ideologies of reform. Specifically, Nazr's narrative does not converge on any center but is a tale of disparate episodes and experiences from her life. When I started reading GBKB, I mistakenly assumed that Qurratulain Hyder had compiled a single serialization of Nazr's diary published in *Tahzib-e Niswan* several years ago. But the unusual form of GBKB unsettled this impression quickly. There were gaps between stories and the entries were not continuous, leaving out months and even years in between. Furthermore, the narrative sometimes read like a diary written at the end of the day and sometimes like a retelling of memories authored several years later. As we have seen, Nazr's telling of her life story was interrupted several times because of forces beyond her individual control, which not only ruptured continuity of the record but also compelled her to generate letters as another form of autobiographical writing for the public. Rather than adhering to one recognizable format for articulating the self, we therefore need to interrogate and subvert traditional autobiographical genre in order to fully incorporate Nazr's life writings. Nazr's self-narratives thus cannot be limited to any particular genre but involve multiple styles of writing and emerge from different historical conditions. If diary, memoir, letters, and Qurratulain's reorganization are all taken together, the narrative becomes a kaleidoscope of its genres and its contexts.

NOTES

1 Francesca Orsini, *The Hindi Public Sphere, 1920–40: Language and Literature in the Age of Nationalism* (Delhi: Oxford University Press, 2002), 31–43; Anindita Ghosh, *Power in Print: Popular Publishing and the Politics of Language and Culture in a Colonial Society* (Delhi: Oxford University Press, 2006), 14, 40–44, 59–65.

2. Kh. H. "Roz-namchey ki zaroorat," *Tahzib-e Niswan* 14.9 (March 4, 1911): 99–100; Syed Mumtaz Ali, "Roz-namcha," *Tahzib-e Niswan*, July 10, 1920, 437–38; Noor-un-nissa Begam, "Diary," *Tahzib-e Niswan*, May 22, 1943, 321–22.
3. See, for example, Siobhan Lambert-Hurley and Sunil Sharma, *Atiya's Journeys: A Muslim Woman from Colonial Bombay to Edwardian Britain* (Delhi: Oxford University Press, 2010). Also see Siobhan Lambert-Hurley, "Life/History/Archive: Identifying Autobiographical Writing by Muslim Women in South Asia," *Journal of Women's History* 25.2 (summer 2013), 61–84; and Siobhan Lambert-Hurley, "The Heart of a Gopi: Raihana Tyabji's Bhakti Devotionalism as Self-Representation," in this volume. For a general account on autobiography, see David Arnold and Stuart Blackburn, eds., *Telling Lives in India: Biography, Autobiography and Life History* (Delhi: Permanent Black, 2004).
4. Nazr S. Hyder, *Guzashta Barson Ki Baraf* (*GBKB*), ed. Qurratulain Hyder (Delhi: Educational Publishing House, 2007), 124. "Tahzibi sisters" here refers to the fictional kinship of *Tahzib-e Niswan* readers.
5. Nazr S. Hyder, "Roz-namcha," *Tahzib-e Niswan* 45.32 (August 8, 1942): 514.
6. Nazr S. Hyder, *GBKB*, 124. Raziq-ul Khairi was editor of *Ismat* when it shifted to Karachi, Pakistan.
7. Nazr S. Hyder, *Tahzib-e Niswan* 46.16 (April 17, 1943): 253.
8. Imtiaz Ali Taj, "Mrs. Nazr Sajjad Hyder ka Roz-namcha," *Tahzib-e Niswan* 46.19 (May 8, 1943): 294.
9. Taj, "Mrs. Nazr Sajjad Hyder ka Roz-namcha," 294.
10. Raziq-ul khairi, "Chand baatein," *Ismat* 79.4–6 (October–December 1947): 194.
11. Nazr S. Hyder, "Roz-namcha," *Ismat* 84.3 (March 1950): 119.
12. Nazr S. Hyder, "Roz-namcha," *Ismat* 84.3 (March 1950): 119.
13. Nazr S. Hyder, "Roz-namcha," *Tahzib-e Niswan* 27.52 (December 23, 1944): 769.
14. Nazr S. Hyder, "Roz-namcha," *Tahzib-e Niswan* 27.52 (December 23, 1944): 769.
15. Nazr S. Hyder, "Roz-namcha," *Tahzib-e Niswan* (July 7, 1945): 441.
16. Nazr S. Hyder, "Ayyam-e Guzashta," *Ismat* 95.5 (November 1955): 254.
17. Nazr S. Hyder, "Ayyam-e Guzashta," *Ismat* 99.1 (July 1957): 37.
18. Nazr S. Hyder, *Ismat* 101.3 (September 1958): 448.
19. Nazr S. Hyder, "Grami Name," *Ismat* 116.1 (January 1963): 116; Nazr S. Hyder, "Grami Name," *Ismat* 112.6 (June 1964): 324.
20. Nazr S. Hyder, "London se khat," *Ismat* 106.5 (May 1961): 249.
21. For Qurratulain Hyder's understanding of time and history, see Fateh Muhammad Malik, "Kar-e Jahan Daraz Hai," in Irtiza Karim, ed., *Qurratulain Hyder: Aik Mutala'ah* (Delhi: Educational Publishing House, 1992), 350–61.
22. Qurratulain Hyder, "Sada-e Aabsharan Az Faraz-e Kehsar Aamad," *GBKB*, 33.
23. Qurratulain Hyder, "Sada-e Aabsharan Az Faraz-e Kehsar Aamad," *GBKB*, 11–12.
24. The first diary entry of Nazr in *Tahzib-e Niswan*, published in the issue of August 8, 1942, has no resemblance to the first one and a half pages of Nazr's narrative in *GBKB*.
25. Abrams and Brown argue that "every day is constituted by the daily patterns of activity with which we fill time and space." In *A History of Everyday Life in Twentieth Century Scotland*, ed. Lynn Abrams and Callum G. Brown (Edinburgh: Edinburgh

University Press, 2010), 3. See the full four volumes of *A History of Everyday Life in Scotland*. Series editors: Christopher A. Whatley and Elizabeth Foyster.

26 Geoff Eley, foreword to *The History of Everyday Life: Reconstructing Historical Experiences and Ways of Life*, ed. Alf Ludtke, trans. William Templer (Princeton, NJ: Princeton University Press, 1995), vii–viii.
27 Eley, foreword, viii.
28 Dorothee Wierling, "The History of Everyday Life and Gender Relations: On Historical and Historiographical Relationships," in *The History of Everyday Life: Reconstructing Historical Experiences and Ways of Life*, ed. Alf Ludtke, trans. William Templer (Princeton, NJ: Princeton University Press, 1995), 153.
29 Sharif Muslims or Ashraf is often used to refer to the community of Muslims who worked at the Mughal court and were later employed with the colonial government.
30 Nazr S. Hyder, "Roz-namcha," *Tahzib-e Niswan* 45.32 (August 8, 1942): 515.
31 Nazr S. Hyder, *GBKB*, 36.
32 Nazr S. Hyder, *GBKB*, 37.
33 Nazr S. Hyder, *Tahzib-e Niswan* 45.33 (August 15, 1942): 534.
34 Nazr S. Hyder, *Tahzib-e Niswan* 45.35 (August 29, 1942): 558.
35 Nazr S. Hyder, *Tahzib-e Niswan* 45.34 (August 22, 1942): 550–51. Qurratulain Hyder mentions that this niece is Waheeda Begam, daughter of Syed Mumtaz Ali, editor of *Tahzib-e Niswan*. Qurratulain Hyder, *GBKB*, 40.
36 Nazr S. Hyder, "Roz-namcha," *Tahzib-e Niswan* 45.35 (August 29, 1942): 558.
37 Nazr S. Hyder, "Roz-namcha," *Tahzib-e Niswan* 45.35 (August 29, 1942): 559.
38 Nazr S. Hyder, *GBKB*, ed. Qurratulain Hyder, 60–61.
39 Nazr S. Hyder, "Roz-namcha," *Tahzib-e Niswan* 46.8 (February 20, 1943): 124.
40 After Musatfa Baqr's death, she wrote a novelette called *Herman Naseeb*, which explored the death of a sibling.
41 Bint Maulavi Abdul Qalum, "Tarbiyat-e Aulad," *Ismat* 9.6 (December 1912): 31–42; Hamsheera Ahmad "Bacchon ki Parvarish," *Ismat* 19.5 (November 1917): 35.
42 Begam, "Bimari aur Timardari," *Ismat* 3.2 (August 1909): 43.
43 Nazr S. Hyder, *GBKB*, 61.
44 Nazr S. Hyder, *GBKB*, 57.
45 Nazr S. Hyder, *GBKB*, 70.
46 Nazr S. Hyder, *GBKB*, 163–65.
47 Nazr S. Hyder, *GBKB*, 168.
48 Nazr S. Hyder, *GBKB*, 215.
49 Nazr S. Hyder, *GBKB*, 218.
50 Nazr S. Hyder, *GBKB*, 45.
51 Nazr S. Hyder, *GBKB*, 46.
52 Nazr S. Hyder, "Roz-namcha," *Tahzib-e Niswan* 43.45 (October 24, 1942): 689.
53 Nazr S. Hyder, "Roz-namcha," *Tahzib-e Niswan* 43.45 (October 24, 1942): 691–92.
54 Nazr S. Hyder, "Roz-namcha," *Tahzib-e Niswan* 45.45 (November 7, 1942): 717. Syed Mumtaz Ali (1860–1935) founded the journal *Tahzib-e Niswan* in Lahore in 1898 along with his wife, Muhammadi Begam. See Gail Minault, *Gender, Language*

and Learning: Essays in Indo-Muslim Cultural History (Ranikhet: Permanent Black, 2009), 35–63.
55. Gail Minault, *Secluded Scholars: Women's Education and Muslim Social Reform in Colonial India* (Delhi: Oxford University Press, 1998), 243–44; Siobhan Lambert-Hurley, *Muslim Women, Reform and Princely Patronage: Nawab Sultan Jahan Begam of Bhopal* (London: Routledge, 2007), 80–81, 83, 86.
56. Nazr S. Hyder, *Tahzib-e Niswan* 45.43 (October 24, 1942): 690.
57. Bint Nazr-ul Baqr, "Muslim University Fund," *Khatoon* 8.2 (February 1912): 29–41.
58. Syed Karamat Husain (1854–1917) was an advocate for women's education and founded a school for girls in Lucknow in 1912. Gail Minault, *Secluded Scholars*, 216–28.
59. Nazr S. Hyder, *Tahzib-e Niswan* 45.50 (December 12, 1942): 798–99.
60. Nazr S. Hyder, GBKB, 93.
61. Malavika Karlekar, "Showcasing the Family," in *Visualizing Indian Women, 1875–1947*, ed. Malavika Karlekar (Delhi: Oxford University Press, 2006), 1–38.
62. Nazr S. Hyder, GBKB, 105.
63. Nazr S. Hyder, GBKB, 107.
64. Qurratulain Hyder, *Kar-e Jahan Daraz Hai* (Delhi: Educational Publishing House, 2003), 387–92.
65. Nazr S. Hyder, GBKB, 247.
66. Nazr S. Hyder, GBKB, 91.
67. Nazr S. Hyder, GBKB, 310.
68. Atiya Fyzee (1877–1967) belonged to the Tyabji clan and was the daughter of Amirunnisa (1829–78) and Hasanally Feyzhyder (1838–1903). In addition to her involvement in women's education, she was also deeply interested in cultural activities like dance and music. Siobhan Lambert-Hurley and Sunil Sharma, eds., *Atiya's Journeys: A Muslim Woman from Colonial Bombay to Edwardian Britain* (Delhi: Oxford University Press, 2010): 17–41.
69. Nazr S. Hyder, GBKB, 76–77.
70. Aparna Vaidik, *Imperial Andamans: Colonial Encounter and Island History* (New York: Palgrave Macmillan, 2010), 161–84.
71. Nazr S. Hyder, GBKB, 223.
72. Aparna Vaidik, *Imperial Andamans*, 71–72.
73. Nazr S. Hyder, GBKB, 310.
74. Muhammad Shibli Nomani, *Safarnama-e Rome, Misr, Sham* (Lahore: Bisat-e Adab, 1992); Aiyid Ahmad Khan, *Sir Saiyid ka Safarnama: Musaferan London*, ed. Asghar Abbas (Aligarh: Educational Book House, 2009).
75. Nawab Begam Hjira, "Ser-e Europe," *Ismat*, August 1908, 23–38; Shaista Suhrawardy, "Holland ki Ser," *Ismat* 62.5 (May 1939): 345–48.
76. Nazr S. Hyder, GBKB, 180.
77. See Judith Walsh, *Domesticity in Colonial India: What Women Learnt When Men Gave Them Advice* (Lanham, MD: Rowman and Littlefield, 2004), 131–38; Meredith Borthwick, *The Changing Role of Women in Bengal, 1849–1905* (Princeton, NJ: Princeton University Press, 1984), 205–10.

78 Nazr S. Hyder, *GBKB*, 196–97.
79 Syed Mumtaz Ali, "Talim aur Khanadari," *Tahzib-e Niswan* 14.49 (December 9, 1911): 598.
80 Nazr S. Hyder, *GBKB*, 199.
81 Shaista A. Suhrawardy, "Apna Ghar," *Ismat* 55.4 (October 1935): 298–300.
82 Antoinette Burton, *Dwelling in the Archive: Women Writing House, Home and History in Late Colonial India* (New York: Oxford University Press, 2003), 5.
83 Nazr S. Hyder, *GBKB*, 306.
84 Nazr S. Hyder, *GBKB*, 307.
85 Nazr S. Hyder, *GBKB*, 309.
86 Nazr S. Hyder, *GBKB*, 288, 121.
87 Joan W. Scott, "Experience," in *Women, Autobiography, Theory: A Reader*, ed. Sidonie Smith and Julia Watson (Madison: University of Wisconsin Press, 1998): 60.
88 Nazr S. Hyder, *GBKB*, 48–49.
89 Jahan Ara Shahnawaz, *Father and Daughter: A Political Autobiography* (Karachi: Oxford University Press, 2002); Begam Qudsia Aizaz Rasul, *From Purdah to Parliament* (Delhi: Ajanta Publications, 2001); Shaista S. Ikramullah, *From Purdah to Parliament* (Karachi: Oxford University Press, 1998).
90 Nazr S. Hyder, "Mohsin-e Niswan ki Yaad mein," *Ismat* 84.2 (February 1950): 59–61.
91 Nazr S. Hyder, "Swadeshi Tahreek aur Musalman Khwateen," *Tahzib-e Niswan* 24.51 (December 17, 1921): 801–4; Nazr S. Hyder, "Zanana-e Swadeshi Bhandaar Aligarh," *Tahzib-e Niswan* 25.1 (January 7, 1922): 3–5.

4. KAILASHBASHINI DEBI'S JANAIKA GRIHABADHUR DIARY
A Woman "Constructing" Her "Self" in Nineteenth-Century Bengal?

SHUBHRA RAY

Kailashbashini Debi (1829 [?]–1895) wrote a diary from 1847/BS 1253 (when she was around seventeen or eighteen years old) to 1873/BS 1280,[1] while she accompanied her husband, Kishori Chand Mitra (1822–1873), an employee of the East India Company, on his tours of undivided Bengal. Her diary was written at a critical juncture of Bengal's history when the "women's question" was being debated, even though it was published posthumously. It has consequently been read as that of a "new woman": someone who had been "recast" according to the needs of reformist politics of cultural nationalism.[2] In readings of her diary and other autobiographical writings from this period, the focus has been on constructing "a more comprehensive picture of the times,"[3] or for contributing to our understanding of "the process of social change which conventional history has so far overlooked."[4] Her diary has also been read for giving a glimpse of an unusual relationship between a couple in nineteenth-century Bengal and for throwing light on a "hitherto unknown or at any rate invisible aspect of family life."[5] However, in my reading of it, I intend to concentrate on the nature of her self-expression while contextualizing her within the larger debates regarding women's education and their subjectivities. The article is divided into four sections. In the first section I introduce Kailashbashini Debi, her familial background, and the limited opportunities that she had for education. In the second section I contextualize her diary against the social and literary developments of the period that influence her self-expression. The third section is a close reading of the diary, while the fourth section is the conclusion. In giving primacy to her self-expression, the attempt is not to imply that her diary is a chronicle of her complete life history or an account of the development of her "self"; rather it is to retrieve her voice—however fragmented or elusive—which has probably been sidelined in the search for an alternate historiography. Further, I wish to reflect on the tensions that are generated by her being molded by reformist politics and her contestations of these dominant discourses. The reading is not only concerned with the individual act of a woman writing her "self," but also with its being determined by the ideas of the possible reception of such a text even when it is not being written with the explicit idea of publication, as is the case here.

While not much is known about Kailashbashini Debi's early years or her natal family, she was married into a family that was known for its reformist zeal. Her husband as well as her illustrious brother-in-law, Peary Chand Mitra, were propagators of women's education and closely involved in its promotion. One of the followers of Henry Louis Vivian Derozio, Peary Chand was a part of the Young Bengal movement in his early days. He is remembered primarily for his book *Alaler Gharer Dulal* [The pampered son of a prosperous household], written under the pseudonym Tek Chand Thakur, which revolutionized the usage of Bengali. He also ran a school and, together with Radha Nath Shikdar, brought out a magazine in colloquial Bengali called *Masik Patrika* [The monthly magazine], in which, along with advocating "the abolition of various superstitious practices among Hindus" and publishing "historical anecdotes and dialogues on various useful subjects," he supported the cause of women's education.[6]

Peary Chand and Kishori Chand are both depicted by Mary Carpenter in her book *Six Months in India*, as ardent supporters of school education for women. Peary Chand was said to be against the idea of "educating females by Pandits" and in favor of having "good books and good teachers" to promote "female education" in Bengal.[7] Kishori Chand, again, comes across as a keen enthusiast for school education as opposed to the *zenana* system: "The zenana system may, in the beginning, be necessary in many cases—I do not depreciate it, I rejoice in its intention—but I can advocate it only as a tentative and a transitory measure, not as a finality and an ultimatum. It is dull and lifeless, whereas the other is instinct with life and admiration. Fancy, sir, a governess teaching one or two girls within the four walls of a dark and perhaps ill-ventilated room! Why, it is very dull work, and both the teacher and the taught participate in the dullnes."[8]

Yet it is the practice of women being taught at home in the seclusion of the *antahpur*, or the inner quarters, that was followed in Kailashbashini's case: she was taught by English tutors and her husband. While Peary Chand sent his daughter, Bindubasini, to the newly opened Bethune School, there is no mention of his brother's daughter going to school. Kailashbashini talks about "teaching" her daughter in her diary, but nothing more is mentioned about her education. However, we do find references to the books that she was reading— Bankimchandra Chatterjee's *Mrinalini*, for instance. In an interesting aside, she also compares her loneliness to that of Robinson Crusoe—even though she gets his name wrong, referring to his surname as "burush."[9] It is pertinent to note that Kailashbashini represents herself as being more than happy with the kind of education that she received. She mentions that her husband took a lot of care in educating her, reading out to her from the newspapers, and giving rational explanations of rituals. But she does not forget to mention that her personality was as much an outcome of her "fertile mind" as it was of the "seed of knowledge that was being planted."[10]

Structurally, Kailashbashini's diary is episodic: events of nearly three decades are compressed in random jottings. However, it is difficult to deduce from the printed text whether these events were recounted from memory as Karlekar assumes.[11] To me, it seems more likely that at least some of the events had been recorded as and when they were occurring in her life, as Kailashbashini mentions that writing the diary was her way of spending time while her husband was away on his tours, indicating that this might not be a retrospective account.[12] She uses the present tense in general and writes in the same vein even if she is writing after days or years.[13] While this creates an effect of immediacy, it certainly takes away from the cohesive unity of the text. The language is colloquial, and there are a number of spelling mistakes, which had been retained by the editor of *Masik Basumati*, to keep it close to the original; the same text is used in *Atmakatha* as well.[14] As a diary, then, it is certainly not a "self-contained literary artefact" with a "unifying vision"; rather it reflects on and is "contingent on lived experience."[15]

Contextualizing Kailashbashini Debi's Diary

Before going on to discuss the specific case of Kailashbashini, it is important to situate her within the larger context of the rapid changes that characterized the social landscape of her times. For a greater part of the nineteenth century, with the formation of new voluntary associations, there was a genuine attempt to ameliorate the perceived deplorable condition of women through the questioning of child marriages, prevention of sati, endorsement of the idea of the remarriage of widows, advocacy of women's education, or raising the age of marriage. Still, the way in which the new, educated, Hindu, middle-class woman was to be "constructed" was very much in keeping with their traditional roles as wives and mothers. This becomes especially evident if one takes a look at the kind of education that women were expected to receive. It consisted mostly of basic reading and writing skills, elementary arithmetic, and lessons in "domestic economy" and needlework.[16] As Partha Chatterjee argues, discouraging women from pursuing higher education was necessitated as much by the need to maintain status quo as the propensity to see them as "true" symbols of "Indianness." They had been able to maintain their "purity" because of their relative distance from the colonial powers, which the men had not been able to do.[17] This "remolding" that was being done was solely in accordance with the ideas and desires of the male reformers. The "women's question" was thus being decided without taking into consideration what women themselves wanted—even if male posturing suggested that changes were being brought about, as Tanika Sarkar puts it, "in the name of the consent and the will of the subjected." Sarkar makes the point that since the colonial order was criticized for not taking into consideration the point of view of the subjected, there had to be a charade that suggested that the will of the woman was not being overlooked when it came to gender-based legislation.[18]

Thus, it is precisely for this reason that, despite the predominant idea that women's writings were insignificant, their views still had a certain space within the newly formed public sphere of print. Conflicting attitudes come out clearly in the coexistence of praise and denunciation in the context of women's writings. One finds forewords by eminent men in books written by women; for instance, Jyotirindranath Tagore wrote the introduction to Rassundari Debi's *Amar Jiban* [My life].[19] But there are innumerable examples of rabid denunciations, patronizing attitudes, and expressions of doubts about the ability of women to write at all in the newspapers of the times. One could consider, as an example, a review of Prasannamayi Debi's *Adha Adha Bhashini* [An inarticulate speaker] published in *Amritabazar Patrika* in 1870 in which the reviewer says that "the book was received well by them because it had been composed by a woman; if it had been written by a man they wouldn't have bothered criticizing it."[20]

While women wrote fiction, anthologies of poems, and critical tracts—*Hindu Mahilaganer Heenabastha* [The woeful plight of Hindu women] by Kailashbashini Gupta[21] published in 1863, for instance, was highly acclaimed—it is the problematic relationship that they had with the genre of life writing that interests me. On the one hand, with institutionalized formal higher education being denied to them (barring a few), most women were expected to write about themselves and their immediate domestic worlds. Yet between the period 1856 and 1910, *Amar Jiban* by Rassundari Debi was the only autobiography to be published in Bengali.[22] Today, of course, we have a list of more than sixty autobiographies by women who were born in the nineteenth century and wrote these either in the nineteenth or in the early decades of the twentieth century. Chitra Deb has compiled a number of these in her groundbreaking work published in 1984—*Antahpurer Atmakatha* [The autobiography of the inner world of women)—while others have been discovered and published as late as the first decade of the twenty-first century.[23]

As has been pointed out earlier, the primary interest in these texts has been from the sociological point of view, rather than as texts that bring out the "construction" of the individual "selves" of these women. In retrospect it seems that the reception of these texts was probably determined by the way they were named. If we look at the autobiographies by male autobiographers, most of them were named either *Atmacharit* or *Jibancharit*. For instance, the autobiography of Debendranath Tagore is called *Swarachita Jiban Charit* [Self-composed biography] (1898); that of Shibnath Shastri is named *Atmacharit* (1918); and Rajnarayan Basu also calls his autobiography *Atmacharit* (1909). Partha Chatterjee has pointed out that while "atmacharit" was a literal translation of the word *autobiography*, it was also an "allusion to the entire body of *carita* literature of the classical and medieval eras in which the lives of kings and saints were recorded."[24] As opposed to self-proclaimed importance of the titles of male autobiographers, the titles of autobiographical writings by women are conspicuous for their desire to not stand out or draw too much attention to themselves—though whether these titles were chosen by them or by their sons or husbands or simply by the editors is not known. If we consider these autobiographies—*Sekele Katha* [The story of earlier times], by Nistarini Debi (1833–1916); *Purbakatha* [The story of earlier times], by Prasannamoyi Debi (1857–1939); *Pitrismriti* [The memories of my father], by Saudamini Debi (1847–1920); *Puratoni* [Old stories], by Gnadanondini Debi; *Amader Katha* [Our story], by Profullamoyi Debi (1852–1940)—to name only a few, it is evident from the titles of their texts that they were meant to be read as part of a collective rather than as individual voices in their own right. As Ishita Chakravarti points out, by using plurals instead of a singular number in the title ("our story"), presenting the self as one among many ("one housewife's diary"), or presenting one's account as irrelevant or trivial, space was being sought for women in an arena where, in accordance with the dictates of reformist politics, the individuality of women hardly had any primacy.[25] Even when Sarada Sundari Debi calls her autobiography *Atmakatha*, in a review that is otherwise favorable in the magazine *Bharatbarsha* in 1915, it is read as a text that provides useful information about her son, Krishna Bihari Sen, the younger brother of the reformer Keshab Chandra Sen, rather than as one where she expresses her subjectivity.[26]

The trend continues well into the latter half of the twentieth century. When Kailashbashini Debi's diary is published posthumously in a serialized form in the Bengali magazine *Masik Basumati* in 1952, it can only be called *Janaika Grihabadhur Diary*, with its raison d'être being to provide information about the previous century. The editor of the magazine writes that the diary was brought to him by the author's great grandson Sushil Kumar De, and the diary had been edited by his daughter, who had also copied the text from the original manuscript. It was reprinted in the magazine *Ekkhan* in 1981 and was finally published in the form of a book in 1982. It is interesting that it was published as *Atmakatha* in the second volume of a five-volume collection of autobiographies written in the nineteenth and early twentieth centuries. As no explanation was given for the change in its nomenclature, it is probably safe to assume that it was no longer problematic to call a woman's autobiography "Atmakatha." In a literal translation, *Atmakatha* would mean "My Story" but the story being sought was certainly not that of the "self" of Kailashbashini, rather of the times in which she had lived.

These texts were meant to provide details about domesticity or, if the autobiographers happened to be daughters, wives, or daughters-in-law of important individuals, information about the interior world of these men; they were never meant to be read as expressions of their personal opinions or worldview. This becomes clear if we take into consideration Girish Ghosh's introductory comments on the first published version of the autobiography of the actress Binodini Dasi, where, to put it in Rimli Bhattacharya's words, he "faults Binodini's life story for being too personal, for containing too many details about her self, *and* for being a bitter social critique; it is simply not professional enough, he says, and wishes it were more concerned with the details of her performances."[27] This attitude is evident in Somendranath Basu also, who edited *Smritikatha*, a collection of autobiographical tracts by women of the Tagore family in the latter half of the twentieth century. As late as 1987, when the third edition of the book came out, he treats these texts in his introduction as narratives that would provide access to the domestic lives of great men, crediting these women for being infused with the spirit of "calm submission," rather than seeking to "interpolate" these narratives with any "personal opinions" of their own![28]

In retrospect, recognition of the subjectivity of women was probably too much to expect from a society in which the very act of writing was considered transgressive by popular norms if not the scriptural ones. That women would become widows if they learned to read or write was one of the beliefs that had to be contested for women to be educated.[29] The very fact that these women could write was monumental; for most women probably, having a notebook of their own was problematic if not impossible. Ashapurna Debi, for example, makes Subarnalata, the eponymous protagonist of the second volume of her fictional trilogy, the victim of jibes and derision by her own husband and sons for "neglecting" her duties toward the house, in order to write. She is ridiculed for daring to publish her autobiography in which she had written, among other things, "I have a mind, intelligence, a brain, soul, but no one acknowledges my entity."[30] Rabindranath Tagore, in his short story "Khata" [The exercise book], similarly talks of the restrictions that are imposed on a young girl, Uma, who wanted to write in her notebook for her own pleasure. She is first mocked for having literary ambitions and finally is deprived of this prized notebook by her husband, Pyarimohan.[31] There are instances of husbands taking interest in their wives' education (as was the case with Kailashbashini Debi) or even taking the initiative in getting their wives' works published (as was the case with Mankumari Basu).[32] But these were exceptions.

However, deliberation over the reception of these texts becomes important if we take into consideration the view that the self is far from being a fixed entity that is available to be written about at any point of time. Rather, it may be understood, as Paul John Eakin puts it, as a "dialectical interplay between an autobiographer's impulse to self-invention and the received mode of selfhood in the surrounding culture."[33] In other words, with the realization that the "self that is being written" is not necessarily "the self which exists prior to the act of writing" comes a greater awareness of the factors which go into the making of this self. These could be the language one writes in, the possible reception of it, and the modes of censorship that it would be subjected to, to name only a few.

The censorship need not be overt coercion all the time; it can very well be implicit, imbibed by the autobiographer as a result of social conditioning. For Nabaneeta Dev Sen, for example, writing toward the latter half of the twentieth century in a very different literary climate in Bengal, the censorship remains largely self-imposed: "Because of her (Nabaneeta's mother) I couldn't write about a lot of things that I would have liked to write, would have written, but for her. . . . If you talk of censorship, there she was—*she was, you know, the censoring officer* in my life, and she stood there as a representative of all the social mores."[34]

When women like Sara Aboobacker or Nabaneeta Dev Sen writing in the later decades of the twentieth century often foreground the limited space that a woman has access to in writing about her life, it can perhaps be assumed that the perceived space available to a text in the public domain did determine to a great extent the kind of text that it was going to be. Aboobacker was probably voicing the concerns of a large cross section of women when she stated in an interview that she had concentrated only on her childhood in her autobiography, *Muslim Hudugi Shale Kalithaddu* [A Muslim girl goes to school], as writing about the rest of her life would be problematic. To put it in her own words, "still we women cannot write like men, without giving a thought to the after-effects. I don't know why only women are so hesitant."[35]

Reading Janaika Grihabadhur Diary

While it is impossible to determine for sure the exact kind of pressures that an autobiographer writing her "self" could have faced in the latter half of the nineteenth century, it is possible to read into her writing the kind of audience that she was expecting, the perceived norms of selfhood and her contestations of these very ideas in subtle but effective ways—factors that I intend to keep in mind while reading Kailashbashini Debi's diary. However, before taking a close look at her diary, it would be pertinent to note that, while Persian and Bengali had indigenous versions of the diary in *rojnamcha* or *karcha*, it is unlikely that Kailashbashini, given her location and her educational background, either had access to or could model her text on these traditions.[36] In his discussion of personal narratives from Kerala, Udaya Kumar has pointed out that diary writing, in its early days among Malayalis, "was often linked to projects of education. In addition to its usefulness as a mnemonic, the diary helped in the cultivation of literary competence and a disciplined survey of everyday activities."[37] In Kailashbashini's case, her practice of diary writing would certainly have been the product of a favorable climate; even though she never went to school she was educated at home by English tutors. Still, she does not tell us whether she was encouraged to keep a diary or started doing it of her own accord. The form that her diary takes—with its rambling and random entries, its vacillation between the colloquial idiom and the more acceptable one—can then be ascribed to her, especially since it is not known for sure whether her husband had access to it. Like the other memoirs written during this period, her life narrative was not about the consistent development of an individual consciousness, and, in that sense, it is analogous to this genre, one that "required the writer only to tell her readers, mainly women from a younger generation, how the everyday lives of women had changed."[38] This requirement, which was encouraged by the existing literary climate, was more than adequately met by the various descriptions of rituals, marriages, and educational practices that make up the corpus of Kailashbashini's narrative. And yet, apart from the everyday events, there is an attempt to capture the uncommon and the extraordinary, with Kailashbashini mentioning time and again that she was ending the topic as there were no more "interesting" events to narrate. These could be a beautiful sunset, a Nawab's mother being buried with a lot of fanfare, or even a storm that almost killed them.[39] This desire to stand out in chronicling the unusual when women writers were expected to do little more than narrate the quotidian is typical of the tone of her writing, as will be evident in this reading of her diary. She starts her diary with an account of her travels through different parts of what was then undivided Bengal. One place after another is mentioned and praised—

> In the year 1253, on the sixth day of the month of Āshād, I went to Rampur first.[40] I left Neemtala at eight. . . . That night we halted at a place beyond Suksagar. The next day we left for Kalna. We saw the temple of Kalna with its one hundred and eight Shivalingas . . . . [41] It was really beautiful and very clean. Beside that was the abode of Nalji and Ram-Sita. There were many other Gods and Goddesses which we saw. That night we ate and slept there. The next day we stayed in Ghoshalpur. Wherever we go the places appear to be very pleasant. The day after we stayed at the battlefield of Plassey, where the Nawab and the British had fought.[42] I was extremely happy on seeing that place and the various thoughts which arose in my mind cannot be expressed in words.

This could have been an ordinary beginning to any diary but for what follows. Immediately afterward she writes that at the time she was "overwhelmed with grief at the death" of her son and was in mourning while she was traveling through these aforementioned places. She does say that "as I write now, the page is wet with my tears," but compared to the details that she gives of the kind of agony that her mother-in-law and husband experienced on account of this death, and even her own pain at the sight of her husband's suffering, she is reticent when it comes to talking about her own sorrow.[43] There are some scattered references to her grief much later in the diary—for example, after the birth of her grandson she says that she has finally been compensated for the death of her son.[44] And even then, when her loss is mentioned—it is in a matter-of-fact tone—lacking the effusiveness that had marked the description of her grieving family earlier.

In the lines that begin her diary, her joy and excitement at being outdoors come out in the almost breathless recall of the places that she had been to rather than her sorrowful state. This curious absence of grieving can be explained by citing her age—she was only seventeen or eighteen—or even her relative immaturity. It could also be that the imposition of *purdah* had led her experience of travel in "open" spaces—in howsoever restrictive a manner—to get precedence in her scheme of things. She did resent the constraints of not getting out of the palanquin or "seeing" places as she wanted to: this becomes especially clear when later in the text, while describing another tour she criticizes the restrictions that were usually imposed on her while traveling with her husband.[45] In drawing attention to this incident the intention is not to critique her reticence; rather it is to note the manner in which her desire to suppress her resentment against the restrictions that she was expected to imbibe leads to a sense of ambiguity in her, something that will hold true for a number of other events in her diary.

The same reticence about expressing her feelings marks the birth of her daughter too. She mentions the displeasure of her mother-in-law, who felt that she had given up "gold"—referring to the death of her grandson—and had received "glass" in return. She also mentions the joy of her husband, who writes to her advocating an attitude of nondiscrimination between a girl and a boy as that was the will of God.[46] Apart from mentioning the time and day of her daughter's birth, she remains silent about her own emotions on becoming a mother again.

Given the fact that she was extremely proud of her daughter, it strikes me as curious that she does not say anything regarding the death or birth of her children. Is the reticence on account of uncertainty regarding the propriety of demonstrating one's grief or joy in public, or is it simply an oversight? There is no way of finding out for sure, but the fact that social codes were in transition thereby complicating the behavioral norms expected of women can be pointed out by considering another instance of such restraint. Nabaneeta Dev Sen points out in her personal narrative *The Wind Beneath My Wings* that when her mother, Radharani Debi, was widowed at the age of thirteen, she controlled her tears with great difficulty as she knew that it was immodest to weep for her husband in public—but then she was criticized and called hardhearted for not shedding a single tear.[47]

The idea of the *bhadramahila* was being "constructed," and this phase of transition in which neither the social codes nor the identities had taken a definite shape is brought out repeatedly in the contradictions that form the depiction of Kailashbashini's life and times. For example, she chooses the occasion of the birth of her daughter to bitterly criticize the kind of confinement that postpartum women had to endure. Giving a detailed description of the *sutikaghar*, which she compares with a jail, she goes on to criticize the social system, where money could be spent on eunuchs and on hiring musicians to celebrate the arrival of the newborn, but the mattress on which the new mother would lie was considered a waste as that would have to be thrown away once the confinement period of a month was over. She complains that the room she was in would often get flooded and it was almost like being incarcerated. It is interesting to note that her criticism of this practice is more from the point of view of her physical discomfort than any inherent ideological position about the sufferings of women.[48] Her basic problem is that, despite being the wife and daughter-in-law of a rich family, she had to stay as a "commoner," and, in her weak state after the birth, it was comparable to hell for her. It was all the more problematic for her as she did not have access to pen and paper and could not write to her husband, who was away on a tour. He, without knowing her situation, kept on complaining in his letters that she was not writing just to torture him.[49]

This is followed by an explanation as to why she mentions this and then she goes on to temper her criticism by making banal statements about how happiness and sadness coexist at all times, and also points out the benefits of living in that period. It is interesting to note that every instance of criticism of social mores—be it that of criticizing ungrateful children who torture their mothers in old age or the hypocrisy of letting men get away with blatant disregard of scriptural and social injunctions while women were ostracized for the same—is followed by ameliorative statements about the times.[50] It is not known whether she had intended her diary to be published, but, even while penning her thoughts in solitude, she cannot help but keep in mind the possible injunctions of her perceived audience. In a particular incident when she comes back from a marriage and her husband takes care of some household activities, she imagines people questioning her about her inability to handle those things and gives explanations in an imaginary dialogue.[51]

On the one hand, there is this overarching awareness of the possible readership, and, on the other, there is defiance of a number of parameters that were expected of her. Unlike fictional characters created in the same time frame, Kailashbashini has no qualms in admitting that she derived pleasure when her husband took care of her in her illness. There are stories where women have nursed their husbands back to health, but since the wife was not comfortable with the husband taking care of her and because of lack of proper medical care and attention, the woman subsequently passes away.[52] And again, she gives primacy to her desire to "see" places rather than blindly obey her husband. In one instance, where she reveals that she had not been permitted to visit a particular temple even though her mother-in-law was going, she manipulates the situation in her favor, even though it angers her husband.[53]

This intense desire to "see" places, which leads her even to dissimulation at times, marks her narrative. Travel is not the mainstay of Kailashbashini's account, unlike Krishnabhamini Das's journey to England, which resulted in the first full-fledged travelogue by a Bengali woman.[54] However, her eagerness to experience places in the limited way that she is allowed to do so comes through very clearly: "When cooking used to be done on the bank then we used to roam about everywhere. In the month of *Agrahayan*, the open field was quite full, wonderful to look at. The heat of the sun was less. We used to sit in the field and watch its beauty. The pleasure that it gave me is difficult to put in words!"[55]

This description of her pleasure in being out in the open while she was traveling with her mother-in-law and a big group of relatives is better understood if it is contrasted with her earlier way of moving about with her husband: "The *ghat* in which I was supposed to get down, the palanquin was wrapped in the sail—so that nobody would be able to see me."[56] As has been noted earlier, she describes the temples that she visits and gives some information about the historical places that she is visiting, but there is not much other than that that she says about the impression that these journeys leave on her mind. Her travels fall in the interstices of traditionally accepted ones for pilgrimage and the newer modes of travel for work. Given the fact that there were restrictions on travel for women, Kailashbashini, as is typical of her, does not consider it a privilege to be able to travel with her husband—for her it is a fact of life.

She continues to react in this vein on a number of fronts. If one considers the debates surrounding domesticity, it was an accepted fact that the main aim of a woman's life was to consider her husband god and obey his every dictate. This was propagated not only by the traditional ideologues but also by the newly educated women themselves in exhortatory tracts.[57] Against this background, Kailashbashini strikes a discordant note when she states that had she followed his wishes "he would have been pleased, but I chose not to give him that pleasure."[58] She is talking about the desire of her husband to defy tradition and not keep a Brahmin for cooking their meals, but it is only on her insistence that they continued to follow the caste injunctions. She states that she chooses to follow such customs not for any inherent belief in them, but simply because she has to keep in touch with her relatives. She is the mother of a daughter and therefore could not afford to sever her ties with them—if she had sons she would not have bothered with adhering to any such norm! She is scared of being ostracized; her biggest fear is that "people would stop eating food cooked by her." She goes on to say that as "I follow the dictates of Hinduism there are no problems. My husband can do whatever he likes but no one says a word. This is the religion of Bengalis, which is why anybody who is intelligent doesn't follow it. I certainly do not."[59]

Partha Chatterjee reads in this passage a statement of the reformed woman's duty. In doing so, he is continuing his argument that the women's question had been "resolved" by sublimating her with the spiritual domain, that of "tradition," rather than the material domain controlled by the British:

> Kailashbashini, speaking from within this emergent middle-class home, is not telling us that religious beliefs and practices are private matters and that what is important for the life of the nation is the public behaviour of its citizens. On the contrary, she has discovered that the practices of the outside world which men have to get used to are in the end inconsequential, since what truly matters in the life of the nation are practices in the inner space of community life. Here it is the duty of women to hold fast to the religious practices of the community: even "private" beliefs are of no consequence.[60]

In other words, he considers her to be a woman who has completely been determined by the reformist politics. My reading of the text, however, brings out that, far from considering it her duty and being determined by her education, she actually demonstrates that she can have her own voice and express her own thoughts in her diary. She considers the necessity of the maintenance of caste injunctions a classic example of hypocrisy prevalent in nineteenth-century society. She continues her exposure of this hypocrisy when she gleefully mentions that, during her daughter's marriage in 1858/BS 1264, none of the caste injunctions were followed: "There was dancing on the day of the marriage. And the British and Bengalis ate together. Nobody said anything. I have stated before that Bengalis cannot do anything to important people. Ramgopal babu said that you made the tiger and the cow drink from the same ghat."[61]

The only reason for her agreeing to follow rules is the demands of practicality. The unstated eventuality for which she takes this position is widowhood—a common enough occurrence given the state of medical affairs. This event—the death of her husband—marks the end of the diary, with Kailashbashini wishing that her life would come to an end soon too. This desire of death is not only because of the sufferings of widowhood, but also because of the quality of relationship that she had shared with her husband.

The relationship between Kailashbashini and her husband is shown to be perfect—he is the loving husband who cannot imagine life without her, and she is a person who cannot bear even the slightest of his sorrows. The best doctors are brought in—both British and Indian—every time she is ill; he keeps in mind her discomfort while taking decisions and refuses to get his daughter married to anybody simply to maintain the purity of the lineage.[62] This could have been read as Kailashbashini's representation of the relationship, but inclusions of conversations verbatim and quotations from a letter that her husband had written to her allow a different reading of it. For instance, in the letter that he had written to her while he was away on work and she and her daughter had been caught in a storm, he had praised his wife and daughter in effusive terms. He had stated that he would have committed suicide if something had happened to them, going on to add, "Most people don't get a wife like mine even after praying to God."[63] Kailashbashini, too, carries out her duties to the fullest—be it that of accompanying him wherever he is posted on account of his administrative duties, or taking care of him and his family. But she is subtly critical of him, of the restrictions imposed on her of not going out of the house or traveling with a lot of constraints. She is also critical of his habit of drinking and names his companions who were important figures socially.[64] She garbs her criticism in apparent happiness at her condition when she says, "being women our minds are inferior and therefore we are satisfied with very little."[65] Interestingly, she does not consider herself inordinately lucky for being in the position that she is—rather considers these her due. In a dialogue where her husband asks her whether he has ever been unjust to her, she replies by saying that she has not done anything unworthy to deserve any kind of censure. She puts the onus on him and his intelligence by adding, "Are you going to scold me, belittle me when there is a mistake, or just like that?"[66]

This conversation is to be viewed against the background of contemporary ideas of marriage—where a woman's importance lay in her ability to bear sons—in fact it was the raison d'être of her existence. If we look at the memoirs of Nistarini Debi or Prasannamoyi Debi, who were chronicling the same time period, we find that their depiction of their marriages was very different,[67] plagued as they were by the curse of "Kulinism"—where the woman had no value whatsoever. Kulins were families among the upper castes in Bengal who were considered to occupy the highest ritual status. It was a matter of prestige to have such a son-in-law. The women of such families were the worst sufferers; since a Kulin girl could not marry a non-Kulin, they were often married off to much younger or much older bridegrooms. The high demand for the Kulin bridegroom led to the practice of polygamy with some of them marrying more than one hundred women.⁶⁸ As Tapan Raychaudhuri puts it, "It is not clear exactly when Kulin polygyny assumed its exaggerated form, but it was a fact of Bengali social life by the early years of the nineteenth century. For the poorer Kulins, marriage became a profession: the wives lived in their parental homes and the husbands visited their in-laws for a few days each year, if that, to collect their stipend."⁶⁹

Under the colonial gaze of criticism, the idea of the companionate wife did take shape, but even this kind of a marriage was firmly rooted in the traditional ideas of male supremacy and the unconditional submission of a wife to her husband.⁷⁰ While this was not unusual given the contemporary social climate, what is interesting is that this kind of an expectation is effortlessly aligned with a desire for mutual companionship, by women themselves. These views were espoused in some of the most acclaimed critical tracts written by women toward the latter half of the nineteenth century. Kailashbashini Gupta, for instance, in her *Hindu Mahilaganer Heenabastha* [The woeful plight of Hindu women], published in 1863, had lamented the lack of compatibility between a married couple because of existing customs: "Would that one could have a spouse after one's own heart—boundless good fortune would then result. Pity! How unjust that the act of marriage is authorised only by the parents or some relative!"⁷¹ She however, had also stated categorically that a woman could "never be of a comparable status to a man," and it was pointless for a woman to seek freedom:

> Till now, women of no country have achieved freedom; why then would Bengali women seek it?
> If one could be liberated by being educated and traveling about as one wished, the women of Europe would have inducted themselves long since into high positions in the government, thus enhancing the glory of their nation. Women, therefore, will never have freedom.⁷²

It needs to be noted that she was arguing for the necessity of women's education and had made this statement to ward off criticism that women should not be given that opportunity because then they would not want to be submissive. Considering the context makes us aware of the complexities of the position that any ideologue for women's education occupied; what is also clear is that for the limited opportunities of education, to continue to come women's way, the prevalent beliefs regarding the inherent inferiority of women had to be perpetuated.

So, even when Bamasundari Debi, writing in 1861, extols the benefits of having an educated wife, she clearly has the man's interests in mind—"If a learned, liberal, broad-minded man marries an ignorant, quarrelsome, and mean-minded wife the company of that illiterate spouse can never give him any mental satisfaction."[73] Her advocacy of the woman's role is not very different from that of traditional marriages: "the wife who serves her husband gladly and without anger in spite of being continually greeted with her husband's cruel words and wrathful eyes alone succeeds in winning her husband's heart."[74]

However, in later writings like Krishnabhabini Das's *Swadhin O Paradhin Nari Jiban* [Independence and subjugation in women's lives], published in 1897, education is not seen as the sole remedy to every problem. Rather, Das argues for the need of self-reliance in women's lives in order for them to have "greater strength and courage." She believes that women have "infinite rights" like men, but their work spheres need to be separate so as to avoid "possibility of conflict and quarrel among them."[75] Similarly, Saratkumari Chaudhurani defended the "modern" educated women of her times against a plethora of accusations in her *Ekal O Ekaler Meye* [The modern age and the modern woman]. Published in 1891, this critical tract brings to the fore, amid various other issues, the changing nature of the relationship between married couples:

> In the past, women respected, loved and also feared their husbands. Today's woman loves and respects her husband. . . .
>
> The modern woman looks upon her husband more as a friend. Since most men have to husband their own households, their wives are their best advisers because the well-being of the family concerns them both. It is largely for these reasons that the woman of today is not in awe of her husband; moreover, since she is the mistress of the household, the husband receives her constant care and attention. The element of fear is thus largely absent from the wife's love and respect.[76]

She also points out that it would be wrong to expect the "modern" woman to behave like women of earlier ages and that "with education there is bound to be a change in her thoughts and taste," thus putting an end to the illogical expectation of maintenance of status quo in women's mentality despite their exposure to education, at least in writings by women themselves.[77]

Kailashbashini writing between the years 1847 and 1873 seems to have lived and chronicled the kind of relationship that writers like Saratkumari Chaudhurani espouse as late as 1891. Even toward the last decade of the nineteenth century such relationships would have been a rarity; and during Kailashbashini's times, they were certainly not the norm. Kailashbashini must have been aware of the existing social conditions, and yet when she portrays her marriage she does not draw attention to the exceptional character of the events; rather she considers these her due and commonplace. From the very beginning of her diary, she has created the impression that she is "special"—be it in her popularity among her family members, the nature of her daughter, or the kind of experiences that she has—and it seems that she internalized the idea to the extent that she can claim for herself a position that was not readily available to other women of that period.

Conclusion

Kailashbashini Debi was very much a product of the times that she lived in. The reform movements, the debates surrounding women's education, the evolution of the nuclear family, the changing definitions of marriage, as discussed above—all contributed in making her the person that she became and the particular form that her diary took. She believed that it was a husband's prerogative to educate his wife and had imbibed the injunctions that were being imposed on the "new" woman, and she proclaims that the most important dharma for a woman was that of "satitva."[78] This is an issue that she discusses with her husband, who rationally explains to her how satitva is present in all other religions as well and why strictures regarding widowhood are necessary.[79] That her diary ended with her husband's death and she considered her life to be over despite having years to live shows that she had inculcated the predominant values of her times.

And yet, this is also a woman who had written in her diary: "In the first place, we are young and on top of that our husbands are in high positions. And they are very much in love with us; they live and die when we tell them to. When husbands like that are under one's control,[80] can one be unhappy? Our bodies are always in a state of pleasure."[81]

She clearly defies any attempt at being classified as somebody who had been completely determined by reformist politics. Coming as she does at the interface of various currents in Bengal's social history, she is embedded in the older ways of living, while imbibing the newer modes of thought. In the midst of it all, she gives glimpses of a voice that is highly unusual for the times that it belongs to.

In my reading of Kailashbashini Debi's diary, I have tried to show that she is clearly contesting the attempts of "self-definition" that were at work, albeit in a subtle manner. I have discussed the ways in which she tries to conform to the expectations and noted her attempts of catering to an imaginary audience. However, in spite of showing her awareness of the limits of acceptability, she nevertheless goes on to stretch the confines of that domain in the manner in which she views and constructs her "self." In the public domain of print she of course gets subsumed in the rhetoric of being an alternative informant about the times that she was living in, but she was doing much more than that in her diary.

NOTES

1 Kailashbashini Debi's diary was published for the first time in 1952 with the title *Janaika Grihabadhur Diary*, and this is the title that I use in my article, despite the text later being published as *Atmakatha*. See Kailashbashini Debi, "Atmakatha," *Atmakatha*, vol. 2, ed. Naresh Chandra Jana et al. (Calcutta: Ananya Prakashan, 1982). BS stands for *Bangiya Shatabdi*, the Bengali era.

2 I have used a term that figured in the title of Sangari and Vaid's book and aptly captured the politics of the resolution of the women's question. See *Recasting Women: Essays in Colonial History*, ed. Kumkum Sangari and Sudesh Vaid (New Delhi: Kali for Women, 1989).

3 Chitra Deb, Malavika Karlekar, and Sambudhha Chakraborty, to name only a few scholars, discuss women's autobiographies with the aim of constructing a picture of the times. See Chitra Deb, *Antahpurer Atmakatha* (Calcutta: Ananda, 1984); Sambudhha Chakraborty, *Andare Antare: Unish Shatake Bangali Bhadramahila* (Calcutta: Stree, 1995); and Malavika Karlekar, "Constructions of Femininity in Nineteenth Century Bengal: Readings from *Janaika Grihabadhur Diary*," *Samya Shakti: A Journal of Women's Studies* 4 and 5 (1989–90): 11–29. Karlekar also tries to construct "a more comprehensive picture of the times we can only know at second hand" in her readings of Kailashbashini Debi's diary and other autobiographical and exhortatory literature of the period in her monograph. Malavika Karlekar, *Voices from Within: Early Personal Narratives of Bengali Women* (Delhi: Oxford University Press, 1993), 2–3, 122–31.

4 Srabashi Ghosh, "'Birds in a Cage': Changes in Bengali Social Life as Recorded in Autobiographies by Women." *Economic and Political Weekly* 21.43 (October 25, 1986): WS88–WS96, http://www.jstor.org/stable/4376267.

5 Karlekar points out that the description of a nuclear family that one gets here is highly unusual for its times. See Malavika Karlekar, "Constructions of Femininity in Nineteenth Century Bengal," 25.

6 This description of Peary Chand Mitra's *Masik Patrika* is from Reverend Long's *A Catalogue of Bengali Newspapers and Periodicals from 1818 to 1855*, cited in Saurindra Kumar Ghosh, *Peary Chand Mitra O Samakalin Bangla* [Peary Chand Mitra and contemporary Bengal] (Calcutta: Anandadhara, 1985/BS 1392), 46.

7 Mary Carpenter, *Six Months in India*, vol. 1 (London: Longmans, Green, 1868), 217.

8 Carpenter, *Six Months in India*, 215.

9 Kailashbashini Debi, "Atmakatha," 15.

10 The translation is mine from the original Bengali. All Bengali extracts have been translated by me unless stated otherwise. Kailashbashini Debi, "Atmakatha," 35.

11 Karlekar had assumed that the writing happened at a later period of her life. In her reading of the diary, she had stated, "It would appear that she kept rough notes which she organized only after her husband's death in 1873, when she was forty-four years old. . . . [She] clearly wrote selectively on issues which she remembered well and had been most influenced by." See Malavika Karlekar, *Voices from Within*, 122.
12 Kailashbashini Debi, "Atmakatha," 15.
13 For instance, there is a gap of nearly three years between the events on page 14 of the diary: her husband's posting in Natore and his transfer to Jahanabad (1849/BS 1256–1852/BS 1259), but the writing does not acknowledge that. She had discussed her husband's stay for fifteen days in Kashi (Benaras) just before this: both time frames are dealt with in the same vein. Kailashbashini Debi, "Atmakatha," 14.
14 In a footnote to the second part of the serialized text, the editor of *Masik Basumati* had mentioned that the mistakes were being preserved to keep it as close as possible to the original text. This is cited in Naresh Chandra Jana et al. eds., "Lekhak Ebong Rachana Prasange" [About the authors and the texts], *Atmakatha*, vol. 2, ix–x.
15 This is precisely the function that Rita Felski had in mind for the confessional diary. See Rita Felski, "On Confession," in *Women, Autobiography, Theory: A Reader*, ed. Sidonie Smith and Julia Watson (Wisconsin: University of Wisconsin Press, 1998), 86.
16 Radha Kumar, *The History of Doing: An Illustrated Account of Movements for Women's Rights and Feminism in India 1800–1990* (New Delhi: Kali for Women, 1993), 16.
17 Partha Chatterjee, "The Nationalist Resolution of the Women's Question," *Recasting Women: Essays in Colonial History*, ed. Kumkum Sangari and Sudesh Vaid (New Delhi: Kali for Women, 1989), 233–52.
18 See Tanika Sarkar, *Words to Win: The Making of* Amar Jiban; *A Modern Autobiography* (New Delhi: Kali for Women, 1999), 114.
19 Sarkar, *Words to Win*, 137–39.
20 See "Adha Adha Bhashini," *Amrita Bazar Patrika*, March 24, 1870, cited in *Sambad Samayik Patre Unish Shataker Bangali Samaj*, vol. 2, ed. Swapan Basu (Calcutta: Pashchim Banga Bangla Academy, 2003), 428.
21 This is a different Kailashbashini, married to Durga Charan Gupta, who was primarily famous for her critical tracts. See the note on Kailashbashini Debi in Chitra Deb, *Antahpurer Atmakatha*, 134.
22 Tanika Sarkar, *Words to Win*, 2.
23 The memoir of Haimabati Sen (1866–1933) was discovered and translated by Tapan Raychaudhuri as late as 2000. See Haimabati Sen, *"Because I Am a Woman": A Child Widow's Memoirs from Colonial India*, trans. Tapan Raychaudhari, ed. Geraldine Forbes and Tapan Raychaudhari, intro. Geraldine Forbes (New Delhi: Chronicle Books, [2000] 2011). Again, the diary of Indubala Majumder was discovered by her grandson Rathindranath Majumder, long after her death, among "old papers." Even though she was born in 1889/BS 1296 and started

writing her diary in 1911/BS 1318, it was published only in 2000. See Indubala Majumder, *Ek Aparachita Briddhar Dinlipi* [The diary of an unknown old woman] (Calcutta: Ananda, 2000).

24 See Partha Chatterjee, "The Nation and Its Fragments: Colonial and Postcolonial Histories," in *The Partha Chatterjee Omnibus* (New Delhi: Oxford University Press, 1999), 138.

25 See the introduction by Ishita Chakravarti, "Pinjar theke Pinjare: Jautha Itihasher Khoje," in *Naishabda Bhenge: Atmakathane Bharatiya Nari* [Breaking the silence: Autobiographical writings by Indian women], ed. Ishita Chakravarti et al. (Calcutta: Khoj Ekhon Parishad and Stree, 2005), xix.

26 See "Pustak Parichay" [Introduction to books], *Bharatbarsha*, Magh (1915/BS 1321), 341.

27 Rimli Bhattacharya, ed. and trans., *My Story and My Life as an Actress: Binodini Dasi* (New Delhi: Kali for Women, 1998), 19.

28 Somendranath Basu, ed., *Smritikatha* (Calcutta: Baitanik Prakashani, 1987/BS 1393), 85.

29 Tanika Sarkar discusses this in the chapter Strishiksha *or Education for Women*. See Sarkar, *Words to Win*, 76.

30 See Ashapurna Debi, *Subarnalata* (Calcutta: Mitra and Ghosh, 1967/BS 1373), 331.

31 Rabindranath Tagore, "Khata," in *Galpaguchha* (Calcutta: Viswabharati Granthalay, 1957/BS 1363–64), 216–20.

32 See the note on Mankumari Basu in Chitra Deb, *Antahpurer Atmakatha*, 139.

33 Paul John Eakin, *Fictions in Autobiography: Studies in the Art of Self-Invention* (Princeton, NJ: Princeton University Press, 1985), 7.

34 Ammu Joseph et al., eds., "Nabaneeta Dev Sen," in *Storylines: Conversations with Women Writers* (New Delhi and Hyderabad: Women's WORLD (India) and Asmita Resource Centre for Women, 2003), 74.

35 Ammu Joseph et al., eds., "Sara Aboobacker" in *Storylines*, 109.

36 Bhaskar Mukhopadhyay has posited that subaltern travelogues "resulted" from negotiations with earlier "diurnal" forms like *tirthya-mahatyas*, *rojnamcha*, and *charitkatha* and the emergent travelogue in nineteenth-century Bengal. For a detailed discussion see Bhaskar Mukhopadhyay, "Writing Home, Writing Travel: The Poetics and Politics of Dwelling in Bengali Modernity," *Comparative Studies in Society and History* 44.2 (April 2002): 308.

37 Udaya Kumar, "Autobiography as a Way of Writing History: Personal Narratives from Kerala and the Inhabitation of Modernity," in *History in the Vernacular*, ed. Raziuddin Aquil and Partha Chatterjee (Ranikhet: Permanent Black, 2008), 418–19. I am thankful to Siobhan Lambert-Hurley and Anshu Malhotra for drawing my attention to this point.

38 Partha Chatterjee, "The Nation and Its Fragments," 140.

39 Kailashbashini Debi, "Atmakatha," 4, 7.

40 Sixth *Āshād* 1253 would correspond to June 20, 1846, with *Āshād* being the third month in the Bengali calendar.

41 A *Shivalinga* is a representation of Lord Shiva in Hindu temples for worship.

42 The reference is to the 1757 Battle of Plassey, in which Robert Clive had defeated Nawab Siraj-ud-daulah, leading to the establishment of the rule of the British East India Company in India. Kailashbashini Debi, "Atmakatha," 3.
43 Kailashbashini Debi, "Atmakatha," 3–4.
44 Kailashbashini Debi, "Atmakatha," 32.
45 Kailashbashini Debi, "Atmakatha," 13.
46 Kailashbashini Debi, "Atmakatha," 4.
47 Nabaneeta Dev Sen, "The Wind Beneath My Wings." *Indian Journal of Gender Studies* 6.1 (January–June 1999): 225.
48 Criticism of prenatal care, the birthing room, and health care for women was common in the writings of European missionaries and reformers. For a discussion of this, see Malavika Karlekar, "The Antahpur," *Voices from Within*, 52–55. Karlekar points out that the *antahpur* (inner quarters) was made out to be the scapegoat and was held responsible for the lowly position of women. When women like Bamasundari Debi started criticizing these practices in their critical tracts they placed the onus on women themselves, especially their lack of education. The assumption was that once they were educated they would not indulge in practices that were harmful for the child or for the mother. See Bamasundari Debi, *Ki Ki Kusamskar Tirohito Hoile Edesher Sreebriddhi Hoite Pare* [What are the superstitions that must be removed?], 1861; trans. Malini Bhattacharya, *Talking of Power: Early Writings of Bengali Women from the Mid-Nineteenth Century to the Beginning of Twentieth Century*, ed. Malini Bhattacharya and Abhijit Sen, School of Women's Studies, Jadavpur University (Calcutta; Stree, 2003), 19–20. But the criticism was always of the practice in general and not confined to any social class or caste.
49 Kailashbashini Debi, "Atmakatha," 5.
50 Kailashbashini Debi, "Atmakatha," 4, 25.
51 Kailashbashini Debi, "Atmakatha," 22.
52 Rabindranath Tagore, "*Nishithe*," in *Galpaguchha* (Calcutta: Viswabharati Granthalay, 1957/BS 1363–64), 263–72.
53 It is interesting to note the manner in which this particular incident has been recorded. Her husband had given very clear instructions about who were to go to see a particular temple including the officers and bearers of palanquins. Initially she writes that she had wondered to herself, "I have come so far; wouldn't I get a chance to see it?" She tries speaking to her mother-in-law, who refuses. She then accompanies her when two palanquins arrive for them. She writes that she goes along only because she believed that one of the palanquins was for her, even though the instructions given by her husband in the beginning had been to the contrary. And then she writes that she was scared because she knew that her husband would not be pleased. Later when her husband asks her in anger why she went, she replies, "All the womenfolk went, I was scared which is why I went with them." The dissimulation is very clear even if we go by the literal content of her diary. She does not bother to defend herself against the charges of mendacity: either she is not aware of it (which is highly unlikely), or she

believes her readers would take her at face value. Kailashbashini Debi, "Atmakatha," 16–18.

54 It was called *England- e Bongomahila* [A Bengali lady in England] and was published in Calcutta in 1885.

55 Kailashbashini Debi, "Atmakatha," 13–14.

56 The term *ghat* refers to a series of steps leading down to a pond or a river. Kailashbashini Debi, "Atmakatha," 13.

57 See the range of advice for women in *Bamabodhini Patrika*, one of the leading magazines of late nineteenth-century Bengal, published monthly from Calcutta, 1863 onward for sixty years. See Bharati Ray, comp. and ed., *Nari O Paribar: Bamabodhini Patrika 1270–1329* [Woman and family: Bamabodhini magazine, 1863–1922] (Calcutta: Ananda, 2002).

58 Kailashbashini Debi, "Atmakatha," 25.

59 Kailashbashini Debi, "Atmakatha," 25.

60 Partha Chatterjee, "The Nation and Its Fragments," 147.

61 Kailashbashini Debi, "Atmakatha," 30.

62 This was a major step to take as girls were married off indiscriminately to maintain the purity of the lineage to "Kulin" Brahmins. Kailashbashini Debi, "Atmakatha," 28.

63 Kailashbashini Debi, "Atmakatha," 8. He acknowledged her worth once again when he lost his job in 1858, and was worried about keeping up their lifestyle. On being reassured by Kailashbashini about her ability to adjust to any situation, he praises her with the words, "I came to know from your words that you are more courageous, more intelligent and have greater powers of endurance than me" (31).

64 Kailashbashini Debi, "Atmakatha," 11.

65 Kailashbashini Debi, "Atmakatha," 11.

66 Kailashbashini Debi, "Atmakatha," 29.

67 The marital lives of both writers were plagued with problems arising out of early marriage and Kulinism. See Nistarini Debi, "Sekele Katha," in *Atmakatha* 2: 3–49. See also Prasannamayi Debi, "PurbaKatha," Calcutta: n.p., 1917/BS 1324.

68 Nistarini Debi's great grandfather had married 108 women while her grandfather had married fifty-four. She states that in those times whosoever could marry more (women) was known as a good Kulin in the society. See Nistarini Debi, "Sekele Katha," *Atmakatha* 2: 7.

69 Tapan Raychaudhuri, "Love in a Colonial Climate: Marriage, Sex and Romance in Nineteenth-Century Bengal," *Modern Asian Studies* 34.2 (May 2000): 354.

70 For a discussion of the idea of the companionate marriage, see Malavika Karlekar, "Education of a Civil Servant's Daughter: Readings from Monica Chanda's Memoirs," in "Reconstructing Femininities: Colonial Intersections of Gender, Race, Religion and Class," special issue of *Feminist Review*, no. 65 (summer 2000): 129.

71 Kailashbashini Gupta, "Hindu Mahilaganer Heenabastha" [The woeful plight of Hindu women], 1863; trans. Kumardeb Bose, in Bhattacharya and Sen, *Talking of Power*, 38.

72 Gupta, "Hindu Mahilaganer Heenabastha" [The woeful plight of Hindu women], 47.
73 Bamasundari Debi, *Ki Ki Kusamskar Tirohito Hoile Edesher Sreebriddhi Hoite Pare* [What are the superstitions that must be removed?], 1861, trans. Malini Bhattacharya in Bhattacharya and Sen, *Talking of Power*, 21.
74 Bamasundari Debi, *Ki Ki Kusamskar Tirohito Hoile Edesher Sreebriddhi Hoite Pare* [What are the superstitions that must be removed?], 20.
75 She does not specify the kind of self-dependence that she is talking of, nor does she speak of the need for them to go out and work. She just outlines the need for them to have greater responsibilities so that they can earn the respect that they deserve. Krishnabhabini Das, *Swadhin O Paradhin Nari Jiban* [Independence and subjugation in women's lives], 1897, trans. Sourin Bhattacharya, in Bhattacharya and Sen, *Talking of Power*, 78.
76 Saratkumari Chaudhurani, *Ekal O Ekaler Meye* [The modern age and the modern woman], 1891, trans., Swati Ganguly, in Bhattacharya and Sen, *Talking of Power*, 65–66.
77 Chaudhurani, *Ekal O Ekaler Meye* [The modern age and the modern woman], 68.
78 For instance, she describes a woman called Lokkhimoni, who had traveled with them to Benaras. She is critical of her loquaciousness but puts the onus on Lokkhimoni's husband, who had not "trained" her. See Kailashbashini Debi, "Atmakatha," 33.
79 Kailashbashini Debi, "Atmakatha," 35. For Kailashbashini Debi, "satitva" or sati-ness consisted primarily in being devoted to one's husband, a widely prevalent view at the time. The notion can be found reiterated in "Satitva O Patibratyo Dharma," where it is stated that "in this country being rid of the sin of adultery is known as the religion of Satitva" even though in this article the attempt was to critique the idea with the writer pointing out that there had to be more to a "good" woman then merely being slavishly faithful to one's husband. See "Satitva O Patibratyo Dharma" [Sati-ness and the religion of being devoted to one's husband], *Bamabodhini Patrika*, Sravana 1280 (July 1873), Bharati Ray, *Nari O Paribar*, 63. It needs to be pointed out here that "sati" is a Sanskrit term meaning a virtuous woman who was devoted to her husband, and not simply one who "self-immolated" after her husband's death. However, as Vasudha Dalmia points out in a note, "Sati" came to be associated primarily with the act of self-immolation because in intervening to end the practice in nineteenth-century Bengal the "British usage restricted the term to the sacrifice alone, the act as well as the agent." Vasudha Dalmia, " 'Sati' in the Mirror of Post-Enlightenment Discourse," in *Orienting India: European Knowledge Formation in the Eighteenth and Nineteenth Centuries* (Gurgaon: Three Essays Collective, 2007), 75. "Satitva" came to have a similar association as well with Paul B. Courtright, who pointed out in his discussion of the iconography of Narayani Satimata, "The myth says that the fire was ignited by her satitva, her "sati-ness"; the heat of her devotion and single-mindedness sufficed to light the fire." See Paul B. Courtright, "The Iconographies

of Sati," *Sati: The Blessing and the Curse; The Burning of Wives in India*, ed., John Stratton Hawley (New York: Oxford University Press, 1994), 34.

80 The term that she uses is "padanata"—literally, prostrate at one's feet. Kailashbashini Debi, "Atmakatha," 16.

81 She was describing her condition as well as that of the wife of the deputy magistrate, with whom she had become friends. Kailashbashini Debi, "Atmakatha," 16.

PART II. **FORMS AND MODES OF SELF-FASHIONING**

5. BETRAYAL, ANGER, AND LOSS

Women Write the Partition in Pakistan

UMA CHAKRAVARTI

Mumtaz Shah Nawaz's growth is not only apparent in her political life but in her writings, of which *The Heart Divided*, like many first novels, is partly autobiographical. It was published several years after her death. Those who knew her have often wondered how she would have reacted to the "iron curtain" which had grown up by then between India and Pakistan. It was not what she had envisaged in the closing chapters of *The Heart Divided*. —AHMED SHAH NAWAZ, Mumtaz's brother, foreword to Mumtaz Shah Nawaz, *The Heart Divided*

The Birds have destroyed the garden
They picked it clean
Not a leaf has been left on the boughs
—ITINERANT SINGER AANGAN, in Khadija Mastur, *Aangan*, translated as *Inner Courtyard*

The wheel of time had scattered families, crushing and displacing peoples as it hurtled along, spreading havoc in its wake. The stroke of a pen divided countries, sharing out the severed pieces among contending parties and men hunted men like beasts of prey transforming homesteads and communities into towers of silence watched over by vultures. —NA JUNOON RAHA, in Zaheda Hina, *Na Junoon Raha*, translated as *All Passion Spent*

. . . .

Why do women write? Why do they write *what* they write? And why do they write what they write *when* they do so at a particular moment in their lives? How do these questions inform the way we read what has been written by women—specifically fiction writers who create "primary" texts and others who try to draw meanings from the primary texts? How does the authorial self insert itself into the narrative self—if it does at all? How do collective memories of events and experiences work themselves out in what we write? What are the circuits that link the double processes in women's writing on a subject like the Partition of the Indian subcontinent in 1947 that bring individual biographies into a dialogue with collective experiences? Do these circuits allow us to understand the complicated history of the subcontinent? Is writing a way to transcend national boundaries that allow us, as women on the subcontinent, to speak to each other in the same way as fictional or real characters did in the past? And why am I writing this chapter at this point in my life? In other words, why am I *choosing* to write on the Partition when I have never done so before? Instead, it has lain in my mind as an inexplicable event that I, as a six-year-old living in Delhi, had experienced secondhand—through snatches of conversation, through the accounts of my best friend at school, through my sister's account of witnessing a killing outside our home, and through my own delirious cries at night recounted by my mother in later years. In this context we may bear in mind that all the recent feminist *scholarship* in India on the Partition has emanated from the personal histories of the writers: all had families that had originated on the other side of the border and had moved to this side. Further it was the 1984 anti-Sikh pogrom that triggered memories of the earlier violence and dislocation leading to some of these feminist Partition studies.[1]

For these and many other reasons, though located across the border from Pakistan in India, I will in this chapter explore Pakistani women's writing on the Partition written at different moments in the history of Pakistan. The texts I have chosen are Mumtaz Shah Nawaz's *The Heart Divided* (1948), Khadija Mastur's *Aangan* (1952), and Zaheda Hina's *Na Junoon Raha Na Pari Rahi* (1996). While the first was written originally in English, the latter two were written in Urdu and translated into English only recently.[2] I chose these novels out of a larger body of writings by Pakistani women mainly because these three novels have been picked up by feminists on both sides of the border between India and Pakistan for republication, translation, and dissemination. These works have not yet been written about, although Partition studies have used short stories and novels in recent years to write about dislocation, trauma, and memory.[3] The choice of the novels and the focus on Pakistani women's writing is itself an aspect of my own "biography," an outcome of a phase in my life, now sadly ended, when I taught women's history at a women's studies course in Lahore to South Asian students between the years 1998 and 2004. During these sessions I was struck by the way in which the same traumatic Partition narratives, remembered from my childhood, were now coming back to me, but through being told from the "other" side. It was a poignant and chastening moment because we are often so bounded by nationalist considerations that we fail to genuinely acknowledge the distinctive yet generic ways in which history is experienced across borders. It forced me to think about the Partition from the standpoint of Pakistani women.[4]

As a feminist historian reading these texts, I am particularly interested in the way in which history, personal and political, appears in this body of writing. Overall, the texts are marked by complex feelings of anger at how history came to unfold on the subcontinent. We also see, however, how loss of land, home, and family, as well as nostalgia for a larger subcontinental ethos now gone forever, figure in their writing. Though these writings are not autobiographies in the strict sense of the term, they are deeply autobiographical in sentiment, enabling the women to speak for a larger feminine self beyond personal experience. This larger feminine self is, in a sense, more poignant as the individual self cannot exist outside history, particularly at its most intensely violent moment in the Indian subcontinent.[5] And yet the violence is not the driving emotional force of the writing; instead, it is the household as the web of relations at the individual and the larger political level that is the locale of the intensely felt experiences of the female protagonists. It may be that through these narratives we can understand something about the cultural memory of the subcontinent in a way that helps us as individuals to mediate or modify difficult moments in our pasts.[6]

In this chapter I will outline in brief the main story line of the novels that I am using and then pick up the themes that interest me in these writings, given the way I see how Partition figures in their narratives: it is the "public" event that shapes the lives of the protagonists, as it did the lives of the authors. Thus while there will be a necessary move away from the "autobiographical" in terms of my own memories of the Partition, the writings that I have chosen speak back to me through the protagonists of the novels and the ways they have been shaped by the writers for whom the Partition was a central event.

The Narratives

THE HEART DIVIDED

Mumtaz Shah Nawaz (also known as Tazi) was born in 1912, and so, in a sense, she lived through the most intense phase of the anticolonial movement that swept the Indian subcontinent. Her family was important in the political life of the country from the time of her grandfather, and, as a child, Tazi met the nationalist and poet Sarojini Naidu, who was delighted to meet the budding child-poet whom she proclaimed to be her "spiritual" daughter. This political and social context imbues her novel *The Heart Divided* with its historical importance because the political events of the subcontinent are the larger backdrop in which the narrative of two households, one Muslim and one Hindu, is embedded. This makes it an unusual text that is able to address a number of themes as it crisscrosses the lives of the two families. Mumtaz wrote the novel between 1943 and 1948, even though it ends in 1942; after 1942 Mumtaz threw herself into the struggle for independence, and went on to finish the novel only between 1947 and 1948. When she died tragically in 1948 in a plane crash, she was on her way to New York to speak on the Kashmir issue. She was also carrying a first draft of *The Heart Divided*, in the hopes of finding a publisher, that was lost in the air crash—but, fortunately, a copy had been left behind at home, which her family published in 1957.

The Heart Divided was republished in 1990 by a feminist publisher who had come to acknowledge its relevance on the basis that students, and especially women students, found the novel a much better way of understanding the recent history of Pakistan than the official school textbook versions with their top-down focus on historical figures. Since *The Heart Divided* is a novel written by a woman, Mumtaz looks at history from that standpoint. This is what appealed to the young women studying history as they could relate to the main protagonists' political journey in the 1930s and 1940s because it was also the immediate history of their mothers and aunts.[7] Many of these young women asked that the book be republished so that it could circulate more widely and also be prescribed in schools and colleges. In a sense the subcontinental audience—which is the extended community of readers that all the books that I will focus on here desire to speak to, because this is the ethos they grew up in or absorbed—was fulfilled when the book was republished once more in India this time. The Indian edition has been well received and has made a small impact on understanding political events in the subcontinent in the last two decades before Partition precisely because it is so historical in essence with its focus on Hindu-Muslim relations.[8]

The 1990 republication from Lahore has a striking image on its cover: against an orange background, itself divided by a green band, we have a map of pre-Partition India divided now into three parts by two roughly hewn boundaries representing India divided through its "heart."[9] These political divisions are presaged by the manner in which the two families in this story, joined together through almost a century of close interaction forged anew by the young women of both families who share their growing into womanhood years, begin to move apart as the struggle for independence intensifies. Zohra, the main protagonist of the novel, through whose eyes we make sense of the political events, shares a deep friendship with Mohini, a Kashmiri Pandit whose family is fully involved in the struggle for independence and has been in and out of jail for their political acts.

As the novel opens Zohra tries to step out of *purdah* by speaking in a debate in a coeducational space, but her deeply conservative grandfather will not hear of it. Zohra makes a slow hesitant beginning in trying to find her own voice and her own sense of self as distinct from her father, mother, brother, and sister. We see this only in glimpses, but the sense of an individuated self that is strongly political does crystallize by the end of the novel. This is as it should be as the journey out of purdah is also a journey into the public sphere—into the political world that is dominating the world outside the *aangan*, the courtyard, which is the title of one of the other novels I will explore below. But it is not as if the inside spaces are untouched by the events outside: these are often the subject matter of discussions between generations, a device Mumtaz uses to recall histories before the contemporary moment of the text. Mohini is already out in the public world giving speeches and getting arrested for her actions at school. Among the ways in which Zohra negotiates purdah is to wear the burka, but to use it as an armor that allows her to carry an important press statement to the newspapers when Mohini is arrested.

Two narrative strands allow the author to weave her own life with the life of the Muslim community, the political events taking place, and the insurmountable tensions generated for the community during the 1930s. Specifically, Zohra's brother falls in love with her Hindu friend Mohini, causing a storm in both families, and Sughra, Zohra's sister (who functions in the novel to represent Zohra's/Tazi's split self),[10] becomes increasingly drawn to her uniquely Muslim past. Eventually, even before the Hindus and Muslims fail to resolve their differences in the early 1940s, the Hindu-Muslim romance comes to a tragic end, metonymically working to evoke the failure of the undivided nation to emerge.

AANGAN: INNER COURTYARD

Khadija Mastur's *Aangan* was published in 1952 and is regarded as the author's best work. She was born in a small town near Lucknow in 1927 and grew up in an atmosphere where learning and literary activities were valued. Among her companions in her childhood were children from the working class, which may have made her acutely sensitive to class dynamics both within the household and outside it. Early on, she developed an interest in storytelling, which was enhanced at the early death of her father and the financial difficulties the family was faced with, leading to her decision, as well as her sister's, to take to writing as a means of earning a livelihood. She began writing seriously in 1942 at age fifteen. A few years later she became part of the left-leaning Progressive Writers' Movement, which drew a number of Urdu writers into its fold. As part of the anticolonial struggle Khadija and her sister joined the Muslim League in 1946, and the family moved to Pakistan in 1947, where she became the secretary of the Lahore branch of the Progressive Writers' Movement. She wrote several collections of short stories and two novels, including *Aangan*, and received many awards for her writing. Friends remember her enthusiastic participation in demonstrations and struggles against martial rule but always rushing back home to return to her writing. The Progressive Writers have often been critiqued for having an "immigrant imaginary" valorizing the homes they left behind.[11] While Khadija shared some of this social milieu, she also wrote about the betrayed ideals of the Muslim homeland with a "pained lucidity" in her works.[12]

Set in the 1930s, *Aangan* has been described as the "story of a dystopic home,"[13] within which the battles of the world are played out. Powerful women characters make this novel an extraordinary account of the politics of the household, over whom the male patriarchs of the family preside and whose destinies they seek to rule, sometimes with tragic consequences. The child Aaliya, through whose eyes the story of the declining fortunes of the family unfold, and who seems close to Khadija's own persona as autobiographical details match,[14] is deeply influenced by the patriarchs, her own father and then her uncle, Bade Chacha, even as she can see how they bring tragedy into the household through their political beliefs. Amma, Aaliya's mother, is deeply implicated in upholding class and feudal arrangements, bringing the first tragedy into the household as Aaliya's sister, Tehmina Apa, who is deeply in love with her cousin Safdar, a poor relative supported by her liberal father, is to be given in marriage to another, more respectable cousin, Jamil, son of Bade Chacha. As the day approaches for Tehmina's marriage, she kills herself, unable to reconcile herself to her situation. When Aaliya's father goes to jail, Aaliya and her mother go to live in the family home, now in the "protective custody" of Bade Chacha. Here, the grandmother waits for her youngest son, who went away to Turkey at the height of the Khilafat movement, to come back. Sadly, he has simply disappeared.

At the family home live others: a female cousin named Chammi, whose father has abandoned her, and Jamil, a male cousin. When Amma and Aaliya come to live in the family house, Jamil begins to develop an interest in Aaliya, which makes for both an awareness of the erotic charge that he displays for her and for the tension it generates all around, doubling Chammi's pain. In turn, she discharges her pain through anger and recalcitrant behavior against Bade Chacha, who is part of a "heathen" party, according to Chammi. She openly and noisily supports the Muslim League, thus bringing the bitter ideological war right into the household. Aaliya keeps studying at home over all these years, finally going to Aligarh for a course in teacher's training.

By the time Aaliya returns to the family home, Partition is taking place, and, since Amma's dearly beloved brother is going to Pakistan, Amma too decides to go. Bade Chacha is heartbroken and will not even see his niece off as she leaves, as he cannot bear the pain of separation. Aaliya herself is torn between duty to her mother and mixed feelings of loss, uncertainty, and also a desire to simply leave the tormented past behind.

NA JUNOON RAHA: ALL PASSION SPENT

Zaheda Hina was born in 1946 in Sasaram, Bihar. In 1947, she was taken to Karachi by her mother to join her father, who was already there to build a business, while the rest of the mother's natal family stayed on in India. Divided by the newly carved boundaries and travel regimes set in place by the two nations, Zaheda's mother did not return to the parental home for nearly a decade. In Zaheda's words, her creative writing was triggered by the sight of her ever silent and apparently emotionless mother clinging to her elder sister and weeping uncontrollably, unable to contain her emotions when she went back to the natal home for the first time after Partition.[15] According to Zaheda, writing came naturally to her after witnessing that high moment of emotional anguish given vent to by her mother. This primeval sense of loss of the undivided homeland is the imprimatur of Hina's *Na Junoon Raha*.

All Passion Spent is actually a novella. Though apparently small in size, it evokes the *dastan go* tradition of storytelling, where one story after another unfolds as the protagonist, Birjees Dawar Ali, journeys through life.[16] Its opening pages are set in Karachi in the mid-1990s (after the Babri Masjid has been demolished in India), with Birjees's arrival in Karachi: the moment is marked within the text by Birjees registering the slogans on the walls that evoke hatred against India, but there are also other slogans against the Mohajirs, expatriates from India, Qadianis, and Shias (both are minority sects in Pakistan). Birjees is on a visit to the Cowasjee family, whose presence in recent decades in her life is marked only by a card at the turn of each year. With the passing of time, Mrs. Cowasjee—or "Bano Aunty"—who opens the door to her, cannot remember Birjees, aged and disconnected with reality as she is. The story then flashes back to forty-five years before, when Birjees first came to Karachi in search of an uncle and her cousin to whom she was betrothed as a child—sealed with a piece of silver—only to find no one at the address she has. Alone and homeless, confused and tired beyond measure, Birjees takes shelter from the pouring rain in the stairway of a block of flats where the Cowasjees live, and they give her shelter, not just for the night but until her relatives can be located.

As the narrative unfolds, we are told that Birjees was left homeless in India when her father died a few months after Partition (he refused to leave for Pakistan after Partition, though other relatives did) and Birjees's stepmother, to whom the house had been left, decided to sell the property and move back to her parents' home. Alone, and anchorless, Birjees decided to go to Karachi in search of the fiancée and her uncle. A chance encounter with Pervaiz, whom she could not locate on arrival, makes it clear that the fiancée has moved on, and is soon to be married to Pervaiz's boss's daughter, as she will bring half the business as a dowry. Pervaiz has calculatedly kept Birjees in the dark, lying to her and betraying her trust. Shocked at this betrayal, Birjees falls ill and is nursed back by Manuchehr, the doctor son of the Cowasjees, who tries to persuade her to stay on in Karachi, but Birjees decides to return to India.

A parallel story tells us the tragic account of Minu, the daughter of the Cowasjees, who fell in love with a Sindhi Hindu whose family left for India after the Partition. Minu leaves home against the will of her family for India in search of her lost love and has never returned. The kind Cowasjees carry their own burden of grief, and Mrs. Cowasjee begins to see in Birjees her own lost daughter. India for her is where Minu went, and she lives in the hope of her return. Years later when she opens the door to Birjees on her second visit, Bano Aunty thinks alternately that Birjees has brought news of Minu and that Birjees herself is Minu. The long awaited return of her lost daughter lets the mother slip gently into death. There is a closure to Minu's story. For Birjees, the journey of her life continues even though Manuchehr finally declares his love for her. It is too late now. Birjees must go back on her unfinished journey, perhaps continuing the search for herself: this is a journey she must make alone.

History: Past, Present, and in the Making

In a sense all three novels are about history: most often about events in the twentieth-century Indian subcontinent that shape the lives of the protagonists, particularly the women, whether they directly participate in the events or are shaped by them through what is happening in the world outside. Partition looms on the horizon, threateningly, unwantedly, and desirably depending on the political positions that different characters espouse. *The Heart Divided* foreshadows Partition, *Aangan* ends just after Partition when the migration to the new land has been completed, and *Na Junoon Raha* begins after Partition and explores its consequences for one young woman on the threshold of her adult life. At the time of Partition all three are young women trying to find themselves in tumultuous times. *The Heart Divided* opens with Zohra looking back on her life in later years and marking the moment of change in her life as the day she stepped out of purdah to a life of independence and adventure—precisely the way the Muslim communities of South Asia were combining independence from colonial rule with an "adventure" in the form of seeking a self-identity within the nation that was in the making. Zohra describes the moment of change thus: "It was not easy to define when it began, for the lives of all of the girls of her generation had changed so much and were woven together in such a manner, like many coloured threads of an intricate pattern. . . . Perhaps it started on a quiet November evening in 1930."[17]

Aaliya and Birjees too are growing into womanhood in the years before Partition, finding themselves—or at least trying to, as the communities into which they are born also struggle to make a distinctive place for themselves in the subcontinent as it moves toward independence. The history of our protagonists and the histories of the subcontinent are narratively linked in all three novels.

But history also presses on the narratives in other "smaller" ways within the larger backdrop: as change sweeping households, as new professional possibilities, through women's struggles for education, and through challenging social customs enforced on the younger generation desperately seeking change. Freedom from foreign rule thus seamlessly melds into freedom and liberation from the prison-house of custom especially for the young women in the narratives. Zohra startles everyone by going off to work in a city away from home;[18] Sughra leaves her husband, unhappy with her cloistered life, and goes on to throw herself into the work of the Muslim League;[19] Aaliya goes to Aligarh to train as a teacher;[20] and Birjees refuses to give up her passion for singing.[21]

The Heart Divided blends these elements of history together in complex ways, so I will focus on this work to explore in depth the ways history figures in it: the distinctive ways in which history dominates the narrative unfolds through the two sisters, Zohra and Sughra, who take oppositional positions in the history that is in the making. The first is drawn into the heady excitement of the anticolonial movement represented by the National Congress of the 1930s—as Tazi herself was, according to her biographical details.[22] The second quietly accepts marriage with a cousin but is also firmly embedded in a distinctly "Muslim" history and its glorious past in the Indian subcontinent. This past is evoked by Sughra through the powerful Mughal rulers, whose visible testimony is found in beautiful architecture: the *masjids*, the palaces, the tombs that dot Lahore and Delhi; and a visit to each is the occasion to recount some aspect of Muslim rule; thus a visit to the Qutab, built by a slave king, is an occasion to highlight the principle of equality within Islam. But there are other powerful memories too, of Muslim glories from stories she has heard sitting on her grandfather's lap as a child. Sughra, whom I have suggested could be a figure based on Tazi's split self, dreams of distant lands—Arabia, Syria, Turkey—and she wonders if she will ever see them, the very lands whose "history beat in her blood."[23] The glorious past was so different from the drab present, a reality she retreats from, losing herself in dreams: "She could see the armies of Salahuddin marching across the desert, drums beating banners flying, with row upon row of knights and heroes mounted on restless chargers ready to die for the greater glory of Islam. And in front of them, always in front of them the unknown knight with the crescent banner."[24]

Years later Sughra attends a meeting of the Muslim League in Delhi, where she hears a fiery speech in which a young man is evoking the glorious Muslim past to exhort his audience out of their apolitical inertia: "Have you forgotten your past? Cannot the walls of the Red Fort, and the minarets of the Shahi mosque remind you of the glory that was yours? Oh sons of Islam who have learnt to be slaves, what if your enemies be many and your arms be weak? Have you forgotten how Tariq landed in Spain and told his men to conquer or perish? Does not the blood of Tariq and Ghazi and Babar flow in your veins? Arise, awake and unite."[25]

Sughra is not only fixated on the past, but she is also deeply concerned about the fate of the Muslims in the subcontinent now and in the future. Her anxieties about growing Hindu mobilization and the leadership of the Congress in the anticolonial movement sets her up as counterfigure to Zohra to present two distinctive views that dominate Muslim discourses during the 1930s, which the author would have heard in her own strongly politicized household. Sughra argues with Zohra about supporting the Congress, even as Zohra has her own fears but still hopes for a way to achieve an understanding between Hindus and Muslims. Instead there is a growing divide between the two communities, especially after the Congress assumes power in many states after the 1937 elections. This is the moment when fears of Hindu rule begin to overwhelm the Muslims with their distinctively Hindu drive. For Sughra the depressing situation is compounded by the feeling among elite Muslim households about Muslim "backwardness"—especially of their women—when compared with the Hindu community, and so she begins to do social and political work for the regeneration of the Muslim community. She also becomes an ardent Muslim Leaguer, as does the rest of her family, and especially the men. Only Zohra remains ambivalent, still drawn to the Congress and especially to Nehru's socialism, hoping for a united onslaught on the British by Hindus and Muslims, hoping also for united India thereafter. Her own growing personal struggle takes place against the backdrop of the political events between 1930, when the mass mobilization phase of the Congress is initiated, and 1942, when she begins to be disillusioned by the Congress. She turns slowly leftward, supporting workers' struggles—but the Left in Lahore is also drawn toward the Muslim League. Indeed self-determination is a position endorsed by the Communist Party, and some of its cadres were officially told to join the League by the party leadership once Pakistan has become a reality. Though the novel ends in 1942, it presages the years immediately before the Partition. This is evident in the following dialogue between Zohra and Sughra, where the former says: "Oh Apa, I . . . for so many years believed and trusted in the Congress leadership . . . and now . . . now I . . . they should have risen to the occasion. They should have accepted the principle of self-determination . . . I am so unhappy!"

Sughra tries to persuade Zohra to join the League: "We need people like you. . . . The doors of the League are open to all; they've joined together for a national ideal, people of all views are there, socialists, democrats, fascists, communists, *maulvis* and modern men. . . . All for the right of the Muslim people to assert their will in their homelands where they are in a majority."[26] The parallel and seemingly irreconcilable political positions of Zohra and Sughra are ultimately resolved by the way each of the two sisters shifts from their earlier position, moving toward bringing the two opposing trends in the history of the subcontinent in terms of the Muslim "question." Zohra moves to appreciate the Muslim League's position because the class question is incorporated by Sughra, so there is a bridging of the gap in their respective positions. Zohra is able to give up on her vision of a united subcontinent and her belief in the Congress's ability to address the Muslim question. The split/divided self of the Muslim community, as represented by the two opposing positions of the sisters, which are ultimately reconciled, substantiates my reading of the two sisters as the split self of the author as a representative of her community at a particular moment in history.

Zohra's own personal struggle is to marry her left-wing comrade, whose social origins are low. Zohra's father begins by objecting to her relationship but finally gives in, saying he is so disgusted by the spectacle of disunity in the country that he is determined not to have his family rent by it at least. As the events close in 1942, Zohra has moved in to work in the Muslim League, even as she hopes for an eventual settlement between the League and the Congress, for which she believes that people with goodwill on both sides will continue to try. Zohra's Hindu friend Mohini's younger brother is heartbroken on hearing that the settlement fails to be forged that year: his anguished cry decries the principle of vivisection that is almost taken for granted by many Muslims: "it would be like cutting up one's own body. We shall never allow it, never!"[27]

History betrays Zohra's hopes of self-determination for the Muslims within a single geographical and political entity on the subcontinent. The heart is divided.

Class, Gender, and the Declining Fortunes of the Muslim Family

The dynamics of class and gender permeate all the novels and make for a different way to explore the framework of history that provides the backdrop for the unfolding of personal histories in them. The dynamics, however, are most sharply etched in *Aangan*. Fortunes are changing under new social and economic processes in the colonial regime, with emerging opportunities for some and growing exclusions for others. Set in a small town in North India, the collapsing fortunes of the family of the narrative voice hark back to another time, when patriarchal power is part of a larger set of social relations, with land as the basis of class power. That power is now going, leaving patriarchal social power stripped of its material base but otherwise intact, though challenged from within. But as the debris of that power remains, the dominant emotion in *Aangan* becomes one of anger, an anger that sometimes has a focus but is so embedded in the dynamics of the "traditional" family that it needs no tangible object to set it off. Aaliya is the archetypal Muslim woman, set in a terrifying transitional moment in history, where anger is as much, if not more, about the family within than it is about social and political events outside, from which she consciously stands apart.

It is a dystopic household because its existence in history is now seen with a different sensibility, stripped of its earlier veneer of paternalism in terms of class and gender. The complexities of the situation are rendered with such consummate skill that each of the characters draws both sympathy and anger in Aaliya's perception. Thus even Amma, who is the least likable character in the novel, continues to receive a degree of sympathy and filial loyalty from Aaliya, whose own persona is otherwise so at loggerheads with her. At the same time the patriarchs of the family, Aaliya's father and her Bade Chacha, are seen with sympathy and love by her even as she can see the damage they inflict on the women of the household. In terms of the dynamics of class relations within the family, both men conduct themselves with better old-world paternalism with those dependent on them (whether as servants or other waifs and strays), while Amma is vicious in her outpouring of venom against the more vulnerable members, tied into the household through servitude or through the assertion of feudal patriarchal privileges by its earlier patriarchs. Aaliya's deep discomfort with, and gradual awareness of, the hierarchies of power within the family and household as she grows into womanhood is the dominant motif of the novel. I think the authorial self of Khadija has created a masterpiece in Aaliya: anger against feudal regimes and sympathy for the underclass unites them both. Aaliya *is* Khadija—or at least imbued with her spirit.

Apart from Aaliya, who both challenges the structure of social relations and lives it out, three figures are superbly etched: Chammi, the half-orphaned dependent of the family, who rebels against her circumstances; Kariman Bua, the one family servant left, given the household's declining fortunes; and Israr Mian, the "illegitimate" child of Aaliya's grandfather by a concubine. Instead of being subservient as a dependent, Chammi becomes the challenger of Bade Chacha's political subservience to the "Hindu party"—in other words, the Congress— making fun of him. When chastised, Chammi refuses to be cowed down merely because she lives in Bade Chacha's household and under his protection. Though she observes purdah, she throws the burka over herself whenever she feels like it, dashing out of the house to mobilize the Muslims of her *mohalla* to defy her uncle by publicly countering his political views and defying his authority: As Aaliya comments: "What kind of talk is this, Chammi? It's certainly made me see through your political fervour. You're no Muslim Leaguer. This drama has been staged only to hurt Bade Chacha."[28] Ultimately though, however much she rebels against Bade Chacha, *he* has authority over her and marries her off to the first person he can arrange a marriage with. Chammi's resistance comes to nothing and, except for Aaliya, no one mourns her departure from the family home. Chammi herself has no critique of the patriarchal household. Aaliya, however, becomes increasingly desperate about the need for economic independence, without which she can see that she too could be trapped in a similar fate.

Even in Aaliya's own generation, the workings of male desire within settled patriarchal structures creates fury in Aaliya. Jamil, her cousin, can marry either of his two cousins: Chammi, who loves him and has helped him by lending him money, lives on hope, but Jamil turns his attention to Aaliya, also his cousin, and pursues her. When Id comes, he gifts Aaliya alone with a suit of clothes and raises a storm of emotion in Chammi (to whom he ought to be beholden), who turns her ire on Aaliya. A horrified Aaliya stuffs the clothes into a trunk and thinks to herself: "God forbid that she should be such a fool. Men were by nature mercurial, a little heat was enough to ignite their passions. Yesterday it was Chammi, today she had found favour, tomorrow it would be someone else's turn. . . . [29] Did he think that with a suit of clothes he had established ownership over her?"[30]

It is in the depiction of internal class relations where *Aangan* is at its best. Kariman Bua is a magnificently portrayed figure: her nomenclature ironically captures the contradictions of the feudal household. Given a fictive kinship relationship—she is called *bua*, or father's sister, and is so totally integrated into the family that there is no mention of her relatives. She had come into the household as part of her mistress's dowry when Aaliya's grandmother was married to her grandfather. When the grandmother, Kariman's mistress, dies, it is she who reads the Qur'an and observes the death rituals. Aaliya is struck by this devotion, presuming that this is a sign of affection that she had for the mistress and a reciprocation of the mistress's love for her, a way of acknowledging her loss. To Aaliya's horror, Kariman stoically recounts the real basis of their relationship, thus giving her an insight into the coercive power of feudal ties: "What! Mistress love me? Beta you do not know grandmother's time. We are servant folk, Aaliya beta, we don't have any standing."

Then lifting her shirt, she bared her back to Aaliya, showing great wheals on it. Kariman explained to Aaliya how she got them: "My mother came with the mistress's dowry. My father died when I was still a little girl. When I grew older mistress married me to a servant. I was newly wed and became a little remiss in my duties. This was my punishment."[31] But even the wretched location of Kariman as a feudal servant is not so low that she has no power within the household. Below her in the hierarchy is Israr Mian, the unwanted member of the household who eats last and must ask each day for his food from Kariman with his servile plea—"if everyone has had their meal, can I have mine now?"—which invariably draws a sharp insult from Kariman, and peals of laughter from others: "All in good time, Israr Mian. The delay will only serve to whet your appetite. In this time of scarcity what would we do if your hunger was not assuaged."

Anguish pierces Aaliya's heart when she witnesses this. What fault had Israr Mian committed that for him hearts turned to stone. He was no kin to anyone. Though Bade Chacha is invariably courteous to Israr Mian, everyone else is part of the general humiliation heaped on him. And though Aaliya's heart is wrenched by compassion for him, never once is she able make her feelings visible or reach out to him: that is the reality of power within the household and the codes of etiquette that allow little possibility of challenging it if you are yourself a dependent, except in the deflected and anarchic ways that Chammi does. You cannot even position yourself ideologically against the repressive system that exists, except to seek a complete exit from the household.

Partition comes almost as a relief into this structurally flawed "dystopic" household, and this is, in part, Aaliya's necessary escape route. The mud dolls' house that Aaliya played in as part of the way young Muslim girls are schooled into marriage and householding is not the real world of the "family," with its tensions and bitterness. Does Pakistan hold promise of a different future? Is it anger and the inability to change things in India that explains Aaliya's wanting to go to Pakistan, her way of making a transition from the old to the new? She says to herself as the family debates her mother's decision to go to Pakistan: "Aaliya Begam, if you stop here now, you will forever be caught in quicksand." And a while later we are told, "Already feeling like a traveler, she began to think of what the future would hold for her. Perhaps their going away would be for the best. She was sure to find happiness once she left this house."[32] *Aangan* makes the history of one household set in a larger political reality its narrative center: anger at the inability to shape either family or nation makes for the personal story of Aaliya, caught at the intersection of the two.

History/Partition as Loss: Journeys into the Unknown

Na Junoon Raha is a work with an entirely different sensibility, permeated by an indefinable air of sadness, a sense of an irreparable loss that is an inevitable consequence of Partition. As the novella opens, the dominating emotion Birjees Dawar Ali experiences is fear and aloneness. At this moment it is about being in a strange place looking for a place to stay the night, so that she can decide what to do with herself, as the home and anchor she came in search of has disappeared into thin air. But, as the narrative unfolds, there is a larger sense of homelessness that pervades the writing: the uprooting from the *babul*, the father's home, so much a part of women's culture on the Indian subcontinent, aestheticized in folk songs and songs sung at the *rukhsati*, when a girl leaves her home after marriage. But the father's home in *Na Junoon Raha* is also the land of the birth, the home of the ancestors' graves, the culture in which one has grown up, the loss of which makes one not only homeless but also in a strange way nameless, and with nowhere to go. As Birjees looks at herself in the mirror in her refuge for the night, she says to herself: "Is this really I? Without a name and with nowhere to go?"[33]

A sudden rush of tears takes over. The archetypal homeless figure—apart from women—is the migrant. And the archetypal migrants of history, the Parsis who came in search of a refuge in times long past, are Birjees's refuge for the night, and ultimately for the time she is in Pakistan. Now, in the moment of separation, of divisions, the Parsis are not part of the making of boundaries: they are invested neither in Pakistan nor in India and see no reason to move, staying on where they are even as others leave or are made to leave. It is part of the narrative logic of the text that it is a Parsi family home that becomes the surrogate for the lost home of the father: these new bonds of humanity transcend the ties of blood that have betrayed Birjees by their denial of the past. The Parsi migrant metaphor also enables Birjees to evoke other histories of losses and movements of people, placing the Partition within a larger history of religious and community tensions that the world bears witness to: "In times long past a huge flood of humanity had moved from one place to another. There were the good and the bad among the exchange of the populations that took place. . . . Sunk deep in thought, Birjees struggled with her own dilemma. It was not so long, after all, when the high wall of the citadel had been breached and its inhabitants had seen their world destroyed."[34]

Cowasjee, with his own migrant history, and his own lost daughter, whom he and his wife are acutely reminded of as Birjees is sheltered for the night in a land of strangers, finds comfort in history, reading it and writing about the Zoroastrians. He reflects on this new turn of history that has brought Birjees to his door: What were the circumstances that had led her to their door, a supplicant for a night's shelter? Such things had never happened before. Life that had flowed like a placid river, unchanged and unchanging, was now a whirlpool of muddied waters, uncertain, unpredictable."[35]

Birjees herself had never dreamed that she would live anywhere except her own land. Birjees's journey to Pakistan in search of home and anchor was driven by multiple losses: first the death of her father, perhaps because of heartbreak, who had survived Partition and the beginning of the great migration, sadly watching people leaving the land of their birth exhorting them to stay: "This dust is our mother. It is the leaven in our blood, and we can sleep peacefully only on its breast. You will never find peace away from it."[36] But now Birjees's father himself had gone, and with him had gone the family home. Sadly, her father's closest Hindu friend too cannot stop his son from turning into a right-wing Hindu fundamentalist, so he cannot safely shelter her. Alone and homeless in the land of her birth, Birjees bemoans her situation: was she to leave the land that was her birthright because the fiancée had gone away? But she must. And so she bid farewell to the mound of earth beneath which her father lay and began her journey away from the land that had given her everything.[37]

The journey ends in disaster. Betrayed in the new land by her kin disregarding blood ties and ties of commitment, shocked at the lies and the naked greed that drives her fiancée, for whom women are merely pawns in the lives of men, she cries out for her Abba, cries out too that she had sold her house for a piece of silver, sold her birthright for nothing as she is cast aside midstream by her closest relatives. It was better to go home even if Abba was dead; at least the land that holds him remains, while in Pakistan there were other kinds of graves, graves of hopes. How could she make a home among them, where her relationships, her culture, and her way of life now lay buried. The divided self in her cries out: "to which God Shall I make my appeal?" In an elemental sense, Birjees bemoans the loss of the civilizational ethos of the subcontinent built over many centuries, having transcended the boundaries of religion and cultural practice that is Birjees's own heritage but now can no longer be. That is the meaning of Partition for her; it has turned both sides of the border into towers of silence. How can she be anything but a migrant? In this Birjees, as a migrant persona, echoes the refusal of Attia Hossain, author of *Sunlight on a Broken Column* and "Phoenix Fled," who refused the division of the subcontinent in terms of having to choose between the two newly carved countries: unable to accept hard borders and the exclusive citizenship that each new state offered, she chose to live in a third country rather than live as a divided self. But in doing so she also lost her place in the original "home"—an exile must perforce remain a migrant.[38]

And Finally

This chapter has come to be something of a three-way interaction between the authors of the novels, the female protagonists they have created, and my own investment in reading these works by picking up themes from them.

In conclusion, a recent work on life writing and the novel may illumine the different threads that I have explored.[39] All three novels featured here are a narration of the personal and political histories of the protagonists created by the authors without making truth claims or hard divisions between past, present, and future. By anchoring the novels in their own temporal, geographical, and cultural worlds, the authors blur the boundaries between the autobiography and the novel: works on the Partition make it difficult for the forms adopted to be fixed in any rigid manner. When we as scholars engage with works such as those that I have chosen, we make it even more complicated because we then create a new autobiographical pact not just between authors and protagonists, but also between them and their readers, who too bring in their own personal histories, as I have done here. There is then a coming together of the authorial self, the protagonist self, and the political self of the feminist reader/scholar that illumine the primary texts that we read. The public archive of memories, carried by us of the Partition, allows us to somewhat hesitantly both recall its trauma as well as engage with its multiple meanings more than six decades after it divided us here on the subcontinent.

The public archive of memories in the subcontinent is also a repository that binds the writers of the novels with its readers in a way that allows for a cathartic release of the congealed emotions of a generation or more of women affected by that tragedy. Further, such an archive can be deployed to capture the otherwise elusive voices and experiences of women when writing about the past through the memories women (and men) carry of an event like the Partition. Through these shared memories, something like a collective biography of a "people" can perhaps emerge.

On a personal note, in writing this chapter I have been able to move beyond the terrible lived trauma of the violence of the Partition, a trauma that each one of the authors would also have experienced in their own lives so much more intensely than I. And yet they have not written explicitly on the violence of the Partition even as the violence is feared or alluded to by the protagonists. If the act of writing is a way to understand what has happened and why it may have happened, that itself may help to heal wounds that we all carry of the Partition. The writing of this chapter has been a way of sharing loss, so poignantly expressed in Hina's novella: Birjees, Zaheda Hina, and I have been bound together in our losses, so different though they are, *despite* the borders that seek to divide us—at least in my engagements with the three novels that have been the subject of this chapter.

NOTES

1 See Urvashi Butalia, *The Other Side of Silence: Voices from the Partition of India* (New Delhi: Penguin, 1998); Ritu Menon and Kamala Bhasin, *Borders and Boundaries: Women in India's Partition* (Delhi: Kali for Women, 1998); and Veena Das, *Critical Events: An Anthropological Perspective on Contemporary India* (Delhi: Oxford University Press, 1996).
2 Mumtaz Shah Nawaz, *The Heart Divided* (Lahore: ASR Publications, 1990); Khadija Mastur, *Aangan*, translated as *Inner Courtyard* (Lahore: Simorgh Publication Centre, 2000); Zaheda Hina, *All Passion Spent* (Delhi: Zubaan, 2011).
3 Ravikant and Tarun K. Saint, *Translating Partition* (Delhi: Katha, 2001).
4 This chapter was in a sense born in Lahore, and I wish to acknowledge my debt to my students and my colleagues in the women's studies course conducted at the Institute of Women's Studies, Lahore.
5 The central protagonists in all three novels seem to be close to the writers of the novels in sentiment and experience: in that sense they are somewhat autobiographical. But because they are distinct from the writers, and yet based on real characters and events in the experience of the writers, it allows the writers to move away from the specifics of events experienced by particular individuals circulating in the community and turn these individual experiences into a collective experience of the community as a whole.
6 Mieke Bal, cited in Ananya Jahanara Kabir, "Gender, Memory, Trauma: Women's Novels on the Partition of India." *Comparative Studies of South Asia, Africa and the Middle-East* 25.1 (2005): 177–90, 182.
7 Nawaz, *The Heart Divided*, vii; also personal communication by N. S. Khan, the publisher of the 1990 edition of *The Heart Divided*.
8 See Krishna Kumar, *The Battle for Peace* (Delhi: Penguin, 2007), 81.
9 Nawaz, *The Heart Divided*.
10 This is my reading of the two sisters in *The Heart Divided*—the title itself bears this out as does the Congress–Muslim League binary as well as the Hindu-Muslim *tehzib* (culture), all of which are braided as the central contradiction of the novel. The author's desires are split down the middle through these binaries because the novel shows the impossibility of fully being a self on either side of the divide in the major part of the novel. In the closing segment of the novel an attempt is made to create a single self by the reconciling of the political positions of the sisters. I owe this point to Shad Naved to whom I remain indebted as the first commentator of this chapter. I have also drawn freely from Karen F. Stien, "Monsters and Madwomen: Changing Female Gothic," in *The Female Gothic*, ed. Julian E. Fleenor (Montreal: Eden, 1983), 123–37. I am indebted to Anupama Chandra for drawing my attention to this essay. As a literary device the split self is a way to explore the good/bad dichotomy in protagonists, but I am reading the split self of the author in the creation of two women/sisters, who represent parallel but oppositional political stances in the making of history.
11 Mastur, *Inner Courtyard*, 4.

12 Mastur, *Inner Courtyard*, 4.
13 Mastur, *Inner Courtyard*, 3.
14 Mastur, *Inner Courtyard*, 3.
15 Plenary session on South Asian Women Writers, Indian Association of Women's Studies National Conference, Wardha, January 24, 2011.
16 Samina Rehman, "Birjees: The Daastan Go," in N. S. Khan et al., eds., *Locating the Self* (Lahore: ASR Publications, 1994), 179–90.
17 Nawaz, *The Heart Divided*, 1.
18 Nawaz, *The Heart Divided*, 387.
19 Nawaz, *The Heart Divided*, 260, 262.
20 Mastur, *Inner Courtyard*, 185.
21 Hina, *All Passion Spent*, 129.
22 Nawaz, *The Heart Divided*, ii–iii.
23 Nawaz, *The Heart Divided*, 115.
24 Nawaz, *The Heart Divided*, 115.
25 Nawaz, *The Heart Divided*, 337.
26 Nawaz, *The Heart Divided*, 470–71.
27 Nawaz, *The Heart Divided*, 435.
28 Mastur, *Inner Courtyard*, 154.
29 Mastur, *Inner Courtyard*, 100.
30 Mastur, *Inner Courtyard*, 102.
31 Mastur, *Inner Courtyard*, 98.
32 Mastur, *Inner Courtyard*, 220–21.
33 Hina, *All Passion Spent*, 20.
34 Hina, *All Passion Spent*, 21.
35 Hina, *All Passion Spent*, 25.
36 Hina, *All Passion Spent*, 67.
37 Hina, *All Passion Spent*, 71.
38 Attia Hosain, *Sunlight on a Broken Column* (London: Virago, 1988); Attia Hosain, "Phoenix Fled," 73–78. "Pheonix Fled" is a story, part of the collection cited in note 3; *Translating Partition*, ed. Ravikant and Tarun K. Saint (Delhi: Katha, 2001), 71–78.
39 Sidonie Smith and Julia Watson, *Reading Autobiography: A Guide for Interpreting Life Narratives* (Minneapolis: University of Minnesota Press, 2010), 9–11.

6. TAWA'IF AS POET AND PATRON
Rethinking Women's Self-Representation

SHWETA SACHDEVA JHA

The *tawa'ifs* have long been compared to the mythological *apsaras* or *devadasis* (temple women) in medieval courts as women of the "oldest profession of prostitution and seduction."[1] Despite the ubiquitous tawa'if of Bombay cinema, writing the history of the tawa'if is a necessary exercise to trace their subjectivity and rethink grand narratives of colonial history and traditions in courtly cultures. The subject of this chapter is Mah Laqa Bai "Chanda" (c. 1767–c. 1824), a wealthy tawa'if in the princely court of late eighteenth- and early nineteenth-century Hyderabad. An experienced Urdu poetess, Mah Laqa Bai was the first woman to compile an entire volume or *diwan* of Urdu poetry in 1798 and a powerful courtesan.[2] She earned revenue from her many *jagir* (gifted) lands and had an extensive library of manuscripts. A patron of poets and performers, Mah Laqa Bai resided in a grand *haveli* or palace, which was home to a large retinue of servants as well as a salon to upcoming performers, chroniclers, and poets.[3]

Unlike contemporary understanding of the autobiography as a literary genre, the "autobiographical" articulations of tawa'ifs such as Mah Laqa Bai are not in the form of memoirs or diaries. In earlier courtly contexts, historians have shown how royal women such as queens employed imperial means of self-articulation through the use of public pageantry; traveling with large retinues; commissioning artists or painters; building inns, tanks, and mosques; or minting coins in their own image.[4] Through the *narration* of Mah Laqa Bai's life history in this chapter we will explore the means through which tawa'ifs negotiated their position as courtesans or women of culture. Their reemployment of "conventional" acts of imperial image making such as composing poetry, architectural patronage, and commissioning chronicles will be shown as significant acts of authorship and autobiographical articulation in the context of emerging regional courts of the late eighteenth and early nineteenth centuries and the decline of Mughal control.

While reading Mah Laqa Bai's life history and that of her family from the time of her grandmother, we will focus on the lives of those generations of women who chose to become tawa'ifs. Their agency, it will be argued, lay in their attempt to transform their identity through deliberate "erasure" of their past history of displacement and the taking on of new names and movement to different courts or cities in search of livelihood.[5] For many women from displaced backgrounds, self-fashioning was possible only in the context of performance and mobility to different courts. Many among these women tried to ensure a brighter future for their daughters by getting them professional training in the arts of music, dance, and poetry, thus enabling their transformation into highly cultured, talented, and politically powerful courtesans or tawa'ifs in regional courts. As artists, the tawa'ifs were known to excel in specific repertoires of poetry (*ghazal*), music (ghazal, *thumri, dadra, tappa*), and dance (*nach, kathak*). The elite among them had sexual relations with rich and successful patrons such as *nawabs, taluqdars* (revenue contractors), and *nabobs* or Europeans who had adopted local lifestyles. For example, in nineteenth-century Awadh, *deredar* tawa'ifs referred to skilled courtesans who shifted from one camp to another in search of patrons.[6]

A study of the origins of the Urdu term *tawa'if* is necessary to see the complexity of the "category" of women called tawa'ifs and their self-fashioning in the context of performance and mobility in the late eighteenth century. The etymology of the word *tawa'if* with its roots in the Arabic word *tawaf*, which means "moving round the Mecca," reinforces the itinerant nature of the lives of these women. In her study of courtesans and women performers, Katherine Butler Schofield points out that the earliest record of the term *tawa'if* to "designate a unitary meta-community of elite female performing artists in North India . . . was probably only widely co-opted for this purpose around 1800."[7] In late eighteenth-century Persian, the term *tawa'if* was sometimes used to refer to "tribes" of female performers or as a generic term, and different communities of women and men performers were categorized under their vernacular communities or castes. The earliest use of the term *tawa'if* for a group of female and male performers in English was in John Gilchrist's 1787 dictionary.[8] John Platt's 1884 dictionary, which is considered the most authoritative dictionary of Urdu to English, listed the *tawa'if* as tribes and a single "dancing girl."[9] By the late nineteenth century, *nachne wale tai'fe* meant bands of singers and dancers in contemporary Urdu vocabulary, and *domnis* and *mirasans* were women who sang or played on instruments only for women.[10] When it came to prostitutes or women of the bazaars, a range of Urdu terms had become popular from *bazaari aurat* or market maid to *randi* and *kasbi*, which meant someone who worked. The term *randi* earlier referred to women in general, but by the late nineteenth century it had become a term for the lowly prostitute.[11] By the late nineteenth century, for some the *tawa'if* meant a cultured courtesan; to others it became synonymous with *prostitute*. The years following the Rebellion of 1857 saw a decline in the position of the tawa'ifs as most began to be perceived as a threat to security and governance by the British colonial authorities.[12] Yet parallel to this decline in their cultural status was the popularity of myriad literary representations of tawa'ifs in Urdu print culture, including texts such as biographies of Mah Laqa Bai and compilations of their poetry in biographical dictionaries of poets called *tazkiras* and novels or fictional narratives such as the famous *Umrao Jan "Ada."*[13] "Reading" the specific biographical representations and traces of authorship left behind by Mah Laqa Bai "Chanda" offer us means to reconfigure authority and agency in the life of a woman who became a powerful tawa'if.

*Reinterpreting the Autobiographical:
Multiple Acts of Reading and Self-Fashioning*

....

In an essay published in 1984 aptly titled "Autobiography as De-facement," Paul de Man questioned the status of autobiography as a genre in itself. For de Man, the author reads himself in an autobiography, but what he sees in this self-reflexive moment is a figure or a face formed by the substitutive trope of "prosopopoeia," the giving of a face. Often we think of "fiction" as "created," therefore untrue and distinct from reality. However, de Man challenges the claims of the genre of an autobiography to be different from fiction by saying that:

> Autobiography . . . *is not a genre or a mode, but a figure of reading or of understanding that occurs, to some degree, in all texts*. The autobiographical moment happens as an alignment between two subjects involved in the

process of reading in which they determine each other by mutual reflexive substitution. The structure implies differentiation as well as similarity, since both depend on a substitutive exchange that constitutes the subject. This specular structure is interiorised in a text in which the author declares himself the subject of his own understanding, but this merely makes explicit the wider claim to authorship that takes place whenever a text is stated to be *by* someone and assumed to be understandable to the extent that this is the case. Which amounts to saying that any book with a readable title page is, to some extent, autobiographical.[14]

Reinterpreting autobiography as an act of reading can help historians of women interpret a wide range of material such as biographies, poetry, chronicles, and even buildings as "autobiographical." Therefore, in this chapter we will read Mah Laqa Bai's autobiography through her many "acts" of fashioning the self, which include composing ghazals or Urdu lyrical poems. The act of reading the ghazal as autobiographical has its problems, which we will address later in the chapter, but we will attempt to trace feminine subjectivity through a combination of reading the ghazal along with other apparently "conventional" modes of self-articulation such as imperial communication or political image making through architectural patronage.

For an analysis of sources other than literature, we take a cue from D. Fairchild Ruggles's study of architecture as potential source of self-representation. In her work on women in Islamic societies, Ruggles posits that the choice of strategic modes of public visibility and architectural patronage form part of the autobiographical authorship of women. Discussing the relationship between vision and power in relation to modes of representation, she suggests that the act of building is one such negotiated process whereby the choice of a woman patron to use regional or historical techniques and styles and the response of the audience can often become ways to glean agency. In contrast to written sources, Ruggles elucidates that buildings can denote "a representational presence" as they "stand, in the sense of synecdoche, in place of their donors, and enjoy a public profile denied to the woman herself."[15] This chapter follows from the work of Ruggles to a "representational presence" of Mah Laqa Bai through architectural structures such as mausoleums and gardens, all of which bear her unique authorial signature. These acts of self-representation were, conventional in their similarity with Mughal imperial traditions, a facet that can be understood only when we study emergence of courtly cultures in the late eighteenth- and early nineteenth-centuries regional princely states such as that of Hyderabad.

Patronage and Courtly Culture in the Princely States

With the decline of the Mughal Empire in the late eighteenth century, erstwhile governors of regions such as Awadh and Hyderabad emerged as rulers of independent states. Initially a Mughal province, Hyderabad was governed by Nizam ul-Mulk Asaf Jah from 1713, but by 1724 he had gained a major victory over a rival in the Deccan and centralized the administration of the region. After his death in 1748, following a series of succession disputes, Nizam Ali Khan acceded to the throne and took up the title of Asaf Jah II (r. 1761–1803) and shifted his court from Aurangabad to Hyderabad in 1763. During his reign Hyderabad flourished as an independent court as the initial tussle between the court and the French East India Company over the coastal regions finally got settled when the Nizam lost these regions to the growing power of the British East India Company (hence forth British EIC).

A period of cultural efflorescence and economic growth, the eighteenth century was marked by the decline of Mughal supremacy and imperial control leading to the emergence of regional courts and the growth of the cities of Lucknow, Hyderabad, and Banaras, which attracted merchants, traders, artists, and soldiers, inspiring new patterns of urban consumption and lifestyles.[16] Tawa'ifs like Mah Laqa Bai "Chanda" became influential female elite in these Hindu and Muslim regional courts, which emulated the Mughal model of imperial culture and tradition of public display and courtly ritual in their patronage of artists and performers like the courtesans. However, these regional courts of Hyderabad, Jaipur, and Awadh were also "modern" in the way they exercised musical and dance patronage. All these courts ran a special department of music or entertainment where they employed tawa'ifs. Although these courtesans were central to the ritualistic display of kingship for princely rulers, their patronage was also a key means for other groups such as the *taluqdars* or landed elite and European officials, to display aristocratic status.

The cosmopolitan court of Hyderabad comprised diverse new nobility including courtiers who had served the Mughals, the Marathas, earlier Deccani states, and Hindu *kayasths*.[17] The increasing dominance of the British EIC in the politics of the Deccan by 1801 had led to a greater need for new officials who controlled and ran various sections of the court administration in liaison with the British Resident. Intermediaries such as controller of records and courtiers became power brokers in the socially complex court of Hyderabad, with its multiple tiers of power. The Nizam and his courtiers ran similar court establishments where consumption of luxurious goods, exchanges of gifts, grand lifestyles, and cultural patronage of courtesans became a means of asserting connoisseurship and elite identity. Aspiring artists usually sought employment and then recommendation from the parallel courts run by these courtiers in search of recognition and employment by the Nizam.

Like other princely states, Hyderabad also began to employ large numbers of tawa'ifs or courtesans in the *daftar-i-arbab-i-nishat* or the Office of Masters of Pleasure, which also employed a range of male performers.[18] Any matter of legal jurisdiction regarding the performers was dealt by a special office called Kanchan Kachehri. The word *kanchani* was used for women performers in the Mughal times and *kachehri* is still the Hindi word for "court." In its use of a department for musicians and dancers, Hyderabad was similar to other princely states in the late eighteenth century. Jaipur had a department of music called *gunijankhana* or "house of melody," and Baroda had its *kalawant kharkhana*.[19] In the case of nineteenth-century Baroda, Janaki Bakhle reveals that the court was "exemplary" in its colonially influenced modernization, which included bureaucratic departments with rule books, rules of conformity, official costumes, and a system of recruitment for musicians to be employed as salaried employees of the court.[20] Courtesans performed at religious functions and in courtly processions in all these courts. In Hyderabad, the tawa'ifs received salaries, owned properties, and were exempted from paying taxes. However, after their death, their properties and houses were auctioned and the money collected was deposited in the Nizamat treasury or at the office in the region where the erstwhile performer belonged.[21]

The protagonist of our history, Chanda, began as a performer in the court of Nizam Asaf Jah II (r. 1761–1803) and was later honored with the title Mah Laqa Bai ("with an angelic face like the moon") in 1815 in the court of his successor Nizam Sikandar Jah Asaf Jah III (r. 1803–1829). Later her adopted daughter Haseen Laqa Bai was also employed by daftar-i-arbab-i-nishat of Hyderabad and performed at the households of other courtiers.[22] Chanda gave her first performance at the tender age of fifteen in Aristu Jah's (1732–1804) establishment, who was the prime minister of Hyderabad in 1778 and held that position until 1795. During her career, she performed in the courts of Nawab Mir Alam (1752–1808), Raja Rao Rambha Sahib, and Raja Chandu Lal (1761–1845), all of whom held separate courts and held positions as ministers at various times in the court of the Asaf Jah II and Nizam Sikandar Jah Asaf Jah III.[23] Chanda had been recommended to the Nizam's court by Aristu Jah, and once an elite courtesan, she performed in six courts in a span of about sixty years.[24] It was her musical training, her artistic talents, and her strategic understanding of contemporary court politics and the rising power of the British EIC that made it possible for her to negotiate her status as a courtesan. The story of her upbringing in a family of performers and concubines is a history that reveals the itinerant lifestyle of women performers and their ability to transform their status as displaced women to elite courtesans by using specific acts of self-representation following protocols of courtly culture.

Born into a family of Iranian descent, Mah Laqa Bai's maternal grandfather, Khwajah Hussain, came to Delhi during the reign of the Mughal ruler Shah Jahan (r. 1628–58). Of Shi'a faith and a resident of Ahmedabad, he was an employee under the Nawab of Gujarat. A lavish spendthrift, Khwajah Hussain had to embezzle money from the royal treasury to pay for his debts, which soon set off a series of enquiries by the Nawab. Khwajah Hussain escaped to avoid potential arrest, but his wife, Chanda Bibi (Mah Laqa Bai was initially named Chanda after her grandmother), and five children, two sons and three daughters, were put under house arrest for a few years.[25] With no money left, no valuables to sell, and no source of income, Mah Laqa Bai's grandmother escaped her house arrest with her children. After an arduous journey through various towns, they finally sought refuge in a colony of *bhagats* (mimics and dancers) in the *qasba* or small town of Deolia. The bhagat community was hospitable and supportive and managed to convince Chanda Bibi that training her daughters in music and dance could offer her a source of income and sustenance. Biographers often portray the bhagats as conniving performers who slyly persuaded Chanda Bibi to let her daughters be part of their troupe. The bias against the bhagats is meant to elicit reader sympathy for Chanda Bibi as a decent woman who was "forced" into the profession of music and dance owing to the lack of a husband and family support.[26]

Mirza Muhammad Hadi Ruswa's famous novel *Umrao Jan "Ada"* also highlighted the plight of girls who were sold into *kothas* and therefore forced to take up the profession of tawa'if. Historical evidence such as sale deeds in eighteenth-century Delhi reveals that girls were sold and bought into slavery for domestic households and kothas simultaneously.[27] The distinction between the harem as a private world and the public kotha stands blurred if we note that both bought girls either as slaves or as dancing girls. In her study of Rajput households, Ramya Sreenivasan elaborates that a trained *patar* or dancing girl was an "investment" for a household. She could not be easily transferred to another chief's household or state and was a symbol of the wealth and prestige of her owner. The owner, in turn, became a "proud possessor of an *akhara* (department) filled with beautiful, slender-waisted women who danced for his pleasure at all hours of the day." Some of them were raised in their stature from being performers to *khwasin* or concubines.[28] Therefore many successful performers often chose to become concubines of rich and elite patrons and set up homes with them.

One such woman who became a concubine was Chanda Bibi's youngest daughter Mida Bibi, who did not train in music or dance. While her sisters, Nur Bibi and Polan Bibi, took up the profession of performers, Mida became a concubine of the ruler of Deolia, Salim Singh. A daughter Mehtab was born to them, while the sisters continued to train in music and dance. However, the world of the harem was not so comfortable for Mida. Salim Singh's wife tried to have her poisoned, forcing her to leave Deolia with her family and daughter. Meanwhile her mother, Chanda Bibi, had died, and the three sisters, one niece, and two brothers set off in search of livelihood and sustenance yet again. During this journey, the brothers apparently got separated from the rest of the women and nothing more is known about them. Men actors are never given much significance in these narratives on the tawa'if; they either appear as being responsible for selling girls into slavery or as conniving performers who tempt women to be part of their troupes. Significantly, Oldenburg showed that men were marginal to the lives of the tawa'if in the twentieth century, and even boys born to elite performers had to struggle for sustenance as girls were considered more fortunate. Men were usually musicians who accompanied the tawa'if or became pimps who arranged performances and earned a commission.[29]

It is therefore not surprising that we don't know anything about the brothers. Each sister, Nur, Polan, and Mida, chose to become a tawa'if by taking up new names of Burj Kanwar Bai, Polan Kanwar Bai, and Raj Kanwar Bai respectively once they had reached Burhanpur in 1747. The use of the suffix "Bai" is pertinent as most performers used the suffix and the sisters wanted to assert their identity as professional and traditional performers, while deliberately erasing their past as daughters of a court official. The niece Mehtab was renamed Mehtab Kanwar Bai, while the aunts chose to use their musical talents as a means to earn an income. Soon the talents of the three sisters earned them fame and patronage among the armies of Asaf Jah II, the ruler or Nizam of Hyderabad. When Asaf Jah II shifted his capital to Hyderabad, Burj Kanwar Bai and her sisters also moved with his army and made Hyderabad their home. They had become deredar tawa'if who camped with their patron and had "fixed abodes with two or three sumptuous tents attached to them."[30] Raj Kanwar Bai later gave birth to two more daughters. Of them, the one born to Bahadur Khan "Turki," a soldier in the Nizam's army, was named Chanda after her grandmother.[31] Chanda later became the famous Mah Laqa Bai of Hyderabad. As a small girl she was sent into the care of her elder stepsister Mehtab, who had by then entered the harem of a local *nawab*, Muhammad Yar Khan or Rukn al-Daulah (Pillar of State), a title awarded to him by the Nizam in 1765 and held until his death in 1775.[32] Mehtab was addressed by the honorific title of

"Sahib-ji-Sahiba" in Ruknud-daulah's harem, and famous courtiers visited her to celebrate this occasion. If and when she traveled with the nawab, the army offered her a salute too. A powerful concubine, Mehtab trained her niece well. In fact, Chanda was born into a wealthy household, where she received royal attention from birth. On the sixth day after her birth in the year 1767, the Nizam of Hyderabad had ordered his minister Aristu Jah (1732–1804) to participate in her birthday celebrations.[33] Aristu Jah later became one of the "Pillars of State" and twice became the prime minister, once between 1778 and 1795 and again between 1797 and 1804. In a few years Chanda grew up to be a beautiful girl and acquired training in the arts of music, poetry, dance, archery, and horse riding. The life histories of women in Chanda's family and her own transformation into Mah Laqa Bai reveal the agency and choices made by these women in reinventing themselves as performers, concubines, and courtesans. Central to this reinvention is their choice to undertake the journey from one place to another in search of patronage while following rulers and their camps of soldiers. The transformation from the position of a performer in a camp to a highly respected courtesan was possible only in the upwardly mobile context of emerging princely states such as Hyderabad, which saw the shift from camps at Aurangabad to a more settled court in subsequent years.

"Modern" autobiographies often use the metaphor of life as a journey. In the case of Mah Laqa Bai's ancestors this trope can be seen in both figurative and literal ways as a means of self-transformation. One skill necessary for the transformation of a common performer to a courtesan or concubine was that of composing poetry. Regional vernaculars in the form of Dhundari, Bhasha, and Urdu had gained prominence in the princely states in the late eighteenth century. Urdu had become a language of popular culture and courtly self-fashioning in courts at Lucknow, Hyderabad, and Delhi, which shared a common linguistic and cultural cartography. In this literary milieu of Urdu the tawa'ifs learned poetry and used it as a skill to attract new audiences and establish their own status as artists and poets. Mah Laqa Bai had acquired training to compose poetry in Persian and Urdu while also learning Arabic and Braj.

Poetry, Political Diplomacy, and Power Networks

In the court at Hyderabad, most ministers and the Nizams were poets themselves.[34] The ability to compose Urdu poetry showed the training of a courtier and his sophisticated background. A means to forge relations with a new patron, Urdu poetry could be learned only through the *ustad-shagird* relationship, where the mentor or tutor was the ustad and the disciple or apprentice was called a shagird. A disciple showed his poetic compositions to the mentor, who would often suggest corrections and give literary advice. Sometimes the rivalry between ustads could be carried on between shagirds. Largely patrilineal, the world of Urdu poetry did not consider women to be at par with men. No *ustani* or woman tutor of Urdu poetry is ever mentioned in poetic records. Frances Pritchett gives examples of a few tawa'ifs who were shagirds or disciples of famous poets such as tawa'if Bega "Shirin," who was the disciple of poet "Bahr."[35] In this patriarchal context, choosing a famous male ustad ensured that Chanda acquired training as well as established a poetic identity, both essential attributes to be introduced as a tawa'if to elite connoisseurs. Her first ustad of Urdu was Muhammad Khan Ba-Iman, the chief *akbhar-go* or head of the newspaper writers and a favorite of Aristu Jah. For Persian poetry Chanda trained under Mir Alam, who later became her patron.[36] She used her name "Chanda" as *takhallus* or pen name. Until recently, it was accepted that she was one of the earliest woman *sahib-i-diwan* poets of Urdu. However Scott Kugle believes that another woman poet from Hyderabad, also likely a courtesan, probably published her diwan much earlier.[37]

The tawa'if performed poetic compositions to the accompaniment of music and dance for her patrons on diplomatic occasions and as a means of entertainment. Many such performances were held for European guests. The European guests used the term *nautch girls* for the tawa'if, and *nautches* for music and dance performances hosted by native rulers for them.[38] These performances were occasions for self-fashioning and exhibiting court protocol. The host tried to emulate imperial culture through patronage of the tawa'if, while the guests showed their allegiance or engaged in political liaison while being entertained through music, dance, and poetry. In addition to Sreenivasan's argument that the local rulers organized these performances to showcase their "investments," we need to see how these performances were complexly choreographed rituals where each participant played a certain role.[39] The tawa'if entertained the host and the guest with her performance, while engaging in diplomacy to seek patronage and express loyalty, thereby negotiating her own position.

A proof of her creative literary abilities, Mah Laqa Bai's diwan was also a symbol of culture and luxury as a material object. Prior to the world of print, the status of manuscripts was that of objects of rarity and material wealth. Mah Laqa's diwan was most probably copied by trained calligraphers in her library, and today two copies survive. In the colonial milieu, when aristocratic status was displayed through consumption of luxurious goods and exchanges of gifts, Mah Laqa Bai must have known that her diwan could display her poetic abilities and assert her cultured status. The use of the diwan as a tool of political networking becomes clear when we note that she chose to gift her diwan as a *nazar* or an offering to John Malcolm, a British EIC official, during a dance performance held at the house of Mir Alam Bahadur on October 18, 1799.[40] John Malcolm was the assistant to the English Resident James Achilles Kirkpatrick (1762–1805), the Resident who went "native" and whose story is famously retold by William Dalrymple in the *White Mughals*.[41] Aristu Jah was not a keen supporter of the British EIC, but Mir Alam and later Chandu Lal all became prime ministers because of their ability to negotiate with the British EIC and were powerful allies to them. In this political context, Mah Laqa Bai's gift to the British officer meant that she understood that relationships with the British EIC needed to be cultivated as they could be powerful political allies.

Poetry and its performance thus became a tool of political performance and diplomacy. Her act of gifting the diwan reveals the tawa'if to be a skilled diplomat and shows how *nautch* performances could be used by the tawa'if for her benefit too. Strategic tawa'ifs like Mah Laqa Bai were mediators who promoted aesthetic tastes in poetry and music while blending political diplomacy with performance. Mir Alam, the controller of records for the English at whose house Chanda offered the *diwan* as a gift to Malcolm, later became the next prime minister of Hyderabad with the support of the British EIC.

Courtiers like Raja Chandu Lal invited other elites such as the Nizam for performances where Mah Laqa Bai was the main dancer and the ritual of offering betel leaves or showering *itr* or perfume added to the choreographed aspect of these events. One such performance was hosted in his garden on August 27, 1811, and recorded in the royal calendar: "Sabit Jang Bahadur and his ten companions pay a visit to the garden of Raja Chandu lal Bahadur. The party take their lunch and dinner there and are entertained with music and dance by Chanda Bai and also comical feats by *bhands* (actors). *Itr* [perfume] and *pan* [betel leaves] were offered to them at their departure late at night."[42] Another such gathering took place on September 20, 1820, and the following night, when the ruler Nizam Sikandar Asaf Jah witnessed a dance performance by Mah Laqa Bai at his Moti Mahal Palace.[43]

By the nineteenth century, these performances were preceded by a salutation by the tawa'ifs, who paid obeisance to their patron and saluted him several times in a fashion similar to courtly salutations made to the king. This specific form of salutation before a performance came to be called *mujra* and was inspired by courtly protocol. The central piece of a mujra was a ghazal sung by the tawa'if while being seated.[44] As a performance, the mujra could be an occasion to elicit favor, seduce the patron, or showcase the new talents of an upcoming poet. One can conjecture the nature of these performances even more clearly when we read the ghazals in her diwan; a collection of beautifully composed verses, many of which are addressed to the Hazrat Ali, the first Imam for the Shi'a and dedicated to her patrons, the Nizam of Hyderabad and Aristu Jah. The ghazal was a lyrical form that was used by the tawa'if to express a range of multiple emotions such as her religious adulation for Ali; to seek favors from her patrons in the form of land and gifts; and to express her allegiance and deference to a new political player like the British EIC.

The Ghazal as Autobiographical Utterance

The ghazal was one of the most common genres sung by the tawa'if. Pritchett defines the ghazal as a brief lyric poem, generally romantic and/or mystical in tone, evoking the moods of a passionate lover separated from his beloved. Each two-line verse (*shi'r*) of the ghazal follows the same Perso-Arabic syllabic meter, and the second line of each verse ends with a rhyming syllable (*qafiya*), followed by an optional (but very common) refrain (*radif*) one or more syllables long. Since the ghazal was sung, the first verse usually included the pen name (takhallus) of the poet and set a rhythmic pattern. Each verse is semantically independent, and often these two-line verses are recited or quoted independently instead of the ghazal.[45] Emotions, symbolism, tonality, and repetition are important features of the ghazal, so the recitation or performance becomes extremely significant.[46]

Since the late eighteenth century, there were two popular forms of Urdu poetry; *rekhta* (which means a mixed language), a form in which the speaker's voice was masculine and *rekhti*, in which the speaker's voice was feminine. Scott Kugle rightly points out that in the former the speaker was usually a male lover who "beseeches or berates his beloved (who could be female or male)," and in *rekhti*, the speaker was a "female lover who seduces or titillates the beloved (who could be female or male)."[47] Most rekhti poetry was composed by men who posed as women.

In his perceptive analysis of Mah Laqa Bai Chanda's diwan, Kugle rightly observes that Mah Laqa Bai did not restrict her compositions to a specific female voice or feminine desire."[48] In fact, she excels in using conventional tropes and imagery of rekhta just like any other famous male poet. For the tawa'if the ghazal was a form that offered enormous opportunities to express a range of desires and agency. But she chose to use it not to express any specific "feminine" desire or "lesbian love"; rather she preferred to use it as a means of seeking patronage, expressing devotion to her patron both political and spiritual. For example, in the following ghazal Mah Laqa Bai praises her patron Aristu Jah's benevolence and knowledge while also convincing him to donate land for charity:

> Let Nauroz bring forth ever increasing pleasure and spring
> By your fortune, flowers are strewn in the garden everywhere for eternity
> Don't let anyone end the pleasure and luxury in His reign
> With whose grace each and every home is prosperous and has companion for wine
> Aristu Jah Oh Fortunate, Beautiful faced and Learned One
> Whose abundant beneficence is known throughout the world
> This is a prayer from Maula Ali for charity land
> Let Maula Ali keep you under his love and care always
> Nothing adorns the moon better in this world
> And whatever is visible on Chanda is for you.[49]

Through ghazals she also sought jagirs or revenue lands as gifts.[50] In the following ghazal Mah Laqa Bai poses as the male lover and uses conventional imagery to describe the unattainable beloved who can kill with a mere glance:

> Hoping to blossom (one day) into a flower,
> Every bud sits, holding its soul in its fist.
> Between the fear of the fowler and (approaching) autumn
> The bulbul's life hangs by a thread.
> Thy sly glance is more murderous than arrow or sword;
> It has shed the blood of many a lover.
> How can I liken a candle to thy (glowing) cheek?
> The candle is blind with the fat in its eyes.
> How can Chanda be dry lipped, O saqi of the heavenly wine!
> She has drained the cup of thy love.[51]

In yet another composition we see how Mah Laqa Bai uses the voice of a male lover whose moon-faced beloved toys with him and teases him, leaving him anxious. The moon-faced beauty (*mah ru*) is Mah Laqa Bai's self-referential gesture to herself as the narrator and at the same time the object of love. Sometimes, she composed a ghazal such as the following, which begins as a conventional love lyric, but by the last couplet, the tone changes to show her love for the Almighty, when she seeks blessings from Ali for both this world and the one beyond.

The heart throbs restlessly of this anxious one
Only the moment of our meeting can bring comfort
Promise the heart to meet one day after a drink
To rout the abundant red one in drunkenness
For a lifetime let's be drunk plentiful on the moon faced one
With no control ever on the kisses and the embraces
In almost every way this heart is deep in love
Each day the reward is fame for this spiritless one
O Ali shower Chanda with your majesty
Let there be honour and dignity for this one in both the worlds.[52]

These ghazals reveal the difficulty of reading Mah Laqa Bai's ghazals as historical evidence of self-representation because she does not express a unique "feminine sensibility" in either a single ghazal or the diwan. Even within one ghazal the gender of the speaker changes from one couplet to another and the poet shifts from the posture of a male lover to a devoted believer. In this rare ghazal, Kugle rightly observes, Mah Laqa Bai swerves toward rekhti when the narrator appears to be a woman and the beloved a man.

Will you keep inventing new oppressions every day
You will ruin countless lovers' hearts in this way
Will you release me from your net? But then
You will make someone else your captive prey
Will you truly think only of me, even if
You will entertain other lovers for display?
Will you ever make a heart happy? It seems
You will keep aloof letting hearts in sorrow stay
Will you accept a hundred lives like Chanda's,
Maula 'Ali?
You will help her sacrifice, for this alone
She will pray.[53]

However, although the suggestion is that the lover is male, the gender of the poet remains by and large ambiguous. By and large men chose to write in rekhti by posing as women. For years these compositions were seen as voyeuristic imaginations of lesbian love which only served the purpose of titillation for male readers, although recently some read them as evidence of same-sex love practices.[54]

Connoisseurs of Urdu have often read ghazals as autobiographical utterances expressing the feelings of the poet, whether it be the case of the soulful compositions of the famous poet Ghalib (1797?–1869) or the tragic life of Bahadur Shah "Zafar" (r. 1837–57), the last Mughal emperor of Delhi. Pritchett criticizes this biographical approach of reading the ghazal as a reflection of the poet's love relationships to argue that in a lyric like the ghazal, expression of desire or love cannot be read as a reflection of biographical or sociological reality. Rather love and desire, she suggested, are literary conventions or tropes common to the form itself.[55] Questions of the poet's personal expression and "poetry as self-revelation" never arose in classical Urdu poetics; rather as Shamsur Rahman Faruqi shows these are central to the concerns of the Urdu modernists in the late nineteenth century because of the lack of other evidence on the lives of nineteenth-century poets.[56] C. M. Naim, another established scholar of Urdu poetry, also warns against misreading the relationship between literary practice and contemporary ideas of "women's language" or "feminine" poetry.[57]

Despite the interpretation of feminist and queer theory scholars, Kugle puts it succinctly when he argues that the ghazal, "is not a personal confession; rather, it offers a snapshot of lover and beloved in different postures of love."[58] Although Mah Laqa Bai could have used rekhti as a form, she preferred the rekhta and in "general refused to write poetry that spoke in a typically female voice or was situated in specifically female positions."[59] Mah Laqa Bai made a crucial choice not to express a unique and coherent feminine subjectivity through her ghazals. Rather as a woman, she preferred to write in rekhta, and use the normative masculine voice, which allowed her to participate in the social activity of writing and reciting Urdu poetry.[60] If women wanted to compete with men as poets, compilation of a volume was another act to affirm their status. No wonder that Mah Laqa Bai possessed two manuscripts of her diwan, both of which are available today along with published versions.[61]

Through her diwan of Urdu poems, Mah Laqa Bai's position in literary history of Urdu women poets has become irreplaceable today. As a material possession, the diwan offered her ample opportunities for political strategizing and diplomacy; as a literary form, the ghazals meanwhile offered a means to articulate myriad desires, which could include her need for land, patronage, political affiliation, or the benevolence of the Almighty. The ghazals may not be ideal evidence to trace "feminine desire," however, when located in contexts of performance and political image making in early modern courts; they become a way to reuse imperial modes of self-fashioning such as the commissioning of buildings or traveling with a huge entourage.

Patronage as Authorship and Acts of Self-Representation

Scholars of courtly cultures have shown that women often used imperial conventions of image making such as use of public pageantry and ceremony, being part of escorted processions with large troupes, and through their patronage of artists, building, and performers. As a courtesan, Mah Laqa Bai could choose different ways of expressing her identity as an elite woman. The choice of a specific mode of visibility signified her powerful status. For example, after Chanda was awarded the title of Mah Laqa Bai she was given the honor of the *naubat* or the sounding of the drums that announced her visit: both symbols of being a courtier of high rank. Apart from receiving a sum of one thousand rupees for each performance, she earned salaries from the respective courts. Additionally, she had about three hundred attendants, including slave girls (*kanizen*) and male servants called *khanazads*, who helped her in managing her immense properties and her household. After her death, Nizam Sikandar Jah Asaf Jah III supported these men and women by giving them a pension of ten rupees per month, while other slave girls were given five rupees monthly, and the male attendants in her employment received a fixed pension at seven rupees a month until the death of the Nizam in 1829. Even after her death, her status as a courtesan was preserved in public memory courtesy of the large retinue, which benefited from being in her service.[62]

Mah Laqa Bai fashioned herself to be remembered as a woman of piety. This expression of religious faith and piety appears most pronounced in her choice to build an *ashurkhana*, a temporary prayer house, built by the Shi'a during Muharram.[63] In the context of Hyderabad, where the previous Qutb Shahi rulers had been Shi'a, building of an ashurkhana brought her in the league of royal patrons.[64] Further, through her participation in religious gatherings such as the one near Hazrat Ali's shrine, where she ensured the availability of guest houses during the annual *urs* celebrations, and regular patronage at the *Khat Mela*, a fair where she chose to offer food and money to the visiting *faqirs*, she cultivated her public image as a woman of faith.[65]

Although the tawa'if had a public image as a courtesan, her choice of patronage of certain types of architectural construction signifies a specific vocabulary of visibility that she chose for herself. Having acquired large pieces of land such as the estate Maqta Adi Khet, Mah Laqa Bai built a palace, the Khas Haveli, for herself. A grand residence displayed her position as a courtier at par with other intermediaries in the court of Hyderabad, and the building of a *baoli* (stairwell) and a grand mausoleum for her mother (where Mah Laqa Bai would also be buried later) at the cost of a hefty one lakh, permanently established her identity as a woman from an elite background. Through the construction of a mausoleum complex, Mah Laqa Bai erased the memory of her mother's initial journey as an itinerant performer to showcase her as a woman of stature and rank.[66] Patronage of stepwells, ashurkhanas, havelis, and mausoleums can be seen as autobiographical acts of self-fashioning and representation that were remembered and documented by her later biographers. Biographical texts woven around these architectural signatures became etched in cultural memory, asserting Mah Laqa Bai's status as an accomplished courtesan and a pious woman. As a final act of self-representation, she inscribed her identity as a tawa'if of stature in history when she commissioned Ghulam Hussain "Jauhar," who was originally from Bidar but now in Hyderabad, to write a history of Hyderabad under the Asaf Jah rulers. The history, titled *Tarikh-i-Dilafruz* [History of the heart inflamer], was written between 1814 and 1819. In the preface to the manuscript, Jauhar praised his patron Mah Laqa Bai as a woman from an illustrious family and wrote a paean to her talents in the arts of poetry, music, horse riding, and wrestling.[67] The formal narrative of his chronicle immortalized her status as a patron, a regal woman of talent and honor, and it firmly located her in the context of the courtly culture of Hyderabad. By late nineteenth century women like Mah Laqa Bai inspired fiction and historical narratives that romanticized their lives and celebrated their position as women with *tahzib* or etiquette and cultural finesse while lamenting the end of courtly culture under British rule.

Conclusion

Paul de Man's deconstructive approach to autobiography as an act of reading offers historians interesting ways of rethinking our understanding of self-representation and autobiography in the context of women in early colonial India. This "autobiographical history" of Mah Laqa Bai "Chanda" was based on our reading of her diwan, the manuscript of the history (*tarikh*) of Hyderabad she commissioned, the *durbar* calendars of the court of Hyderabad, and the Urdu biographies that were published in the early twentieth century. Sifting through biographical material on the tawa'if is an act of retrieval ridden with complications. The published biographies included her entire diwan, but the narratives ranged from being nostalgic, to being critical, to bordering on the hagiographic. Ghulam Samdani Gauhar Sahib was an employee of the court of Hyderabad, and his biography *Hayat-i-Mah Laqa* was the earliest Urdu biography published by the Nizam's Press in 1906. In the preface, Gauhar mentioned that his text was a follow-up on her diwan that he had published earlier. His biography expresses empathy and respect for her as a woman of talent and stature. During the late nineteenth and early twentieth century, the tawa'ifs were popular subjects for writers like Ruswa, who wrote in the new genre of the novel.

A tendency to elevate the institution of the tawa'if or to pity the woman performer who belonged to a "decent" family background but was "forced" into the profession became a common trope for biographers like Gauhar. Later authors, including Shafqat Rizvi of *Urdu Ka Classiki Adab Diwan Mah Laqa Bai Chanda*, a printed edition of her poetry, and Rahat Azmi of *Mah Laqa: Halat-i-Zindagi: Mah-i-Diwan*, also expressed empathy for her ancestors as displaced women from "honorable" families. Despite the presence of these biographies, details of Mah Laqa Bai's family and dates of birth and death varied across texts. For example, her year of birth was variously noted as 1764 or 1767. However, the Shi'a origins of her family and the tale of migration remains the same in these narratives. Through the tarikh she commissioned and the mausoleum and gardens she built, Mah Laqa Bai had ensured her reputation as a courtesan for posterity. Later, literary representations and histories reiterated her life history, but anxiety toward the figure of the tawa'if, a woman of talent and economic independence beyond the fold of domesticity and marriage, made them tone down the agency that they showed in their adoption of the cultural institution of the tawa'if to fashion new identities for themselves.

This chapter analyzed the process of reinvention and self-fashioning of a girl from a family of women performers and concubines to become the famous tawa'if Mah Laqa Bai "Chanda" of Hyderabad during the reigns of Asaf Jah II and III. Reading the different "texts" of/on her life such as biographies, her poetry, chronicles commissioned by her, and the "monumental" traces she left behind in conjunction with evidence of her performances displayed the agency of this tawa'if in shaping her subjectivity. Beginning with the etymology of the term *tawa'if* and through Mah Laqa Bai's biographies, we saw how a tawa'if moved from one place to another in search of patronage and continually reimagined herself—sometimes erasing certain aspects of her past, and at others taking on a new identity whether as a concubine to a ruler or a courtier in a princely state—reconstituting herself anew.

The collective biographies of the women of Mah Laqa Bai's family and her own transformation into a powerful courtesan further revealed the significance of the metaphorical and literal journey of self-invention and self-fashioning. While the modernist autobiography may choose the metaphor of journey to highlight the "inner" journey of the self, in the case of Mah Laqa Bai, hers was not only a journey of self-discovery, but centrally one of self-invention and fashioning. The use of the term *autobiographical* that allows for a wider understanding of the representational self (as the introduction to this volume shows)—as acts of reading and reconstituting the self—congeals in the way Mah Laqa Bai, a tawa'if, constructed a meaningful life for herself. This transformation became possible in the early modern court of the princely state of Hyderabad, a court that comprised nobility distinct from that of the Mughals. Upward mobility of courtiers was the norm in the state where new political players like the British EIC were becoming influential and local intermediaries were powerful. Running establishments similar to the ruler, courtiers and intermediaries offered multiple opportunities to the tawa'if to be a successful diplomat, a promoter of new literary tastes, and a political player. Mah Laqa Bai became one such successful courtesan by consciously choosing various modes of self-expression that gave her access to material success and power, and left a cache of traces for posterity. Using a complex vocabulary of authorship, she went far beyond the act of "writing" an autobiography to assert her status as a woman with a voice through acts of patronage and performance.

NOTES

1. Apsaras are mythological performers in Lord Indra's court. Moti Chandra, *The World of Courtesans* (Delhi: Vikas, 1973); Madhu Trivedi, "Female Performing Artistes in North India: A Survey," in Ahsan Jan Qaisar and Som Prakash Verma, eds., *Art and Culture: Painting and Perspective* (Delhi: Abhinav, 2002), 153–64; Pran Nevile, *Nautch Girls of India: Dancers, Singers, Playmates* (New York: Ravi Kumar, 1996).
2. Susie Tharu and K. Lalita, eds. *Women Writing in India: 600 B.C. to the Present*, vol. 1 (Delhi: Oxford University Press, 1991), 180–82.
3. Today Osmania University stands on one of her jagir lands. Ghulam Husain Khan Jauhar, *Tarikh-i-dilafruz*, 1819, British Library manuscript, f.149b–152b.
4. Aurangzeb's daughter Zebunissa Begam (1638–1702) chose to compose poetry, and the courtesan Nur Bai traveled on a grand elephant carriage at the time that Nadir Shah invaded Delhi in 1739, while Nur Jahan (1577–1645), the Mughal empress, got coins minted with her own image. Annie Krieger Krynicki, *Captive Princess: Zebunissa, Daughter of Emperor Aurangzeb* (Karachi: Oxford University Press, 2005); Dargah Quli Khan, *Muraqqa-e-Dehli*, trans. and ed. Chandra Shekhar and Shama Mitra Chenoy (Delhi: Deputy, 1989), 111–14; Ellison Banks Findly, *Nur Jahan: Empress of Mughal India* (New York: Oxford University Press, 1993). The devadasis or temple women in medieval Tamil Nadu were closely involved in the life in the villages and cultivated their status as donors by making donations and commissioning stepwells and tanks. Leslie Orr, *Donors, Devotees and Daughters of God: Temple Women in Medieval Tamil Nadu* (New York: Oxford University Press,

2000). Although despised by chroniclers, the erstwhile tawa'if Udham Bai of Delhi, who also became a queen and was one of the wives of Muhammad Shah (r. 1719–48), built mosques and gardens. For more on the tawa'if and architecture, see Shweta Sachdeva, "In Search of the Tawa'if in History: Courtesans, *Nautch Girls* and Celebrity Entertainers in India (1720s–1920s)" (PhD diss., SOAS, 2008), 68–70.

5 Royal patronage to Shi'a religious gatherings and building of *imambaras* had offered professional musicians and singers opportunities of career building in eighteenth-century Lucknow. In his study of Shi'a Islam in north India, Juan R. Cole argues that these opportunities meant that some low-caste Hindu musicians and women singers such as *domnis* converted to Shi'a Islam during these years. About 85 percent of tawa'ifs in Lucknow and surrounding areas were Shi'as, and many among them, Cole has shown, were former Hindu widows who had converted to Islam in search of increasing opportunities of patronage. Cole, *Roots of North Indian Shi'ism in Iran and Iraq: Religion and State in Awadh 1722–1856* (Berkeley: University of California Press, 1988), 87.

6 Abdul Halim Sharar, *Lucknow: The Last Phase of an Oriental Culture*, trans. and ed. E. S. Harcourt and Fakhir Hussain (Boulder, CO: Westview, 1975), 147–50.

7 Katherine Butler Schofield, "The Courtesan Tale: Female Musicians and Dancers in Mughal Historical Chronicles, c. 1556–1748," *Gender and History* 24.1 (April 2012): 152.

8 Schofield, "The Courtesan Tale," 152.

9 John T. Platts, *A Dictionary of Urdu, Classical Hindi, and English* (London: W. H. Allen, 1884), 754.

10 S. W. Fallon, *A New English-Hindustani Dictionary* (London: Trübner, 1883), 486.

11 Mir Insha Allah Khan "Insha" Dehalvi, *Kahani Rani Ketaki aur Kanwar Aude Bhan Ki* (Karachi: Anjuman Taraqi Urdu Pakistan, 1993). Often seen as the first "Hindi" prose written without using any Perso-Arabic words, in this text *randi* meant a woman.

12 Veena Talwar Oldenburg, "Lifestyle as Resistance: The Case of the Courtesans of Lucknow, India," *Feminist Studies* 16.2 (summer 1990): 259–87.

13 Fasih-al-Din "Ranj," *Baharistan-i-Naz* (Meerut: n.p., 1882), 38; Durgaprasad "Nadir," *Tazkirat-al-Nisa* (Delhi, 1878): 27. The earliest publication of her diwan was by Ghulam Samdani Gauhar, called *Gulzar-i-Mah Laqa* (Hyderabad, Nizams Press, 1906). This chapter is based on the first biography and two recent ones edited by Shafqat Rizvi: *Urdu Ka Classiki Adab Diwan Mah Laqa Bai Chanda* (Lahore: Majlis Taraqqi-e-Adab, 1990); Rahat Azmi, *Mah Laqa: Halat-i-Zindagi: Mah-i-Diwan* (Hyderabad: Urdu Academy Andhra Pradesh, 1998). Several Urdu editions of the story were printed from 1899 to 1938. The best English translations of the Urdu story is Mirza Muhammad Hadi Ruswa, *Umrao Jan Ada*, trans. David Matthews (Delhi: Rupa, 1996).

14 Paul de Man, "Autobiography as De-facement," in *Rhetoric of Romanticism* (New York: Columbia University Press, 1984), 67–82.

15 D. Fairchild Ruggles, "Vision and Power: An Introduction," in *Women, Patronage, and Self-Representation in Islamic Societies*, ed. D. Fairchild Ruggles (New York:

State University Press of New York Press, 2000), 4–5. On building as visibility, see Lucienne Thys-Senocak, *Ottoman Women Builders: The Architectural Patronage of Hadice Turhan Sultan* (Burlington, VT: Ashgate, 2006).

16 C. A. Bayly, *Rulers, Townsmen and Bazaars: North Indian Society in the Age of British Expansion 1770–1870* (Cambridge: Cambridge University Press, 1983); Muzaffar Alam, *The Crisis of Empire in Mughal North India: Awadh and the Punjab, 1707–48* (Delhi: Oxford University Press, 1986).

17 Karen Leonard, "The Hyderabad Political System and Its Participants," *Journal of Asian Studies* 30.3 (May 1971): 569–82.

18 Sheela Raj, *Mediaevalism to Modernism: Socio-economic and Cultural History of Hyderabad, 1869–1911* (Bombay: Popular Prakashan, 1987), 282–84. Andhra Pradesh State Archives, *Daftar-i-arbab-i- nashat* "Mal," file no. 1295. H/23; file no. 1293, H/34, file no. 1294, on notification of the sale of a house of a dancing girl.

19 In her study of late nineteenth-century Jaipur, Joan L. Erdman notes that the *gunijankhana* was still functioning as one of the sixteen *karkhanas*. Her study is detailed in its use of gunijankhana archives in English, Dhundhari, Hindi, and Persian. Joan L. Erdman, "The Social Organization of *Sangit: Gunijankhana*," in *Patrons and Performers in Rajasthan: The Subtle Tradition* (Delhi: Chanakya, 1985), 74–113. Chandramani, "Gunijan khana," in *Cultural Heritage of Jaipur*, ed. Jai Narayan Asopa (Jodhpur: United Book Traders, 1982), 95–103.

20 Sayajirao Gaekward II of Baroda was the head of one such department of musicians called the kalavant karkhana. Janaki Bakhle, *Two Men and Music: Nationalism in the Making of an Indian Classical Tradition* (Delhi: Permanent Black, 2005), 12.

21 Raj, *Mediaevalism to Modernism*, 282.

22 Khwaja Hakim Ghulam Hussain Khan Zaman Khan Dehlavi, *Tarikh-i- Asafjahyiyan (Gulzar-i-Asafiya)*, ed. M. Mehdi Tavassoli (Islamabad: Iran-Pakistan Institute of Persian Studies, 1999), 639–42.

23 Mir Alam was also one of her lovers and wrote a *sarapa* in Persian describing her beauty. Rizvi, *Urdu Ka Classiki Adab Diwan Mah Laqa Bai Chanda*, 24.

24 Azmi, *Mah Laqa*, 40.

25 Even concubines were addressed as Bibi, a title used for married women.

26 Bhagats are mentioned as a group of men who sang songs, dressed in various disguises, were excellent mimics, and performed only at night. Colonel H. S. Jarrett, trans., *'Ain-i- Akbari of Abul Fazl-i-'Allami*, vol. 3 (Calcutta: Asiatic Society of Bengal, 1948), 271–73. Azmi, *Mah Laqa*, 35.

27 Many sale deeds of girls being sold into slavery to tawa'ifs are available in the National Archives of India. For example, *bakshishnama* executed by Najabat 'Ali Rizawi to the effect that he has gifted Gulbahar *kanizak* (slave girl) to Mulayam Bai free of cost on his own accord, October 29, 1762 AD, NAI 2382/42; *Dastawez* to the effect of Himmat Khan, son of Jafar Khan resident of Manikpur, *pargana* Kara has sold one of his *kaniz* (slave girl) aged nine years to Radi tawa'if for Rs 10, December 20, 1754 AD, NAI 2382/39. These records were translated with the help of the catalogue of Persian documents. R. K. Perti, ed., *Acquired Documents*, vol. 3, *1356–1790 AD* (Delhi: NAI, 1992).

28 Ramya Sreenivasan, "Drudges, Dancing-Girls, Concubines: Female Slaves in Rajput Polity, 1500–1850," in Indrani Chatterjee and Richard Eaton, eds., *Slavery and South Asian History* (Bloomington: Indiana University Press, 2006), 140–41.
29 Oldenburg, "Lifestyle as Resistance," 259.
30 Sharar, *Lucknow: The Last Phase of an Oriental Culture*, 33–34.
31 Mah Laqa Bai's grandfather or Bahadur Khan 'Turki's father, Basalat Khan, had started his career in Aurangzeb's court as a caretaker of the royal prince and heir. He was also a close associate of Shah Nawaz Khan, who was also employed at Hyderabad and was the compiler of *Maasir-al-Umrah*.
32 *The Chronology of Modern Hyderabad (1720–1890)* (Hyderabad: Central Records Office, 1954), Index, 31.
33 William Dalrymple suggests that later Chanda also became a mistress to Aristu Jah, although none of the biographers suggest it. William Dalrymple, *White Mughals: Love and Betrayal in Eighteenth-Century India* (London: HarperCollins, 2002), 124.
34 Mir Alam was known to compose poetry in Persian and Urdu, as well as the Asaf Jah rulers. Chandu Lal, another (1833–44) prime minister of Hyderabad, wrote poetry under the pen name Shadan. The famous poet Dagh (1831–1905) was Chandu Lal's ustad in the court of Hyderabad.
35 Frances W. Pritchett, "A Long History of Urdu Literary Culture, Part 1: Histories, Performances, and Masters," in *Literary Cultures in History: Reconstructions from South Asia*, ed. Sheldon Pollock (Berkeley: University of California Press, 2003), 582.
36 Rizvi, *Urdu Ka Classiki Adab*, 42.
37 Both Azmi and Rizvi mention the confusion over her position as the first or second woman poet with an entire diwan. E-mail communication with Scott Kugle, June 26, 2013.
38 Captain Thomas Williamson, *The East India Vade-Mecum or Complete Guide to Gentlemen Intended for the Civil, Military, or Naval Service of the Hon. East India Company*, 2 vols. (London: Black, Parry and Kingsbury, 1810), 2: 423–24. For an extensive survey of English travelogues that describe the nautch, see Ketaki Kushari Dyson, *A Various Universe: A Study of the Journals and Memoirs of British Men and Women in the Indian Subcontinent 1765–1856* (Delhi: Oxford University Press, 2002), 336–56.
39 Sreenivasan, "Drudges, Dancing-Girls, Concubines," 141.
40 The manuscript diwan in the British Library has an entry on the flyleaf that gives these details. John Malcolm played an important role in disbanding the French army in Hyderabad.
41 Dalrymple, *White Mughals*.
42 *The Chronology of Modern Hyderabad*, 143.
43 *The Chronology of Modern Hyderabad*, 161.
44 For detailed analysis of a *mujra* setting, see Regula Burckhart Qureshi, "The Indian Sarangi: Sound of Affect, Site of Contest," *Yearbook of Traditional Music* 29 (1997): 24–28.

45 Pritchett, "A Long History of Urdu Literary Culture," 867–68.
46 Ahmed Ali, *The Golden Tradition: An Anthology of Urdu Poetry* (New York: Columbia University Press, 1973), 3–22.
47 Scott Kugle, "Mah Laqa Bai and Gender: The Language, Poetry and Performance of a Courtesan in Hyderabad," *Comparative Studies of South Asia, Africa and the Middle East* 30.3 (2010): 365–85.
48 Kugle, "Mah Laqa Bai and Gender," 368.
49 My translation of ghazal no. 9 (*bab alif*, the ghazal begins, *rahe hai nauroz ishrat afrin*), quoted in Azmi, *Mah Laqa*, 169.
50 See ghazals on Asaf Jah II. Azmi, *Mah Laqa*, 190, 210, 225.
51 Translated in Tharu and Lalita, *Women Writing in India*, 1991, 180–82.
52 My translation of ghazal no. 3 (begins *tadpe hai dil payam ka*), quoted in Azmi, *Mah Laqa*, 167.
53 Translated by Scott Kugle, "Mah Laqa Bai and Gender," *Gulzar I Mah Laqa* [The garden of Mah Laqa] (Hyderabad: Nizam al-Matabi AH1324/1906), ghazal 109 radif *ye*. The ghazal begins *har roz jo yun hi sitam ijad karoge*, cited in Kugle, "Mah Laqa Bai and Gender," 368.
54 Only recently scholars have attempted to study rekhti, and apart from extremely few compositions by women, most have been by men; see Carla Petievich, *When Men Speak as Women: Vocal Masquerade in Indo-Muslim Poetry* (Delhi: Oxford University Press, 2008). For a reading of rekhti and same-sex love, see Saleem Kidwai and Ruth Vanita, eds., *Same-Sex Love in India: Readings from Literature and History* (London: Palgrave Macmillan, 2000).
55 See issues of *Annual of Urdu Studies* and the responses of Frances Pritchett to Ralph Russell, Ralph Russell, 'The Urdu Ghazal: A Rejoinder to Frances W. Pritchett and William L. Hanway Jr.," *Annual of Urdu Studies* 10 (1995): 96–112.
56 Shamsur Rahman Faruqi, "The Poet in the Poem or, Veiling the Utterance," in Kathryn Hansen and David Lelyveld, eds., *A Wilderness of Possibilities: Urdu Studies in Transnational Perspective* (Delhi: Oxford University Press, 2005), 173–91.
57 For a critique of reading poetry as practice of same-sex love, see C. M. Naim, "Transvestic Words? The Rekhti in Urdu," *Annual of Urdu Studies* 16 (2001): 3–26.
58 Kugle, "Mah Laqa Bai and Gender," 370.
59 Kugle, "Mah Laqa Bai and Gender," 368.
60 Women poets, Petievich suggests, preferred to use rekhta as it gave them access to the otherwise male world of poetry and performance; see Carla Petievich, "Feminine Authorship and Urdu Poetic Tradition," in Hansen and Lelyveld, *A Wilderness of Possibilities*, 234.
61 The manuscripts are available in the Salar Jung Museum Library, Hyderabad, and the British Library, London. *Tazkiras* on women poets or biographical dictionaries of poetesses mention her as the first *sahib-e-diwan* woman Urdu poet or the first woman to have a complete diwan of poetry.
62 Azmi, *Mah Laqa: Halat-i-Zindagi*, 74–79. Her earliest Urdu biography of 1906 mentions her age as fifty-six at the time of her death, but the date engraved on her tomb is 1824.

63 The ashurkhanas and mausoleums built by Chanda and her music ustad are listed by Bilgrami. Syed Ali Asgar Bilgrami, *Landmarks of the Deccan: A Comprehensive Guide to the Archaeological Remains of the City and Suburbs of Hyderabad* (Hyderabad: Government Central Press, 1927), 16–18.

64 For an excellent study of courtly architecture and literature, see Ali Akbar Husain, *Scent in the Islamic Garden: A Study of Deccani Urdu Literary Sources* (Karachi: Oxford University Press, 2000). On Hyderabad, see Raza Ali Khan, *Hyderabad: A City in History* (Hyderabad, 1986).

65 Bilgrami, *Landmarks of the Deccan*.

66 Bilgrami, *Landmarks of the Deccan*, 16–18. The garden tomb of Chanda has recently been renovated by Scott Kugle, U.S. consulate general at Hyderabad, Centre for Deccan Studies and the Muslim Educational, Social and Cultural Organization.

67 Also known as Mahnama in the Salar Jung Library Collections. Ghulam Hussain Jauhar, *Tarikh-i-Dilafruz*, 1819, f.149b–52b.

7. MASCULINE MODES OF FEMALE SUBJECTIVITY

The Case of Jahanara Begam

AFSHAN BOKHARI

In 1631, the Mughal emperor Shah Jahan's empress Mumtaz Mahal died in childbirth, leaving her eldest daughter, seventeen-year-old Jahanara Begam (1614–1681), in her role as head of the imperial harem.[1] As keeper of the imperial seal and manager of the harem, Jahanara functioned as Shah Jahan's "consort queen" and confidant. However, the emperor's detailed biographies are brief and mechanical in their descriptions of the princess and other imperial women.[2] This omission in the emperor's biography makes the contents of Jahanara's anthology of Sufi saints, *Munis al-arvah* (1640), and her autobiographical Sufi treatise, *Risalah-i Sahibiyah* (1641), intriguing and underscores the crucial Mughal-Sufi equation, strategic for imperial rule. Jahanara's writings and sacred commissions aligned with those of Mughal emperors and bestowed a patrilineal biographical record onto their heirs to uphold and served as a form of objectified counsel. The imperial imperative and enduring paradigm begins with Mughal emperor Babur's (d. 1530) autobiographical narratives in his *Baburnama* and continues in Shah Jahan's multiple *Shahjahanama* biographies. The habit of chronicling the deeds of each Mughal king ensured a consistency in governance, public confidence, and sociopolitical praxis.

This chapter considers the crucial Mughal-Sufi relationship of Jahanara Begam with her *pir* Mullah Shah Badakshi (1585–1661), her two Sufi treatises, *Munis al-arvah* and *Risalah-i Sahibiyah*, and her prominent patronage, within a politically pivotal moment during Emperor Shah Jahan's reign (1628–58). It locates the modes of masculine strategies that the princess appropriated to cultivate the multiple subjects of her representation and to uphold the Mughal sociopolitical and religious ideology. The work considers Jahanara's textual and architectural narratives as forms of male Mughal prerogatives and bureaucratic practice that allowed the princess as the emperor's consort queen to advance imperial agendas, sustain sovereignty, and conceptualize her subjecthood/objecthood—hereafter, called "subjectivity."

The concept of the imperial self as both a synecdoche of royal subject/hood and self-representation has been determined by recent scholarship on first-person narratives to craft and conceptualize identity as both physical and ephemeral and one that simultaneously imbues textual and physical space.[3] Jahanara Begam's contributions are located at the intersection of Sufism, political legitimacy, and Mughal-Sufi historiography-hagiography. Her writings denote how an imperial female attempted to subjectively narrate and weave her persona through the religious, imperial, and political values of the court using creative and cultural processes of autobiographical/history writing and architectural commissions. Mughals propagated imperial ideology through sustained patronage of history writing and utilized historiography as a means to legitimize and sustain empire. Though the unmarried princess's book and architectural commissions conformed to the imperially sanctioned modes for promoting the sovereign's propaganda and ethos, they were historically and by custom permissible only for Mughal kings to sponsor. Jahanara personally engages historical and religious narratives through her two treatises and crafts a public and private brand of imperial subjectivity through the male-only creative practice. The two texts and Jahanara's bold commissions function simultaneously as rhetorical devices for articulating and perpetuating Mughal ideology and at the same time objectify an imperial female's representation within Sufi hagiography and Mughal historiography. In her hagiographic representation, Jahanara explores the full dimensions of her female identity in a spiritual context through the use of sexual metaphors and her "mystical union" with her male pir, Mullah Shah Badakshi. In her historiographical articulations, however, she resists, and to some extent subsumes, her gender to consciously and boldly appropriate masculine modes to represent her imperial persona.

Though there is insufficient space here to flesh out the tensions between her various gendered appropriations and articulations, this chapter will focus on her subjectivity/ies as represented in her Sufi treatises and architectural patronage. Between her articulations as a Mughal princess imbued with and expressing imperial agendas, and her mystical Sufi religiosity as an utterance of the spiritual self, Jahanara embodied and expressed multiple identities/subjectivities. Furthermore, she wasn't the only imperial female to fashion the self through the use of conventional, stylized modes—a treatise or a monument; others like Nur Jahan, the queen of Jahangir (r. 1605–27) did so before her.[4] Concepts like *autotopography*, which point to personal objects that relate to the psychocultural body, may help us make sense of the relation between corporeality and the sensorial self. The material artifacts through which it may be expressed, but are perhaps inadequate to show the monumental and imperial scale through which Jahanara expressed the self.[5]

Jahanara's contributions are the most symbolically potent of imperial idioms that fashion her subjectivity and graft her legacy onto the male-dominated bureaucratic state's governance and patrilineal history. The autobiographical *Risalah-i Sahibiyah* describes the mid-seventeenth-century Mughal spiritual ideology and associations, dream narratives, networks of kinship, and political alliances. It legitimizes Jahanara's assigned imperial authority and her elevated spiritual rank within the Sufi Qadiriyah order. Unlike the emperors' auto/biographies, Jahanara's writings are not tedious chronological collations of imperial deeds and sociopolitical events but are engaging and simple personalized ruminations of her spiritual development in response to significant historical and sociopolitical events. Serving as the counterbalance to the worldly successes of Shah Jahan, Jahanara uses Sufi ideology and mystical semantics to cultivate an aura and also perceptions of her spiritual subjectivity that cast her in a leading role on the male-dominated Sufi-Mughal stage. While the Mughals' political expansion was achieved through diplomacy, sociopolitical alliances, and military campaigns, it also involved the meticulous projection of Islamic religiosity informed by conventional and mystical Islam. Jahanara's investment in her relationship with a Sufi *shaikh* through her religiosity, writings, and sacred commissions was strategic in advancing her personal and imperial agendas.

During Babur's conquest of India in 1526, Sufi orders occupied a central position in the sociopolitical and cultural life of Indian Muslims. The strength, sustainability, and expansive schemes of the Mughals over northern India into the eighteenth century depended to some extent on forging alliances with key Sufi shaikhs who maintained extensive networks throughout the region.[6] This vital Sufi-sovereign dynamic harkens back to the Mughals' Timurid heritage and the imperial propaganda around which Indo-Islamic concepts of kingship were constructed. Jahanara's younger brother, the heir-apparent prince Dara Shikoh (1615–1659), introduced the Qadiriya shaikh, Mullah Shah Badakhshi, to his sister Jahanara, and together they actively sought Sufi pirs for spiritual discussions and guidance, and each wrote mystically inspired treatises.[7] However, the Sufi-Mughal relationship was not central to Shah Jahan's political ambitions and may have given Jahanara the impetus to resurrect their Sufi-sovereign heritage through her textual and physical assertions that objectified her subjectivities. The aggregate of the princess's political and spiritual immersions into the Mughal landscape projected a nuanced and gendered sovereignty that is heavily textured by Timurid-Mughal imperatives, ideologies, and idioms of empire.

The Mughal legacy hails from the Central Asian Turkic-Mongol Timurid dynasty and its founder, Amir Timur, who employed folk traditions, pre-Islamic spiritual concepts, symbols, and rituals to craft an imperial ideology and concepts of kingship to establish semidivine authority.[8] The emperor was perceived as perpetuating the divinely ordained "flame" of kingship, the *farr-i izadi*, and the aura and radiance of his "flame" were maintained through multiple public/private and sacred/secular modes for the legacy to continue with each successive dynastic ruler.[9] History writing in the form of emperors' auto/biographies became a principal Timurid convention adopted by Mughal emperors that contributed to the farr-i izadi mythification of the emperor and was habitually practiced until Emperor Aurangzeb (1618–1707).[10] The earliest *namas* had among them Timur's fifteenth-century biography, *Zafarname*,[11] written thirty years after Timur's death, and Babur's sixteenth-century autobiography, *Baburnama*.[12] Through this chronicle, Babur entreated the memory of his ancestor, Timur, as central to claims of sovereignty in the newly conquered India and forged links with his patrilineal past.

Another mode to "history writing" was imperial sponsorship of prominent public and charitable projects and endowments. Such works can be seen as the composite objectification of the patron and the design and details of the prominent commissions as the "coded" narratives of stock Mughal-Timurid iconography that communicated through the object of the structure, the subject of the male sovereign, and his subjectivities. The imperial, illustrated biographies and patronage were instruments that recorded imperial history and ideology, and inscribed authority and governance through physical and textual narratives. These modes of communication instructed and reminded each ruler of good governance and rules of kingship. Both architecture and book production sustained imperial ideology and policies and also exemplified Mughal grandeur as a cultural expression and a component of noble and absolute governance. The documented Mughal in his illustrated auto/biographies exemplified male imperial authority and persona. The record made kingship accountable to their lineal descent and legacy. Thus, official narratives written during the Mughal reign were conditioned by subjectivities "that existed simultaneously" as personal and imperial prerogatives.[13]

In this work, I interrogate and superimpose the imperial, male-centered framework onto Jahanara Begam's modes of textual and architectural representations that are seemingly learned and observed responses of the imperial male prerogatives of her day and the Mughal past. The princess's commissions, and particularly her Sufi treatise, the *Risalah*, a rare autobiography of an imperial female in premodern Islamic history, are embedded within a larger imperial narrative structure and ethos while also being specific to her ambitions, agenda, and persona. In addition to emperors' biographies and commissions serving as tools of governance, control, and omnipresence, imperially sponsored miniature paintings also played a key role in objectifying the subject of the patron. Only one painting has been identified as the princess Jahanara Begam and is included in Dara Shikoh's album, commissioned for his wife Nadira Begam.[14] The painting shows Jahanara holding an open book and facing a Sufi figure on the opposite page (see figure 7.1). The formal elements of the work underscore Jahanara's penchant for writing and mysticism, and her close relationship with her pir, Mullah Shah Badakhshi. Dara Shikoh deeply influenced Jahanara through his devotion to Sufism and his intellectual pursuits.[15]

Mughal women's agency served a complementary role in promoting empire and legacy-building initiatives through public acts of piety and dynastic reproduction. These contributions ensured an enduring polity and were intrinsic to practical politics. Women promoted personal and state piety by distributing alms, visiting saints' tombs, and endowing state-sponsored sacred and secular buildings. Though Mughal women had the fiscal means to commission public monuments and structures, it was not conventional for elite women to formally articulate their subject/subjectivities in the public realm. Women also were not encouraged to preserve or project the self in memoirs or biographies as emperors had through the nama genre. Major monuments and memoirs/biographies were imperial male prerogatives that articulated the subject of the emperor throughout his domains and the history of power in the private and public realms. As noted earlier, auto/biographies and architecture are imperial idioms referred to as "subjectivities" of the sovereign in this work.

Mughal monuments and memoirs/biographies were conceived by sovereigns and received by their subjects, as resilient literary and lithic narratives that conveyed the subjectivities and endurance of the ruler and his reign. The role of early Mughal women was secondary in this regard to that of the king. Women promoted imperial ideology and were guided in their contributions by the imperial dictates expected of their gender and rank. A woman's role in Mughal

FIGURE 7.1. *Jahanara*, attributed to Lalchand, c. 1631–33. © British Library Board. Add.Or.3129.f.25v. Used by permission.

FIGURE 7.2. Agra *jami* (congregation) Friday mosque, east elevation, pishtaq entrance to mihrab and prayer hall at forecourt. Photo by author.

FIGURE 7.3. AND 7.4. (Above, Top) Mullah Shah Badakhshi Mosque. Courtyard view of pishtaq leading to mihrab. (Above) Mullah Shah Badakhshi Mosque. View from southeast corner and entry pishtaq. Both photos by author.

statecraft was not diminished in power by her seemingly subordinate position to the emperor; rather, she articulated female authority in ways that were not as publically profound or politically motivated as the male counterparts. In the case of Jahanara, a textured, nuanced, and distinctive subjectivity is conveyed through what the author calls "masculine modes." As her father's confidant, Jahanara was not allowed to marry and thus avail herself of an advantageous matrimonial alliance, or perpetuate herself through dynastic reproduction. The primary means for projecting and perpetuating her political position and authority was through concepts of kingship in the sacred and secular milieu. Jahanara's imperial "semantics" to convey her subjectivity and objectify her persona are her Sufi treatises, *Munis*,[16] an anthology of Sufi saints, and the autobiographical *Risalah*; and her commissions, including the Agra congregation mosque (1648), her documented relationship with her pir, Mullah Shah Badakhshi, and her commemorative commission of his namesake the *khanaqah* complex (1650) in Srinagar, Kashmir. The intertexuality of the treatises and the iconic Mughal commissions exploit the prevailing masculine forms of imperial subjectivity and conventions, thus asserting the princess's political and spiritual imperatives that uniquely privileged her ability to illuminate Shah Jahan's divinely ordained flame, or farr-i izadi, and kingship (see figures 7.2, 7.3, and 7.4).

Jahanara's Sufi Treatises

SUFI-SOVEREIGN AFFILIATION IN MUGHAL INDIA

Sufism and its mystical belief system had a significant influence on the sociopolitical psyche of the Mughal dynasty, and the Sufi-sovereign dynamic forged links with the Timurid past.[17] Genealogical imperial portraits were popular illustrative methods to document and convey the Sufi-Mughal relationship and started with the Timurid patriarch, Amir Timor, and ended with the Mughal emperor Shah Jahan. In figure 7.5 the privileged moment of the thirteenth-century poet and Sufi shaikh Sa'di is recorded as he presents Timur with a book, possibly the *kulliyat*.[18] Sa'di functioned as the moral Sufi barometer that guided and ensured good governance and sound kingship. Starting from the Mughal's great ancestor Timur's fourteenth-century relationship with the Naqsbandhi order, Sufi pirs viscerally attended to the social, spiritual, and political needs of the Timurid elite and also facilitated the politically motivated Sufi-indoctrinated concepts of semidivine kingship. The Sufi-sovereign relationship was primarily modeled on a spiritual relationship of a *murid* (seeker/disciple) with a *murshid* (guide/preceptor). The fundamental relationship of the pir-murid changed in fifteenth-century Herat, between a Naqshbandi master and his disciples. The murids with imperial or political power assumed unprecedented social and political significance and functioned in effect as political advisors to kings. The Naqshbandi pir was also the spiritual preceptor and advisor who promoted the political agenda of his disciples, primarily Timurid rulers and their nobles in Central Asia.[19] Further, the pir and his descendants/disciples claimed that they were not simply spiritual masters, but were also a source of otherworldly strength needed in politics and power struggles.

The Sufi-sovereign politico-spiritual relationship was sustained in Mughal India through the India-based Chishtiyah order. In pre-Mughal India, the Chishtiyah had established an effective and efficient hierarchical ordering with deputies (*khalifas*), disciples (murids) and ordinary associates (*mutawassils*) to manage and minister the entire upper northern Indian plains.[20] Grafting Mughal governance along the Chishtiyah networks legitimized and expanded Mughal rule and politically sustained their visions of power along spiritual lines. The long-standing popular tradition of Sufi orders and saints in pre-Mughal India provided the strategic sociopolitical support for the Timurid-Mughal rulers in the nascent empire and allowed them to establish rightful rulership similar to Timur's status in the ancestral lands of Herat and Balkh, Afghanistan. The sovereign's inextricable connection to Sufi institutions was political and spiritual, solidified through the sponsorship of Sufi saints and their shrine complexes and through the magnanimous and visible support by the royal family.[21]

Mughal alignment with Sufi institutions, specifically the Chishtiyah order,[22] was formally established during Akbar's reign (1540–1605). The exclusive relationship between Sufis and sovereigns was reflected in what Ebba Koch regards as "exponents of worldly and spiritual powers."[23] Though the Central Asian and Timur-sanctioned Sufi Naqshbandi order was favored by Babur and the Timurids, their presence and influence among the later Mughal emperors was marginal. The populist dimension of the Chishtiyah among Indians of all sects qualified their membership as chief advisors in Akbar's sacral-secular political cabinet. Akbar's affiliations with the order allowed him to graft the Chishti network of support and its venerated spiritual leadership to his sovereignty. Akbar assigned Shaikh Salim (d. 1572) as his son Jahangir's "protector and preserver,"[24] and he extended the long and powerful reach of an emperor by linking a living pir with his heir-apparent.[25] Jahangir's auspicious birth was mystically anointed by Shaikh Salim and perceived as divinely ordained and

FIGURE 7.5. *Timur Enthroned with His Descendants from Babur to Jahangir*, signed by Hashim, c. 1620. © British Library Board. Johnson Album, 64, 38, 174 x 116 mm. Used by permission.

thereby legitimized Akbar's sovereignty and Mughal legacy. By extension, the Sufi-sovereign affiliation established an aura of sanctity around the imperial family and a metaphysical link to Mughal-sponsored shrines and mosques.[26]

Babur and Akbar's modes of subjectivity, personalized narratives as auto/biographies (*Baburnama* and *Akbarnama*), and direct and personal Sufi affiliations, established imperial frameworks that informed and guided later emperors in crafting their visions and also served Jahanara's literary and lithic undertakings. Jahanara's earliest commission was the ladies-only Begam Dalani portico and enclosure in the Khwaja Moinuddin Chishti shrine in Ajmer in 1638,[27] alongside Shah Jahan's commission of a small community mosque. The Chishti shrine's improvements and additions can be analyzed as an architectural datum. The allegiance of each Mughal emperor from Akbar to Shah Jahan can be viewed through their consistent contributions to the complex. Jahanara's embedded patronage of the portico and its placement within male-sponsored works to honor a male Sufi saint assigns and legitimizes her subjectivity through the historical and contemporary modes of sovereignty.

In 1635, Dara Shikoh introduced Jahanara to the Chishtiyah pir Mian Mir (d. 1636) for mystical initiation.[28] However, according to the *Sahibiyah*,[29] Mian Mir conveyed both brother and sister to Mullah Shah of the Qadiriyah order.[30] The choice of the Qadiriyah order may have been politically motivated, or a matter of convenience, as it was based in Lahore, an important provincial site of Shah Jahan's governance and a military checkpoint en route to the outer imperial domains of Kashmir and Kabul. Jahanara Begam describes her desire to enlist in the Chishti order, but gratefully accepts the Qadiriyah and is eager to begin her spiritual journey: "Since my twentieth year I have had a sincere intention and firm belief in the order of the masters of Chisht. . . . Although my entire wish was to find a shaikh of this kind in the respected Chishti order, it is better and more appropriate, for in this time there will be many perfect, wise, accomplished, and monist shaikhs in other exalted orders."[31] Seventeenth- through nineteenth-century Mughal paintings frequently depict pirs Mian Mir and Mullah Shah in conversation. The repeated visual documentation of the two figures confirms their close relationship and Mian Mir's endorsement of Mullah Shah (see figure 7.6).

Jahanara's Sufi initiation from 1638 to 1641 coincided with Shah Jahan's accelerated military campaigns in the ancestral lands of Balkh, specifically Mullah Shah's hometown, Badakhshan. The "Timurid Renaissance" was further motivated by Shah Jahan's vision of kingship, in which he formally proclaimed himself the second Timur and appropriated Timur's regnal title, *Sahib Qirani-i sani*, "the second lord of the auspicious planetary conjunction," a title he inscribed on his coins.[32] Further, Shah Jahan's aim to regain Balkh would link

FIGURE 7.6. Sufi saints Mian Mir and Mullah Shah Badakhshi seated under a tree in discussion, seventeenth century, Mughal. © Ashmolean Museum, University of Oxford, EA1990.1287. Used by permission.

his rulership and sovereignty to his lineal descendants in his ancestral lands. The mandate to keep the "eternal flame" and legacy of the Timurids burning bright through successive emperors was not lost on Jahanara, as she details in the *Sahibiyah* the names of Mullah Shah's extensive network of pirs in Balkh/Badakhshan: "Among all the disciples of Hazrat, Mulla Muhammad Sa'di is outstanding. His origins are also from the area of Badakhshan and he has . . . kinship with Hazrat. . . . Among his other disciples was Mulla Miskin, who was also from Badakhshan and master of austerities and efforts, and great states and stations. Among the other felicitous disciples of my Hazrat are Muhammad Halim. . . . Muhammad Halim's father is Gul Beg, also from Badakhshan."[33]

Jahanara expresses her disappointment about Dara Shikoh's numerous failed military campaigns in Badakhshan: "During that time my great father . . . also turned toward Badakhshan, and I always received letters from my powerful brother. My dignified brother had seen other shaikhs on the way, and he wrote the truth about them to me so that I would be informed."[34] Jahanara, Dara Shikoh, and Shah Jahan politically and spiritually favored the Sufi Qadiriyah order. Mullah Shah Badakhshi's network was vital to the emperor's objective to regain a political foothold in his ancestral lands. Mullah Shah and his network of pirs in Balkh may have been conscripted into Shah Jahan's retinue and political infrastructure to support the empire and the emperor's expansionist schemes.

JAHANARA AS KHALIFA

Jahanara's political and spiritual motivations/aspirations and Sufi connections extended beyond the imperial dictates and pietistic roles expected of imperial females. The princess sought an elevated Sufi state not just a connection with a shaikh and order. Jahanara claimed a *piri-muridi*, or de facto khalifa rank, which legitimized her self-professed spiritual authority and made claims to an enduring Timurid-Mughal legacy. The princess's claim and documentation of her spiritual ascension to metaphysical heights was unprecedented for any imperial male or female, and predates her to her great-grandfather Akbar's assumption of a semidivine concept of kingship as crafted by the chronicler Abu Fazl's literary and ideological propaganda. Akbar reportedly had several mystical visions that deeply impressed on him the divine intimations of his rule, and Jahanara was likely knowledgeable of the *Akbarnama* and the legitimizing concepts of her great-grandfather's sovereignty.[35] The assumption of the khalifa role in the Qadiriyah order was historically a mode of male subjectivity that Jahanara appropriated from the spiritual and imperial realms. In Sufi institutions the khalifa is the successor to his master/pir and had been a male-dominated role. Akbar claimed the authority of a khalifa in 1579 while embroiled in a religious debate with conservative Afghan religious leaders.[36] To Akbar's divine kingship, the princess adds the ultimate expression of her spiritual authority and transcendental experience: "In our family no one took the step on the path to seek God or the truth that would light the Timurid lamp eternally. I was grateful for having received this great fortune and wealth. There was no end to my happiness."[37]

Jahanara invokes the pre-Islamic notion of divine kingship, farr-i izadi, by lighting the Timuria's lamp of "divine effulgence," making manifest the pre-Islamic Persian concept of fire or light that evinces the legitimate ruler. The illumination is Shah Jahan's subjectivity, and Jahanara is the privileged igniter and keeper of the flame of effulgence. Abu Fazl's *Akbarnama* conflates the Timurid concept of kingship and the Sufi doctrine of illumination to craft Akbar's rightful rule. By lighting the Timurid lamp, Jahanara claims her divinely ordained place on the same spiritual mantle as Prophet Muhammad and his revered companions and documents her dream narrative:

> I was overtaken by a state in which I was neither asleep nor awake, and witnessed the holy assembly of the prophet.... The prophet ... was seated there and the four great friends.... I expressed a thousand thanks because I had been honored by the blessing of the Prophet ... and because I had heard the words, "You have lighted the lamp of the Timurids" from the miraculous tongue of that leader.... Only we brother and sister from the family of Timur, Lord of Two Conjunctions, set upon the path of God and extended the hand of devotion to ... Hazrat [Mullah Shah]; no one from the nobility has been honored by this felicity nor ... by seeking God and the truth.[38]

Jahanara, in a reverie between wakefulness and sleep, is seated with Islam's holiest figures, the Prophet Muhammad, and his four companions, later khalifas. The structure of the dream narrative in the *Sahibiyah* follows the literary conventions in "mirror for princes" literature. Mirror for princes literature in the context of Persian and Indian kingship is best known as textbooks that instructed kings on aspects of rule and behavior. The term is also used to cover histories or literary works aimed at creating "reflective" images of kings for emulation or avoidance.[39] According to Sholeh Quinn, "dream narratives and accounts of miraculous events" were included in the introductions of Mughal and Safavid historiographies.[40] Quinn cites the introduction of Mohammad 'Aref Qandahari's *Tarikh-i Akbari*, with an account of Akbar's deeds and dream visions that became instant truisms and were considered divinely ordained.

FIGURE 7.7. From the *Akbarnama—Akbar Ordering the Slaughter to Cease in 1578*, attributed to Miskina, c. 1595. © British Library Board. Johnson Album 8, 4. Used by permission.

In the *Akbarnama*, Akbar is captured in a "mystical trance" during a hunting expedition and is in a daze that Abu'l Fazl describes as Akbar receiving divine revelation, upon which he freed all the animals in captivity (see figure 7.7).[41] Such mystical experiences legitimized Akbar's semidivine authority, giving him the ultimate power over all sacred and secular matters, including issuing divinely ordained *mazhars* (religious decrees).[42]

Accustomed to the imperial value of the dream narrative, Jahanara documents in the *Sahibiyah* her mystical reverie and visions in the company of Islam's illustrious "heroes" and thereby legitimizes her khalifa ascension and authority. Further, the princess cites Shah Jahan's reading the *Akbarnama* about Sufi leadership: "he was reading the *Akbarnama* and his auspicious eyes fell on the part where Abu'l Fazl describes ... the guiding master being a Sayyid."[43] The Timurid-Mughal's lineal descent from Sayyids (descendants of Prophet Muhammad) confirmed and sanctioned her pir/khalifa assertion and is substantiated in the writings of Mullah Shah's biographer and disciple Tawakkul Beg:[44] "She passed through all the normal visions and attained a pure union with God and gained an intuitive perception. Mullah Shah said of her, 'She has attained so extraordinary a development of the mystical knowledge that she would be worthy of being my representative if she were not a woman.'"[45] Jahanara's gender impedes her spiritual prominence and excludes its formal investiture by Mullah Shah as his successor. Regardless of the formality of her ascension, the textual subjectivity and documentation of her two treatises objectifies her spiritual and divinely ordained status.

LEGITIMIZING DARA SHIKOH'S EMPEROR CANDIDACY

Dara Shikoh and Jahanara Begam's corpus of first-person Sufi narratives and literature enable historians to develop renewed perspectives on imperial social, political, and spiritual life, and emotional attitudes, during the waxing and waning of the Mughal dynasty at the end of the seventeenth century. Considering the dominant Sufi element in the intellectual and spiritual life of the emperor's two eldest children, a social change and aspects of spiritual dislocation are discerned, and one that may have been brought on by an ulterior sense of dynastic disorder and decline among the members of the royal house. The seemingly "chaotic" climate may have provoked Dara and Jahanara to look inward and be more self-conscious in their observations of empire. This new imperial orientation inward indicated by the plethora of mystical literature produced by both brother and sister generated new conventions of history writing, as both the heir-apparent and consort queen consciously dismissed the production of their auto/biography, and conventional Islam.

The *Sahibiyah* details the crucial elements of Jahanara's life and is a textured recollection of sacred and secular themes: Dara Shikoh as the heir-apparent, Shah Jahan's military campaigns in Badakhshan, the personal details of Mullah Shah's habits and his network of pirs, divine presence, and Jahanara's transcendental experiences and khalifa claims. The accrual of facts and subjects in the *Sahibiyah* and *Munis* are the threads that Jahanara weaves to fabricate an imperial retinue that serve her Sufi devotion, filial piety, empire, and legacy. Finally, the mystical narratives are veiled pronouncements of the unmarried princess's intimate and spiritual feelings of love for the Beloved/beloved and her support for Shah Jahan's "Timurid Renaissance," and Dara Shikoh's right to accession. Jahanara relied on the Timurid protocol to legitimize Dara's rightful inheritance of the throne in response to their youngest sibling, Aurangzeb's contestations and declaration of his own candidacy. He defeated Dara on the battlefield for the throne and reigned from 1568 to 1707. The itemization of Dara's "kingly virtues" is the requisite affirmation employed by the Timurids, Mughals, and Safavids to legitimize an heir's rightful claims to the throne.[46] Aurangzeb's tumultuous and vocal avowal for his own candidacy prompted Jahanara to dutifully support Dara's bid and rightful claim. Jahanara's personal brand of imperial propaganda includes semidivine concepts of kingship drawn from Akbar and other pre-Mughal sources and is presented through a "mirror for princes" framework. In the narratives of the *Sahibiyah*, Jahanara uses her textual agency and authorial authority to aggrandize her brother and father's imperial worthiness. The princess inextricably aligns the sovereign's kingly virtues with her own subjectivity by binding her soul and person to Dara Shikoh: "I had and have a lot of personal love, extreme notional affection, perfect religious and worldly accord, and a unity of form and meaning for my powerful and successful brother, the true heir, the sage of secrets, the master of zeal and presence, the light of the eye and source of light, full of meanings and illustrious actions, heir to the internal and external kingdom, felicitous in his search for God, one of lofty rank, Sultan Muhammad Dara Shikoh.... We both are one spirit blown into two forms and one life has come forth in two bodies."[47]

Dara Shikoh and Aurangzeb's contest for power escalated from 1640 to 1645. Aurangzeb used his successful military campaigns and governorship in the Deccan to legitimize his claims against Dara's administrative experience at court. The *Sahibiyah* details Dara's significant military campaign in Balkh and Badakhshan with a cavalry of fifty thousand.[48] Dara's military achievements and imperial virtues are dramatized and underscored with poetic gravitas:

Until . . . [1641–42] when . . . my great father sent off my powerful brother to Balkh . . . there was a necessary physical separation between us . . . and seemed very bitter and difficult for me, and when we said farewell we both wept, . . . and my brother the perfect sage also felt great sorrow. . . . Weeping we said goodbye . . . and I composed a couplet:
>That heart that is the pride of the garden does not last.
>Indeed, it is always burnt by pain and separation.

. . . My great father also turned towards Balkh, and I always received letters from my powerful brother. My dignified brother had seen other shaikhs on the way, and he wrote the truth about them to me so that I would be informed.[49]

Dara Shikoh's communication about his meetings with shaikhs in Balkh indicates that the shift of loyalty from the Chishtiyah Sufi order to the Qadiriyah may have been politically motivated. The campaign in Balkh was not successful, and Jahanara defends the valiant loss: "For the sake of . . . the large army . . . my esteemed father and successful brother left them a few stations behind and went ahead to determine their strategy. . . . A famine occurred, and the plan of conquering Balkh . . . was abandoned. The revelation of this gift . . . brought joy and happiness in my heart. . . . From obtaining this desire my zeal increased a thousand-fold, and the fire of zeal for divine gnosis was thrown in me."[50]

Dara's kingly virtues remained intact and were recounted in the *Sahibiyah*, couched in mystical and political rhetoric. Jahanara uses her literary agency to supplant Dara's military failure with prowess by exemplifying his benevolence, compassion, justice, and spiritually inspired judgment. Dara's just and sympathetic character is a prerequisite for establishing a legitimate and stable kingship and that which distinguishes him from Aurangzeb's military achievements.

THE SACRAL-SEXUAL ENCOUNTER

By the end of the thirteenth century, with the institutionalization of the Sufi *tariqahs*, the relationship between masters and disciples crystallized, and Sufi manuals included an elaborate code of conduct (*adab*) and prescriptions for governing sociopolitical and spiritual relations. The manuals describe the training and rituals of a disciple's passage from novice to Sufi adept and are reiterated in the *Sahibiyah*. The advice narrative in Jahanara's treatise details her transformation as a Sufi adept and concludes with sexual awareness as a function of the sacral-secular modes of courtship/initiation, affirmation, and finally consummation/mystical union. A devoted and trusted disciple/murid was expected to have intimate knowledge of the habits of his/her pir: "His customary way is to sit on his knees... and sometimes leaning. Sometimes he stretches his legs, sometimes he sits in the moonlight, and sometimes in a dark house.... He performs ablutions by mostly pouring water with his own hands... and it is seldom that a servant pours the water for him."[51] Mullah Shah wrote Jahanara a quatrain in praise of her devotion: "The light of God that shines on your face, from it opens a path to the faces of everyone. Your friends are all saints of the time. I am proud of you, the king of saints, Mulla Shah."[52] Jahanara responds with a short "courtship" poem for her pir: "If that sun-like visage becomes accessible to me I will make a claim of lordship, not just kingship. Oh Shah, come on to me like the light of the sun."[53]

Jahanara prepares food for Mullah Shah, and he returns a half-eaten naan, which she consumes with zeal; she exchanges bodily fluids with her "beloved" as a first kiss: "Knowing that sending of gifts to be a breach of form... I sent naan and *saag* cooked with my own hands along with a note.... His servant returned with a piece of naan which I consumed immediately."[54]

Jahanara's first meeting with her pir takes place in seclusion, where only she can see him and imagine that he has seen and touched her: "I saw his great beauty from a hidden place.... My great father summoned him.... From the shining light that emanated from his clear forehead... from the auspiciousness of seeing him, my belief, sincerity, and devotion increased thousand-fold.... I myself touched his skirt of felicity with my hand of devotion, and he, with affection that a perfect master has for his sincere disciples, accepted my touch."[55]

The use of Sufi hermeneutics, pir-murid dialectics, and the mystical language of passionate love and union conveys Jahanara's sacral-sexual experience as a metaphorical aid that facilitates her divine-human encounter. A homology exists between normative relations among Sufis and what Jahanara longs to have in her spiritual world and her worldly existence. The young princess will never marry or enjoy the joys of carnal love and sexual intimacy. She uses her "auto-hagiographical" text to draw correspondence from and satisfy the gap in her lived experience with divine awareness. Jahanara invokes her authorial authority in *Munis* and *Sahibiyah* to legitimize her sacral-sexual encounter and spiritual transference with both B/beloveds.

Imperial and Islamic codes of etiquette prohibited private meetings between unmarried women and men without the requisite chaperones. The *Sahibiyah* indicates two meetings with Mullah Shah; one indirectly when she visited Shah Jahan and another when she personally requested to see him en route to Kashmir. Otherwise, to make the absent pir present, his portrait was used to objectify spiritual and sexual longings: "After seeing the perfect beauty of my Hazrat outwardly, my exalted brother had given me his portrait that a master painter had painted.... I kept this portrait by me ... and continuously studied that noble portrait ... and ... I imagined his auspicious form ... as if present before me ... and it was fixed in my mind ... to meditate on and imagine the portrait of the pir."[56]

Portraits of Sufi saints and mystics were frequently commissioned by patrons and devotees to commemorate their pir as a form of respect and adoration. Portraits were also collected in imperial albums to document affiliations. Mullah Shah's portrait appears in several Mughal paintings, and it is plausible that one was commissioned by Dara Shikoh for his sister. Jahanara uses the pir's portrait as a witness to her piety (see figure 7.8). A charismatic pir had the ability to arouse intense devotion, and these formal qualities are captured in Mullah Shah's portraits. The delicate and sublime formal elements portray the pir as a benevolent, sensitive, and charismatic master who lovingly inspires devotion. Sufi treatises frequently relate how love or longing for the pir, attachment to him, and contemplation and/or visualization of him in prayer can lead to absorption or annihilation (*fana*) in God. Jahanara wrote the *Sahibiyah* when she was twenty years old, complete with the passions of a woman in her prime. It is not unreasonable to surmise that she may have redirected/diffused her intense and unrequited amorous desires and carnal longings from mortals to God through mystical conveyance and the spiritual agency of her pir. Jahanara embraced and kissed the image of Mullah Shah to activate and project her spiritual passions and carnal desires to invoke divine presence: "My beloved came easily into my arms on the nights of parting.... I was a crazed lover.... My yearning has finally rewarded me with you in embrace.... Your passion takes me in embrace and caresses me.... Every moment I am anointed by your rapture.... Oh Shah! You have finished me with one glance. Bravo to you, my Beloved, how well you showed me your gaze.... Separation is good whose end is union."[57]

The dialectic between spiritual possession and material dispossession, femininity and masculinity, the inner and outer realms, the sexual and the spiritual, are the main modalities through which Jahanara experiences and documents her mystical transcendence from a murid to a khalifa. Upon her ascension, Mullah Shah bestowed his mantle as a form of investiture: "He took off his *dupatta* (headscarf) ... and gave it to me.... I rubbed it over my eyes, lips, and chest, and then placed it on my head. I experienced immense joy.... Although it was a manifestly wondrous miracle ... God ... has gifted me with the rank of sainthood and station of kindness."[58]

FIGURE 7.8. Portrait of Mullah Shah Badakhshi, Mughal, c. 1650. The Art and History Collection, courtesy of the Arthur M. Sackler Gallery, Smithsonian Institution, LTS2002.2.4. Used by permission.

Jahanara continually links the spiritual and sexual during this pir-murid exchange. The dupatta plays the role of the pir's hand and physically touches and caresses parts of her body. Jahanara's ascension is a metaphor for sexual climax and achieving mystical intent through her divine interface with spiritual B/beloveds.

IN PARALLEL TO EMPERORS of the past and Dara Shikoh, Jahanara Begam forged and documented her alliances with powerful Sufi saints to advance her multiple agendas. The imperial protocol allowed the princess to extend her position through what Munis Faruqui has analyzed as the conduits of political, economic, religious, and social networks.[59] The particular modes that Jahanara employed to promote imperial ideology in the religious and political realms were in alignment with and specific to the polity of the princes and Mughal statecraft. This study maintains that Jahanara's contributions were in concert with the prevalent imperially sanctioned masculine modes of representation, and were used as rhetorical devices by her to advance her legitimacy and ideology, and as material vehicles of her subjectivities. The princess relied on and exploited the established social, spiritual, and political networks to support the inner workings and vital extranetworks of empire and the Mughal enterprise. The role of Sufi linkages as support for the Mughal enterprise and the maneuvers of the ruling elite in provoking a Sufi support was largely the domain of male sovereignty, and an unprecedented privilege that a Mughal princess appropriated for her subjectivity and self-representation. Jahanara's unprecedented initiatives expand the gendered princely retinue and shed light on the crucial contributions of imperial females in intradynastic partnerships to ensure empire.

Architectural Representation

THE AGRA MOSQUE

In 1640, prior to completing her two treatises and with a "spiritually heavy heart," Jahanara left the aura of Mullah Shah in Kashmir and returned to Agra, the Mughal capital. Shah Jahan's building projects in Agra were in progress, including the Taj Mahal. The court chronicler, Inayat Khan, recorded in the *Shah Jahanama* the plans to construct a large forecourt, bazaar, and congregation mosque across from the Delhi gate of the imperial fort.[60] Jahanara appealed to her father that he fund the building of the only congregation mosque in Agra, which would form a critical link between the imperial fort and the main bazaar and/or the sovereign and the subject.[61] In its manifold meanings, the essential function of the mosque and Jahanara's subjectivity as an intercessor and an extension of Shah Jahan's sovereignty are fashioned through her prominent philanthropic patronage. The commission to create a public area for prayer was the ultimate act of benevolence expected from the sovereign. The "mirror for princes" literature requires the emperor to build impressive buildings to legitimize and assert imperial powers and to exhibit compassion for his subjects.

The Agra mosque is a standard "Shahjahani" archetype and well-established imperial idiom that integrates Timurid-Persian design and details with indigenous iconography and craftsmanship.[62] The Shahjahani style is one of the emperor's physical strategies to cultivate an official imperial typology that objectified his sovereignty and governance. Two design elements in particular, in the Agra Mosque, convey the sovereign's subjectivity and are employed in their modified form. The Shahjahani baluster column has a rectangular, or round, shaft from which emerge an organic mass of acanthus leaves up and along the column, changing into rhythmically arranged striations that culminate at the capital in an arrangement of leaves. The organic nature and vitality of the baluster column became an intrinsic part of the imperial vocabulary and also represented the emperor and the munificence of his rule that promoted "growth, fecundity and well-being."[63] The balusters represent the emperor's support and strength for empire and his subjects. The column is a perfect balance of organic and rigid elements and conveys the desirable warrior-aesthete characteristics for a just and exemplary sovereign. The oblong prayer hall is entered through a central Persianized *pishtaq* (high portal) surmounted by three domes (see figure 7.2). The courtyard entrance is on axis to the pishtaq and extends thirty meters.

Jahanara's structured and inscribed subjectivity in the format of the mosque and the verses framing the pishtaq were unprecedented features in mosque architecture. The Persian eulogies prominently praise the details of the mosque as the person of the princess: "It [the Jami Masjid] was built by her order who is high in dignity, who is as elevated as the firmament on which it sits, screened with curtains bright as the sun, possessing a glorious palace as illuminated as her wisdom, veiled with chastity, the most revered of the ladies of the age, the pride of her gender, the princess of the realm, the possessor of the three domes as worldly crowns, the chosen of the people of the world, the most honored of the issue of the head of the Faithful, Jahanara Begam."[64] The eulogy ends with Jahanara Begam's name prominently displayed on the apex of the arch, alongside Emperor Shah Jahan. The encomiums that follow her name start with the emperor's name and are viewed equally, in structure, subjectivity, and authority.

The Agra mosque inscriptions include seven of the eleven kingly virtues listed in Qandhari's *Tarik-i Akbari*: piety, authority, judgment, wisdom, public works, building achievements, and good fortunes. The laudatory verses and virtues are woven, metaphorically, into the mosque's features and emerge as Jahanara's synecdoche in a public, spiritual, and politicized context, due to the Red Fort's proximity and linkage to the mosque. The dialectic of verse and structure projects Jahanara's body politic and persona and creates a symbiotic relationship of patron, place, and patronage. The princess's name is not merely inscribed but profusely eulogized on the congregation mosque of the capital city and seat of government. The encomiums make transparent the imperial female's characteristics in a public space. They uphold her as a spiritual and imperial exemplar among women and as a counterweight to Shah Jahan's kingship.

Inscriptions on Mughal mosques were regulated by the Muslim scholars and played a sociopolitical role in conveying the sovereign's religious policies and attitudes and the allegories of his rule.[65] The self as narrative subjectivity records and projects Jahanara's persona in the built landscape and is aligned with that of sovereignty and empire. A congregation mosque commission was an imperial male privilege and underscored the patrons' religiosity and philanthropy. The Agra mosque is attributed to Jahanara's largesse and therefore is an appropriated masculinized mode of subjectivity. Conventional Mughal standards for mosque epigraphy were complete *surah*s or individual chapters from the Qur'an. Persian encomiums on the pishtaq of the Agra mosque were unprecedented and distinguished the princess's patronage and persona as inextricable to the sovereign's subjectivity.

THE MULLAH SHAH BADAKHSHI COMPLEX

In 1650, Jahanara commissioned the Mullah Shah Badakhshi (see figures 7.3 and 7.4) complex, located in Srinagar, Kashmir. It included a mosque and residential quarters (*khanaqah*) for Sufi masters, disciples, and students. Drawing on the newly articulated epi/biographical idioms in Agra, Jahanara applied the fullest expression of her nuanced personal piety in the Mughal provincial stronghold by commissioning a spiritual retreat dedicated to her pir. The mosque is a modified Shahjahani plan and includes the imperial idioms: baluster columns, multicusped arches, a centralized pishtaq, and a high-relief panel with a distinctive modified *bangla* (canopy) form. To complement the organic

FIGURE 7.9. Bangla projection in qibla wall and mihrab, Mullah Shah Badakhshi Mosque. Photo by author.

and leafy characteristics of the baluster column, a Shahjahani floriated multicusped arch was added to the imperial repertoire. On the western elevation is the projection of a bangla form emerging from the *mihrab* on the *qibla* wall (see figure 7.9).

The Bengali curved bangla roof form was appropriated by Shah Jahan and translated as the square-edged *jharoka*. The form was strategically implemented and used to frame the emperor's privileged position high above his public audience and frequently captured in paintings.[66] Shah Jahan always appeared under the jharoka balcony in a formal setting with members of his retinue. The baldachin was highly visible, and the consistency of the emperor's appearance framed by the jharoka made direct associations of the form as the sovereign's subjectivity, particularly in absentia. The jharoka was intrinsic to Shah Jahan's imperial ideology and propaganda, where architecture and structure were used in the service of sovereignty and *as* the emperor himself. In the Mullah Shah complex, the jharoka/bangla feature is a "visual quotation," however divorced from its explicit imperial function. The resilient patterns and performativity of sovereignty appearing in public under the jharoka is recalled by the high-relief form and is concomitant to Jahanara's patronage. The overall design conveys

FIGURE 7.10. Band of Persian poetry over blind arches, north exterior elevation of Mullah Shah Badakhshi Mosque. Photo by author.

FIGURE 7.11. *Prince Dara Shikoh with Sages and Sufi Saints in Garden Pavilion*, c. 1649–50, Chester Beatty Library. CBL In 07A.7, "Dara Shikoh and Sages in Garden Pavilion." Used by permission.

Shahjahani semiotics and imperial idioms and is perceived as the sovereign's benevolence and distant/provincial reach of altruism in the hinterlands through Jahanara's agency. The complex is distinctive due to its primary function as a khanaqah and not a pure mosque. The Mullah Shah and the Ghaziu'd-Din (Delhi College) khanaqahs are the only two of their kind in India.[67]

Four bands of Persian poetry are inscribed in the paneled arches on the exterior elevation of the mosque that rises above the Kashmir valley and Dal Lake below. The siting of the complex replicated the Shahjahani riverfront design scheme with vistas to a valley below and a distant lake. The riverfront was an imported exclusive-use, Persian feature that restructured the Timurid-Mughal conquered territory of India and distinguished sovereignty from the subject. The support brackets on the elevation indicate the support of a (now missing) terraced pavilion below the verses. Terraces and garden pavilions hosted religious debates among mystics, religious leaders, imperials, and disciples. The panel verses above the spiritual discussions are in a parenthetical relationship to the mystical musings of the discussants and the patron's inscribed self as narrative and subjectivity. Based on the stylistic composition of each verse, Shah Jahan's court poet Abu Talib Kalim (d. 1650) may be the author.[68] A complete translation of the verses is challenging because of the panel's ruinous state; however, the following verses are intact: "The guide for the lost heart has come. The conquest of the hearts is all in His hands. The Beloved, to fill the goblet has come. This is the second Mecca. For circumambulation the enlightened King has come. The chronogram from God has come" (see figures 7.10 and 7.11).[69]

During the Timurid era, Persian poetry was frequently inscribed on sacred monuments within well-defined borders in large *thuluth* script. This convention increased under the Safavids' patronage. Poetry reached literary and aesthetic heights during Shah Jahan's reign and the metacreative poetry-architecture dialectic functioned as an instrument of imperial ideology and sociopolitical messages.[70] Persian poetry translated Jahanara's piety into the discursive realm of Sufi ideology and her religiosity. The abstract language of love in the poetic verses inextricably links Jahanara's relationship with Mullah Shah as both her "beloved" and pir. The panels exalt the spiritual attributes of the pir and, by proxy, Jahanara.

JAHANARA'S MAUSOLEUM

Jahanara was laid to rest in 1681 in an enclosure with mystically informed design details that remained faithful to Sufi conventions of modesty. The princess is buried under a raised cenotaph in a small, open-air, ninety-square-foot,

FIGURE 7.12. Jahanara Begam's tomb, seventeenth century, Nizamuddin, Delhi. Photo by author.

marble-latticed grave enclosure across from the *dargah* of Delhi's beloved Sufi saint Nizam al-Din Awliya (d. 1325). The Sufi-sovereign pact and inextricable sociopolitical and spiritual codependency is indicated by the proximity of Jahanara, and twenty-six years later Aurangzeb's grave, to the dargah of notable Sufi saints. Jahanara's tomb precinct is made of white marble, the imperial and mystical funerary uniform. The simplicity of the grave departs from the lavish Taj Mahal tomb mausoleum and is indicative of the Sunni modesty that informed Aurangzeb's ideology and rule. The inscriptions on the grave marker are the Sufi princess's authorship: "Let nothing cover my tomb save the green grass, for grass suffices well as a covering for the grave of the *faqira* (lowly/impoverished one)."[71] Faqira is frequently used in her treatises as a form of self-effacing Sufi modesty and to excuse her bold authorial authority. The faqira, humbled by abject poverty, articulates the submissive modality of her sovereign/subject and pir/murid roles. The verses eulogize Jahanara's khalifa status, and the stark, white, unadorned tomb precinct projects the highest level of mystical intent: *fana*, or annihilation that allows the pure, liberated, enlightened self to emerge (see figure 7.12).

FIGURE 7.13. Aurangzeb's tomb enclosure, eighteenth century, Aurangabad. Photo by author.

Aurangzeb's reign is laced with Sunni conventions of Islam and grounded his modesty, authority, and imperial image and exemplified the shifting perceptions of the sovereign's subjectivity. Aurangzeb's remains are interred in a humble open-air grave that is identical to Jahanara's, and he also is buried near a Sufi pir, Sayyid Zayn al-Din (see figure 7.13). His preference for simplicity in his life may have been influenced by his orthodox Sunni proclivities or Sufi allegiances. The epitaph, like Jahanara's reads: "No marble sheets should shield me from the sky as I lie here one with the earth." The tomb remains open to the sky and the compact marble lattice enclosure is covered with only cloth sheets. The grand-scale display of imperial power and the sovereign's subjectivity that was used to index, gauge, and sustain the Mughal Empire was not on Aurangzeb's agenda. Aurangzeb managed the waning Mughal empire at its most basic and quotidian level, unlike the formal imperial schemes, ethos, visions, and concepts executed by Shah Jahan and his consort queen, Jahanara Begam. The Mughal domains, once indexed through monumental designs and embellished auto/biographies, waned with the flickering light of the Timuria at the close of Aurangzeb's reign.

Conclusion

The masculine modes of Jahanara's subjectivity, expressed through her first-person historicized narratives as forms of history writing in her two Sufi treatises and her prominent mosque and khanaqah commissions, successfully promoted the self, emperor, and empire through the appropriated "image" or subjectivity of the male sovereign merged with perceptions and conceptions of Jahanara's social and spiritual personas. *Munis al-arvah* and *Risalah-i Sahibiyah* are nuanced forms of autobiography/hagiography with narratives of self. The Agra mosque and the Mullah Shah Badakhshi khanaqah complex are structural "narratives" of her imperial and spiritual subjectivity and interiority modeled on prevailing Mughal masculine modes. Jahanara's writing and patronage of prominent philanthropic commissions preserve and perpetuate the imperial enterprise, but most important, the princess wrote herself into the Timurid-Mughal patrilineal history and imperially sponsored spirituality. Imperial women indirectly grafted their blood lines through dynastic (male) reproduction but did not directly promote the self within the Mughal framework, making Jahanara's pronouncements exceptions to the rule. The princess's ascendancy and her role as the consort queen encouraged and pressured her to seek alternative means to proclaim her subjectivity and to negotiate her role in the imperial apparatus.

The mystically informed intertextuality of the treatises and Jahanara's prominent commissions laced with imperially coded architectural features document and project her imperial and spiritual authority and employ the resilient patterns used by Mughal males to assert and legitimize their kingship, governance, and empire. Jahanara uses mystical language to sanction and stage her autobiographical narratives and articulates the specificity of her mystical descriptions and promotes the Sufi-sovereign dynamic that supports and perpetuates Mughal rule. The *Risalah* is influenced by Mughal emperors' auto/biographies and "mirror for princes" literature.[72] Jahanara Begam's recordings are brief textual moments narrated in the mystically informed spaces of her Sufi treatises as forms of counsel for good governance, and also itemize the stable, heroic, and benevolent characteristics of Emperor Shah Jahan and his heir-apparent, Dara Shikoh.

The very act of writing the narrative self into history aligns Jahanara's treatises with the autobiographies of past Timurid and Mughal emperors and allows her pen to personalize the narratives of empire through which she and the composite self emerge and converge with sovereign's subjectivity. Jahanara's writings follow Timurid patterns of legitimizing sovereign authority and include reflections of her lived and imagined personal and spiritual experiences, articulation of authority, and subjectivity that is grounded in specific historical moments during Shah Jahan's reign. In the *Sahibiyah*, Jahanara legitimizes Dara Shikoh's imperial accession by including the requisite details and particular aspects of his emotional character and physical strengths. The *Sahibiyah* includes acts of valor, military triumphs, benevolence, kindness, and spiritual affinities. Both treatises employ Sufi semantics and mystical language to record Jahanara's personal and public history, and through this framework we gain access to an understanding of the interstices of Mughal life and the fashioning of the princess's subjectivity.

As time, space, and patrilineal links to Timurid ancestors became dislocated and weak, Jahanara "lights the lamp of the Timuria" and illuminates Shah Jahan's farr-i zadi. This act links them to their Timurid heritage and locates the subjectivity of the Sufi princess's sovereignty at the center of this privilege.[73]

Jahanara used first-person narratives in the *Sahibiyah* to enlist her sacred and secular autobiographical narratives within the Mughal historiographies that align her authorial self with her imperial male counterparts. The *Sahibiyah* represents a princess and not an emperor; the text forms a major subset within the broader category of historical writing that conveys a nuanced and textured understanding of the imperial and spiritual landscape and the place of women in this male-dominated category. In comparison, the emperors' namas are quantifiable and/or chronological details and entities of state administration and imperial ethos. The *Sahibiyah*'s authorship, format, and transparency indicate the nuanced, textured, and changing nature of the imperial convention of first-person narratives within the Mughal Empire, imperial ideology, and the expansive nature of sovereignty.

NOTES

1 'Abd al-Hamid Lahawri, *The Badshah Namah*, vol. 1, ed. Kabir al-Din Ahmad and 'Abd al-Rahim (Calcutta: Bibliotheca Indica, 1867–68), 384.
2 On Jahanara's life, see Nausheen Jaffrey, "Jahanara Begam: A Biographical Study 1614–81 A.D.," (MPhil diss., Jamia Millia Islamia University, 1997).
3 For non-Western autobiographies in postcolonial contexts, see Afsaneh Najmabadi, *Women's Autobiographies in Contemporary Iran* (Cambridge, MA: Harvard University Press, 1990); Dwight F. Reynolds, ed., *Interpreting the Self: Autobiography in the Arabic Literary Tradition* (Berkeley: University of California Press, 2001); David Arnold and Stuart Blackburn, *Telling Lives in India: Biography, Autobiography, and Life History* (Delhi: Permanent Black, 2004); and James Olney, *Memory and Narrative: The Weave of Life Writing* (Chicago: University of Chicago Press, 1999).
4 Ellison Banks Findley speaks of Nur Jahan's "matronage" of various monuments, but specifically the Serai Nur Mahal in Jullundur as an expression of her sense of

herself. See her "Women's Wealth and Styles of Giving: Perspectives from Buddhist, Jain, and Mughal Sites in D. Fairchild Ruggles, *Women, Patronage and Self-Representation in Islamic Societies* (Albany: State University of New York Press, 2000), 92.

5   Sidonie Smith and Julia Watson, *Reading Autobiography: A Guide for Interpreting Life Narratives* (Minneapolis: University of Minnesota Press, 2001), 262.

6   The Sufi-Mughal/Timurid dynamics and the Naqshbandi relationship are discussed in S. A. A. Rizvi, "Sixteenth Century Naqshbandiyya Leadership in India," in Marc Gaborieau, Alexandre Popovic, and Thierry Zarcone, eds., *Naqshbandis: Historical Development and Present Situation of a Muslim Mystical Order* (Istanbul: Institut Francais d'Etudes Anatoliennes d'Istanbul, 1990), 153–65; Stephen F. Dale, "The Legacy of the Timurids," *Journal of the Royal Asiatic Society*, 3rd series, 8.1 (1998): 43–58; and Arthur F. Buehler, "The Naqshbandiyya in Timurid India: The Central Asian Legacy," *Journal of Islamic Studies* 7.2 (1996): 209–28; K. A. Nizami, "Naqshbandi Influence on Mughal Rulers and Politics," *Islamic Culture* 39 (1965): 41–52.

7   Among Dara Shikoh's works are *Safīnat al-awliyā'* [Anthology of Sufi saints] (1639); *Sakīnat al-awliyā'* [The peace of the saints] (1640–43), a hagiography of the Qadri saint Miyan Jiv, which includes a short biography of the saint's devout sister, Bibi Jamal Khatun. See Muḥammad Dārā Shikūh, *Sakīnat al-awliyā'*, trans. Carl W. Ernst, in *Religions of India in Practice*, ed. Donald S. Lopez Jr. (Princeton, NJ: Princeton University Press, 1995), 509–12; and *Majma-ul-Bahrain* [The mingling of two oceans—Comparing Hindu and Islamic mysticism] (1643).

8   Abu Fazl (1551–1602) refers to Akbar as the "glory of the Gurgan (Timur's) family" and the "lamp of the tribe of Timur." Abu Fazl b. Mubārak (1551–1602), *Akbarnāma*, translated from the Persian by H. Beveridge (Calcutta: Asiatic Society, 1897).

9   *Farr-i izadi* is a Zoroastrian/Persian concept of a manifestation of the sacred element of fire/light in the person of the ruler. Mosque lamps are perceived to "visualize" God in a religious setting. Ebba Koch, ed., *Mughal Art and Imperial Ideology: Collected Essays* (New Delhi: Oxford University Press, 2001), 174.

10 Taymiya Zaman's dissertation details the reasons for Aurangzeb not sponsoring his biography. "Inscribing Empire: Sovereignty and Subjectivity in Mughal Memoirs" (PhD diss., University of Michigan, 2007).

11 See Yazdi Sharafuddin Ali, "Zafarnama," in *A Century of Princes: Sources on Timurid History and Art*, trans. W. M. Thackston (Cambridge, MA: Aga Khan Program for Islamic Architecture, 1989), 63–101.

12 Wheeler M. Thackston, trans., ed., and annotator, *The Baburnama: Memoirs of Babur, Prince and Emperor* (New York: Modern Library, 2002).

13 Zaman, "Inscribing Empire," 124–31.

14 This album is a collection of paintings and calligraphy assembled during the 1630s by Dara Shikoh, the eldest son of the emperor Shah Jahan, and presented to his wife, Nadira Banu Begam in 1641–42. British Library Add. Or. MS 3129.

15 Jahanara's two treatises, the *Risala* and the *Munis*, were written between 1640 and 1643, when Dara Shikoh also wrote his Sufi manuscripts.

16 Jahān Ārā Begam (d. 1681), *Munis al-Arvāh* (Persian) 1048/1639 (Bodleian Library, "Ms. Fraser 229," University of Oxford.
17 See John F. Richards, *The Mughal Empire* (Cambridge: Cambridge University Press, 1993).
18 A *kulliyat* is a compilation of moralistic lessons on appropriate behavior. J. P. Losty and Malini Roy, *Mughal India, Art, Culture and Empire* (London: British Library, 2012), 113–14.
19 Hamid Algar, "A Brief History of the Naqshbandi Order" and "Political Aspects of Naqshbandi History," in Gaborieau et al., *Naqshbandis*, 3–44 and 123–52.
20 Muzaffar Alam, "The Mughals, the Sufi Shaikhs and the Formation of the Akbari Dispensation," *Modern Asian Studies* 43.1 (January 2009): 138.
21 Koch, *Mughal Art*.
22 The mystical tradition was brought to India by Khwajah Moinuddin Chishti in the twelfth century. The Chishtiyah gained prominence during Emperor Akbar's rule (1540–1605) and became intrinsic to Mughal imperial ideology. See J. F. Richards, "The Formulation of Imperial Authority under Akbar and Jahangir," in *Kingship and Authority in South Asia*, ed. J. F. Richards (Delhi: Oxford University Press, 1988), 252–85; and D. E. Streusand, *The Formation of the Mughal Empire* (Delhi: Oxford University Press, 1989), 89–91.
23 Koch, *Mughal Art*, 176.
24 Nuruddin Muhammad Jahangir, *Tuzuk-i Jahangiri*, trans. H. Beveridge (Delhi, 1989), 1: 2.
25 A *pir* (usually male—women were not conferred this revered status) is a Sufi master who is well-versed in the philosophy of his particular order. A pir guides and counsels others on the Sufi path. However, women who did become pirs through observance of Sufi doctrines would informally earn the status of *pir-murid* (master-disciple). See Kelly Pemberton, "Muslim Women Mystics and Female Spiritual Authority in South Asian Sufism," in Pamela J. Stewart and Andrew Strathern, eds., *Contesting Rituals: Islam and Practices of Identity-Making* (Durham, NC: Carolina Academic Press, 2005), 3–39. Though the term *piri-muridi* is not used in the context of Sufism before the twentieth century, I have classified Jahanara's spiritual persona in this way to facilitate discussion and to distinguish her rank within the Qadiriyah order.
26 Kishwar Rizvi, "Gendered Patronage: Women and Benevolence during the Early Safavid Empire," in *Women, Patronage, and Self-Representation in Islamic Societies*, ed. D. Fairchild Ruggles (Albany: State University of New York Press, 2000), 123–53.
27 On the Ajmer shrine complex, see Syed Liyaqat Hussain, *The Chishti Shrine of Ajmer: Pirs, Pilgrims, Practices* (Jaipur: Publication Scheme, 2004).
28 Hasrat Bikrama Jit, *Dārā Shikūh: Life and Works* (New Delhi: Munshiram Manoharlal, 1982), 28.
29 Jahanara Begam, *Risalah-i Sahibiyah*, 15–16. This analysis relies on an unpublished translation of the *Risalah-i Sahibiyah* by Dr. Sunil Sharma. An annotated translation is planned as Afshan Bokhari, *Mughals and Mystics: A Sufi Princess; Jahan*

Ara Begam (1613–1681) (Louisville, KY: Fons Vitae, forthcoming). Several translated and original copies of Jahan Ara Begum's *Risalah-i Sahibiyah* (1640–41) Sufi manuscript have been consulted for this study. The original Persian manuscript has been cited in the Apa Rao Bhola Nath Library at Ahmadabad (India). The author was unable to locate this document in the library's holdings. See citation in the bibliography of Qamar Jahan Ali in her published PhD dissertation (Aligarh Muslim University, Department of Persian): *Princess Jahan Ara Begam: her life and works* (1950), published by S. M. Hamid Ali in Karachi, 1991. A typed Persian copy of the original manuscript was published by Professor Muhammad Aslam in the *Journal of Research Society of Pakistan*, 16/4 and 17/1; an Urdu translation of the original was published by Professor Tanvir Alvi in *Nava-yi-adab*, October 1986 (*Anjuman-i-Islam* Urdu Research Institute of Bombay, India), 34–51. An unpublished English translation of Alvi's Urdu work was completed by Dr. Yunus Jaffrey and Afshan Bokhari in Delhi, January 2007, and an unpublished English translation of Aslam's Persian copy was completed by Dr. Sunil Sharma in Cambridge, MA, 2007.

30 The Qadiriyah order, considered the earliest of the formal Sufi orders and based primarily on the principles of the *shari'ah*, was founded by the Hanbali theologian 'Abd al-Qadir al-Jilani (1078–1162) in Baghdad. On the Qadiriyah order, see Arthur Buehler, "The Indo-Pak Qadiriyya," *Journal of the History of Sufism* 1–2 (2000): 339–60; and Fatima Bilgrami, *History of the Qadiri Order in India during 16th–18th Century* (Delhi: Jayed Press, 2005).

31 Jahanara Begam, *Risalah*, 8.

32 Dale, "The Legacy of the Timurids," 46; Stanley Lane Poole, *The Coins of the Moghul Emperors of Hindustan in the British Museum* (New Delhi: Inter-India Publications, 1983), 104.

33 Jahanara Begam, *Risalah*, 10.

34 Jahanara Begam, *Risalah*, 11.

35 Jahanara Begam, *Risalah*, 12.

36 Richards, *The Mughal Empire*, 40. Also Iqtidar Ali Khan, "The Nobility under Akbar and the Development of His Religious Policy 1560–1580," *Journal of the Royal Asiatic Society* 1 (1968): 29–36. The term *khalifa* was used to refer to the Prophet Muhammad and his spiritual authority. After the prophet's death, the leaders of Muslim lands became known as *khalifa*s (caliphs, the institution, the caliphate); the office represented both spiritual and political authority.

37 Jahanara Begam, *Risalah*, 15.

38 Jahanara Begam, *Risalah*, 16.

39 The best-known "mirrors for princes" precedent for Timurid works may have been the eleventh-century *Siyasat-nama* written by Nizam al-Mulk, a minister working under the Seljuks.

40 The Safavid dynasty ruled from 1501 to 1722, and at the height of their power, they controlled all of modern Iran, which included the Timurid state. Sholeh Quinn, "Through the Looking Glass: Kingly Virtues in Safavid and Mughal Historiography," *Journal of Persianate Studies* 3 (2010): 150–51.

41 Abu'l Fazl ibn Allami, *The A'in-I Akbari by Abul Fazl 'Allami*, vol. 3, trans. H. Beveridge (Calcutta: Asiatic Society, 1897–1939), 345–47.
42 Anne-Marie Schimmel, *The Empire of the Great Mughals: History, Art and Culture*, trans. C. Attwood (New Delhi: Oxford University Press, 2005), 36–37.
43 Jahanara Begam, *Munis*, 18. This analysis relies on an unpublished translation of the *Munis al-arvah* completed by the author under the guidance of Sunil Sharma.
44 Tawakkul Beg, *Nuskhah-i Ahwal-i Shahi*, MS British Museum, 3203, Rotograph (No. 138), 1667.
45 Tawakkul Beg, *Nuskhah-i Ahwal-i Shahi*, fol. 32.
46 Quinn, "Through the Looking Glass," 144–46.
47 Jahanara Begam, *Risalah*, 15–16.
48 *Padshahnama*, 2: 292; *Shahjahannama*, 293; *Amal-i Saleh*, 2: 302.
49 Jahanara Begam, *Risalah*, 14.
50 Jahanara Begam, *Risalah*, 18.
51 Jahanara Begam, *Risalah*, 10.
52 Jahanara Begam, *Risalah*, 22.
53 Jahanara Begam, *Risalah*, 21.
54 Jahanara Begam, *Risalah*, 22.
55 Jahanara Begam, *Risalah*, 22.
56 Jahanara Begam, *Risalah*, 16.
57 Jahanara Begam, *Risalah*, 23.
58 Jahanara Begam, *Risalah*, 28.
59 Munis D. Faruqui, *The Princes of the Mughal Empire, 1504–1719* (Cambridge: Cambridge University Press, 2012), 134–80.
60 W. E. Begley and Z. A. Desai, eds. and trans., *The Shah Jahan Nama of 'Inayat Khan* (Delhi: Oxford University Press, 1990), 205–6.
61 Begley and Desai, *The Shah Jahan Nama*, 205.
62 Koch, *Mughal Architecture*, 54.
63 Ebba Koch, "The Baluster Column: A European Motif in Mughal Architecture and Its Meaning," *Journal of the Warburg and Courtauld Institutes* 45 (1982): 251–62.
64 Muhammad Latif, *Agra: Historical and Descriptive* (Calcutta: Oriental Publishers, 1896), 186–88. I have relied on Latif's Persian text of the *pishtaq* inscriptions on the Agra mosque and compared these to my English translation. This translation was completed in December 2006 with the invaluable assistance of Dr. Yunus Jaffrey in Delhi.
65 Wayne E. Begley, "The Symbolic Role of Calligraphy on Three Imperial Mosques of Shah Jahan," in *American Studies in the Art of India*, ed. Joanna G. Williams (New Delhi: Oxford University Press, 1981), 7–18.
66 Ebba Koch, "Shah Jahan and Orpheus: The Pietra Dure Decoration and the Programme of the Throne in the Hall of Public Audiences at the Red Fort of Delhi" in Koch, *Mughal Art and Imperial Ideology*, 66–70.
67 On the Ghaziu'd-Din complex, see Margrit Pernau, *The Delhi College, Traditional Elites, the Colonial State and Education before 1837* (New Delhi: Oxford University Press, 2006), 1–58.

68 A comprehensive analysis of the Persian poetic verses from the exterior of Mullah Shah Mosque with Dr. Sunil Sharma in Cambridge, MA, in December 2006, and with Dr. Yunus Jaffrey in Delhi in January 2007, confirmed the court poet Abu Talib Kalim as the likely author of the inscriptions. Thackston's dissertation provided supporting literary evidence that further identifies Kalim as present in Kashmir in the late 1640s. See Wheeler Thackston for an analysis of Kalim's work, "The Poetry of Abú-Tálib Kalim: Persian Poet-Laureate of Shahjahan, Mughal Emperor of India," PhD diss., Harvard University, 1974.
69 Translation of stone panels by Afshan Bokhari under the guidance of Sunil Sharma.
70 Sunil Sharma, "Celebrating Writing and Books in Safavid and Mughal Court Poetry," in *Écrit et culture en Asie centrale et dans le monde turco-iranien, XIVe–XIXe siècles*, eds. Francis Richard and Maria Szuppe (Paris: Association pour l'Avancement des Études Iraniennes, 2008), 12–13.
71 Z. A. Hasan, *Guide to Nizam-ud Din, Memoirs of the Archaeological Survey of India Office*. Issue: 10 (Calcutta: Archaeological Survey of India, 1922), 16.
72 Sajida Sultan Alvi, A*dvice on the Art of Governance: An Indo-Islamic Mirror for Princes* (Albany: State University of New York Press, 1989), and Ann K. S. Lambton, "Islamic Mirrors for Princes," in *Theory and Practice in Medieval Persian Government*, ed. Ann K. S. Lambton (London: Variorum, 1980), 6: 419–42.
73 Zaman, "Inscribing Empire," vii.

PART III. **DESTABILIZING THE NORMATIVE**
The Heterogeneous Self

8. PERFORMING A PERSONA

Reading Piro's *Kafis*

ANSHU MALHOTRA

We will go to a foreign land, friends, far away from Turaks and Hindus
We will sacrifice the doctrine of the Hindus, nor keep anything of the Turaks
Where neither Hindus nor Turaks can reach, friends let us reach such a place
Piro says sitting on Ram's window [*Ram jharokre*] we'll dance [*mujra*] away the norms of the clan and the world.
—SIHARFI PIRO JI LIKHAYTE, in Sant Vijendra Das, Sant Kavyitri Ma Piro

....

This chapter focuses on Piro's *Ik Sau Sath Kafian* (160 *Kafis*)[1] to understand what it was the author was attempting to accomplish through its composition, and make sense of the themes she explores and the obsessions she displays in its pages. Piro (d. 1872) was self-confessedly a prostitute, and a Muslim, who came to live around the 1830s in the Gulabdasi *dera* (establishment) of Guru Gulabdas (1809–1873) in Chathianwala, near Lahore. The Gulabdasis were a marginal "Sikh" sect, who were significant enough, nevertheless, to find a mention in both an important "vernacular" history of the Sikhs compiled toward the end of the nineteenth century, the *Panth Prakash* of Giani Gian Singh,[2] and in various colonial ethnographies of Punjab. The Punjabi verse with which this chapter opens captures the themes played out repeatedly in Piro's *160 Kafis*. These included fulminations against the empty religiosity of the guardians of the Hindu and the Islamic faiths; her disclaimers of belonging to either of the two religious configurations while simultaneously giving them primacy in social life; the acknowledgment of her background in prostitution, apparent here in the evocation of the dance form *mujra* associated with courtesans; and her recourse to a complex of ideas associated with the Bhakti movement, with Ram as a favored god.

The *160 Kafis* is not the usual compilation of philosophical ruminations, homilies on moral living, or advice on adopting an uncluttered life of devotion that one may expect from a text produced in a religious establishment, and one that purportedly borrows from Bhakti, and even Sufi ethics. It is a text constructed with a specific and limited agenda—to elucidate Piro's move from a brothel to a religious establishment, and lay to rest the misgivings of those opposed to it. The process of its composition may have helped Piro understand and digest what she made of her unusual move. It also allowed her to explain, justify, and popularize her version of the events, besides scotching the egregious rumors that followed in the wake of her unprecedented move that not only touched her, but cast aspersions on her guru. The personal tone of Piro's *160 Kafis* can be further gleaned from her preoccupation with noting, indeed emphasizing, the acrimonious relations between "Hindus" (inclusive of Sikhs) and "Turaks," a theme around which she frames her own story of flight and asylum. This chapter attempts mainly to study this "autobiographical" content of Piro's *Kafis*, while commenting on the literary and rhetorical strategies she adopts to narrate her tale, and highlight the cultural and historical repertoire she mines to do so.

At a first glance, Piro's angst-ridden *160 Kafis* appears to appositely occupy the cultural threshold to the colonial world in a temporal and historical congruence. Piro and Gulabdas's time straddled the precolonial and colonial eras of Punjab, a region that witnessed full-scale colonization only from 1849. The *160 Kafis* ostensibly anticipates the social and cultural change one has come to associate with the Punjabi society of the mature Raj—the assertion of separate and "pure" religious identities of "Hindus," "Sikhs," and "Muslims" that eschewed porous "fuzziness" of communities. The 1870s in Punjab, the decade that saw Piro's demise, was a period of enormous turmoil, when foundations were laid for new identity-based politics. Piro's foregrounding of the apparently hostile relations between Hindus and Muslims suggests her work to be a harbinger of the time to come. Yet this remains a superficial reading of her oeuvre. The essay delves on Piro's (and Gulabdasis') debt to cultural practices and mental habits that belonged to an earlier episteme. This was a time free of neither religious conflict nor the promotion of certain identity markers, but one in which sharply etched exclusive group identities were rarely sought, and life could be lived in the intersections of various exclusionary orders. For Piro this meant adapting and intersecting Bhakti, Sikh, and Sufi inheritance to her own existential needs at one level, and sifting them for her philosophical contemplations on the other, even while being aware of the specificities of her own sect's theological predilections.

Piro's mental cosmos in many ways is in fact best described as "premodern." This means not only that her manner of negotiating the apparent cleavages between Hindus, Muslims, and Sikhs was substantially different from the "communal" polemics that came to dominate the late nineteenth century in Punjab, but that the concept also has to be understood in the context of her literary output. Piro's *160 Kafis* showed a world free of modern obsessions with autonomy and originality. Here the process of creativity unfolded through negotiation with earlier literatures, forms, and themes, a process of "reflexivity" and "intertextuality" that A. K. Ramanujan has familiarized us with.[3] Such engagements did not preclude innovation. Piro's crafting of her own story through other well-loved ones demonstrates that. Piro's moment of self-appraisal then has to be located in a universe comprehended through emulation, allegory, and allusion.[4]

The "autobiographical" content of the *160 Kafis* merits further comment. Though the poetic insertion of the "self" in the signature line of various literary genres is common, one rarely encounters in premodern literatures an attempt at narrating one's own story. As mentioned, the *160 Kafis* was written to justify an extraordinary train of events in Piro's life; in other words, it speaks of an "autobiographical moment" that was transformative. Since Piro wrote it in retrospect, that is, after the events she describes had occurred, *if they happened at all*, self-fashioning and self-representation are important aspects of it. The employing of a term like *autobiographical* to describe the *160 Kafis* is done with a caveat, for Piro did not have the impulse to lay bare her whole life. It was only a particular set of events she went through and experienced, or her hope of gaining something by putting her version of events, real or imaginary, in the realm of the society that mattered to her, that compelled her to put them down in writing. It is tempting to use a metaphor that Piro often deployed to describe her motivation, following a long literary tradition in Bhakti poetry, of "crossing over," the making of a boundary transaction to gain the inward eye. The spiritual quest for crossing over from the mundane to the transcendent, when encountered in quotidian life, pushed Piro to capture its momentousness and organize its meaning.

Piro's *160 Kafis* is a text available easily today as multiple print versions have surfaced in recent years in both Gurmukhi and Devnagari scripts, attesting to her growing popularity.⁵ The literary-minded Gulabdasis preserved handwritten manuscripts of her works, one of which was consulted by this scholar. This manuscript, unembellished in appearance and displaying ordinary scribal skills, may indicate Piro to be just another member of her sect. Her importance in her sect, however, is underscored by the fact that her works are preserved along with those of her guru in a single, revered book as seen by this author in a contemporary branch of her sect in Haryana.⁶ It is more difficult to speculate on the circulation of her text(s) in her own time. The justificatory tone of her *160 Kafis* minimally indicates that it was circulated among her peers, the guru's disciples, as probably among other kindred sects of the time, as Piro eased her way into the Gulabdasi establishment. I have also suggested in this chapter that Piro in her former life as a courtesan may have been on the periphery of Lahore's courtly life, and it is possible that the text circulated in those circles as well.⁷

The chapter is divided into four parts. The first deals with why Piro's sojourn from prostitution to a life of contemplation may have been perceived as scandalous by her contemporaries. It discusses the many counts on which her move was seen as transgressive and suggests that the cumulative effect of her various indiscretions may have made her desperate to end her isolation by seeking a secure place for herself in the *dera* of Gulabdas. The second section comments on Piro's use of the genre of kafis and goes on to recapitulate the overt story Piro embarks on in her *160 Kafis*. Her personal trauma and her relating of the charges of apostasy made against her by her former coreligionists are placed in the regional framework that helps us grasp their significance. In the third part Piro's impersonation of Sita, the heroine of the epic Ramayana is discussed—its import highlighted for her, for the community that provides her a refuge, and for the one that apparently maltreats her. Piro's silences and subtle hints on the life of prostitution are also examined. The last section treats the religious differences that animate Piro's text, raising the question if we should see them as reflecting the vituperations of her age. The context in which Piro's utterances may be viewed is sketched, and her debt to the Bhakti and Sufi heritage of her sect is explicated.

Courting a Scandal

The borders that Piro may have "violated," despite some degree of opposition, were many. The late nineteenth-century source—Giani Gian Singh's *Panth Prakash*—highlighted some. He referred to Piro as a *kasbi* (prostitute) and a *Musali* (low-caste Muslim),⁸ who came to live in the dera of a guru, Gulabdas, Jat by caste, and falling within Sikh lineage. Since deras were normally monastic establishments, a woman's presence inside them was anomalous, not to speak of a "disreputable" prostitute, and also a "Muslim" within "Sikh" precincts.

Two points need to be made here, one that illustrates the serious nature of Piro's defiance of social strictures, and another that mitigates and renders acceptable the daring overstepping of boundaries observed in her move. The first relates to the tangled history of relations between the remnants of the Mughal state in eighteenth-century Punjab and its violent history of Sikh rebellion, Afghan invasions and rule, and the jockeying for power among multiple Sikh confederacies.[9] From the time of the establishment of the Khalsa in 1699, some from within the Sikhs, more specifically the Khalsa, tried to create religious norms and codes of behavior that worked toward imparting a distinct Sikh identity partly by distancing from the Muslims. A stream within the Khalsa set about creating codes of conduct, the *rahit* literature, that began "othering" the Muslim/Turak (used interchangeably), passing tenets that included the avoidance of *halal* meat associated with the Muslims, and sleeping with Muslim women.[10]

That Piro and her guru, Gulabdas, shared intimate relations is attested by almost all our sources. Gian Singh reported that the two lived *abhed* (without distinction, in unity).[11] Ganesha Singh, a member of the Nirmala sect, closely associated with the Gulabdasis, noted almost fifty years after the death of Gulabdas (d. 1873) that the two believed in the goodness both of *yog* (asceticism) and *bhog* (sexual pleasure and other corporeal appetites).[12] The colonial accounts stressed the epicurean ways of the Gulabdasis.[13] It was not then just the presence of a woman in a dera that created the ill will that Piro noted, though that must have been condemnatory on its own. It was also the flouting of norms of expected behavior on the part of a "Sikh" guru who was intimately associated with a "Muslim" woman that breached social etiquette, brewing a scandal that Piro sought to stem by explaining her and her guru's conduct. It also tells us something of Piro's insistent need to frame her text in language that assumed an agonistic relationship between "Hindus" and "Turaks."

And so the second point that explains and puts into perspective the enormity of Piro's daring step is that of the heterodox tendencies of the Gulabdasis. Gulabdas was a maverick guru, flouting social norms, and determinedly paving his spiritual path. Born in 1809 in the village Ratol of the Tarn Taran district of Punjab,[14] he received his early education, training in philosophy and prosody, under the auspices of scholars associated with the Udasi and Nirmala orders of the Sikhs.[15] However, he broke free of both, neither adhering to the more stringent asceticism of the Udasis, nor keeping the symbols of the Khalsa that the Nirmalas adopted. Gulabdas followed a form of monism that denied duality between God and the world, and veered toward solipsism that saw the self as the only knowable truth. From Piro's writings it is apparent that the Gulabdasis' philosophical inspiration was from diverse sources, including Sikh, Bhakti, and marginal Sufi ideas.

It is also important to point out that philosophical eclecticism and eccentric singularity in charting out a spiritual path that was the hallmark of the Gulabdasis was matched in part by defying given norms of social behavior. If Piro was transgressing codes of social interaction between people of different religions, she was equally flouting tradition that shaped appropriate caste relations by stepping into the dwelling of a holy man. Piro as a prostitute *was* low caste. It is difficult to say what caste Piro may have originally belonged to, in case she had not been born into prostitution. Newly constructed hagiographical literature acknowledges her past in prostitution, tracing her early life among *mirasis* (musicians and genealogists), and her being sold into a *vaishyalaya* (neologism for a brothel) in Hira Mandi (prostitutes' quarters) in Lahore.[16] Among the terms employed by Gian Singh to refer to Piro, and prostitutes in general, were *kasbi, besya, kanchani, ganka, randi,* and *kanjari*.[17] Piro too used terms like *veswa, randi,* and *ganka* to connote a prostitute, not drawing out the differences between who might be a courtesan, a dancing girl, or a low-rung whore soliciting customers. However, the low status of the prostitute was obvious enough, Piro calling herself a *sudar veswa* (k.9) when presenting herself to her guru, mindful of the diffident demeanor suitable for a woman, but also underlining her low status as a prostitute.[18]

That the Gulabdasis admitted into their ranks men from all castes was in keeping with many ascetic orders, among them the Udasis of Punjab.[19] Though Gulabdas belonged to the dominant agrarian caste of Jats, he chose as his successor an adopted son from *Kumhar* (Potter) caste.[20] The Gulabdasis seem to have been unique in admitting a prostitute among their numbers. They were also open to recruiting from different religious communities, and a contemporary noted a Sayyid Shia as a disciple.[21] Nor were the followers of Gulabdas punctilious about maintaining various distinguishing marks that set them apart from other ascetic groups. Ganesha Singh, the Nirmala, frowned on such laxity,[22] while Gian Singh noted that Gulabdas's followers could keep unshorn hair or have it cut short, observing that there were no restrictions on what could be consumed and with whom.[23]

It must have been the outcome of such a relaxed attitude that attracted Piro to the Gulabdasi sect, though she does not mention in any explicit way her motivations for a remarkable move. However, she does detail her landing into trouble by the boldness of her move. In her own writings she also tries to highlight this distinguishing characteristic of the Gulabdasis from other kindred sects, underscoring Gulabdas's attitude that opened the spiritual path to women.

However, despite the comparatively lenient attitude visible among the Gulabdasis, there is evidence to point that the induction of Piro into the sect caused consternation. This is revealed in the writings of the disciples of Gulabdas, including the references to rumor mongering that Piro alluded to. The very writing of the *160 Kafis* can be understood to be a response to this crisis. However, while Piro chose to frame her *160 Kafis* in terms of speaking of the conflict that revolved around issues of religious differences, others picked up the impropriety of a holy man's relationship with a woman and a prostitute to air their ire. There is also a hint of creeping corruption into the sect in the wake of the Piro episode in the writings of those who commented on the sect later, in that other prostitutes too became the disciples of Gulabdas, a development that evoked further opprobrium and may have also led to an effort to put down the sect.

Sant Ditta Ram, a Gulabdasi to begin with, in a career of prolific writing, most of it in the service of the Singh Sabha movement (and as Giani Ditt Singh), penned a verse that seemed to point an accusing finger at Gulabdas for his relationship with a prostitute. In condemnatory tones he ridiculed an ascetic who succumbed to the charms of a prostitute and destroyed the accumulated advantages gained from the practice of celibacy.

> A prostitute and a *faqir* are enemies forever
> When she comes to the house of an ascetic where could there be wellbeing
> ... his ascetic radiance is lost
> No one respects him and dishonor greets him everywhere
> Says Ditt, friend of Hari, the world exposes such charlatans
> There is no honor for the ascetic who keeps a prostitute.[24]

It is important, however, to bear in mind that Ditta Ram may not have been in direct contact with Gulabdas. He was born in 1852 and spent his early life in Ambala and may have come to Chathianwala, the abode of Gulabdas, only closer to the time of the latter's death.[25] Nevertheless, a simmering resentment against the guru's actions cannot be ruled out, though Ditta Ram may be simply commenting on proper roles and stations in society as the lines appeared in a text called *Abla Nind* [Insulting women], a conventional genre that enumerated the evils of a woman's sexuality and the dangers that men faced from it. Since the date of its publication is not given, it is possible that Ditta Ram may have written it after the breakup of the main dera of the Gulabdasis and when he was an advocate of the Singh Sabha reforms with their new sexual norms.[26] A later disapproval of a sect that he was earlier associated with is also possible, just as we cannot be sure that he may have genuinely castigated his guru for lapses in his ascetic makeup. Indeed the comparison in the verse to his guru's position is too sharp to be merely coincidental.

A second type of evidence that there may have been a debate about giving Piro asylum, and that a serious degree of infamy came to be associated with her admittance into the dera, comes from the writing of another disciple who defended his guru, Kishan Singh Arif. To explain his guru's choice he placed him at par with Hindu gods who were associated with consorts and noted that Gulabdas did not commit any abomination by having relations with a woman, but adhered to a set pattern. Arif wrote:

> A *sant* can keep a woman if he pleases no one should think badly of him
> This is not a new wonder it is quite the norm;
> Shiv had Gori, Krishna Radha, and Sita was beloved of Ram
> Bhagat Kabir had Loi in his home, all sants kept a woman.[27]

In her *160 Kafis* Piro also repeatedly raises the issue of her guru bearing humiliation. In a set of three kafis (k.157–59) toward the end of her text, she brings the question of his bearing the insults of the world, presumably on her behalf. On the one hand she expresses her gratefulness toward him by stating that he "purified" (*pak*) a "fallen" (*palit*) woman like her; on the other she accuses others of looking at a pure and blameless relationship from a polluted viewpoint. She also speaks about her guru allowing such rumor mongering (*charcha karvai*) to highlight his good deeds in the manner of godly avatars that live out their human lives in order to restore dharma and defeat evil. Her unrestrained expression of gratefulness toward the guru, followed by a humble assertion of her being his slave, tells us why Piro put down in writing the *160 Kafis*.

> Beholden to *satguru* I'm enamoured of him
> Many like me the guru has ferried across
> Where do I have any virtues being a sudra woman
> He bore the humiliation of the world the benevolent guru. (k.157)

What was also obvious from her text is that during her trying period Piro showed herself as one trapped with little choice. It seems Piro had firmly rejected the option of her going back to her older life and was not sure of her acceptance within the dera. There are lines in the *160 Kafis* that weigh down with a note of desperation, telling us about the limited choices for a woman on her own and the need to have a protective male figure to ensure a genuine refuge.

The odor of scandal that came to attach itself to the Gulabdasi dera—partially because of their general nonconformism, but mostly because of Piro—continued to color the perceptions about the sect. If Piro was unwilling to wholly repudiate her past in prostitution, people were equally unforgiving, never really assigning respectability to the sect despite recognizing immense talent in Gulabdas and his personal intellectual capacities. Both Gian and Ganesha Singh recounted the attempt at suppressing the sect by the prince of Patiala, Ganesha Singh additionally noting the same treatment at the hands of the British between 1855 and 1857.[28] Though subsequent to this the Gulabdasis apparently settled down, many calling themselves Udasis and Nirmalas,[29] their notoriety for risqué life may not have detached from them completely. Piro continued to live in the dera at Chathianwala until her death, and the guru did not renege on the refuge he offered her.

A Web of Stories

The first part of this chapter has suggested the compelling urge Piro may have felt for self-representation—the transgressions implicit in her move from a brothel to the sanctuary of a religious sect created discord that needed to be mitigated. However, in a society unfamiliar with the self-absorption required of an autobiography, how was one's life to be written? How does one look at the *160 Kafis*, conventional in so many ways, yet breaking the mold?

Employing traditional verse and regurgitating at one level sagas beset with conforming meanings and expected denouements in the cultural landscape of mid-nineteenth-century Punjab, Piro nevertheless innovates persistently these stories to put across her own tale. What may seem at one level oxymoronic perversity, using well-known tales in order to fabricate one of your own, in effect etched out a space to unfold one's own drama, where the theatrical props and the drift of the story were well known. The *160 Kafis* weave a web of stories, some overtly related, others explicitly used to arouse habitual and given moral constructions. There were still others unsaid and hesitatingly hinted, available in the interstices, ambiguous in their intent and ambivalent in their interpretive load. It is through this messy maze, but one charged with multivalent meanings, that we try to grasp at some aspects of Piro's life, and speculate on others.

The paradoxical juxtaposition of convention and innovation is visible in the very naming of Piro's text—*Ik Sau Sath Kafian*. The poetic expression referred to as kafis is a form that incorporates any rhyming lines. The Punjabi verses of Piro are written in the Gurmukhi script in a six-line format, following a simple metrical pattern where the last words of every two lines rhyme. What is exceptional about Piro's kafis is that she picks up the genre of kafis, nonnarrative traditionally, to tell tales. Annemarie Schimmel described kafis as "little songs composed by the Sufis for their followers."[30] Explicating the Sufis' use of this poetic form, Carla Petievich has emphasized the use of the feminine voice in these compositions, giving examples from the kafis of Shah Hussain in the sixteenth century, and Bulleh Shah in the eighteenth century in Punjab. Noting that kafis are set to music, until at least the advent of print culture, their most notable feature being the refrain (*rahao*) repeated after every stanza, she also points out that their distinctive feature, much like the *ghazal*, is that they do not follow a narrative sequence.[31] Piro made the kafi pliant to her need to narrate her life, and in the use and arrangement of varied tales, she deploys the rhetorical skills at her command to create her story.

At an overt level Piro narrates a sequence of events that had ostensibly occurred, the saga that she wishes to tell. The obvious and patent narrative relates the arrival of Piro, humble and deferential, at the door of Gulabdas, seeking refuge. Noting her disenchantment from material goods, she introduces herself as one disinclined from the world. She also emphasizes breaking all her previous relations before coming. However, the Turaks she had left behind follow her, importuning that Piro as their daughter/sister (*dhi bhain*) be sent back with them. Piro then suggests that she herself asked her guru to send her back with them, saying that she would be back if the guru would offer shelter. Immediately thereon Piro hints at the harsh treatment she would meet at the hands of the Turaks. She also shows the primary concern of the Turaks was apparently a putative "conversion" of hers, or rather her apostasy, her giving up/taking off of her (earlier) faith. To rectify things the Turaks then call the mullahs, upholders of religious orthodoxy, the authority figures who come with their religious and legal books to question Piro on her transgression and expect her to "reconvert" to Islam. Piro put these words in the mullahs' mouth to underscore their anger—"Say the mullahs O' infidel, who spoilt you and made you eat pig?" (k.26). Piro then speaks of the mullahs asking her to read the *kalma* and other Islamic prayers in order to reassimilate her into Islam. In the ensuing dialogue of Piro with mullahs and *qazis*, in charge of Islamic jurisprudence, she presents herself not only as capable of defending the choice of her guru, but also as repeatedly insulting them, and getting the better of them in tête-à-tête. Thus Piro depicts herself as using speech and argument to outdo those traditionally used to talk down to people.

The failure of the mullahs to win her back was followed by the clan (*kutumb*) making an appeal to her to reincorporate her in the Islamic faith. Importantly, the clan is composed of friends (*saheliyan*), hinting at those in her former profession—"the virtues in their Vedas are in the Koran too, leave the path of the infidels and come back to your faith" (k.33). Piro is able to outargue her friends, persuading them about the rightness of her chosen path.

The failure of the friends then gets "Muslim men" (*Musalman nar*) angry, whom Piro taunts by ridiculing their religion as one devoted to outward appearance—"snipping the penis and the moustaches" (k.40). The humiliation at the hands of a woman frustrates the men—"how is she going on humbling our religion" (k.41). After further cursing these men Piro presents herself as so strong in her determination and will that the Turaks are hard-pressed to find a way out—"seeing her strong all feel helpless, she's not going to turn she follows her will" (k.47). Through these exchanges Piro also shows her interlocutors to be conscious of the power of her guru, both as an accomplished person (*kamal*) and as one who commanded loyalty in the vicinity of Lahore. Seeing Piro's unwavering loyalty to her guru, she presents her opponents as then hatching a plan to abdicate her and take her away from Lahore to Wazirabad, which they accomplish against her will.

The next part of her narrative moves to Wazirabad, where Piro says she is kept imprisoned in a four-storied building with locks put in place and sentinels posted to guard her. In the midst of enemies, due to the equanimity, liberality, and fearlessness of her character, Piro says she befriends two women, Jaanu and Rehmati. With their help she is able to get an amanuensis (*munsi*) to her and makes him write a letter to her guru pleading to be taken out of her difficult situation. She says the letter reaches her guru on the third day and generates wrath among his disciples on the treatment meted to her. The guru dispatches two of his disciples, Gulab Singh and Chatar Singh, on a rescue mission to Wazirabad. On arriving there, the two encamp in an orchard and befriend its gardener, whom they are able to send to the house of Piro's captivity. The disciples, according to Piro's narrative, make quite a splash, alerting her captors to their presence. The fallout of this is that Piro's condition of imprisonment is made harsher. Piro introduces at this stage a woman called Mehrunissa, who, once again, is presented as offering Piro a choice of accepting Islam or facing incarceration in chains—"She said leave the religion of the infidels and become a Muslim woman, or wear chains on your feet and sit in jail" (k.102).

Before these plans could be set into motion, Piro speaks of her escape from her captivity because of the support of the two disciples of the guru, the efforts of the loyal friends Jaanu and Rehmati, and the gardener. However, her actual escape from the prison Piro presents as a miracle unfolded by her guru, the locks falling away at her touch and the guards rendered blind. Remarkably the whole town of Wazirabad is unable to perceive the three disciples making good their escape, as they cannot see them. It is only after they move away from the gates of the city that the enormity of the occurrence is understood, and Piro's captors begin the pursuit of the three disciples. The three however do not rest until they reach the banks of river Ravi, on the outskirts of Lahore, its sight giving them reassurance of the passing off of danger.

In the dera Piro presents the three as giving proof/being a witness (*sabati*) to each other's bravery and good conduct. Significantly, the Muslims at this juncture are referred to as *mlechha*, a term connoting those outside the indic civilization context, perhaps Piro wishing to overcome the ambiguity of her recently converted status by drawing attention to her not belonging to the "outcastes." The steadfast loyalty to the guru on Piro's part is highlighted by Gulab Singh, who speaks of her resisting their efforts of converting her—"they undertook a lot of trouble to make her adhere to the Sharia, she suffered their incarceration but did not leave your feet" (k.124).

The last part of Piro's narrative praises her guru, emphasizing his glory, the radiance of his personality, and his nonbiased attitude toward all, whether high caste or low, man or woman, Hindu or Turk. Besides a fulsome critique of the religion of the Hindus and the Muslims, this part of the text also censures other sects, presumably competitors to the Gulabdasis in offering salvationist choices. Piro also dwells on the salience of the consort, the *Shakti* (power/force and goddess) of the Lord, a role that she envisages for herself. While thanking her guru for enlightening her, she expounds on her understanding of the unique doctrines of her sect, ending her narrative with reiterating her fidelity and servitude to her guru.

This summary paraphrasing of the overt story that Piro wished to relate has a ring of plausibility. Piro emphasizes the suffering she underwent in order to see the manifestation of her spiritual desires in a sequence of episodes that could well have occurred. Piro creates a throbbing reality, naming the personae involved in the events, and the places that featured in the escapade. If we follow one of her statements, the advice she gives to Gulab and Chatar Singh when in Wazirabad, asking them to be cautious by warning them of the rule in those parts of the *firangi*—"here the firangi rules don't be riotous" (k.97)—it may even help us place the "incident" in the early 1830s. That Piro was comfortably ensconced in the dera at Chathianwala at the time of the sanguinary battles between the Sikhs and the British is apparent from Gian Singh's reference to the "Satluj" clash (the Anglo-Sikh wars of the 1840s), when many a soldier deposited his wealth with Gulabdas and went and fought in the war. Also the bid to tame and suppress the sect in the 1850s as mentioned by Ganesha Singh makes the Piro incident into a Sikh-period affair. Furthermore, Ganesha Singh made an important observation about the anecdote of a conflict around Piro's arrival in the dera, his version almost matching that of Piro's, but with some significant additional details. Ganesha Singh gives an account of how Piro kanjari came to stay with the guru after she "fell for his charms," an occurrence resented by her guardians, who took her away. He also notes that Gulabdas dispatched Kala Singh and Chatar Singh to bring her back, a train of events and cast of characters that resemble Piro's account of the happenings. Ganesha Singh added a detail that spells out the incendiary and scandalous nature of the affair when he notes that another "friend" of Piro's, one Ilahi Khan, promised the help of the army (*fauj*), and urged Piro's "brothers" to take on Gulabdas. Gulabdas, according to this account, was surrounded near the tomb of the saint Mian Mir in Lahore where, however, two hundred of his own supporters arrived to help him and a skirmish followed. According to Singh, the fighting came to an end only at the intervention of "Maharaj," presumably Ranjit Singh himself, and subsequent to that Gulabdas and Piro settled in Chathianwala.[32] Some scholars have identified Ilahi Khan with Ilahi Baksh, an important general of Ranjit Singh, who commanded his artillery.[33] If that was the case, we can actually understand the furor Piro's departure to the dera of Gulabdas must have caused, though according to her own telling, the guru was already settled in Chathianwala when she first joined him. The firangi can then be identified with Paolo de Avitabile, an Italian general of Ranjit Singh, who controlled Wazirabad in the 1830s.[34]

Looking at the strong parallels in Piro's and Ganesha Singh's accounts and giving due consideration to the garnishing of the story the two may have taken recourse to—one to perform her persona and loyalty to her guru, and the other a victim of time, rumor, and hearsay—we can still conclude that some disturbance had occurred at the time of Piro's arrival at the dera. If that is true, what made Piro's narrative so exceptional, her embellishments a strain to comprehend and present her story? There are several reasons that suggest the extraordinary effort Piro made to push the envelope of self-representation, her account of events presented within a carefully chosen cultural palimpsest that set the tone for their reception, drawing on contexts that gave her story the cultural links she favored and a moral aura she sought. Firstly, the account of her "abduction" drew linkages to the primary, if not originative, kidnapping, that of Sita, the queen of Lord Ram at the hands of the demon Ravana in the epic Ramayana, a parable that sharply cleaved good from evil. Secondly, Piro's version of her confrontation with the mullahs/qazis drew on region-specific as well as pan-regional traditions of questioning the authority of religious figures. It specifically links her to the episode of Hir's refractory showdown with the qazi who tried to preach good womanly conduct to her while she questioned the legitimacy of his pronouncements in the amazingly popular *qissa* of Hir and Ranjha in Punjab.[35] It simultaneously drew on the Sufi tradition of Punjab, especially the Qadiriya Sufis and their reviling of the mullahs, some doing so by taking on the persona of Hir.[36] The pan-regional links are visible in a similar strain within the Bhakti movement and its ridiculing of the religious authority figures. It might be underscored that for Piro the Bhakti inheritance of her sect was significant, and she constantly tries to legitimize her own actions by seeking parallels from the Bhakti legacy. The appropriation of the Bhakti, and to an extent the Sufi, traditions in her repertoire of cultural resources opens up, thirdly, the reasons why Piro chose to submit her personal conflict in the language of a religious face-off. The charges of conversion and apostasy made by Musalman/Turak men in Piro's narrative may well resemble the situation as she saw it, but her interpretation also carries the metaphoric weight of a Bhakti and Sufi inheritance that opened up for questioning external religiosity of men of formal faith as against the sants' and faqirs' own interiorized spirituality. This story in turn may provide clues to decipher the incipient and often incoherent voices that appear in Piro's text, along with meaningful silences, hinting at life as a prostitute, a woman with sometimes frustratingly little say in the matter of how she may live her life. Let us then try to unravel this web of Piro's stories, and see what Piro hoped to gain by making the connections she did.

Piro as Sita
....

Quite audaciously for a Muslim low-caste prostitute, Piro took on the role of the prima donna of "Hindu" wifely devotion and chastity, Sita, the wife of Lord Ram, the prince-king of Ayodhya, in the epic Ramayana. The juncture at which she introduces herself as Sita in her narrative is of course after her "kidnapping," comparing her own ill-judgment at persuading her guru to let her go with her clan to Sita's ill-considered lust for the golden deer—

> My bad sense has created the difficulty
> You too are feeling helpless because of me
> Like Sita made Ram wander in search of the deer
> Please do not upset yourself or put yourself to trouble. (k.67)

Though the last line of the verse purportedly refrains the guru from bothering himself over her, the intention of the lines was, in fact, to galvanize him into action. She manipulates her words to simultaneously create the effect of illustrating that his reputation was at stake, as it was for Ram, and therefore the divine analogy was used to underscore the significance of undertaking her own rescue.

> Piro says satguru I have no recourse
> My honour is in your hands and your reputation is at stake
> As Ram used force to secure Sita's release
> Piro asks satguru to bestow his magnanimity on her. (k.79)

The ambience of the epic is further created by direct and indirect allusions to people and events from the text. Thus if Piro was Sita, and the guru Ram, then the disciples, Gulab and Chatar Singh, who came to Wazirabad for her rescue, were Hanuman and Angad, loyal supporters of the Lord who breached the defenses of Lanka/Wazirabad to carry back Sita—"said Angad and Hanuman we seek your permission, if you permit we'll burn Lanka and bring Sita home" (k.74). In Piro's writing the orchard where the disciples sought refuge in Wazirabad resembles the Ashok Vatika, the site of Sita's captivity, and the gardener who helps the disciples is rewarded among other things with a golden ring, which again has a distinct recall of the one Hanuman presented to Sita.

Through these narrative strategies Piro became the self-fashioned Sita, endowing her own character and her version of events with ethical righteousness, depicting herself as the wronged person in the saga she relates. The irony of her portrayal of Sita was not just that of a prostitute taking on the mantle of a chaste wife, but also unlike the conventional Sita, silent and suffering, Piro was neither, putting down in writing her complaints against her supposed tormentors, and in the long run living out a fairly comfortable life. Furthermore, though conventionally shown as the loyal shadow of her husband-god, there existed other traditions that sought to critique patriarchal institutions through taking a sympathetic view of Sita's suffering. For instance, women have chosen to lament their ill treatment at the hands of their husbands by mourning the fate of Sita, thereby undermining the moral claims of patriarchy,[37] the fascinating Chandravati Ramayana or "Sitayana" of Bengal of the sixteenth century even indicting Ram for cruel treatment by pushing out a pregnant wife.[38]

Yet we find a highly traditional portrayal in Piro's rendition of Sita's story. For she chose to draw attention away from what may have been perceived as a "promiscuous" past, toward the more acceptable and orthodox Sita-like fiber of chaste loyalty, free of sensuous temptations. She was thus worthy of not only the shelter of the guru, but in the long run as a practitioner of ascetic lifestyle, of being the guru's partner, and a "mother" to his disciples. But the more immediate reason to cast herself as Sita may have been to accuse her former community, clan, and their religious heads of cruel and abhorrent behavior toward her. The epic Ramayana, as some scholars have noted, is suited to drawing out implacable lines between the morally upright and the ethically repugnant and could be used historically to mark out the "divine" and the righteous world from that of the licentious and illicit "demons."[39] Scholars have also shown that such rhetorical practices were well established and formulaic, and purportedly bore little resemblance to the lived reality, yet as literary devices they served varied purposes.[40] Piro, it seems, chose to demonize her former community and associates. Her account may also be read as a "conversion narrative,"[41] frequently employed in hagiographies of *bhaktas*, where everything noteworthy occurs after undergoing "conversion" of some sort, whether through a chance meeting with the guru, or through a supernatural happenstance. Piro's "conversion" carried the double load of her spiritual inspiration after encountering the guru, and also a putative conversion/initiation into his sect, stepping away from her given faith. It might be worth recalling her use of the term *mlechha* at this point in her text to denote the "Muslim" men who abduct her, underlining their alien nonbelonging as against the community of dharma represented by her guru and his disciples. Piro sutured the cultural flavor that the epic carried, the clash between good and evil, to her own story. She painted a stark image in black and white for the consumption of her chosen audience, the Gulabdasi disciples and other ascetic orders, perhaps the politically powerful that mattered and may choose to arbitrate in the matter.

However, the calumnious charge that Piro makes against those with whom she lived as a community until recently does sound like a protest too loud, ridden with anxiety to prove her case. While on the surface Piro gave a particular story of her ill treatment and abduction and made specific allusions to illustrate her tale, her account was nevertheless riddled with half-said reproaches and brief utterances. These betrayed another tone, one not overtly spoken by Piro, but posing questions that punctuated her text with another set of possibilities not always easy to understand or create a coherent tale from. Fairly early on in her story, for example, it becomes quite clear that Piro *chose* to go back with her "clan" when they came to collect her, promising to return, one would assume, after "persuading" her people of the seriousness of her intent toward an ascetic life. That somewhere she felt herself betrayed, misled, even "tricked" into leaving comes through repeatedly; but what also emerges is that she herself did not have the discernment to see what was right. A fair question that then can be posed is that did she leave in the first place because of an attractive offer of some sort placed before her? Or because life in the dera did not seem appealing enough and she chose to go back only to be let down, and so became desperate to reenter the dwelling of the guru, a task made all the more difficult by her initial departure, and in the new situation her complete lack of choice? At least some of these varied nuances in her account are caught in the tone of these lines:

> I did not recognize your worth having become negligent
> Seeing my faults the guru pushed me
> Forgive my previous sins for I am helpless
> I have no place to go satguru except yours. (k.66)

Though the previous sins Piro refers to could be an allusion to her earlier life, the first line does suggest a more recent misjudgment on her part.

It is undoubtedly difficult to put a finger on the nature of this betrayal whose refrain stays with Piro. Yet another manner in which it emerges is the subtle reference to the unacceptable way in which "daughters" are treated by Piro's relatives and associates, which point a finger at her own treatment. Right in the beginning of her narration, when her clan comes to the dera looking to take her with them, they assert their rights over her by calling her their daughter/sister. This address of her clan to the guru is presented as a supplication (*araj*) to return their "daughter," questioning her reasons to leave, having taken off her jewels and good clothes, when all material things were available to her?

> Accept our supplication Maharaj we have come to your door
> Piro is our daughter sister so we ask for her gift . . .
> She has taken off her (beautiful) clothes and ornaments
> Ask her Maharaj what she seeks. (k.15)

Daughters in high-caste Hindu society are "gifted" in marriage, a meritorious act that all fathers hope to perform.[42] The symbolic transfer of the right to gift a daughter from the clan to the "Hindu" guru here creates two possibilities. On the one hand, the guru is pressured on a dharmic scale to treat "his" daughter well, "gifting" her to her rightful claimants; on the other, it is clear that the clan's daughter must go back to her jewels and clothes, the accoutrements a part of her profession, to further their traditional trade.

At two other instances Piro mentions daughters' ill treatment. At the moment of her conversation with mullahs, she abusively calls them "daughter fuckers" (*dhi de laure*) (k.42), indicating their "exploitation" of daughters. What this statement achieves is, again, to toss up two different expectations of daughters into conflict with each other. Piro, it seems, sought to appropriate for herself the high-caste model of treating a daughter with care and earning merit through following prescribed behavior toward her. This was set against, assumedly in her worldview, the condemnable act of making a living or earning any advantage through her. The second reference reinforces this interpretation when Piro makes a more direct statement accusing the same religious figures of using daughters to further the cause of their religion—"they give sixty daughters to strengthen their religion" (k.45). Sixty may be a figurative way of underscoring the willingness to "trade" in several daughters in order to serve faith/community. However, what remains unclear is how religion/religious community is served in this sordid bargain as against the benefit accruing to her professional clan.

While Piro's foregrounding of her personal conflict in religious terms will be discussed subsequently, we may speculate where her background in prostitution placed her in terms of expectations from a daughter. Louise Brown in her study of the contemporary life in Hira Mandi in Lahore has shown the dominance of Shia Islam in this prostitutes' quarters, noting the many "temporary" marriages that a prostitute is expected to enter, and the way a good-looking and healthy daughter is treated as an asset and a security for the rest of her family.[43] Though it would be difficult to project on to Piro's time the realities of contemporary Hira Mandi, Piro's own narrative does fuel speculation on similar lines. When she speaks of her being forced to leave Lahore for Wazirabad, she accuses her captors not only of taking her against her will, but also perhaps of tricking her into a potential relationship (of temporary wifehood/concubinage?)—"I know your wickedness/wiliness of finding a man/lover (*chhaliya*) for me" (k.50)—and then asserting that she would never interact with him. Was Piro kept captive in order to make her succumb to a demand she refused to bow to? Was the turning to the guru a way of escaping a situation she did not relish? Did she fall for the charms of the guru as disingenuously suggested by Ganesha Singh? Or was a spiritual urge on her part a genuine one? We do not know the answers, though the truth might have been a combination of all the above. However, it is evident that by assuming the role of Sita she ensconces herself in a moral order that had echoes in the society she wished to persuade toward her own attitude of restraint and rectitude, and pushed her clan and its demands, hopes and expectations in the realm of the illegitimate and the unethical. Piro's masquerade of Sita may be read as primarily aimed at her new community, persuading them of the purity of her intent, of her consort-like devotion to the guru, but significantly also of her irreconcilable differences with her former associates. Piro's careful self-fashioning on the one hand, and her recusant self on the other, not only in her presentation of her conflict with authority figures of her former community, but also from the point of view of her clan to whose authority too she refused to bend, show a person of exceptional will and self-worth. It was surely this remarkable sense of selfhood that allowed her to live and maneuver her extraordinary circumstances, as glimpsed in her writing, to her advantage.

Religious Conflict and an Alternative Legacy

If the above outlined suggestion that Piro's *160 Kafis* can at one level be interpreted in terms of her personal choice of moving away from the demands and circumstances of her old profession be accepted, though her desire to pursue a spiritual path cannot be overlooked, the question that begs an answer is why she represented her dilemma in terms of a rabid confrontation between herself and religious authority figures, and why she posited an implacable hostility between religions. Did such conflict in some manner reflect her times, or did Piro have something to gain through the presentation of such a canard?

The question of religious identity, in its affirmation as in its rejection, was a central concern in Piro's writing. For instance, Piro often highlights in her writings her guru's openness toward both Hindus and Turks—"I seek the master of Turaks and Hindus" (k.16)—while at other times she vehemently denies being either a Hindu or a Muslim—"I am neither a Muslim woman nor a Hindu" (k.150)—emphasizing her sect's distinct philosophy, though the rejection itself attested to the dominance of the two religious denominations of India.

One can suggest several reasons of Piro's that surely worked at a personal level, to understand why she portrayed a collision of religious affiliations when she spoke of her tribulations. Her "abduction" and its denouement were, for example, shown as the triumph of her new loyalty to her guru, akin to the eagerness of a recent or an unlikely convert, against insistent hostility toward it, and against the will to reclaim her for Islam. One obvious reason for her to depict such contentiousness was to display her sincerity toward the new life of asceticism. The overcoming of her previous identity, and the many obstacles that splitting from it threw up, also gave her the opportunity to put on display her steadfast loyalty in the face of overwhelming pressure to recant. Moreover, it was important for her to show that her conversion to a spiritual life was a serious undertaking, and by rejecting her older religion, she was also turning away from her previous friends, and the life they represented. The louder her denunciations of the mullahs, *miyans*, and mlechhas, the more resolute she could show herself to be in her chosen path.

Yet the question remains as to her choice of showing trenchant hostility between religious communities and her assumption of a sympathetic audience to such assertions. The habitual conflict between Hindu and Muslim authorities was a commonly and frequently used trope within the Bhakti and the Sufi traditions in Punjab and elsewhere, that allowed the challenging of religious authority, condemning it as inspired by nothing more than outward ritual practice to ensnare innocent people, as against the truly universal and inwardly turned spirituality of the sants and faqirs, the latter's appeal lying in inclusive catholicity. Piro could thus appropriate an indic and a regional alternative tradition to stitch legitimacy to her own rebellion, her cause the cause célèbre of many before her.

Piro specifically evoked the Bhakti tradition in order to make a statement about the availability of a spiritual life to low castes. It was with the figure of the fifteenth-century sant Kabir, the most popular of the Bhakti saints of India, that Piro sought inspiration, even equivalence. As a recalcitrant personality, nominally Muslim, but more critical of its theology than accepting of its tenets, the hagiographical person depicted constantly at loggerheads with religious authorities, both Muslim and Hindu, Kabir seemed to Piro a person after her own heart.[44] Kabir was both overtly and covertly present in Piro's kafis. Piro's refractory statement of being neither a Muslim nor a Hindu can be taken to be a reiteration of the sentiment of Kabir—"I am neither Hindu nor Muslim, Allah-Ram is the breath of my body." Similarly, Piro's confrontation with the mullahs had a distinct recall of Kabir's hagiographic tale of being tied and thrown into the river Ganges on the orders of Sultan Sikander Lodi at the behest of qazis,[45] the upholders of the Shari'at or Muslim law. One of Piro's kafis made a reference to the torture of Kabir, and also of the Sufi mystic martyr of West Asia, Mansur-al-Hallaj, at the hands of authorities. It may not be far-fetched to assume that Piro imagined her own ordeal along similar lines, the trial that all truly evolved figures go through in order to come out victorious:

> Piro says satguru they love the Shari'a,
> Without giving it a thought they tried to drown Kabir,
> They hung Mansur flaying him,
> What more suffering shall I relate? (k.22)

Moreover, Kabir, famous for his mocking of pandits and mullahs, shaming them on the outward orientation of their religiosity, fuelled a parallel reaction from Piro. It is from this Bhakti trope that Piro, even though she relates the account of her adversarial encounter with the mullahs, nevertheless questions the sincerity of both the Hindu and Muslim religious authority figures concurrently. Importantly, Piro uses this sharp interlocutory mode to insert a question that was not relevant to Kabir or to most other Bhakti saints, but a central query of Piro's, the religious identity of women:

> They make false religions making false promises
> Snipping the penis and the moustache they call themselves Turks;
> Hindus are made by wearing the sacred thread and keeping the topknot
> Women can't be made thus, they are both wrong. (k.44)

However, for Kabir the question of women's religious identity was unimportant as he equated women with illusory *maya*, distracting from the spiritual path rather than seeking soteriological resolutions of their own.[46] The question of women's religious identity was a significant aspect of Piro's spiritual journey and personality, one of the reasons for her rejection of Islam resting on the impossibility of women to be Muslim (or Hindu). By focusing on the fetish for outward and somatic religiosity, a persistent theme in her kafis, Piro shows why women were denied power within the community, remaining on the margins of a religiously defined identity, though control over them was deemed important.

If the evocation of the Bhakti voice allowed the opening of the issue of the ambiguity of women's belonging to religious communities, and the rejection of ritualistic religion, Piro equally resorts to Punjab's Sufi legacy to further link her ideas to a popular culture tuned to assail religious authorities.

The polysemous relationship of Sufi legacy with Punjabi popular culture apart, the Gulabdasis had a deeper linkage with a Sufi tradition through the ideas of Bulleh Shah (1680–1758).[47] The latter's establishment in Kasur was a strong influence on Gulabdas. Besides his training with the Udasis and the Nirmalas already mentioned, Gulabdas apparently spent some time with faqirs, Muslim holy men, referred to by both Gian and Ganesha Singh, the latter identifying them as "Bullehshahi." Interestingly, the reference in Gian and Ganesha Singh to the faqirs is negative, both calling them *rind* (debauched), and their habits as *khulasa* (living outside social norms and taboos, literally in openness or frankness).

It is apposite that the unorthodox Gulabdasis should have been attracted to the ideas of Bulleh Shah known for integrating "Hindu" elements in his poetry that borrowed from Nath traditions and Krishnaite images,[48] and the imprimatur of whose kafis was the thwarting of the dyed-in-the-wool self-important religious establishment. It is here that Piro, by her insistent challenge to the mullahs and the qazis, sought to re-create the magic of Bulleh's poetry. The ridiculing of Hindu and Muslim orthodoxies, with its unique resonance in Punjab, was captured effectively in Bulleh Shah and replayed in Piro. To give one example, Bulleh wrote:

> We are tired of reading the Vedas and the Koran
> We've damaged our foreheads doing *sijda*
> God is neither at pilgrimage nor Mecca.[49]

The same sentiment echoed in Piro:

> Qazis trapped the Turks in the honour of the Koran,
> Hindus are tricked by the pandits who read the Vedas to them. (k.152)

A topos within the Sufi tradition of Punjab was what Petievich has referred to as the "masquerade" in women's voice, the Sufi faqirs speaking as women to their master/God, emphasizing the annihilation of self/ego through taking on the feminine voice. Shah Hussein and Bulleh Shah, for instance, often took on the persona of Hir in some of their kafis, the heroine of the qissa of Hir and Ranjha, the romantic tale circulating in Punjab from at least the sixteenth century. The exploration of the dialectic between a temporary recourse to one's feminine self and the regular male demeanor, and the unavailability of such self-abnegating/elevating switching to a woman poet is not attempted here, but the idea is to draw attention to how Hir's voice was exploited by Piro too. Among the many famous episodes of the qissa were of Hir's two confrontations with the qazi, Hir accosted by him for flouting social norms, particularly overstepping the proprieties of women's guarded sexuality.[50] Piro's own harangue with the mullahs, besides imitating Kabir and Bulleh's mien, is also in the image of Hir/Bulleh in contestation with the religious authorities. Through the insertion of this particular topos in her narrative, Piro could reap the emotional recompense of what was understood in Punjab as wrongly applied power for social control. This single episode in Piro's own tale, of her inexorable opposition to the religious authority figures, could evoke polyvalent chords in Punjabi culture, something that Piro banks on to create for her story an audience in agreement with her rendition of it.

Conclusion

This chapter has raised the issue of self-representation in premodern Punjab for a woman who would have been on the edges of her society. The multiple conditions of liminality that defined Piro's life—of occupation, gender, caste—combined with a sense of feeling persecuted, may have goaded her into writing, as much as such a situation may oppress another into silence. To what extent the autobiographical content of the *160 Kafis* was a product of speaking from the periphery is a question that requires serious consideration. However, her act of putting down in writing aspects of her life, and a story she wished to tell in the process of fashioning a self and a life, rescued her from anonymity and marginality.

Piro made deft use of cultural resources at her command—qissas and kafis, epic sagas and their characters, Bhakti sants' songs and their hagiographies—to mold a story of her life. Thus Piro's *160 Kafis* can be seen at one level to be relating stories that everyone knew and empathized with—the abduction of Sita, the challenge of Bulleh or Hir to religious establishment, Kabir's harsh and rhetorical taunting of the socially powerful. Yet at another level she also used these fables and parables to narrate her own life, garnishing her narrative with stories woven around ethical questions to generate the right chord. The significance of her life did not lie in the uniqueness of her tale; rather it lay in the repetitiveness of the events of history, in the living out of mythology through ordinary and everyday lives, the manner in which the good are accosted and troubled by the malevolent only to emerge victorious, but after prolonged suffering that tested their mettle and so by proving one's worthiness. Whatever transgressions prompted Piro to put the *160 Kafis* in writing, she did ultimately have the satisfaction of finding a prominent place for herself in the life she chose.

NOTES

1 *Ik Sau Sath Kafian*, ms. 888, Bhai Gurdas Library (Amritsar: Guru Nanak Dev University) (hereafter GNDU).
2 Giani Gian Singh, *Sri Guru Panth Prakash* (Patiala: Bhasha Vibhag, [1880] 1970) (hereafter *PP*).
3 A. K. Ramanujan, "Where Mirrors Are Windows: Toward an Anthology of Reflections," in *The Collected Essays of A. K. Ramanujan*, ed. Vinay Dharwadker (New Delhi: Oxford University Press, 1999), 6–33.
4 On tradition stressing emulation over autonomy see B. D. Metcalf, "The Past in the Present: Instruction, Pleasure, and Blessing in Maulana Muhammad Zakariyya's Aap Bitii," in David Arnold and Stuart Blackburn, eds., *Telling Lives in India: Biography, Autobiography and Life History* (Ranikhet: Permanent Black, 2004), 116–43.
5 Vijendra Das, ed., *Sant KavyitriMa Piro* (Panchkula: Satluj Prakashan, 2011); Shaharyar, "Kalaam Mata Piro Ka," *Hun* (January–April 2009); Vir Vahab, ed., *Piro Kahe Saheliyon* (Jalandhar: R. B. Printing, 2012).
6 Interview with Sant Vijendra Das, Sonepat, Haryana, June 10, 2010. He heads the Gulabdasi dera of Hansi, Haryana.
7 On Piro's works, see Anshu Malhotra, "Bhakti and the Gendered Self: A Courtesan and a Consort in Mid Nineteenth Century Punjab," *Modern Asian Studies* 46.2 (2012), 1506–39.

8 A low-caste Muslim Chuhra (scavenger) was called a Musali. D. C. J. Ibbetson, *Panjab Castes* (Patiala: Languages Department Punjab, [1883] 2000), 294–95.
9 J. S. Grewal, *The Sikhs of the Punjab* (Delhi: Cambridge University Press, [1994] 2002), 82–98.
10 Harjot Oberoi, *The Construction of Religious Boundaries: Diversity in Sikh Tradition* (Delhi: Oxford University Press, 1994), 67.
11 *PP*, 1293.
12 Ganesha Singh, *Bharat Mat Darpan* (hereafter *BMD*) (Amritsar: Viadyak Bhandar, 1926), 187.
13 L. S. Saunders, *Report on Revised Land Revenue Settlement of the Lahore District 1865–69* (Lahore: Central Jail Press, 1873), 54.
14 *PP*, 1292.
15 *PP*, 1292–93; *BMD*, 187.
16 Interview with Sant Vijendra Das, March 28, 2007. Das is invested in "reinventing" Piro as a "pure" woman, spiritually inclined, but caught in difficult circumstances. In *Sant Kaviyitri* he creates her hagiography.
17 *PP*, 1293–95.
18 Ms. 888. The *kafi* numbers of quoted verses are in parenthesis.
19 H. A. Rose, *A Glossary of the Tribes and Castes of the Punjab and the North-West Frontier Province* (Patiala: Languages Department Punjab, [1911] 1970), 479–81.
20 *PP*, 1295.
21 Mufti Ghulam Sarwar Qureshi "Lahori," in *Tarikh Makhzane Punjab* (Lahore: Dost Associates, [1877] 1996), 567–68.
22 *BMD*, 128.
23 *PP*, 1294.
24 G. I. Sewak, *Gulab Dasi Sampradaye: Rachna Ate Vichar*, PhD diss., GNDU, 1984), 102–3.
25 Giani Amar Singh, *Jiwan Chariter Singh Sabha Lehar de Ughe Sanchalak Giani Ditt Singh Ji* (Amritsar: Gulab Singh Malak Firm, 1962).
26 Anshu Malhotra, *Gender, Caste and Religious Identities: Restructuring Class in Colonial Punjab* (Delhi: Oxford University Press, 2002), 179–91.
27 This verse from Arif's *Kotre Khatpade* is quoted in Sewak, *Gulab Dasi Sampradaye*, 104.
28 *PP*, 1295; *BMD*, 127.
29 *BMD*, 127.
30 Schimmel quoted in Carla Petievich, *When Men Speak as Women: Vocal Masquerade in Indo-Muslim Poetry* (New Delhi: Oxford University Press, 2007), 9.
31 Petievich, *When Men Speak*, 16.
32 *BMD*, 128.
33 Sewak, *Sampradaye*, 96–97.
34 Edward Thornton, *A Gazetteer of the Territories under the Government of the East India Company and the Native States of the Continent of India*, vol. 4 (London: W. H. Allen, 1954).

35 On the popularity of this qissa, see Farina Mir, *The Social Space of Language in Punjab: Vernacular Culture in British Colonial Punjab* (Ranikhet: Permanent Black, 2010), 123–49.
36 Petievich, *When Men Speak*.
37 Velcheru N. Rao, "A Ramayan of Their Own: Women's Oral Tradition in Telugu," in *Many Ramayanas: The Diversity of a Tradition in South Asia*, ed. Paula Richman (Delhi: Oxford University Press, 1994), 114–36.
38 Nabaneeta D. Sen, "Chandravati Ramayana: Feminising the Rama Tale," in *Faces of the Feminine in Ancient, Medieval, and Modern India*, ed. Mandakranta Bose (Delhi: Oxford University Press, 2000), 183–91.
39 Sheldon Pollock, "Ramayana and Political Imagination in India," in *Religious Movements in South Asia 600–1800*, ed. David N. Lorenzen (New Delhi: Oxford University Press 2004), 153–208.
40 Cynthia Talbot, "Inscribing the Other, Inscribing the Self: Hindu-Muslim Identities in Pre-colonial India," *Comparative Studies in Society and History* 37.4 (1995): 692–721.
41 Arnold and Blackburn, *Telling Lives*, 14.
42 Malhotra, *Gender, Caste*, 47–81.
43 Louise Brown, *The Dancing Girls of Lahore: Selling Love and Saving Dreams in Pakistan's Pleasure District* (New York: HarperCollins, 2006).
44 On Kabir's personality in his hagiography, see J. S. Hawley and Mark Juergensmeyer, *Songs of the Saints of India* (Delhi: Oxford University Press, [1988] 2008).
45 Charlotte Vaudeville, *A Weaver Named Kabir* (New Delhi: Oxford University Press, [1993] 2005), 45.
46 Kumkum Sangari, "Mirabai and the Spiritual Economy of Bhakti," in two parts in *Economic and Political Weekly*, July 7, 1990, 1464–75, and July 14, 1990, 1537–52.
47 Namwar Singh, ed., *Bulleh Shah ki Kafian* (Delhi: National Institute of Punjab Studies, 2003).
48 Denis Matringe, "Krsnaite and Nath Elements in the Poetry of the Eighteenth-Century Panjabi Sufi Bulhe Sah," in R. S. McGregor, ed., *Devotional Literature in South Asia* (Cambridge: Cambridge University Press, 1992), 190–206.
49 Singh, *Bulleh Shah*, 37.
50 Mir, *Social Space*, 140–49.

9. THE HEART OF A GOPI
Raihana Tyabji's Bhakti Devotionalism as Self-Representation

SIOBHAN LAMBERT-HURLEY

In 1924, a young woman called Raihana Tyabji "suddenly felt," in her own words, "a tremendous, an irresistible urge to write." She sat down at her desk "with sheets of foolscap and poised pen" and, over the next three days, poured out the story of Sharmila, a gopi, or milkmaid, enraptured by Krishna in his guise as the cowherd at Vrindavan. At the time she understood this narrative to be, as she called it, a "Fragment of a Gopi's Diary." But in time she recognized that what had been revealed to her—for she understood herself to be "possessed" at the time of writing—was the very "soul," the inner self, of the gopi and, through that, an understanding of Lord Krishna himself. Hence, when her tale was eventually published in 1936, she gave it the evocative title, *The Heart of a Gopi*.[1] Subsequently, her little book went into several reprints and editions in its original English (1941, 1953, 1971), while also being translated into several European languages, including French (1938), German (1977), and Dutch (1995).[2] Excerpts from the French edition, *L'Âme d'une Gopi*, were even crafted into songs sung by Raihana herself, certainly in a recording for the American composer and choral singer Catherine Urner (1941–42).[3] Today the book is still available and often quoted in a most diverse set of contexts—from academic studies of Hinduism and websites on spirituality to a blog on "Godwriting" and the "official George Harrison message board."[4] Most recently, it has even been made into a musical that takes dialogue directly from the original text.[5]

The ongoing interest in *The Heart of a Gopi*—right into the twenty-first century—points to the success of this at least nominally Muslim woman in having her spiritual writings accepted within other religious traditions. With this achievement, we are reminded of other individuals and communities in South Asian culture and history that have inhabited the shifting ground between faith groups and thus rejected an exclusively "Hindu" or "Muslim" (or, indeed, "Sikh" or "Christian") paradigm.[6] Perhaps the most popular of these liminal figures would be the fifteenth-century poet and saint Kabir. In mocking both *pandit* and mullah, he rejected ritualistic forms of religion as practiced in the *mandir* or the *masjid*, the temple or the mosque. It is this trope of resistance to organized Hinduism or Islam that makes him so important not only as a foundational figure within certain Sikh sects, but also in the Bhakti movement, with its emphasis on spontaneous expressions of devotion, as directed at Rama or especially Krishna.[7] One may also think of Sufi poets, like Bulleh Shah in eighteenth-century Punjab, who, to the extent of none before, absorbed "Hindu" elements, including Krishnaite images, into his "Muslim" devotional poetry.[8] Perhaps the best model here, though, in that his "elegant and impassioned verses in praise of Krishna" did not just borrow "Hindu" imagery but, in the words of Rupert Snell, demonstrated a "complete commitment to Vaishnava sentiments," is the sixteenth-century poet Raskhan. Like Raihana, this Muslim Pathan's "transcendental persona" was that of a gopi endowed with such "urgent passion" that his devotion to Krishna is conceived as "conversion."[9]

Yet *The Heart of a Gopi* is not just of interest as an example of "crossing the threshold," to borrow the phrase of Dominique-Sila Khan.[10] It also attracts interest as part of a literary and historical project of theorizing the relationship between gender, history, and the self. As seen in this volume's introduction, historians of South Asia have been at the forefront of those scholars going beyond conventional autobiography to examine the diverse ways in which individuals—including those from marginalized groups and premodern societies—have found means for self-fashioning and self-representation.[11] To draw out women's conceptualizations of self has proved more difficult within the specific cultural conventions and constraints of a society that privileges the silencing of female voices—to the point that Gayatri Spivak has indicated that the South Asian woman has no real "voice," at least within traditional sites of knowledge, like the colonial archive.[12] And yet, where the effort has been made for recovery, it has pointed to the creative ways in which women have been able to narrate their life stories, or at least aspects of them, by "negotiating" with entrenched gender ideologies to manipulate the specific cultural resources at their command.[13] As Anshu Malhotra writes of the recusant Piro's *160 Kafis*, this may be a "convoluted and metaphorical path" to "unfold[ing] one's own drama," but it still represents "careful self-fashioning" in a "universe comprehended through emulation, allegory and allusion."[14]

Raihana Tyabji left to history not a memoir per se, but, rather enigmatically, a few letters, some recordings, a couple of thin books in Hindi, plenty of memories and reminiscences, and *The Heart of a Gopi*. To be considered in this chapter is how far then this piece of Bhakti devotionalism may still be read as a kind of personal narrative, an evocation of the self. A starting point will be to gain some insight into Raihana's personhood by piecing together some biographical information about her life from family, interviews, the national archive, and her own writings. It will then consider her recourse to Bhakti as a trope of the liminal self. Does the referencing of a great tradition give the author's feelings and experiences, especially as a nominal Muslim devoted to Krishna at a time of increasingly religious rigidity and communal strife, a kind of validity not achievable otherwise? The third section considers the text itself within the context of the gopi tradition. Is it possible—and, if so, how—to separate out the author's "self" from the literary conventions that structure the story? The chapter will then ask in conclusion if, in the tradition of Islamic life writing, the gap between the miraculous and the mundane can be breached in order to understand the mystical experience charted here as a kind of autobiography? Even from the rationalist's perspective, should not the life of the imagination still be considered part of the life?

Raihana's Personhood

So, who is this Raihana Tyabji? As her surname may suggest, she was born into the prominent Tyabji clan that was at the forefront of Bombay's Sulaimani Bohra community in the late nineteenth and twentieth centuries. Her father, Abbas Tyabji (1853–1936), was the grandson of the clan's founder, Tyab Ali (also known as Tyabji Bhoymeeah), through his father, Shamsuddin. Though Abbas was first married to his elder paternal uncle Camruddin's daughter, Ashraf-un-Nissa (with whom he bore two sons), upon her death he married Ameena Begam, the eldest daughter of the Tyabji clan's perhaps most famous son (and Abbas's younger paternal uncle), Badruddin (1844–1906). With his second wife, Abbas produced four children (one son and three daughters), including Raihana (1901–1975). The family was based, not in Bombay like most other Tyabjis, but instead in the princely state of Baroda in Gujarat, ruled in Raihana's youth by the larger-than-life figure of Maharaja Sayaji Rao III (1863–1939, ruled 1875–1939). In 1879, the maharaja, or at least his dewan, was responsible for appointing the then young Abbas, fairly recently returned from studying law in London, to Baroda's judicial service. By 1885, Abbas had risen to the top of this service as a judge of the Baroda high court, a position that he retained until his retirement in 1913.[15] In Baroda, Ameena too distinguished herself, not just as a hostess and a companion to the maharani (including on a trip to Europe in 1894), but also as an educationalist. Specifically, she oversaw the Muslim girls' school established by the maharaja at her encouragement in the mid-1890s.[16]

According to Abbas's recent biographer, Ameena should also be attributed with involving her husband and children with India's preeminent nationalist leader, Mohandas Karamchand Gandhi, soon after his return from South Africa in 1915. Seemingly, she had "great respect and affection" for the Mahatma-to-be, having known him ever since the early 1890s, when her esteemed father, Badruddin, himself a president of the Indian National Congress in 1887, had befriended the unknown lawyer before he left Bombay for Natal.[17] Abbas too had been a member of Congress from its establishment in 1885, even attending the historic sessions held in 1889, 1906, and 1907, but always, in his own words, as a representative of the "Moderates" committed to achieving concessions for the Indian population by working with the British government.[18] A first meeting with Gandhi at an elegant party in Bombay in 1915 did not change his views, instead leaving him "not particularly impressed."[19] The following year, however, a budding friendship between Abbas and Gandhi seems to have blossomed when they met first at Ameena's brother Salman's house in Bombay and then again at the home of Ameena's youngest sister, Safia, and her husband, Jabir Ali, in Tavoy in Burma.[20] In time, Abbas—referred to within the context of the nationalist movement as the "Grand Old Man of Gujarat"—was to become one of Gandhi's most dedicated lieutenants, even leading the famous Dandi salt march after Gandhi's arrest and being jailed for his political activism.[21]

If the occasion was the same as the party referred to above, the teenaged Raihana was rather more drawn to the saintly Gandhi on first meeting than her father. As she recalled in an interview with Ved Mehta at some point in the 1970s: "I caught a glimpse of him in the midst of silks and brocades, frills and sparkling jewels. He was dressed in a coarse khadi dhoti and looked like a small-time tailor who'd wandered in by mistake. I lost my heart to him. He became my father, my mother, my girlfriend, my boyfriend, my daughter, my son, my teacher, my guru."[22] In subsequent weeks, the rising politician and the cosseted young girl sought one another out at a number of other parties in Bombay and then privately, quickly establishing what Raihana described as a "very intimate" relationship that was to last until the Mahatma's tragic end.[23] Their amity is evident in that his *Collected Works* contain over eighty epistles from Gandhi to Raihana over the twenty-year period from 1927 to 1947—and these appear to be only a fraction of their original correspondence. Indeed, Gandhi's diary suggests that he actually wrote to her at least every couple of weeks and sometimes as often as twice a week, especially from prison.[24] Unfortunately, we do not have Raihana's side of the exchange beyond a few extracts in published articles; as Gandhi explained to her in a letter from 1927, "I destroy all your letters after replying."[25] Still, one gets a good sense of their familiarity and fondness for one another in that Gandhi addressed Raihana affectionately, if unusually, as "Raihana the Crazy" or, more conventionally, as "beloved daughter," and often finished his letters with "a slap" if not "a kiss."[26]

It is perhaps no wonder then that Raihana was inspired to become, in her own words, one of "Bapu's brahmachari soldiers."[27] Reflected here was her decision not to marry, but instead to live according to Gandhi's principles while serving the nationalist cause. According to family sources, her commitment to celibacy was made after a possible engagement to a first cousin was broken, perhaps on account of her father's concerns about the medical effects of intermarriage within families (discussed in more detail below) or perhaps on account of her skin condition, a pigment deficiency known as leucoderma, that took the form of white patches all over her body.[28] Interestingly, this medical condition gave Raihana an aura of exceptionalism that led one Tyabji descendant, quite approvingly, to describe her as "more than normal": one who "knew so much more than we do."[29] Yet Raihana's poor health often left her bedridden and sometimes in need of medical intervention (including an operation on her displaced nasal septum in 1930).[30] Her body's fragility thus interfered with her "public work" at least until the early 1930s—a cause of great frustration, if Gandhi's letters to her on the subject are anything to go by.[31] Still, she was responsible for acting as president of the Youth League (or Yuvak Sangh) in Baroda in the late 1920s,[32] picketing liquor shops and fasting against foreign cloth merchants during the civil disobedience movement of the early 1930s,[33] and serving as a trustee of the Kasturba Gandhi National Memorial Trust in the mid-1940s.[34] During the Quit India movement, she was even imprisoned on at least two occasions for participating in banned processions.[35] Hence, Gandhi was inspired to write of her in *Navajivan*: "Raihana, poor cripple, spends her days and nights thinking of India only."[36] To Raihana herself, he opined: "What a strange girl you are! You fall ill, return home, go out again to work and again fall ill. What wonderful enthusiasm [for] the cause!"[37]

Though generally resident at her parents' home in Baroda (where she appears to have written *The Heart of a Gopi*), Raihana often visited Gandhi's ashram at Sevagram and, a year after her mother's death in 1940, settled at Wardha with two of Gandhi's other disciples, D. B. Kalelkar (popularly known as Kakasaheb) and Sarojini Nanavati (shortened to Saroj). Raihana seems to have met the latter, the daughter of Judge D. D. Nanavati, while doing some sort of work at the Oriental Research Institute in Pune in 1932, and the two had soon become inseparable.[38] As Gandhi wrote to Saroj fourteen years later, "May your devotion to service go on increasing and Raihana's with yours, or yours with Raihana's. You may be separate in body, but are not you one in spirit?"[39] In Wardha, Raihana also became very involved alongside Kalelkar in an organization to advance Hindustani as a national language for India, the Hindustani Prachar Sabha.[40] This cause was perhaps surprising in light of her earlier preference for English, Urdu, and even Gujarati—and all the more so because Gandhi's letters and articles on the subject indicate that Raihana was "rigidly" in favor of Hindustani being written in the Nagari script only (rather than the Urdu script as well). Apparently, she felt that the latter encouraged a "separatist tendency" among Indian Muslims.[41] After independence, Raihana, Saroj, and Kalelkar relocated to a house in Gandhi's ashram in Delhi, from where Raihana dedicated her latter years to offering spiritual guidance as comfort to those with mental difficulties.[42] Part of the service, it seems, was to recount the past incarnations of visitors as she "saw" them.[43]

In the context of Gandhian mythology, the Muslim-born Raihana is attributed with having taught Urdu to the Mahatma and for having encouraged him to incorporate verses from the Qur'an into his prayer meetings—two contributions that are well documented in Gandhi's *Collected Works*.[44] Feminist scholars also sometimes point to the way in which Raihana influenced Gandhi's writings on women's rights.[45] What Raihana is best remembered for, however, is the *bhajans*, or devotional songs associated with the Bhakti movement, that she sang at the commencement of meetings at the ashram or on tour with Gandhi and even at annual sessions of the Congress.[46] On this account, many around Raihana apparently considered her to be a "reincarnation of the legendary Mirabai," a reference to the sixteenth-century songstress and Krishna devotee that will also resonate with contemporary readers.[47] Gandhi's love of Raihana's singing is recorded in many of his letters to her. As he wrote to her from jail in 1932, "The bhajan you have sent will seem good only when I can hear it sung, and that can be when you come and sing it to me."[48] It is perhaps not surprising then that Raihana, along with her father, Abbas, and niece Hamida, was one of the chosen few permitted by Gandhi to see him in jail—his explanation being that they were "like blood relations to me."[49]

More racy accounts of Gandhi and Raihana highlight their shared interest in Tantric practices. This sexual fixation was alluded to by Raihana herself when, in her interview with Ved Mehta, she referred to *brahmacharya* experiments (which involved sleeping naked with members of the opposite sex) that later inspired Gandhi's own.[50] This strange juxtaposition of eroticism and celibacy is something that emerges in Gandhi's correspondence with Raihana as well. On one occasion, he referred to her as a "stranger to sensuous passion."[51] And yet, on another, he offered sympathy in response to a letter in which she had clearly unburdened herself about the difficulties of "discipline"—before admitting that he too was not "too pure for sex-consciousness."[52] Much later in life, Raihana explained in her interview with Blum that she had come *not* to accept the principle of brahmacharya as practiced by Gandhi. "Abstinence in an army," she explained "was a necessity," but "abstinence must not be made the rule of life for everybody." Their point of departure seemed to be Gandhi's insistence on celibacy within marriage—an idea that, in her opinion, contradicted the "sacredness of the marital relationship." From her experience of watching others, she had come to believe that a man who practiced abstinence would become a "sadist": someone who would be "violent on the mental or emotional plane."[53]

Accounts of Gandhi's closest associates thus cannot avoid mentioning Raihana. In characterizing her religious allegiances and identities, however, the depictions are varied. Sometimes she is recognized as a "devout Krishna bhakt," or devotee, though "born in a Muslim family."[54] Elsewhere, she is described as a "devout Muslim," but "with respect for all religions."[55] Ved Mehta, on the other hand, opens his section on her in the oft-quoted *Mahatma Gandhi and His Apostles* with: "By birth and upbringing she is a Sufi Muslim, and by inclination and choice a Vishnuite Hindu."[56] In contrast, contemporary Tyabjis now tend to depict her as a Sufi, or at least "influenced by Sufism," seemingly in an attempt to contain her unusual religious beliefs and activities within the Muslim fold.[57] This characterization resonates with Raihana's *own* account of her spiritual practice in her interview with Blum in 1973 in which she asserted: "The Sufi is quite different from the Mussalman. I am Sufi. I don't call myself Mussalman because I don't believe in and do not belong to the Mussalman sect. But I am Islamic, in that I accept whole-heartedly the blessed tenets of Islam, and the way that I live my way of living, is that of a Muslim monastery."[58] And yet, earlier in the same interview, she had accounted for differences with

Gandhi over the importance of *ahimsa*, or nonviolence, in terms of her preference for a "middle path": one that was "both of the *Gita* and of the *Koran*."[59] On other occasions, the balance swung in the opposite direction in that she portrayed herself as "80% Hindu," "though born a Muslim," on account of believing in karma and samsara, or the cycle of birth and rebirth.[60] In that she continued to describe Lord Krishna appearing and speaking to her (even in the course of her interview with Mehta carried out shortly before her death), one may assume that—however her religious identity was constructed by her and others—the passion aroused in the course of "writing" *The Heart of a Gopi* in the 1920s did not leave her.[61] What this recourse to Bhakti reveals in terms of self-representation will be explored in the following section.

The Recourse to Bhakti

According to Raihana, she had no role in crafting the story that came through her hand. As she specified from the outset with the certainty of any life writer depicting his or her outpouring as "truth-telling," "the truth is that this story is not mine except in that it has been written by this hand." She went on: "During the three days that it took to write I had a distinct sensation of being possessed by something from outside myself and of being compelled to write even in spite of myself."[62] Her abdication of responsibility for writing smacks of a "convention of passivity" within the long tradition of writing life stories and journeys with Islam by which no suitably modest author should really be seen to be writing at his or her own initiative.[63] Barbara Metcalf has pointed to this phenomenon with reference to the *hajj* narrative of Pakistani novelist Mumtaz Mufti. He records that he wrote about "what happened in Mecca," though "not knowing what happened," because "God grabbed him."[64] In this context, we may debate how appropriate it is to speak of choice per se in the form of the story that Raihana told. Perhaps it is better to treat it simply as part of that corpus of Islamic literature concerned with dreams and visions, revelation and prophecy.[65] And yet, within the religious context in which she was writing, her recourse to the Bhakti tradition—so often associated with a rejection of religious authorities and the false spirituality in which their rituals could trap the pious individual—in itself seems highly revelatory of a liminal self caught between increasingly monolithic conceptions of "Hinduness" and "Muslimness."

Of course, to seek a more personalized relationship with God by depicting oneself as a female lover in relation to the divine, as Raihana does in *The Heart of a Gopi*, is not exclusive to the Bhakti tradition. In devotional poetry and music associated with Sufi Islam, whether *sufiana-kalam*, *qawalli*, or the *ghazal*—the poetic voice is often indeterminate or female addressing a beloved representative of the divine that also may be of indeterminate gender or identifiably male or even female.[66] The trope is one of longing to be united with the cruel and fickle lover from whom the devotee experiences painful separation. Here we may quote a line from early in Raihana's text to draw a parallel: "That Krishna seems to be a wonderful being! Who he is, what he does, where he lives, where he is now, all this a complete mystery . . . this Krishna, is he, too, full of color, full of light, full of music? Ah, one day I shall know."[67] Yet, as the last line suggests, whereas the highest aspiration of the devotee within Sufic literature is to suffer in the face of the beloved's indifference, the gopi does not, ultimately, remain apart from her God. Worth noting here too is that, while Raihana demonstrated a thorough knowledge of the ghazal tradition in her letters to Gandhi—often sending him favored lyrics (for instance, by Bahadur Shah "Zafar") in Urdu or Gujarati translation[68]—it was bhajans that, as noted previously, she chose to write and sing herself. Raihana thus laid claim to a place within the Bhakti tradition in an act that may itself be read as self-representation.

It has been noted already that, by birth, Raihana was a Sulaimani Bohra, a denomination of especial relevance in this context. The Bohras were a sect of Ismaili Shiism originally established in Yemen, but that probably came to Gujarat in western India at some point in the thirteenth century. Over the many centuries that followed, the community experienced innumerable schisms with the Sulaimani branch to which the Tyabjis belonged, recognizing the leadership of a different *da'i*, or spiritual leader, than others such as the Daudi Bohras or the Jafari Bohras.[69] In *Crossing the Threshold*, Dominique-Sila Khan has explored the way in which Ismaili Islam in Gujarat especially represented an "intricate interface" between supposedly separate and even antagonistic religious groupings in South Asia as represented by the labels, "Hinduism" and "Islam."[70] The ongoing openness of Sulaimani Bohras to a range of different religious practices, even at a time of growing communitarianism and intolerance, is evident from those customs and attitudes recorded in the goodly stash of autobiographical writings produced by different Tyabjis in the twentieth century.[71] Raihana herself wrote in her later book of reminiscences, *Suniye Kakasahib*, of the "inter-communal culture" within her childhood home in Baroda by which the family "celebrated Diwali, *Dussehra*, Holi, *Bhai duj*, *Nagpanchami*, *Utran* (the kite festival), Muharram, Id, *Papeti* (the Parsi New Year), and Christmas with equal enthusiasm."[72] Of her father, Gandhi wrote too: "His Islam had room for all the great religions of the earth."[73]

Nevertheless, by the time of Raihana's birth in the late nineteenth or early twentieth century, the Tyabjis as a family group were, as Khan terms it, "creating orthodoxies."[74] What is meant here is they were seeking to prove their Islamic credentials in a number of different ways. One method was the jettisoning of the clan's mother tongue of Gujarati for the north Indian *lingua franca* of Urdu by family decree in 1859.[75] Another method was through the establishment or patronage of Islamic organizations associated with a broader movement of socioreligious reform—a prominent example being the Anjuman-i-Islam founded in Bombay in 1876.[76] Yet another method was intermarriage with more "mainstream" Muslims, whether Sunni or Shia, from other parts of the Indian subcontinent. Raihana's two elder sisters, Shareefa and Sohela, for instance, were married, not to cousins within the clan as was the usual Tyabji practice, but instead to Hameed Ali, an officer in the Indian civil service, and Muhammad Habib, a university professor at Aligarh Muslim University.[77] According to Theodore Wright Jr., these marriages were less to do with hypergamy than exogamy after Abbas Tyabji read a book on the "undesirable and inheritable physical traits" that could result from "too much inbreeding" within a family.[78] Still, when combined with "Urduization" and reformism, these marriages (and many others besides) had the effect of tying the Tyabjis much more closely to what Wright calls the "old Mughal ruling class"[79]—in other words, making them more identifiably "Muslim."

And yet, for all these efforts, there is no doubt that Raihana's birth community still retained a liminal status within South Asia's complex religious landscape during her lifetime. As evidence we may consider an incident recorded in her *Suniye Kakasahib* in connection with her father. Apparently having found the Jama Masjid in Baroda to be in a poor state of repair, Abbas Tyabji decided to collect donations for it to be renovated, perhaps sometime in the 1890s, in part from the Muslim community and in part by securing a grant from the maharaja. And yet, when the mosque was renewed, he was excluded from entry. As Raihana records: "On the first Friday after the inauguration of the mosque, when *babajan* [her father] together with some Sulemaini Bohras went to offer *namaz*, the Sunnis said, 'You cannot offer *namaz* here. You are not Muslims.' They drove them out with *lathis*."[80] Even as Abbas asserted his Islamic credentials with a great act of piety, so he and his community were denied a place in the Muslim fold. Her disgust at her father's treatment, and by extension the organized and dominant forms of Islam represented by the "Sunnis" at the mosque, is plain from her response to this incident: "What shameful behavior to make such distinctions in the House of God!"[81]

In light of this past, communitarian and familial, Raihana's recourse to Bhakti as a means of telling her story makes much more sense. The very form and practice allowed her to legitimize a sense of self that was not just at odds with increasingly rigid definitions of religious identity, but actually embraced the inclusivity that had been at the heart of the Sulaimani Bohra community and her own family's practice, at least until very recently. Of course, it is important to recognize that the Bhakti movement too was undergoing a process of solidification and sedentarization in this period.[82] An effect of *this* new orthodoxy, in a point of especial relevance for the next section, was that Bhakti was increasingly purged of its eroticism—to the point that the nineteenth-century Bengali mystic Ramakrishna, though willing to dress up as a woman to replicate being a gopi before Krishna (a practice known as *madhura bhava*), often equated sex with defecation.[83] Still, for the Muslim-born Raihana, Bhakti's connotation, even more than that of Sufism, must have been that of a rejection of a formulaic and exclusionary paradigm in favor of a celebration of her inherited and inherent liminality. How and why she then used the gopi tradition specifically to tell her particular story will be explored in the following section.

Using the Gopi Tradition

Those familiar with the Islamic context will know that it boasts a long tradition of recording life stories quite apart from the Western biographical and autobiographical tradition. From the time of the Prophet Muhammad himself, "narrations" of an exemplary life—whether of scholar, saint, poet, or king—were used to didactic purpose: as a model for "ordinary" Muslims. Distinctive to this literary heritage were a number of specific features, not least a humoral understanding of personality, a lack of chronology, an attention to moral lessons, a rejection of individual agency and an emphasis on relations with others.[84] Until the nineteenth century, it was rare for women to participate in the genre, but not entirely unheard of.[85] The onslaught of colonialism accompanied by the introduction of print culture to the Indian subcontinent was still, however, transformative on Muslims writing lives. It inspired, in Francis Robinson's words, a "growth of self-consciousness and reflective habit" among South Asian Muslims, male and female, that was represented, in one form at least, by a proliferation of life writing.[86] Increasingly, Muslims of all walks of life wrote more and different autobiographies in which the emphasis was less on the "Perfect Man" of the

Sufi tradition, to borrow Robinson's formulation once again, and more on the "perfect person": "the manifold nature of the human individual" or, more simply put, the self.[87]

The Tyabji clan offers an excellent case in point, starting with the dynasty's founder. Having established himself as a prosperous cotton merchant in a Bombay flourishing under East India Company rule, Tyab Ali recorded his "rags to riches" story in an autobiography that offered important inspiration to his many descendants.[88] Subsequently, an inordinate number of individual Tyabjis narrated their lives, or fragments of them, in memoirs, autobiographies, and travel accounts that date from the nineteenth century to the present.[89] Among them were a significant number of women. Two out of three daughters of the first generation of the Fyzee branch of the clan, to take a representative example, published full-length travelogues—or, more properly, travel diaries (*roznamchah*)—in which they recounted their journeys, physical and metaphorical, to Britain, Europe, and West Asia in the Edwardian era.[90] The clan's various branches also kept unusual family diaries, known as *Akhbar ki Kitab* (or "news-books"), in which public and private events, quotidian and otherwise, were recorded. Women especially were urged to contribute, and thus it is not surprising that it was here that Raihana's mother, Ameena, wrote a short account of her life that was later published in a prominent women's magazine.[91] Her father, Abbas, too kept a personal diary in which he recorded earlier incidents revelatory of his adult self.[92]

For Raihana then, there was no shortage of autobiographical models close at hand. Hers was not so much a problem, as Malhotra writes of Piro, living in nineteenth-century Punjab, of finding a way to write about her life in a "society unfamiliar with the self-absorption required of an autobiography."[93] And yet, for her first foray into public self-representation—if we may interpret it as that—Raihana explicitly chose *not* to write a memoir, nor even a travelogue. Instead, she elected, like many women before her, to employ a familiar narrative form—in this case, the devotional mode of Bhakti associated with the gopi tradition—as a means of writing about her feelings and experiences. We might draw a parallel here with the way in which women throughout South Asian history have used epic, including the Ramayana, and the afflicted Sita especially, to narrate their own suffering.[94] This narrative strategy could be interpreted as a means of drawing a metaphorical veil over women's voices—not meant to be heard in the South Asian context—while, at the same time, endowing their individual experiences with a kind of validity not achievable otherwise. Where then to find Raihana's "self" in her little book of Bhakti devotionalism so firmly located with the gopi tradition? And what was she trying to relate that she could not say otherwise? What did the gopi tradition offer specifically that other readily available models of life writing did not?

As a starting point, it is important to note that, in many ways, *The Heart of a Gopi* follows conventional, even formulaic, patterns. Great importance is invested in the devotee, Raihana's alter ego Sharmila, gaining a vision of the deity, a *darshan* that cannot help but fill her with "nameless ecstasy."[95] As she exults in the latter stages of the narrative, "before my eyes that incarnation of divine beauty began to shine with greater and with greater brilliance, until there stood before me a Form made, from head to foot, purely of dazzling blue light."[96] There is also that "literal and realistic interaction," to borrow Snell's phrase, between the devotee and the deity himself.[97] Sharmila, like the best of gopis, spends her days frolicking with the other milkmaids and the child Krishna, partaking in his pranks, reveling in his mischief.[98] She is driven to frenzy by the sound of his "Celestial Flute," loses her earrings (if, notably, not her sari) in this state of "madness," and even allows her husband's supper to be pilfered while in a state of having "lost all consciousness of self."[99] Her sister-in-law, representing society's censure of a married woman disregarding "normal social roles," chastises her for her impropriety—for following Radha and the other "vile" gopis into forgetting "their vows and their Pati Vrata" by chasing after Krishna.[100] And yet, ultimately, it is those moments in which Sharmila's earthly soul submits to Krishna's grace that represent, as one would expect, the pinnacle of the narrative. "The world hath been flung off like a soiled garment, I am clad in the shining robes of Bhakti, pure white, gleaming as a white pigeon's wing in sunlight! . . . I come, my lord, I come!"[101]

To find self-representation then, one must look beyond the convention outlined here to the level of emphasis and innovation within this particular telling of the gopi story. We may ask: in what ways, however subtle, *does* Raihana's account diverge from the gopi formula? Is there a sense in which Sharmila is not the average gopi? If so, in what ways and in which contexts? And what do these ways and contexts tell us about Raihana's decision to use the gopi tradition to narrate her own story, her own self? Did the gopi tradition open up avenues for self-representation and perhaps even self-fulfilment not achievable otherwise? To begin answering these questions, let us take two examples of distinctive themes within the narrative—one relating to social status and the other to erotic mysticism—that help illustrate the way in which the self may be revealed in this type of text, and also the reasons why.

The first theme that stands out as distinct in Raihana's telling of the gopi story relates to the leaving behind of social status. Unlike your usual milkmaid, Sharmila is located from the outset in social terms as a "rich man's beloved daughter" who has been married off hurriedly to a Gauli, a keeper of cattle, seemingly to protect her from the "wrath of the King."[102] Whereas yesterday she was "clad in silk," today only a "red rag conceals [her] nakedness."[103] She sleeps on the floor of a poor man's hut when used to a palace, milks cows with the other maidens when accustomed only to picking flowers, waits on the "father, mother, sisters" of her low-caste husband rather than issuing commands.[104] She is "abased, humbled to the dust."[105] The resonance with Raihana's own experience of staying in Gandhi's ashram seems pronounced when set against her later account of arriving there with her own personal commode. Displayed "royally" on top of her luggage, it announced to all others that she, from her privileged background among Bombay's elite—a "spoilt girl," as Gandhi characterized her in 1932[106]—was incapable of "squatting over a trench latrine without a proper seat." "You can imagine how silly I felt," she told Ved Mehta, "how chastened." And yet "because of Bapu," Raihana went on to explain, "I"—like Sharmila enchanted by Krishna—"learned to go anywhere, sleep anyplace, eat anything."[107] Her autonomous self, we come to see, takes form in being removed from social context.

In this connection, it is also worth noting that Raihana's decision to become a disciple of Gandhi was not uncontested. Though members of the Tyabji clan are often celebrated now for their early and consistent espousal of Gandhian ideals,[108] we see from Gandhi's *Collected Works* that Raihana often found herself in conflict with her parents, Abbas and Ameena Tyabji, over her chosen path. Throughout the late 1920s and early 1930s, she wrote lengthy epistles—sadly, not preserved, though they are referred to in Gandhi's own correspondence—in which she complained bitterly that they would not allow her, in Gandhi's words, "to wear whatever you like and to see or be seen by any friends you like."[109] Indicated here is not a young woman's tempestuous assertion of false independence, but rather a political statement in favor of spurning "Western facilities and contrivances" in favor of wearing *khadi*, or clothes made of homespun cloth, and meeting fellow nationalists of different castes, classes, and religions.[110] In response, Gandhi advised Raihana not to oppose her parents openly—not least because they were "rulers of the household" on whom she depended for her "maintenance"—but rather to "convince everybody around you of the justice of your action" through "gentle suggestions."[111] *The Heart of a Gopi* may have fulfilled that very function in a suitably oblique fashion.

A second theme emphasized in Raihana's narrative is the expression of love of the divine through the love of an individual. Despite being chastised by her sister-in-law, Sharmila ultimately convinces her alarmed husband and in-laws that her love of Krishna, though expressed in highly eroticized, earthly terms, is acceptable on the basis that the love of a God and the love of a man may actually be complementary. As Sharmila describes her attraction to her husband: "It is not thy body that I love, it is thy soul, and all the goodness, and sweetness, and strength thereof. I love thee for thy strong manhood; for thy virtue; for thy intellect; thy skill, thy tenderness; for thy simplicity, truth and steadfastness. All of this, yea, every single one of these qualities, is Krishna! All, all is Krishna! All is Krishna!"[112] The gopi tradition is, of course, by nature playful and erotic (regardless of what Ramakrishna made of it). But the connection between the intense passions described in *The Heart of a Gopi* and Raihana's own sexual experimentation, as referred to in the earlier section, seems plain. Consider another quote from her later interview with Mehta: "I often told Bapu that there was a great difference between repressing libido and outgrowing it, and that the only way to outgrow it was to give free rein to it—to indulge it and satiate it."[113] This, she explains, is what she had done in previous incarnations—to the point that even her skin condition was attributed to "recklessly indulging my sexual appetite."[114] In alluding to Mehta's own sexual conquests in a previous life, she also grouped herself with other "passionate, romantic girls."[115] Though a brahmachari, Raihana's self is revealed as sexual.

This second theme especially suggests why the young Raihana may have chosen Bhakti and the gopi tradition specifically as a means of self-representation, rather than participating more explicitly in the autobiographical tradition of her clan or Islamic societies more generally—namely, it allowed her to circumvent prohibited expressions of female sexuality. Contrary to popular perception, Muslim women in South Asia have written autobiographically about their sexual relations in the modern period. We might consider, as just one early example, Nawab Shah Jahan Begam's encyclopedic manual for women, *Tahzib un-Niswan wa Tarbiyat ul-Insan*, first published in 1889. Here, she used her own experiences with her first and second husbands as illustration in a passage on women's right to carnal pleasure.[116] Indicated by this example, it was primarily in a princely context that sexual matters were broached by female memoirists—perhaps on account of the authors' more elite status, a more developed *zenana* culture or the relative autonomy of "native states."[117] In reformist circles like those frequented by the Tyabjis, autobiographical references to sexual matters were much scarcer, most probably reflecting the greater influence of Victorian notions of bourgeois sexuality. Certainly Raihana's female cousins who wrote life histories in a more conventional way were highly modest in their approach—Atiya Fyzee not even alluding to her reputed affair with the poet Iqbal, nor Nazli, the Begam of Janjira, to the problems in her marriage, in their respective European travelogues.[118]

For Raihana then, *The Heart of a Gopi* seems to have offered a means of justifying her unconventional lifestyle—her leaving behind the comforts associated with the Tyabji's social status to live as a brahmachari in one of Gandhi's ashrams—while, at the same time, allowing her to speak of a mystical path expressed through earthly passion. By juxtaposing her individual telling of the gopi story against later accounts of her own life, the seeming contradictions of a brahmachari experimenting with Tantric practices and writing in Bhakti's amorous mode are brought into sharp relief, but also, in a way, resolved. We are given a sense of the innate tensions and even conflict that must have played out in Raihana's mind, if not her body, between her innate desire for sexual indulgence and her vow of celibacy: a sexualized self that she dare not articulate in a more unambiguously autobiographical form. And yet, just as she writes so convincingly of love without ever making explicit any amorous physical encounter between Sharmila and Krishna, so the gopi persona seemed to offer her an erotic outlet without consummation. Krishna—or may we read Gandhi?—is Raihana/Sharmila's salve: the promise of spiritual fulfilment expressed as human desire, *but without the actual indulgence*. We may recall here the quote from the second section in which Raihana identified Gandhi not just as parent and teacher, but also as companion and child. Appropriately then, at the end of her tale, Sharmila is finally reunited with her husband, in-laws, parents, and sister in expressing a common devotion to Krishna. Together, their hearts "thrilling with love," they sing, "Jaya Krishna! Jaya, Jaya Krishna!"[119] This mysticism is considered as a form of autobiography to conclude.

The Marvellous and the Miraculous: Conclusions

I first read *The Heart of a Gopi* in the personal collection of Salima Tyabji, herself a descendant of Tyab Ali, at her home in Delhi. The copy that she generously allowed me to peruse at her kitchen table (while, memorably, drinking the most delicious cinnamon tea) had, apparently, been presented by Raihana herself to Salima's father, Saif. In the back was a handwritten note, perhaps attributable to this Cambridge-educated lawyer, then mathematician. "The only element I personally dislike," it read, "is that miraculous touches have been used. But it is a habitual device with mystics and bhaktas of all times and creeds. Some get so fond of the marvellous and the miraculous they make it the dominant note in all they say or sing."[120] This most eloquent scribble sums up, effectively, what might be the expected response to this text from one rooted in a Western rational tradition. How could Raihana have written this text, and yet not? Does she seriously expect us to believe that she was "possessed" for three days during which she wrote things that even she "could not understand"? How could she have been transformed into a gopi living in Vrindavan at the feet of Krishna? Raihana herself recognized these likely misgivings in her introduction to the text when she wrote: "I must risk being either smiled or sniffed at by 'rationalists' if I am to speak the truth here."[121]

As a trained historian, it would be easy for me, too, to dismiss *The Heart of a Gopi* as little more than a wild and creative tale by a slightly barmy woman. And yet, whatever we may think of it, Raihana *believed* it happened. In that way, it becomes a very personal tale of her mystical experience, not so very different from those highly individualized accounts written by Muslims on hajj, for instance, in the modern period. We may think again here of Mumtaz Mufti. Though a self-proclaimed "nominal Muslim" laying claim to a cosmopolitan intellectual inheritance, he experienced all sorts of "strange things" in the course of his pilgrimage to Mecca—from dreams indicating the future to idols (or *bat*) in the Kaʻaba.[122] Metcalf points out that this "expanded sense of reality" is only to be expected from a text rooted in the long Urdu-Persianate tradition of writing autobiography and biography.[123] Here, as she writes, "the definition of what is presented as part of life's experience is very inclusive. Put differently, magic is on the loose."[124] We may consider, as just one other example, the hajj narrative of one of South Asia's greatest Islamic scholars, Shah Waliullah Dihlawi: "in no sense a travelogue but rather a compendium of visions and dreams."[125] Approached from this perspective, Raihana's little book of Bhakti devotionalism—mediated through a long tradition of Islamic life writing—becomes as valid to those interested in self-representation as any other more identifiably autobiographical text.

The Heart of a Gopi then requires us to rethink what we actually mean by *autobiographical writing*. As seen in the introduction to this volume, standard definitions of *autobiography* elaborated by literary theorists in the context of a Euro-American tradition have tended to celebrate the Enlightenment ideal of the autonomous male individual crafting his own life story into a coherent, retrospective narrative as a function of personality.[126] The historical contingency and gendered representation inherent to these definitions have encouraged a number of postmodern and postcolonial theorists to jettison the term *autobiography* in favor of other monikers considered more accepting of temporal and geographical diversity.[127] Often preferred in the South Asian context in that, in this mode, it is deemed more inclusive of the heterogeneity of autobiographical practice is the term *life history*. As Arnold and Blackburn write in the introduction to their important *Telling Lives in India*, they choose to employ "life histories" to apply to their collection on the basis that it does not "privilege print over orality," nor "ignore the often fragmentary or allusive nature of many life-historical forms."[128] "Fragmentary" and "allusive" are two descriptors that may rightly be applied to *The Heart of a Gopi* too. And yet, if we hope to disrupt the established Western canon of autobiography—as this book seeks to do—it seems only appropriate to employ a term that has resonance on a global scale. In the end then, I would assert that we can read Raihana Tyabji's Bhakti devotionalism as self-representation and even, to take the point further, as a form of autobiography, if only the autobiography of the imagination. The adjective *autobiographical* is thus appropriated as an inclusive hold-all for a wide range of self-referential writing—even "the marvellous and the miraculous."

So what can we say of the self-represented here? Raihana Tyabji is best known to history as a devotee of Gandhi, rather than for her writing or even her singing. But standard narratives of the Mahatma's followers or associates rarely get beyond a brief and rather confused attempt to explain her unusual status as a Muslim-born Krishna bhakt. In this circumstance, *The Heart of a Gopi* provides access to the inner self—the "soul," as Raihana terms it in her introduction—of this particular gopi. Her recourse to the Bhakti tradition itself is revelatory of her experience of growing up with her family's Islamic ambitions, but still ambiguous status as Sulaimani Bohras within South Asia's colorful religious spectrum. Here is a woman, her chosen genre says, who will not be trapped by religious authority or ritual or convention—even to the point of stepping outside her "Muslimness." Yet it is the points of disjuncture with more conventional gopi narratives—whether in terms of emphasis or innovation—that offer the best insights into this liminal self. Only by using the metaphorical language of Bhakti can Raihana explain her rejection of social hierarchy, but acceptance of a mystical path expressed through earthly passion. A creative reading of this miraculous account then allows a woman's resistant voice to be recovered.

NOTES

This chapter is reprinted from *Modern Asian Studies*. Earlier drafts of this chapter were presented at the panel "Speaking of the Self? Women and Self Representation in South Asia," at the European Conference on Modern South Asian Studies in Bonn, Germany, in July 2010; and at the South Asia Studies Seminar at the University of Leeds in March 2011. My thanks to the participants, and especially my coconvenor in Bonn, Anshu Malhotra, for their extremely useful comments on these occasions and after. I am also grateful to Anand Vivek Taneja, Sunil Sharma, and the anonymous reviewers at *MAS* for their suggestions. More generally, this has benefited from lively discussions held in connection with the international research network Women's Autobiography in Islamic Societies (http://www.waiis.org).

1 Raihana Tyabji, *The Heart of a Gopi* (Poona: Miss R. Tyabji, n.d.). The quotes here come from v–vi.
2 Raihana Tyabji, *The Heart of a Gopi* (Bombay: Vora, 1941; n.p.: n.d., 1953; Delhi: East West Publication, 1971); *L'Ame d'une Gopi*, trans. Lizelle Reymond (Frameries, Belgium: Union des Imprimeries, 1935); *Das Herz einer Gopi* (Darmstadt: Synergia/Syntropia, 1977); *Het hart van een Gopi* (Rotterdam: Synthese Uitgeverij, 1995).
3 See *Inventory of the Catherine Murphy Urner Collection, [ca. 1910-ca. 1942]*, Music Library, University of California, Berkeley, accessed December 10, 2009, http://www.oac.cdlib.org/data/13030/5x/tf0z09n55x/files/tf0z09n55x.pdf.
4 See, as examples, René Guénon, *Studies in Hinduism*, trans. Henry D. Fohr (Hillsdale, NY: Sophia Perennis, 2001), 194–95; *Lord Krishna*, accessed July 5, 2010, http://www.ramdasstapes.org/krishna.htm; *The heart of a gopi*, accessed July 5, 2010, http://board.georgeharrison.com/viewtopic.php?q=board/viewtopic.php&f=7&t=4111; and *Heart of a Gopi*, accessed December 10, 2009, http://www.blogcatalog.com/blog/godwriting.
5 Accessed July 5, 2010, http://heartofagopi.org/.
6 Two studies of such liminal communities in a historical context are Dominique-Sila Khan, *Crossing the Threshold: Understanding Religious Identities in South Asia* (London: I. B. Tauris, 2004); and Shail Mayaram, *Resisting Regimes: Myth, Memory and the Shaping of a Muslim Identity* (New York: Oxford University Press, 1997). For a more popular, contemporary study, though with a strong historical element, see Yoginder Sikand, *Shared Spaces: Exploring Traditions of Shared Faith in India* (Delhi: Penguin, 2003).
7 On Kabir and the Bhakti movement more generally, see John Stratton Hawley, *Three Bhakti Voices: Mirabai, Surdas and Kabir in Their Time and Ours* (New York: Oxford University Press, 2005).
8 My coverage of Bulleh Shah here draws on Anshu Malhotra, "Telling Her Tale? Unravelling a Life in Conflict in Peero's *Ik Sau Saṭh Kāfiāṅ (One Hundred and Sixty Kafis),*" *Indian Economic and Social History Review* 46.4 (2009): 572–73, but, for a more comprehensive discussion, see Denis Matringe, "Krsnaite and Nath Elements in the Poetry of the Eighteenth-Century Panjabi Sufi Bulhe Sah," in *Devotional Literature in South Asia*, ed. R. S. McGregor (Cambridge: Cambridge University Press, 1992), 190–206. On "shared philosophical beliefs and imageries" between the Bhakti and Sufi movements more generally, see Bruce Lawrence, "The Sant Movement and North Indian Sufis," in Karine Schomer and W. H. McLeod, eds., *The Sants: Studies in a Devotional Tradition of India* (Delhi: Motilal Banarsidass, 1987), 359–73.
9 Rupert Snell, "Raskhān the Neophyte: Hindu Perspectives on a Muslim Vaishnava," in *Urdu and Muslim South Asia: Studies in Honor of Ralph Russell*, ed. Christopher Shackle (Delhi: Oxford University Press, 1991), 29–37. For particular quotes, see 29, 32, 34. My thanks to Sunil Sharma for this reference.

10 Khan, *Crossing the Threshold*.
11 As an example, see David Arnold and Stuart Blackburn, eds., *Telling Lives in India: Biography, Autobiography and Life History* (Delhi: Permanent Black, 2004).
12 See Gayatri Spivak, "Subaltern Studies: Deconstructing Historiography," in *Subaltern Studies: Writings on South Asian History and Society IV*, ed. Ranajit Guha (Delhi: Oxford University Press, 1985), 330–63.
13 Deniz Kandiyoti, "Bargaining with Patriarchy," *Gender and Society* 2 (1988): 274–98.
14 Malhotra, "Telling Her Tale?," 544–45, 566.
15 On Abbas's judicial career, see Aparna Basu, *Abbas Tyabji* (New Delhi: National Book Trust, India, 2007), 24–42.
16 On this school, see Basu, *Abbas*, 34–36. On Ameena Tyabji's experiences in Europe, I consulted a transcript of a speech delivered by her at the family ladies' club, Akdé Suraya, on August 22, 1904. It is kept in the private collection of Rafia Abdul Ali in Mumbai.
17 Basu, *Abbas*, 43–44.
18 Basu, *Abbas*, 50, 53.
19 Basu, *Abbas*, 43.
20 Basu, *Abbas*, 44; and Safia Jabir Ali, "Manuscript Memoirs of Mrs Safia Jabir Ali," in Badruddin Tyabji Family Papers VI, Nehru Memorial Museum and Library, New Delhi.
21 On this, see Basu, *Abbas*, 67–74.
22 Quoted in Ved Mehta, *Mahatma Gandhi and His Apostles* (Harmondsworth, UK: Penguin, 1976), 211. For another account of their first meeting, see the interview with Raihana Tyabji in Usha Thakkar and Jayshree Mehta, eds., *Understanding Gandhi: Gandhians in Conversation with Fred J. Blum* (Delhi: Sage, 2011), 158–60.
23 Thakkar and Mehta, *Understanding Gandhi*, 160.
24 See, as an example, "Diary, 1932," in *Collected Works of Mahatma Gandhi Online*, accessed April 4, 2011, http://www.gandhiserve.org/cwmg/cwmg.html (hereafter CWMGO). From Gandhi's letters, we know too that, at the least, he began reading *The Heart of a Gopi* in its first incarnation as a "Gopi's diary" before leaving it for the Bardoli satyagraha in 1928. Sadly, there is no record of his opinion other than that he considered it "quite good news" to hear that it was to be first published in the mid-1930s. See letter to Abbas Tyabji, August 4, 1928; and letter to Raihana Tyabji, January 30, 1934.
25 Letter to Raihana Tyabji, July 12, 1927, CWMGO. For an example of a published extract, see "Position of Women," *Young India*, October 17, 1929, CWMGO.
26 See, as examples, letters to Raihana Tyabji, January 25, 1931, October 1, 1932, January 23, 1933, and August 14, 1941, CWMGO.
27 Mehta, *Mahatma*, 211.
28 Mark Devereux, "The Early Tyabji Women," from *Retroblog of Najm Tyabji (1930+)*, accessed November 5, 2009, http://nstyabji.wordpress.com/2008/12/07/the-early-tyabji-women/; and interview with Salima Tyabji, New Delhi, February 3, 2006.

29 Interview with Rafia Abdul Ali, Bombay, December 16, 2005.
30 See, as examples, letters to Raihana Tyabji, December 29, 1930, and April 25, 1945, CWMGO.
31 See, as an example, letter to Raihana Tyabji, June 20, 1932, CWMGO.
32 Letter to Raihana Tyabji, October 10, 1928, CWMGO; Thakkar and Mehta, *Understanding Gandhi*, 204.
33 Letters to Raihana Tyabji, April 11, 1930, and January 25, 1931; Draft Letter to Viceroy, April 27, 1930; and "What Should One Not Do?," *Navajivan*, March 1, 1931, CWMGO; Thakkar and Mehta, *Understanding Gandhi*, 202.
34 Draft of Power-of-Attorney, April 1, 1945, CWMGO.
35 Thakkar and Mehta, *Understanding Gandhi*, 172, 183, 237.
36 "The Spirit of Raas," *Navajivan*, April 27, 1930, CWMGO.
37 Letter to Raihana Tyabji, January 25, 1931, CWMGO.
38 Letter to Raihana Tyabji, June 28, 1932, CWMGO.
39 Letter to Saroj Nanavati, October 1, 1946, CWMGO.
40 Proceedings of the Hindustani Prachar Sabha Meeting, Wardha, February 16, 1946, CWMGO.
41 "Hindustani Written in Nagari Only," *Harijan*, November 9, 1947; and letter to Raihana Tyabji, November 30, 1947, CWMGO.
42 For two separate accounts of these spiritual services offered by Raihana in her later years, see Devereux, "Early Tyabji Women"; and Mehta, *Mahatma*, 3.
43 See "letters concerning past incarnations" from Raihana Tyabji to Mary Cushing Niles, 1954–71, in Niles Family Papers, RG 5/267, Friends Historical Library of Swarthmore College, Pennsylvania, accessed April 4, 2011, http://www.swarthmore.edu/library/friends/ead/5267nile.xml.
44 For an example of the secondary literature, see *Gandhiji's Associates in India*, accessed December 2, 2009, http://www.gandhi-manibhavan.org/gandhicomesalive/comesalive_associates_india.htm#Tyabji,%20Raihana. On Raihana's Urdu lessons and the Qur'an at prayer meetings, see, as examples, letter to Devdas Gandhi, May 11, 1932; and "Speech at Prayer Meeting," Sodepur, December 8, 1945, CWMGO.
45 Thakkar and Mehta, *Understanding Gandhi*, 40. As evidence, see "Position of Women," *Young India*, October 17, 1929, CWMGO.
46 One particularly memorable performance at the Ahmedabad session of Congress in 1921 was recalled in Anil Nauriya's obituary of Raihana's sister, Sohaila Habib, "Memories of another Gujarat," accessed November 5, 2009, http://www.hinduonnet.com/2002/12/24/stories/2002122400941000.htm.
47 Yasmin Lukmani, "The Role Played by the Tyabji Women in the National Movement," in *Women in India's Freedom Struggle*, ed. Nawaz B. Mody (Mumbai: Allied, 2000), 219–36. The page quoted here is 227.
48 Letter to Raihana Tyabji, April 4, 1932, CWMGO.
49 Letter to R. V. Martin, Yeravda Mandir, July 8, 1930, CWMGO.
50 Mehta, *Mahatma*, 5. For just one example of the former, see Nicholas F. Gier, "Was Gandhi a Tantric?," accessed December 2, 2009, http://www.class.uidaho.edu/ngier/gandtantric.htm.

51 Letter to Abbas Tyabji, September 12, 1934, *CWMGO*.
52 Letter to Raihana Tyabji, June 18, 1931, *CWMGO*.
53 Thakkar and Mehta, *Understanding Gandhi*, 175–76.
54 "Gandhiji's Associates in India," accessed November 5, 2009, http://www.gandhi-manibhavan.org/gandhicomesalive/comesalive_associates_india.htm#Tyabji,%20Raihana.
55 "Gandhi: The Last 200 Days (Day 21)—'Who Is My Greatest Follower?,'" accessed November 5, 2009, http://pages.cs.wisc.edu/~vganti/Gandhi/aug4.html.
56 Mehta, *Mahatma*, 207.
57 Interview with Rafia Abdul Ali, Bombay, December 16, 2005; interview with Salima Tyabji, Delhi, February 3, 2006; Basu, *Abbas*, 21.
58 Thakkar and Mehta, *Understanding Gandhi*, 217.
59 Thakkar and Mehta, *Understanding Gandhi*, 179.
60 Basu, *Abbas*, 20.
61 Mehta, *Mahatma*, 211.
62 Tyabji, *Heart*, vi.
63 Barbara D. Metcalf, "What Happened in Mecca: Mumtaz Mufti's 'Labbaik,'" in *The Culture of Autobiography: Constructions of Self-Representation*, ed. Robert Folkenflik (Stanford, CA: Stanford University Press, 1993), 149–67. The quote here comes from 157.
64 Metcalf, "What Happened in Mecca," 158–59.
65 On this subgenre of Islamic literature, see Kate Brittlebank, "Piety and Power: A Preliminary Analysis of Tipu Sultan's Dreams," in her edited volume, *Tall Tales and True: India, Historiography and British Imperial Imaginings* (Victoria: Monash University Press, 2008), 31–41. My thanks to Andrea Major for this reference.
66 On the female voice in the Sufi tradition, see Shameem Burney Abbas, *The Female Voice in Sufi Ritual: Devotional Practices in India and Pakistan* (Austin: University of Texas Press, 2003).
67 Tyabji, *Heart*, 10–11.
68 See, as an example, letter to Raihana Tyabji, July 7, 1932.
69 For a brief introduction to the Bohras, see Ira M. Lapidus, *A History of Islamic Societies*, 2nd ed. (Cambridge: Cambridge University Press, 2002), 377. For a more comprehensive study, see Asghar Ali Engineer, *The Bohras* (New Delhi: Vikas, 1980).
70 Khan, *Crossing the Threshold*.
71 For just one example, see my discussion of Atiya Fyzee's "openness, or at least curiosity, to other religious faiths" in her *Zamana-i-tahsil* in Siobhan Lambert-Hurley and Sunil Sharma, *Atiya's Journeys: A Muslim Woman from Colonial Bombay to Edwardian Britain* (Delhi: Oxford University Press, 2010), chap. 4.
72 Basu, *Abbas*, 41.
73 Quoted in Basu, *Abbas*, 78.
74 Khan, *Crossing the Threshold*, chap. 3.
75 On the Tyabji clan's adoption of Urdu, see Marlen Karlitzky, "The Tyabji Clan—Urdu as a Symbol of Group Identity," *Annual of Urdu Studies* 17 (2002): 187–207;

Theodore Wright Jr.'s "Muslim Kinship and Modernization: The Tyabji Clan of Bombay," in *Family, Kinship and Marriage among Muslims in India*, in Imtiaz Ahmad (Delhi: Manohar, 1976), 217–38, especially 227; and Lambert-Hurley and Sharma, *Atiya's Journeys*, chap. 1.

76 On this organization, see Gail Minault, *Secluded Scholars: Women's Education and Muslim Social Reform in Colonial India* (Delhi: Oxford University Press, 1998), 182–92.
77 Basu, *Abbas*, 20–21.
78 Wright, "Muslim Kinship and Modernization," 229.
79 Wright, "Muslim Kinship and Modernization," 227.
80 Basu, *Abbas*, 36–37.
81 Basu, *Abbas*, 37.
82 On this process, see Peter Van der Veer, *Gods on Earth: The Management of Religious Experience and Identity in a North Indian Pilgrimage Centre* (Delhi: Oxford University Press, 1989); and Sumit Sarkar, "Kaliyuga, Chakri and Bhakti: Ramakrishna and His Times" in his *Writing Social History* (Delhi: Oxford University Press, 1997), 282–357. My thanks to Oliver Godsmark for raising this point during my seminar in Leeds.
83 Sarkar, "Kaliyuga," 313.
84 This summary is based on Barbara D. Metcalf, "The Past in the Present: Instruction, Pleasure, and Blessing in Maulana Muhammad Zakariyya's *Aap Biitii*," in Arnold and Blackburn, *Telling Lives*, 119–21.
85 For a South Asian example, see Ruby Lal's discussion of Gulbadan Begam's *Humayun-nama* in *Domesticity and Power in the Early Mughal World* (Cambridge: Cambridge University Press, 2005).
86 Francis Robinson, *Islam and Muslim History in South Asia* (Delhi: Oxford University Press, 2000), 95, 115.
87 Robinson, *Islam*, 95.
88 Asaf A. A. Fyzee, ed., *The Autobiography of Tyabji Bhoymeeah: Merchant Prince of Bombay 1803–1863* (Bombay: The Government Central Press, 1964).
89 For a well-known example by a male Tyabji, see Badruddin Tyabji, *Memoirs of an Egoist*, 2 vols. (New Delhi: Roli Books, 1988).
90 Nazli Rafia Sultan Nawab Begam Sahiba, *Sair-i-Yurop* (Lahore: Union Steam Press, n.d.); and Atiya Fyzee, *Zamana-i-tahsil* (Agra: Matba' Mufid-i-'Am, 1921). For a translation and commentary on the latter, see Lambert-Hurley and Sharma, *Atiya's Journeys*.
91 "A Page from the Past: Extracts from the Diary of Amina Binte Badruddin Tyabji," special issue of *Roshni* (Delhi), 1946, 69–73.
92 Abbas Tyabji's diaries are now preserved in the Nehru Memorial Museum and Library.
93 Malhotra, "Telling Her Tale?," 555.
94 My thanks to Veena Oldenburg for encouraging me to draw out this point. It has been developed in Velcheru N. Rao, "A Ramayan of Their Own: Women's Oral Tradition in Telegu," in *Many Ramayanas: The Diversity of a Tradition in*

South Asia, ed. Paula Richman (Berkeley: University of California Press, 1991), 114–36.
95 Tyabji, *Heart*, 57.
96 Tyabji, *Heart*, 57.
97 Snell, "Raskhān," 32.
98 See the section entitled "Two Weeks Later," in Tyabji, *Heart*, 62–69.
99 Tyabji, *Heart*, 30, 47, 53. For comparison with the early gopi tradition, see David Kinsley, *Hindu Goddesses: Visions of the Divine Feminine in the Hindu Religious Tradition* (Berkeley: University of California Press, 1988), 83–85.
100 Tyabji, *Heart*, 24.
101 Tyabji, *Heart*, 51–52.
102 Tyabji, *Heart*, 1–2.
103 Tyabji, *Heart*, 1.
104 Tyabji, *Heart*, 1–2.
105 Tyabji, *Heart*, 19.
106 Letter to Dr. Mohammad Alam, November 26, 1932, CWMGO.
107 Mehta, *Mahatma*, 210–11.
108 Lukmani, "The Role Played by the Tyabji Women in the National Movement," 219–36.
109 Letter to Raihana Tyabji, July 12, 1927, CWMGO.
110 Letter to Raihana Tyabji, July 14 and 19, 1927, and March 5, 1930, CWMGO.
111 Letter to Raihana Tyabji, July 12, 1927, and October 19, 1929, CWMGO.
112 Tyabji, *Heart*, 61.
113 Mehta, *Mahatma*, 211.
114 Mehta, *Mahatma*, 209.
115 Mehta, *Mahatma*, 211.
116 Shah Jahan Begam, *Tahzib un-Niswan wa Tarbiyat ul-Insan* (Delhi: Matba'i-Ansari, 1889).
117 I develop this point in "To Write of the Conjugal Act: Intimacy and Sexuality in Muslim Women's Autobiographical Writing in South Asia," *Journal of the History of Sexuality* 23.2 (May 2014): 155–81.
118 Atiya, *Zamana-i-Tahsil*; and Nazli, *Sair-i-Yurop*. For an analysis of these silences, see Lambert-Hurley and Sharma, *Atiya's Journeys*, chap. 2; and Sunil Sharma, "Delight and Disgust: Gendered Encounters in the Travelogues of the Fyzee Sisters," in Roberta Micallef and Sunil Sharma, eds., *On the Wonders of Land and Sea: Persianate Travel Writing* (Boston: Ilex Foundation, 2013).
119 Tyabji, *Heart*, 74.
120 Tyabji, *Heart*, inside back cover.
121 Tyabji, *Heart*, vi.
122 Metcalf, "What Happened in Mecca," 149.
123 Metcalf, "What Happened in Mecca," 154.
124 Metcalf, "What Happened in Mecca," 152.
125 Metcalf, "What Happened in Mecca," 152.

126 See, as an example, Robert Folkenflick, ed., *The Culture of Autobiography: Constructions of Self-Representation* (Stanford, CA: Stanford University Press, 1993), 13.
127 Sidonie Smith and Julia Watson, *Reading Autobiography: A Guide for Interpreting Life Narratives*, 2nd ed. (Minneapolis: University of Minnesota Press, 2010), 3.
128 Arnold and Blackburn, *Telling Lives*, 9.

10. PERFORMING GENDER AND FAITH IN INDIAN THEATER AUTOBIOGRAPHIES

KATHRYN HANSEN

This chapter focuses on the autobiographies of two prominent actors who achieved renown in the first few decades of the twentieth century. These actors were men who performed for years as women onstage. The most famous, Jayshankar Sundari, was a female impersonator who built his entire professional career on his feminine persona. The second, Fida Husain, also played women's parts for over a decade. Then when he assumed masculine roles he starred as a Hindu god and saint, disguising his Muslim identity. In a volume devoted principally to women's autobiographies, what is the place of these two men's life stories? How do they supplement the other narratives in this book?

As representatives of a practice that was once widespread, these examples are useful for understanding how images of women were constructed and displayed in the performing arts before it was acceptable for actresses to play female roles. The context of the theater is especially useful for problematizing the category of gender, insofar as it destabilizes the notion of a fixed sign that might be called "woman." As well, the case of Fida Husain raises the issue of faith and religion, illustrating how religious identity might be constructed or made invisible. This project also brings a different perspective to the concept of performance. These two subjects' livelihood entailed daily acts of mimetic representation, in a distinctive theatrical space. This sense of "performance" is separate from the repetitions of social behavior associated with gender in everyday life, or the performative construction of the self found in autobiographical texts, two theoretical constructs underpinning this volume. To further blur the boundaries, neither of the autobiographical texts I will examine is authored by their subjects in the conventional way. Both are based on oral accounts that were subsequently transcribed, edited, and published. These then are works that enlarge each of the categories at the heart of this edited collection: gender, performance, and autobiography.

Both of the actors in question got their start in the somewhat misleadingly named Parsi theater. Originally spearheaded in the middle of the nineteenth century by Parsi drama buffs in Bombay, the Parsi theater became an extremely popular form of urban entertainment in the days before cinema. It was carried by traveling troupes from one end of the subcontinent to the other, reaching out to diverse audiences through the vernacular languages of Gujarati, Urdu, and Hindi. Fida Husain was associated with the Parsi theater for fifty years, from 1918 until 1968. Jayshankar Sundari first performed with a Calcutta-based Parsi theater company in 1898 and made his Bombay debut in 1901. As "Sundari," or lovely lady, he went on to become a star in the professional Gujarati-language theater, in which he played a leading role until his retirement in 1932.

The autobiographies of these performers join others of a similar nature from the nascent period of modern theater in South Asia. They establish the significance of the theatrical memoir, which emerged as an important subset of autobiography in India. Compared to the life narratives of political leaders or social reformers, these accounts from the world of professional entertainment might seem tangential to the trajectory of India as an emerging nation. Yet they are important sources for the study of cultural formation in the nationalist era from the perspective of those who were embedded in vernacular, largely oral, systems of communication and knowledge. They also are invaluable to the archives of theatrical history and oral performance, and in their own right are colorful documents of a bygone era.

These texts in certain ways are like women's autobiographies in their articulation of muted subjectivities. Yet a close reading reveals that theatrical memoirs construct their subjects as righteous individuals, as defenders of a larger moral order, despite their subordinated status. As I will argue in this chapter, the autobiographies reveal a kind of doubled performativity, by which the actor's self is twice created, both as a stage performer and as a social being. The disjunctures between the two are evident in the silences and gaps that inhabit these texts. Herein I will focus specifically on the doubleness related to gender and faith. Considering Jayshankar Sundari, I will analyze the occlusion of his transgendered self in narrative passages that address romance and conjugality.

In the case of Fida Husain, I will discuss the erasure of his Muslim family background and questions of religious identity. These two examples will complicate the categories of gender and faith and serve to contribute a counternote to a book that focuses on autobiographies of women.

Theatrical Memoirs as a Species of Autobiography

Autobiography as a distinct genre of literature arose and acquired a following in a number of Indian languages in the second half of the nineteenth century. Whereas oral modes of life narration had a longer history, autobiographical texts were predicated on literacy, print culture, and the consolidation of reading publics. The development of commercial book publishing in the mid-nineteenth century made genres like vernacular novels accessible to diverse audiences. Then with the growth of reading communities, the spread of newspapers, magazines, and journals accelerated. First-person accounts enlivened the reportage that filled the pages of the popular press. Many life histories were produced for the print media, usually in the form of brief biographies. During the same period, sustained autobiographical writing in book format began to be produced by reformists and cultural innovators.[1]

Most of the pioneering Indian-language autobiographies were written by men who were public figures affiliated with literary, educational, and political circles. As recent research has shown, early autobiographies were also written in surprisingly large numbers by women, beginning in Bengal with the autodidact Rashsundari. Lesser known are the autobiographies written by actors, actresses, and personnel associated with the vernacular theaters of colonial India. These theatrical memoirs constitute a species of autobiography in their own right. Until now, they have virtually escaped the notice of cultural historians. Many were published by small presses with limited circulation, although some have been reprinted. Nonetheless, men and women of the theater were witnesses of epochal change, and their lives are of inestimable value to historians. Their autobiographical writings capture a turbulent time in India's cultural development from a unique vantage point.

As historical documents, these autobiographies are a trove for those interested in the institution of theater and dramatic practice. The texts abound in the names of actors and companies, titles and dates of plays, and other minutiae vital to constructing a factual record of the stage. Beyond the archive of theatrical history, these documents offer unprecedented insights into India's cultural formation in the nationalist era. They comment on political developments, religious reform, language debates, caste mobilization, changing attitudes toward women, and the spread of education and reading. However, they do so from a humble vantage point, and their insights often seem marginal to the concerns of nationalist historiography. Major historical events are infrequently foregrounded, yet the cultural changes that accompanied the spread of nationalism and their impact on ordinary lives are very evident. These memoirs also contribute to the elusive history of orality in South Asia. They detail a variety of performance genres and explore the social lives of performers at the turn of the nineteenth century.

The theatrical life narrative in print culture evolved over several decades. It first appeared in the colonial context in the form of published biographical sketches about actors on the stages of Victorian England. These profiles of English actors were soon replaced by reports of Indian performers, leading in turn to short autobiographical pieces and finally full-fledged life stories. The biography format in an Indian language, Gujarati, was featured in the daily newspaper *Kaiser-i Hind*. Dhanjibhai Patel penned ninety-seven short essays, each focused on a nineteenth-century Parsi theater personality, probably in the first decade of the twentieth century.[2] A similar set of sixty-two essays by Jahangir Khambata was published weekly in the journal *Parsi*.[3] Although generally quite brief, these biographies preserved luminous memories of performers and performances. They created name recognition for the actors and their companies, celebrating the Parsi theater in its first few decades.

Another forum for the telling of theatrical lives was the theater magazine, associated with the rise of public theater in Bengal.[4] Bengali-language theater journals such as *Rangalay* date to 1901, although theater-related items appeared in ordinary newspapers in Calcutta earlier, as they did in Bombay. Specialized theater magazines documented the golden era of Bengali theater, taking a retrospective view on the past century. It was in a theater magazine, *Natya-Mandir*, that the first autobiography of the celebrated actress Binodini Dasi was serialized. Her *Abhinetrir Atmakatha* [Autobiography of an actress], which came out in 1910, is likely the first of its kind.[5]

In Tamilnadu too, the vernacular theater developed rapidly at the turn of the century. Its founding father, Pammal Sambanda Mudaliar, published his autobiography, *Over 40 Years before the Footlights*, originally in the Tamil newspaper *Swadesamitran*. The Marathi stage also produced a number of theater biographies and autobiographies, including memoirs by Kolhatkar, Tembe, and Varerkar.[6]

In my recent book *Stages of Life: Indian Theatre Autobiographies*, I have assembled and translated four autobiographies of this very type, all related to the

Parsi theater. These texts are historically significant, representative examples of the theatrical memoir. The first is the autobiography of the prolific playwright Narayan Prasad Betab (1872–1945). Betab began writing for the Parsi stage in 1900 and composed over thirty theatrical dramas. He ushered in the turn to Hindi-language plays with his popular versions of the Hindu epics. Radheshyam Kathavachak (1890–1963) was another influential Hindi dramatist who wrote on mythological themes. His autobiography describes his background in religious storytelling and Ram Lila performance and its influence on his dramatic style. Jayshankar Sundari (1889–1975) was the most famous female impersonator of the Gujarati stage. His autobiography, *Some Blossoms, Some Tears*, written in collaboration with his son, Dinkar Bhojak, and Somabhai Patel, recounts his life and times with insightful detail. Master Fida Husain (1899–2001), hailed as the final exponent of the Parsi style of acting, managed several companies in Calcutta, the most successful being the Moonlight Theatre. Theater scholar Pratibha Agraval elicited and published his first-person oral history, entitled *Fifty Years in the Parsi Theatre*.

The cultural context for these four life stories is the Parsi theater, sometimes referred to as the "old Parsi theater," to distinguish it from contemporary dramas (mainly comedies) produced in the Parsi community. Along with other literary and dramatic innovations of the nineteenth century, the Parsi theater was a by-product of colonial modernity, and its origin can be quite specifically traced to Bombay in 1853. It began with a group of young men, the Parsi Dramatic Corps, organizing dramatic shows along European lines. While at first their activities were amateur and affiliated with college dramatics, Parsi drama clubs by the 1870s and 1880s were developing into professional companies. They presented increasingly spectacular productions in purpose-built playhouses in the theater districts such as Grant Road and near the Victoria Terminus. Elsewhere too—in Gujarat, Maharashtra, Bengal, Tamilnadu—hybrid, transitional varieties of theatrical representation came in vogue. All participated in a shared entertainment economy, appealing to spectators in cities undergoing rapid economic growth and cultural change. Everywhere, forms of music, dance, and drama once restricted to aristocratic groups were becoming ready commodities for the price of a ticket. Theatergoing emerged as a defining feature of the urban experience across South Asia.

Although parallel to regional language theaters in Madras or Calcutta in terms of theatrical sophistication and style, the Parsi theater of Bombay took off in its own direction. Its "Parsi-ness" diminished over time, and it achieved widespread popularity beyond regional boundaries. The rubric *Parsi theater*, to clarify, reflected its entrepreneurial base in the Parsi community—but not its performers, audience, language, or content. Initially, performances favored Gujarati and Hindustani, but for many years Urdu was the predominant language of the theater, until the 1920s, when Hindi replaced it. Parsi theater companies contained a mix of Parsis and non-Parsis, as did their audiences. The dramatic repertoire assimilated stories of Asian and European origin, and typically it possessed a middlebrow, eclectic character. Parsi theater companies were large and well organized. They traveled widely by rail and ship, achieving a remarkable degree of popularity across a vast territory. By the end of the nineteenth century, the Parsi theater had become well-nigh ubiquitous in many parts of the subcontinent.

Constructing the Self through Performance

Alongside their value as historical resources, the autobiographies of theater personalities are also the life stories of distinct individuals. Their narrators tell of childhood, of growing up, of entering the wider world and struggling for success. Through these accounts of personhood, the felt quality of the actor's life, his constructions of self and others, his modes of performing his identity are made accessible. The autobiographies present the reader with a medium through which to explore the subjectivity of the theatrical personality, alternately masked and unmasked in its multiple guises.

The self has been variously understood within different periods, schools of thought, and intellectual disciplines. The tradition stemming from the European Enlightenment constructed the self as sovereign, unitary, and universal. The canonical autobiographies, with their narratives of the unified, transcendent self, were later displaced with the advent of modernism. Under the influence of Freud's discovery of the unconscious, theories of economic determinism, and poststructuralism, a more fragmented notion of selfhood took hold. Since the 1980s, the concept of relationality, the self as interdependent and identified with a community, has been invoked as an alternative to the autonomous individual. The role of intersubjective identification has proven important to studies of the life narratives of women, African Americans, Dalits, and other groups.[7]

A further concept holds great promise for the analysis of the autobiographies in this study: the performative self. In the performative paradigm, identities are not understood as fixed or essentialized attributes. Central to this notion is the axiom that the autobiographical subject is produced in performance. As phrased by Sidonie Smith, "Every day, in disparate venues, in response to sundry occasions, in front of precise audiences (even if an audience of one), people assemble, if only temporarily, a 'life' to which they assign narrative coherence and meaning and through which they position themselves in historically specific identities. Whatever that occasion or that audience, the autobiographical speaker becomes a performative subject."[8] The corollary is that different storytelling occasions and audiences call forth different stories from the performative self, yielding sometimes quite divergent narratives of identity.

The focus on performativity gains special salience in the interpretation of oral histories and life narratives of autodidacts and semiliterates. Both Jayshankar Sundari and Fida Husain had minimal schooling, and their life stories were delivered through oral narration. Sundari told his story to Dinkar Bhojak and Somabhai Patel, who compiled the autobiography for publication, and Husain's narrative was elicited and transcribed by Pratibha Agraval.[9] In the case of such texts, the critical writing of Philippe Lejeune is particularly helpful. Lejeune examined the autobiographies of working-class French men from the nineteenth century, and he found that they employed a public discourse structured by class, code, and convention. Such popular autobiographical texts (popular meaning "of the people") did not copy reality; rather, they created verisimilitude by imitating narrative forms that constituted the lingua franca.[10]

In "The Autobiography of Those Who Do Not Write," Lejeune explored the prevalent practice of collaborative authorship in life writing. In ghostwritten autobiographies, the "life" (the written and published story of a person's life) is the product of a transaction or collaboration between two different parties: usually the "author" (the subject) and the writer. When class and other differences separate the writer from the subject, nostalgia and voyeurism play a role. The experience of the "other" (the autobiographical subject) is often converted into an object of the gaze. Lejeune questioned the ethics and authenticity of ethnological projects in which the reading middle-class public became consumers of the "memories" of forgotten people who had been encouraged to "speak," often to prop up an idealized or exotic picture of the past.[11] He concluded that "by no means [is it] clear that the illiterate individual (peasant, artisan, worker) has in fact been enfranchised through . . . ethnographic intervention, achieving 'authority' over his or her own life."[12]

In contrast with Lejeune's skepticism, other critics have been less dismissive of the "failure" of the performative self to create coherence. They consider the autobiographical occasion as an opportunity and the disjunctures between self and other as potential sites of resistance. The multiple demands placed on the autobiographical subject to reiterate conflicting discourses produce gaps, ruptures, and transgressions, which for Judith Butler signal the "possibility of a variation on . . . the rules that govern intelligible identity," according to Sidonie Smith.[13] Michel de Certeau similarly viewed the autobiographical subject as capable of tactically adjusting, redeploying, and transforming the discourses of identity. Smith notes his argument for the capacity of "the weak" to strategically combine heterogeneous elements of discourse and use them to their own ends.[14]

If autobiography is a performance that creates the self, if every self is performative, then what of the lives of professional performers, adepts who play roles onstage, and their autobiographies? My proposition is that a kind of doubled performativity inhabits theatrical memoirs. The actor's self is twice created, or twice born, to adopt an Indic metaphor. Onstage, he becomes the king, hero, warrior, or leading lady, overwriting the abject self of social origins. The act of impersonation is his métier, and he is recognized or identified with his most popular character. His performance even continues offstage, in interactions with fans and patrons. Interiorizing his role, he may alter his presentation of self in everyday life, for example, Sundari's wearing his hair long, or Fida Husain's yogic bodily regimen. At his most successful he becomes an icon; his image circulates independently of his body, through advertising, photography, and the media.

Inscribing this subject in autobiographical writing presents a dual challenge. In the theory of performativity, the self does not exist prior to its recitations, and an autobiographical story is already the recitation of a recitation. Here, however, the self as an actor has one set of recitations, and the self as narrator has another. Congruence is possible, but disjunctures are also common and can be particularly meaningful. In the next section, I will consider the divergence between two discrete notions of gendered identity found in Sundari's narrative, and then turn to the case of Fida Husain, whose oral history reveals the disjuncture between his Muslim background and his signature role as the Hindu saint Narsi Mehta.

Jayshankar Sundari (1889–1975)

In the early twentieth century, the leading Parsi and Gujarati theatrical companies routinely hired men to perform women's roles. Each troupe prided itself on a large number of boys and men who specialized in female impersonation. Jayshankar Sundari (see figure 10.1) was one such artist, and his autobiography is extraordinary in documenting his experience as a female impersonator. No

FIGURE 10.1. Jayshankar Sundari (*right*) acting with Bapulal Nayak, around 1915. Credit: Suresh Nayak, *Gujarati Rangbhumi na Abhinay Shilpi Bapulal Nayak* (Gandhinagar: Nayak, 1980).

other "lady actor," as such performers were sometimes called, has left such an insightful account of his personal process of transformation from man to woman.

Sundari earned his sobriquet—"beautiful lady," or more colloquially, "pretty woman"—at the age of twelve, from his role as heroine of the Gujarati drama *Saubhagya Sundari*. Recalling his debut, he wrote: "It was May 18, 1901, when I first set foot in the Gaiety [Theatre]. This was the same Gaiety that would prove to be a milestone in my life.... When I spotted the stage my feet wanted to dance, the desire to act surged in every limb. A vision of times to come swam before my eyes. The magnificent stage, the rumbling of applause, the form of a woman taking shape! My soul was yearning to take on the features of a Gujarati lady."[15]

Sundari's sense of being destined for the stage is woven into the opening lines of the autobiography, wherein he recounts the origins of modern theater in Bombay: "In the year 1853, before I was born, the Gujarati stage came into being. I was meant to be an actor, and who knows why . . . I was attracted to the profession from childhood. The Gujarati stage was established in Bombay by educated Parsis, and I was, it seems, destined to inherit its great legacy."[16] Coming from a family of singers, Jayshankar grew up in a musical atmosphere: "At the age of 5 or 6, I spent my mornings listening to grandfather singing Anandaghan's *padas* or the *ashtapadis* of the *Gita Govinda*. . . . Listening to grandfather practice every day, we all learned to tell good music from bad."[17]

Although admitted to school at seven like his siblings, he was not fond of studies, and the schoolmaster's beatings further alienated him. He used to run away to attend performances such as Ram Lila (dramatic enactment of the *Ramayan*) and Bhavai (Gujarati folk theater): "I was very fond of listening to stories and tales. Dramas, plays, and especially Bhavai attracted me. Although I had no knowledge of music yet, I enjoyed listening and was more readily affected by music than other children my age."[18] Soon, Sundari was imitating the sights and sounds he heard and creating his own replica of the theater:

> When the Ram Lila came from the city, my happiness knew no bounds. The palaces, jungles, mountains, rivers and natural scenes painted on the stage curtains, and the kings, queens, and princes in their makeup and costumes—all seemed real to me. . . . I forgot school, home, hunger, thirst, everything, and just waited for nightfall when the performance would begin.
>
> Grandfather had an acquaintance in the Ram Lila troupe, and he allowed me to see three or four plays. Then I went into the neighbor's courtyard and made a miniature stage, draping some clothes for curtains

and making cutouts of a king and queen from paper. Standing in front of the curtain, I manipulated the cutouts and imitated the performance. I myself was the producer, director, and spectator.[19]

In this way, Sundari's theatrical imagination was stimulated from his early experiences, and his desire to mime was aroused. He recounts how he identified emotionally with dramatized scenarios. His facility for absorption in mimetic spectacle was unusual, presaging the aptitude for feminine sensibility he displayed later on: "They [bygone stones] washed me away in a sea of emotion. Once, at my maternal grandfather's, my father gave a recitation from Premanand's *Nalakhyan*. In the story, Nal grows suspicious of Damayanti and abandons her. Damayanti laments pitifully in the forest. Hearing her poetic appeal, I lost all emotional control of myself. I was . . . weeping with sorrow at Nal's desertion of Damayanti."[20]

By the time he turned nine, Sundari was disinclined toward formal schooling. His true education occurred while watching rehearsals and performances, and he committed many poems and tales to memory. He also encountered performers of various stripes: Nats, Bahurupiyas, Bhavaiyas. Acting was Sundari's birthright. He was born into a traditional performing caste, the Nayak-Bhojaks. When a Parsi theater recruiter came to the village in search of boys for his Calcutta-based company, Sundari's parents consented, probably swayed by the agent's offer of money. In 1898 Sundari left for distant Bengal, to begin his career as a professional actor.

Working at the Thanthaniya Natak Mandali, he began learning Urdu theater songs and training for the *sakhi* parts. Sakhis were the female companions to the heroine, typically enacted by young boys, who were often engaged onstage in group choreography and choruses. With his adept acting and quick absorption of Urdu, Sundari quickly advanced to the role of heroine. The rehearsal regimen was strict, and the boys were vigilantly watched. At the same time, the company provided a comfortable existence with good food, clothing, and lodging.

After several years, Sundari returned to Gujarat. He was again enrolled in school but soon fell in with theater folk and began spending time in Ahmedabad. Bapulal Nayak, an established actor and director, took him under his wing. Following negotiations with his family, Sundari once more left home, this time for Bombay. He joined the Mumbai Gujarati Natak Mandali and appeared regularly on the boards of the Gaiety Theatre. There Sundari played opposite Bapulal for a number of years to great acclaim.

In Bombay, Jayshankar was carefully coached in the Gujarati language, classical music, and a more realistic style of acting. Offstage he enjoyed special living arrangements with the family of the company owner, a prosperous businessman. With the help of private tutors and interested patrons, he gained wider knowledge of the arts and literature. He also began to develop his own method of acting. His search for a more helpful technique stemmed from his own experience, brought about by the differences he noticed between the language and style of the Parsi theater in Calcutta and those of his new environment, the Gujarati theater in Bombay.

Sundari's extraordinary self-awareness allowed him to lyrically suggest the dynamics of gender transformation in his autobiography. In the following passage, he describes the moment of cross-dressing as one in which a feminine self was born. What is noteworthy here is the way in which the narrator moves back and forth between an external gaze, expressed in the third person, and an exploration of interiority in the first person: "At the moment when Jayshankar first attired himself in a *choli* and *lahanga* [blouse and full skirt], he was transformed into a woman, or rather into the artistic form that expresses the feminine sensibility. A beautiful young female revealed herself inside me. Her shapely, intoxicating youth sparkled. Her feminine charm radiated fragrance. She had an easy grace in her eyes, and in her gait was the glory of Gujarat. She was not a man, she was a woman. . . . Her manner, her gestures, her sensuality shone in every limb of my body. A sweet tingling arose for a moment and then vanished, and for that instant I felt as though I was not a man."[21]

Sundari created his feminine stage persona by watching old dramas, reading Gujarati novels, and hearing others discuss English and Sanskrit literature. He also made a close study of the young women he came into contact with in polite society, and he observed their habits and tastes carefully. One such was Gulab, the girl who became the model for Lalita in *Jugal Jugari* by Mulshankar Mulani. She was staying with an elite family, awaiting her marriage. Her restraint and elegance struck Sundari, and he observed her intently: "I was extremely impressed by this girl's attire and elegant manner of dressing, but above all by her behavior. . . . Her smiling face, her modesty, her open manner of replying—I was going to put all of this precisely into the character of Lalita."[22]

These methods of observation, imitation, and internalization helped him project his female characters successfully to his audience. Because of the correspondence of his characters to real life, his stage movements, attire, and speech became models for women offstage. As a government citation later noted, "it was a fashion for ladies in Bombay to imitate him in their daily lives."[23] His technique of total identification with women produced idealized feminine types and created a visual construct of womanhood that conformed to the norms of bourgeois respectability.[24] During the active years of his career, his personal appearance also embodied fashionable markers of femininity. He kept his hair long and his face clean shaven. He reverted to a masculine public image, growing a moustache and cutting his hair, only upon retirement.

Turning now to the construction of the autobiography, it is perhaps not surprising that Sundari's autobiography is put together largely as a bildungsroman, or more specifically a *künstlerroman*, a chronicle of the development of an artist. Such narratives typically employ the subject's education over the course of a period of apprenticeship, marked by various encounters with mentors. Following these stages of growth, the subject abandons youthful dreams and fantasies and becomes integrated into society. The effectiveness of the bildungsroman as a template for the exemplary life hinges on the eventual resolution of conflicts, such as those that arise in regard to education or social obligations. According to Smith and Watson, narratives of this kind culminate in "the acceptance of one's constrained social role in the bourgeois social order, usually requiring the renunciation of some ideal or passion and the embrace of heteronormative social arrangements."[25]

This underlying pattern is evident throughout Sundari's life story. He appears first as a spirited and gullible child, by nature drawn to music and oral performance. Preternaturally suggestible, he is easily reduced to convulsive weeping by the lament of Damayanti, as enacted by his first mentor, his father. This sensitivity presages his uncanny ability to merge with feminine roles later onstage. When he shows little sign of taking to formal education, his parents indenture him to a drama company in Calcutta. As a youth, he becomes a rebel of sorts, challenging male authority figures such as Dadabhai Thunthi, his mentor and director of the Parsi theater company. Later he converts this oppositional attitude into a search for a rational method of acting, in contradistinction to the rote approach then in favor. His quest to move beyond the teaching of his gurus to his own system of study and self-absorption in the role foregrounds the artist's struggle to define himself, to embrace his inner actor (*antar nat*). His triumph as a female impersonator lies in his ability to apprehend the feminine through his own differentiated sense of self, a self that always deeply identified with women. He thereby asserts his variance from heteronormative gender roles. He claims agency as an artist and aligns his nature and inner being with his chosen artistic role.

As a social actor rather than a stage performer, Sundari in his narrative homes to a rather different—and yet equally compelling—gendered imperative.

His story gives surprising prominence to his seemingly unrequited love affairs with female fans. It also highlights his battle with his unenlightened family and caste fellows to contract a companionate marriage. In the chapter entitled "Married Life," he poignantly recounts a series of romantic attachments, first to a child widow, then to a Parsi girl who is a Theosophist, then to a wealthy married Hindu lady. The latter two are clearly women of superior social status who fall in love with him through his performances; the first seems to be from his own caste. These romances are depicted as full of pathos, tragedy, and melodrama.

The child widow attends his first wedding, sobbing under her mantle. "The shadow of her grief fell on me too, and so my wedding was not the occasion for joy but rather for dejection."[26] Much later, Sundari attends her on her deathbed: "Some years passed. She became a mother and had several children. Then she contracted a serious illness. She was brought to Bombay for treatment, and she stayed in the same building as I. I'd avoided meeting her until then, but she found me alone and beseeched me to come sit with her. 'Read something to me, do something that will help me pass the time. Who can have any doubts about a woman who is on the brink of death, lying on her sickbed?'"[27]

The young Parsi lady courts Sundari by sending him anonymous love letters. Finally they meet in person, and in a voice "thickened with emotion," with her hand on his, she declares: "I wrote those letters, Jayshankar. I love you, and I want to marry you. Will you accept me and save me from ruin? I'm my parents' only child, and they have lakhs of rupees. Even if I have to leave all of that, I'm ready to do so. I'm a Theosophist and so are you."[28] Sundari rejects her, not because he is already married, but because a union with her would be an intercaste marriage, and he knows that his parents would oppose it.

A wealthy Hindu wife also approaches him through correspondence, which Sundari is an expert at decoding: "The letter was written by a woman, and from the handwriting and expression I could tell that this woman was ready to immolate herself like a moth circling a flame."[29] This liaison results in Sundari becoming friends with her husband and going to their home for family dinners on a regular basis.

Interwoven with these romantic episodes, the chapter also describes the rocky course of Sundari's multiple marriages. These are told through a truncated set of references that are to a large extent obscured by the sentimentally drawn affairs of the heart. Sundari's dilemma is stated at the outset: "Though I had little formal schooling, I was self-taught and had gained exposure to educated society."[30] Because of this background, he desires an educated wife, and yet: "Girls were not educated in our community in those days, and I felt suffocated, assuming my bride would be rustic and illiterate. I couldn't reveal these feelings."[31] Twice he is matched with unsophisticated brides from his community according to the dictates of his parents. The first wife contracts several diseases and becomes disabled. The second wife "made no attempt to understand me.... She lacked all capacity for discussion.... It was impossible for us to be compatible."[32] Sundari becomes deeply anguished: "As for domestic life, it was torment. To liberate myself from all of this, I tried several times to commit suicide."[33] Only in his third marriage, which is conducted while the first two wives are still alive (and with no mention of divorce), does Sundari find conjugal happiness. "Today I have a full family—three sons and a daughter—and I owe it all to my wife, who is like the goddess Lakshmi."[34]

One possible reading of the chapter is as the culmination of the künstlerroman. The impassioned voice of protest carries over from the youthful self as Sundari confronts what he deems archaic marriage practices that deny his romantic ideals. Nonetheless, in accord with the resolution noted by Smith and Watson, the artist must eventually capitulate and abandon his personal quest in order to be reconciled with the social order. After finding a compatible marriage partner on the third try, Sundari forsakes his self-centered fantasies and enters the hierarchical order of adulthood. Not entirely by coincidence, he gains wealth and satisfaction after this marriage, which chronologically overlaps with the most active phase of his career.

Although Sundari in this chapter manifests no gender confusion, one still wonders at the disjuncture with the gendered self of earlier chapters. Let us return to Sundari's discovery of his transgender identification as the pivotal moment in the narrative. The autobiography contains additional evidence that support this dimension of his emerging selfhood. As a child, he was called "girl" (*beti*) by his grandfather, although this does not necessarily mean he was considered female. More telling is the period of his adolescence, when he effortlessly portrayed female roles and failed at his only attempt to play a man. For many years he worked closely with his director and leading man, Bapulal Nayak, in an intense professional relationship that may have had an intimate aspect. He enjoyed the adoration of male fans who gifted him expensive objects like books and binoculars. Almost certainly he aroused erotic desire among both his male and female viewers. What erotic desires did he himself experience, and did he act on them? Did he feel obliged to shore up his respectability by stressing his conformity with heteronormative conventions? Did his public iterations of self hide a traumatic past, a history of exploitation and abuse? Were the gaps in his narrative occasioned by amnesia, or should they be read as strategically plotted in an act of resistance?

These kinds of questions, which may suggest themselves to the contemporary reader, were almost indubitably beyond the realm of discourse during Sundari's lifetime. This is not to say we cannot speculate on their answers, but we must avoid imposing our own preferences and desires. What Sundari's narrative does explicitly offer is evidence that changing notions of marriage, conjugality, and female education were widespread in his time. Not only did Sundari through his dramatic portrayals contribute to the circulation of new ideals of gendered conduct: his expectations for his own relationships were influenced by them. In my reading, his autobiography effectively stages the progress of an impoverished lower-caste child from village Gujarat. This poor village boy advanced to become a leading exponent of the art of female impersonation on the Bombay stage. As an aged actor looking back, the autobiography's narrators (Sundari and his collaborators) found an opportunity to promulgate the modern discourses of romantic love and conjugality that had become normative. Both moves—toward transgendered performances (mainly onstage) and toward modern love and marriage (mainly in life)—arguably expanded social boundaries and challenged dominant expectations, despite the instabilities in the interplay of performative identities that may have resulted.

Fida Husain (1899–2001)

Veteran actor, director, and teacher Fida Husain (see figure 10.2) had an extraordinarily long career, and the title of his autobiography, *Fifty Years in the Parsi Theatre*, aptly reflects that fact. The memoir focuses on the span beginning with his entrance into the New Alfred Theatrical Company in 1918 and ending in 1968, when the Moonlight Theatre he directed shut down. The idea of preserving Husain's story was conceived during conversations that theater scholar Pratibha Agraval recorded with him in the 1970s and 1980s. The transcribed and edited text, published in 1986 by the Natya Shodh Sansthan, an institute for theater research in Calcutta, is more an oral history than a conventional autobiography. Like Sundari's *Some Blossoms, Some Tears*, which resulted from a prolonged exchange between the actor and two interlocutor-scribes, Husain's narrative was collaboratively authored. Both texts fall into the category identified by Philippe Lejeune as "autobiographies of those who do not write."[35]

Like Sundari's, Husain's history grew from an early attraction to music and theater. Born in Muradabad in 1899, he grew up with a tremendous fondness for singing. Unlike with Sundari however, his family was strictly opposed to his interest in music. His father was kindhearted, but his uncle thrashed him

FIGURE 10.2. Fida Husain in the role of a Brahmin in a mythological drama. Credit: Pratibha Agraval, *Mastar Fida Husain: Parsi Thiyetar men Pachas Varsh* (Calcutta: Natya Shodh Sansthan, 1986).

every time he was caught attending music sessions. His sister-in-law tried to ruin his voice by feeding him abrasive *sindur* (vermilion) hidden in *pan*. In the face of this opposition, Husain ran away from home to join the New Alfred Theatrical Company as a teenager. He had just married, and his sudden departure aggravated relations with his in-laws, who ostracized his father and uncle from the *biradari* (clan group). Husain's career thus began as an act of defiance, although the autobiography stresses that he soon patched up the quarrel with his family.

Also like Sundari, Husain got his start in the theater by playing female parts. For twelve years, he worked as a female impersonator in the New Alfred, where he was called "Master" in honor of his youth and expertise in cross-dressed roles. The traditionalist New Alfred under Sohrabji Ogra pursued a strict policy of prohibiting actresses from appearing onstage. Its twenty-odd boys who danced and dressed up as girls were allowed out only for an hour or two per week, accompanied by guards. Husain achieved particular popularity as the melodious heroine in *Parivartan*, a social drama by Radheshyam Kathavachak. He assumed the male part in *Laila Majnun* only in 1930, and shortly thereafter his employment with the company ended when it closed permanently.

Yet unlike Sundari, he barely acknowledges this phase in his autobiography. Nor do any published photographs survive of this period. One reason for the difference in narrative approach may be that Husain's early stage persona as a heroine was eclipsed by his subsequent male roles. Sundari, by contrast, played women exclusively until his exit from the commercial stage in the early 1930s. Nonetheless, a certain silence about gender transactions pervades Husain's story, setting it apart from Sundari's more explicit treatment of this area. Husain gives no hint of the relations between the grownups and boys with whom he was clubbed in the New Alfred, aside from mentioning that the latter were heavily guarded. Nor does he discuss how he graduated to playing men's roles, what transpired to enable him to reach that position. His story reproduces the image of a self in harmony with heteronormativity, avoiding the ambiguous zones of gender and sexuality that flourished in and around the Parsi theater.

In terms of style and structure as well, Fida Husain's autobiography differs significantly from Sundari's. Unlike Sundari and his collaborators, Husain resists molding his tale to a linear template such as the bildungsroman. His narrative, based on oral interviews carried out over a period of years, is anecdotal, garrulous, and circular in its movements. In the main body of the narrative, Husain takes on a raconteur's manner, regaling his audience with spicy anecdotes. He improvises, using verbal witticisms, barbs directed at others, and amusing asides.

The content of his tale, however, is often at odds with his joking tone. Whereas Sundari recalled his risqué romantic relationships with women and told of his rebellion against the norms of arranged marriage, Husain presents himself as an upright, abstemious family man. His adolescence was troubled by his passion for music and drama, and conflicts with patriarchal figures resulted on account of it. He tells of beatings and abuse at the hands of close relatives, leading to his decision to run away from home to join a theater company. However, he emphasizes that soon after his departure from home, he was reconciled with his father and adopted the elder man's strict moral code.

Husain, indeed, highlights his compliance with social dictates and stresses his self-control throughout his account. Early on he describes his daily routine:

> No *pan*, no cigarettes, no tea. I go to bed at nine-thirty regardless of whether there's a poetry recitation, a cultural program, or a wedding. I dine only at home. I get up at four-thirty in the morning and immedi-

ately head to the latrine, take care of my business for twenty-four hours. My whole life, I've never needed to go twice. Then I step outside, walk four miles, and attend morning prayers. Next I feed and wash my cow, Sarojini. She's a sweetheart, 5 or 6 years old, gives eight kilos of milk a day. At seven-thirty I eat breakfast: two slices of toast with butter, *panir*, a glass of milk. No snacking in between, just water a couple of times a day. I eat lunch at one and dinner at seven-thirty or eight. After dinner, I stroll outdoors for a while and go to bed at nine-thirty. That is the law I still follow, and everything is fine. The machine is still running.[36]

This description of self-discipline at the very beginning of the oral history dispels the notion (which Agraval, the interlocutor, introduces) that Parsi theater actors are known to be of "defective character." The portrait of oral and anal restraint that Husain paints locates him within a moral system that valorizes self-mastery and purification. In linking these virtues with good health, Husain suggests that his adherence to a yogic regimen is the source of his longevity: "Health is the most important thing. If you are healthy, you have everything. And health comes from self-control. I have always paid attention to that, whether I was at work or resting at home."[37] A related aspect of his self-representation is Husain's devotion to family and financial support for them. A dominant theme in the autobiography is that he was a good husband and provider: "I always stayed in touch with my family and fulfilled my responsibilities toward them. Whenever I got the chance, I went home, at least a couple of times a year. I sent money regularly."[38] The virtue of self-regulation extends to management of his personal finances. "I lived an ordinary life, but I always saved something. Whether it was five rupees or a hundred a month, I made a point of putting money aside. That way I never felt the need to beg from anyone. My sole desire is that I will always be able to look after myself, and whenever possible, that I may serve others as well."[39]

Family life, indeed, seems to have assumed great importance for Husain in retirement, and he seems genuinely fond of his grandchildren and great-grandchildren and proud of his sons. Husain never mentions his wife or his married life, keeping her hidden and preserving family honor. He claims to have avoided relationships with actresses during his career, although his story includes several episodes that cast some doubt on the matter.

Husain's emphasis on self-reliance and family solidarity mirrors his description of the disciplinary regimen of the Parsi companies. In his interviews, he repeatedly alludes to the rules and regulations that framed the daily life of the boys and men in the troupe: "Everything was systematic, fixed. Whether it was eating and drinking, or rehearsals and show times, it was the same attitude.... It was the same food for everybody. In the morning... two chapatis, two eggs, and tea for breakfast.... If the rehearsal was at 9:30, the first bell would ring at 8:30, so that anyone that had not eaten could finish. After the second bell at 9 a.m., breakfast was over. No matter how famous the artist, if he arrived after that it was too late. These rules were strictly observed."[40] Observation of timings was a fundamental rule, but other proprieties were equally important: "No one could chew *pan*, and although smoking wasn't forbidden, it was not allowed in the dressing room or during rehearsals.... During rehearsals, all the actors had to sit for hours at a stretch with full attention to the training given on stage. No talking or looking around were allowed, and both feet had to be firmly planted on the floor."[41] Even audience members were required to behave with respect: "Company discipline was not just for the actors, it was for the spectators too. They couldn't put their feet up on the sofas or sit with their legs splayed or knees apart."[42] Equality of treatment was another basic principle. Husain tells an amusing story of the mistress of a maharaja who tried to sit in the "special class" where women of ill-repute were forbidden. After being cautioned, Shyama Bai, the courtesan, was bodily removed from the theater hall—along with the sofa on which she was seated.

The disdain of highbrow critics for the Parsi theater is thus parried by Husain with examples of discipline, self-control, and self-sacrifice. While his narrative supplies entertaining anecdotes, it also underscores the theatrical life as one lived according to rules and order. Moreover, he stresses that his career involved service, catering to the public, whose tastes demanded what he delivered. This aspect comes into prominence as Husain discusses his years of portraying Hindu gods and saints, the roles for which he earned the greatest acclaim. Before turning to this facet of his career, however, let us consider the autobiography's treatment of his identity as a Muslim.

Fida Husain's account, while in general quite verbose, contains substantive gaps, particularly in regard to his early life and religious orientation. The text does not mention his childhood or education, nor is his family's lineage and traditional occupation addressed. He grew up in Muradabad, a *qasba* famous for its brassware production. On the basis of Husain's sons' involvement in that business, one might assume this was his background as well. However, he makes no mention of this. Nor does the reader learn whether he was a Sunni or a Shia. In passing, he cites Hindu-Muslim violence at the time of Partition and recounts a dispute about performing plays during Muharram. Aside from these stray references, his self-image as a Muslim remains a mystery.

In contrast with the absence of information about his personal roots as a Muslim, he says a great deal about his participation in Hindu-oriented dramas and interaction with Hindu patrons. Fida Husain became well known for his impersonations of Hindu gods and saints. His most famous role was as Narsi Mehta, a fifteenth-century Gujarati saint-poet and devotee of Lord Krishna. The drama about Narsi Mehta was a particular favorite of Gujaratis and Marwari Vaishnavas, and as a result of their patronage, Husain's career took a very successful turn in the 1930s and 1940s. As he tells it: "Some wealthy businessmen based in Kanpur, Padmapat and Kamlapat Singhania, persuaded me through their agent to join the Marwari stage. These Marwaris were devotees of Narsi Mehta. When I performed that role with Ganpat as Lord Krishna, the Singhanias reserved a sofa with their mother for the entire run, paying in advance. The mother used to touch my feet and beseech me to intercede with Lord Krishna on her behalf. In the winter season, they presented Ganpat and me with warm blankets, on the assumption that Narsi and Krishna must feel the cold too."[43] In another passage he tells how he produced *Narsi Mehta* for the Babu Roshan Lal Company: "For 300 nights we performed this play in Delhi.... People saw it twenty times over, and I was awarded 150 medals. The gold ones I turned over to my daughters to wear. The silver ones I melted down; they amounted to Rs 1400. I had no interest in wearing medals, but I kept some as remembrances: the medal from the State of Bikaner, the Maharaja of Patiala's cup, the medal from Tonk, and the Jaipur medal."[44] Because of his stature as a saint on stage, Fida Husain prevailed in a dispute with a maharaja: "The whole of Delhi was on my side, and I feared no one. I was on good terms with all the officials, the court, the magistrate. They were devoted to me because of my role as Narsi Mehta. Kings and princes had no authority over them."[45]

Putting Husain's career within historical perspective, it is relevant that the early twentieth century witnessed the consolidation of the Hindu majority and its growing alliance with the nationalist cause. Compared to the Marathi or Bengali theaters, the Parsi theater was a relative latecomer to adopting Hindu religious themes. Nevertheless, from 1915 on the trend toward production of mythological and devotional dramas grew apace. The advent of the mythological led to a measure of ritualization of the heretofore secular space of the playhouse. The fondness for dramatizing the epics went hand in hand with the new visual regime and trappings of modern stagecraft. As Husain himself articulates, the theater became the locus of spectacle, and the depiction of miracles through illusion scenes became the coin of mass entertainment: "Spectacle was a particular feature of the Parsi theatre, and it was used to attract the public.... I'll describe for you an illusion scene from *Ganesh Janm*. A mirror was used to show that Parvati was taking a bath. She forms a lump of clay and places it on the altar, and then Ganesh is born from it. This illusion involved two mirrors, one with the image of the lump, the other showing a boy. The light was adjusted in such a way that Ganesh seemed to be taking birth from the lump of clay."[46]

The Parsi theater capitalized on the concept of *darshan* as well, offering tableaus of gods in iconic poses as opportunities for worship and the collection of donations. Although the Urdu pageant *Indar Sabha* (1853) arose as a representation of the Nawab of Awadh and his court, the Indar of its title was widely understood as the Vedic deity Indra, king of heaven. Fida Husain recalls the way in which theater companies benefited from gullible audiences' religious beliefs: "You wouldn't believe how incredibly innocent the people of Bihar once were. Raja Indar comes into court at the beginning of the *Indar Sabha*, and all the courtiers sing an *amad* for him. . . . Then an *arti* ceremony is performed and an offering plate is circulated for donations. This was not in the original. It was all the company director's scheme to take advantage of the audience. . . . The income from ticket sales usually amounted to Rs 700, but from the *arti* the company earned another Rs 900 on top of that."[47] As the mythological genre gained in popularity, theatrical discourse and practice were infused with Hindu sacrality, even as the migration of the epics and Puranas to the popular playhouse moved in the other direction as well, toward dilution of the sacred with comic plots and dance sequences.

In general, casting with a blind eye to religious community was common in the Parsi theater. The utilization of non-Hindu actors and actresses for Hindu roles was not considered inappropriate. The Muslim actor Fida Husain playing a Hindu saint worked well and was accepted. The performance of mythic female roles by Muslim actresses was somewhat more contentious. When the famous actress Gauhar played Sita or Draupadi from the Hindu epics, public outrage was occasionally provoked, as Betab and Radheshyam describe in their autobiographies.[48]

Given that Muslims were actively engaged in large numbers in the Parsi theatrical companies, how did they adjust to the surge in devotionally imbued tales of Hindu gods and saints? What internal and external accommodations were required when Muslim actors routinely portrayed Hindu characters? Was there a personal response to the acts of devotion they elicited among their adoring spectator-followers? Although the answers are not to be found in Husain's autobiography, his silence on matters of religious faith and identity invites further reflection. Husain's example suggests that Muslim actors not only embraced Hindu roles onstage but suppressed their Muslimness in nontheatrical public contexts as well. Husain was lauded as a performer who mimed Hindu spirituality through the medium of his Muslim body. In his narrative, he constructs his self as disciplined and pure. Perhaps this performance of identity also served as an icon of integration, an embodiment of India's composite culture. Composite culture in India is widely equated with the confluence of Hindu and Muslim cultural streams (*ganga-yamuni tehzib*) and in recent cultural politics has been reinvigorated as a resource for reclaiming secularism and opposing Hindutva.[49] In the case of Fida Husain, the textual and performative erasure of his Muslim identity points to the communal bias latent within the composite ideal. As cultural historians have pointed out, composite culture discourse encodes a Hindu majoritarian perspective: the Yamuna is always already subordinate to the Ganga.[50] In my reading of Husain's *Fifty Years*, then, his autobiography subsumes his Muslim self within the putatively secular culture of the nation-state. The textual erasure of Husain's religious identity may reflect his tacit acceptance of the official culture of the postcolonial state and its spokespersons in the urban theater world.

Conclusion

In her study of Rashsundari's autobiography, Tanika Sarkar outlines the paradoxical position occupied by "muted groups" such as women in nineteenth-century Bengal. She cites the cultural anthropologists Shirley and Edwin Ardener to argue that muted groups lacked access to public modes of articulation and could not set cultural standards or norms. Instead, they laid claim to "a sliver of existence," to practices and beliefs outside the prevailing culture. Dominant groups viewed the sphere of the muted as a "wild zone" beyond their knowledge and wished to gaze on it, to enter it to fill the gaps in their understanding.[51]

The communities from which the Parsi theater autobiographers hailed could also be considered muted groups. Just as the upper-caste woman violated nineteenth-century norms of female propriety by writing her autobiography, so too the early twentieth-century actor in writing his life could be said to have crossed a line. As Susan Seizer has shown, a long-standing prejudice construes actors as lacking a fixed identity and therefore dangerous in their liminality. Professional actors in Tamilnadu are still stigmatized and must counter mainstream perceptions of being disorderly and of bad character.[52] The actor as autobiographer, however, was in a position to assert self-regard, self-mastery, and self-determination. The knowability of the actor through his writing negated the dominant culture's understanding of the performer as a vessel, a mere mask. His writing could engage the voyeurism of the reader, driven by desire to perceive the actor's secret world.

Theorizing the Parsi theater as a wild zone and the actor as a shadowy subject whose partial visibility exerts a great allure has a certain cogency. It suggests the complex structure of avoidance and attraction that binds the spectator-reader and the actor-author, creating a reading public for theatrical lives. In Sundari's and Fida Husain's stories, the narrators at times play to the voyeurism of their readers by exoticizing the theater world. Yet these memoirs also advance claims for their subjects' bourgeois sensibilities. They articulate the civilizing virtues of theatrical entertainment and testify to their subjects' public reputations. Assuming the roles of narrators, moreover, while they are silent on certain subjects, in their very forthrightness they create an impression of audibility not normally associated with subordinated groups.

Indeed, these autobiographies belie the hypothesis that their subjects were made mute through subordination. Although not univocal, these narratives speak in voices that are often bold, daring, and feisty. Their subjects on occasion talk back to those in power, breaking with conventions of deference. They articulate opposition to systems they deem unfair and unjust. To differing degrees, the autobiographies construct their subjects as righteous individuals, as defenders of a larger moral order. The stylized voices in which the narrators speak are various, but each crafts a performative presence that both entertains the reader and affirms the worth of the self.

NOTES

1 Kathryn Hansen, *Stages of Life: Indian Theatre Autobiographies* (Ranikhet: Permanent Black, 2011), 30–31.
2 In 1931, sixty-eight of the essays and 150 accompanying photographs were compiled in a 422-page volume, *Parsi Natak Takhtani Tavarikh*, published by Kaiser-i Hind Press in Bombay. The sketches begin with the first Parsi Theatrical Company in 1853 and extend through the 1890s.
3 Jahangir Pestanji Khambata, *Mahro Nataki Anubhav* (Bombay: Parsi Ltd. Press, 1914).
4 Rimli Bhattacharya, "Actress-Stories and the 'Female' Confessional Voice in Bengali Theatre Magazines (1910–1925)," *Seagull Theatre Quarterly* 5 (May 1995): 3–25.
5 Rimli Bhattacharya, ed. and trans., *My Story and My Life as an Actress: Binodini Dasi* (Delhi: Kali for Women, 1998).
6 Hansen, *Stages*, 34–35.
7 Hansen, *Stages*, chap. 7. See also Sidonie Smith and Julia Watson, *Reading Autobiography: A Guide for Interpreting Life Narratives* (Minneapolis: University of Minnesota Press, 2010), 193–211.

8 Sidonie Smith, "Performativity, Autobiographical Practice, Resistance," in *Women, Autobiography, Theory: A Reader*, Sidonie Smith and Julia Watson, eds. (Madison: University of Wisconsin Press, 1998), 108.
9 For details on the authorship and compilation of Sundari's autobiography, see Hansen, *Stages*, 176–78; and for similar issues in regard to Fida Husain, see 249–52.
10 Paul John Eakin, foreword to Philippe Lejeune, *On Autobiography*, ed. Paul John Eakin, trans. Katherine Leary (Minneapolis: University of Minnesota Press, 1989), xxi.
11 Lejeune, *On Autobiography*, 207–11.
12 Eakin, foreword, xviii.
13 Smith, "Performativity," 110.
14 Smith, "Performativity," 111.
15 Hansen, *Stages*, 200–201.
16 Hansen, *Stages*, 181.
17 Hansen, *Stages*, 183.
18 Hansen, *Stages*, 186.
19 Hansen, *Stages*, 187.
20 Hansen, *Stages*, 187–88.
21 Hansen, *Stages*, 210.
22 Hansen, *Stages*, 213–14.
23 Bhailal Bulakhidas Panchotia, *Jayashankar Sundari and Abhinayakala* (Bombay: Bharatiya Vidya Bhavan, 1987), 131.
24 Kathryn Hansen, "Making Women Visible: Gender and Race Cross-Dressing in the Parsi Theatre," *Theatre Journal* 51.2 (1999): 127–47.
25 Smith and Watson, *Reading Autobiography*, 189; see also 70, 107.
26 Hansen, *Stages*, 219.
27 Hansen, *Stages*, 221.
28 Hansen, *Stages*, 224.
29 Hansen, *Stages*, 225.
30 Hansen, *Stages*, 217–18.
31 Hansen, *Stages*, 218.
32 Hansen, *Stages*, 228.
33 Hansen, *Stages*, 228.
34 Hansen, *Stages*, 229.
35 Lejeune, *On Autobiography*, 190.
36 Hansen, *Stages*, 256.
37 Hansen, *Stages*, 256.
38 Hansen, *Stages*, 257.
39 Hansen, *Stages*, 257.
40 Hansen, *Stages*, 273.
41 Hansen, *Stages*, 269.
42 Hansen, *Stages*, 272.
43 Hansen, *Stages*, 276–77.

44 Hansen, *Stages*, 278.
45 Hansen, *Stages*, 280.
46 Hansen, *Stages*, 267.
47 Hansen, *Stages*, 267–68.
48 Hansen, *Stages*, 43–44, 139.
49 Kathryn Hansen, "Staging Composite Culture: Nautanki and Parsi Theatre in Recent Revivals," *South Asia Research* 29.2 (2009): 152–53.
50 Kathryn Hansen, "Who Wants to Be a Cosmopolitan? Readings from the Composite Culture," *Indian Economic and Social History Review* 47.3 (July–September 2010): 294–97.
51 Tanika Sarkar, *Words to Win: The Making of* Amar Jiban; *A Modern Autobiography* (Delhi: Kali for Women, 1999), 115.
52 Susan Seizer, *Stigmas of the Tamil Stage* (Durham, NC: Duke University Press, 2005).

SELECT BIBLIOGRAPHY

Abbas, Shameem Burney. *The Female Voice in Sufi Ritual: Devotional Practices in India and Pakistan*. Austin: University of Texas Press, 2003.

Abrams, Lynn, and Callum G. Brown. "Introduction: Conceiving the Everyday in the Twentieth Century." In *A History of Everyday Life in Twentieth Century Scotland*, ed. Lynn Abrams and Callum G. Brown, 1–18. Edinburgh: Edinburgh University Press, 2010.

Abu Fazl, B. Mubārak. *Akbarnāma*. Translated from the Persian by H. Beveridge. Calcutta: Asiatic Society, 1897.

Abu'l Fazl ibn Allami, *The A'in-I Akbari by Abul Fazl 'Allami*. Vol. 3. Translated by H. Beveridge. Calcutta: Asiatic Society, 1897–1939.

Agraval, Pratibha, ed. *Master Fida Husain: Parsi Thiyetar men Pachas Varsh*. Calcutta: Natya Shodh Sansthan, 1986.

Ahmad, Nazir, *Mirāt-ul Urūs* [The bride's mirror]. Karachi: Sultan Husain, 1963.

Alam, Asiya. "Polygyny, Family and *Sharafat*: Discourses amongst North Indian Muslims, circa 1870–1918." *Modern Asian Studies* 45 (2011): 631–68.

Alam, Muzaffar. *The Crisis of Empire in Mughal North India: Awadh and the Punjab, 1707–48*. Delhi: Oxford University Press, 1986.

Alam, Muzaffar. "The Mughals, the Sufi Shaikhs and the Formation of the Akbari Dispensation." *Modern Asian Studies* 43.1 (January 2009): 135–74.

Algar, Hamid. "A Brief History of the Naqshbandi Order." In *Naqshbandis: Historical Developments and Present Situation of a Muslim Mystical Order*, ed. Marc Gaborieau, Alexandre Popovic, and Thierry Zarcone, 3–44. Istanbul: Institut Francais d'Etudes Anatoliennes d'Istanbul, 1990.

Algar, Hamid. "Political Aspects of Naqshbandi History." In *Naqshbandis: Historical Developments and Present Situation of a Muslim Mystical Order*, ed. Marc Gaborieau, Alexandre Popovic, and Thierry Zarcone, 123–52. Istanbul: Institut Francais d'Etudes Anatoliennes d'Istanbul, 1990.

Ali, Ahmed. *The Golden Tradition: An Anthology of Urdu Poetry*. New York: Columbia University Press, 1973.

Ali, Yazdi Sharafuddin. "Zafarnama." In *A Century of Princes: Sources on Timurid History and Art*, trans. W. M. Thackston, 63–100. Cambridge, MA: Aga Khan Program for Islamic Architecture at Harvard University and the Massachusetts Institute of Technology, 1989.

Al-Samman, Hanadi. *Anxiety of Erasure: Trauma, Authorship and the Diaspora in Arab Women's Writing*. Syracuse, NY: Syracuse University Press, 2013.

Alvi, Sajida Sultan. *Advice on the Art of Governance: An Indo-Islamic Mirror for Princes*. Albany: State University of New York Press, 1989.

Alvi, Wahhaj al-Din. *Urdu Khud Navisht*. New Delhi: Maktaba Jamia, 1989.

Arnold, David. "The Self and the Cell: Indian Prison Narratives as Life Histories." In *Telling Lives in India: Biography, Autobiography, and Life History*, ed. David Arnold and Stuart Blackburn, 29–53. Delhi: Permanent Black, 2004.

Arnold, David, and Stuart Blackburn, eds. *Telling Lives in India: Biography, Autobiography, and Life History*. Delhi: Permanent Black, 2004.

Azmi, Rahat. *Mah Laqa: Halat-i-Zindagi: Mah-i-Diwan*. Hyderabad: Urdu Academy Andhra Pradesh, 1998.

Badran, Margot, ed. and trans. *Harem Years: The Memoirs of an Egyptian Feminist*. London: Virago, 1986.

Bakhle, Janaki. *Two Men and Music: Nationalism in the Making of an Indian Classical Tradition*. Delhi: Permanent Black, 2005.

Basu, Aparna. *Abbas Tyabji*. New Delhi: National Book Trust, India, 2007.

Basu, Aparna, and Malvika Karlekar, eds. *In So Many Words: Women's Life Experiences from Western and Eastern India*. London: Routledge, 2008.

Basu, Somendranath, ed. *Smritikatha*. Calcutta: Baitanik Prakashani, 1987.

Basu, Swapan, ed. *Sambad Samayik Patre Unish Shataker Bangali Samaj*. Vol. 2. Calcutta: Pashchim Banga Bangla Academy, 2003.

Bayly, C. A. *Rulers, Townsmen and Bazaars: North Indian Society in the Age of British Expansion 1770–1870*. Cambridge: Cambridge University Press, 1983.

Begley, W. E., and Z. A. Desai, eds. and trans. *The Shah Jahan Nama of "Inayat Khan."* Delhi: Oxford University Press, 1990.

Begley, Wayne E. "The Symbolic Role of Calligraphy on Three Imperial Mosques of Shah Jahan." In *Kaladarsana: American Studies in the Art of India*, ed. Joanna G. Williams, 7–18. New Delhi: Oxford and IBH Publishing Co., 1981.

Bharucha, Rustom. *Rajasthan: An Oral History; Conversations with Komal Kothari*. New Delhi: Penguin India, 2003.

Bhattacharya, Debipada. *Bangla Charit Sahitya*. Calcutta: Dey's, 1982.

Bhattacharya, Malini, and Abhijit Sen, eds. *Talking of Power: Early Writings of Bengali Women from the Mid-nineteenth Century to the Beginning of the Twentieth Century*. Calcutta: School of Women's Studies, Jadavpur University, 2003.

Bhattacharya, Rimli. "Actress-Stories and the 'Female' Confessional Voice in Bengali Theatre Magazines (1910–1925)." *Seagull Theatre Quarterly* 5 (May 1995): 3–25.

Bhattacharya, Rimli, ed. and trans. *My Story and My Life as an Actress: Binodini Dasi*. Delhi: Kali for Women, 1998.

Bilgrami, Fatima. *History of the Qadiri Order in India: 16th–18th Century*. Delhi: Jayed Press, 2005.

Bilgrami, Syed Ali Asgar. *Landmarks of the Deccan: A Comprehensive Guide to the Archaeological Remains of the City and Suburbs of Hyderabad*. Hyderabad: Government Central Press, 1927.

Blackburn, Stuart. "Life Histories as Narrative Strategy: Prophecy, Song, and Truth-Telling in Tamil Tales and Legends." In *Telling Lives in India: Biography, Autobiography and Life History*, ed. David Arnold and Stuart Blackburn, 203–26. Delhi: Permanent Black, 2004.

Booth, Marilyn. *May Her Likes Be Multiplied: Biography and Gender Politics in Egypt*. Berkeley: University of California Press, 2001.

Booth, Marilyn. "Subjectivities on the Nile, 1890s to the 1920s: Intellectual Openings in Egypt and Gendered Representations of the Self." Conference paper, "Women's Autobiography in Islamic Societies: Context and Construction," India International Centre, Delhi, December 16–18, 2010.

Borthwick, Meredith. *The Changing Role of Women in Bengal, 1849–1905*. Princeton, NJ: Princeton University Press, 1984.

Brittlebank, Kate. "Piety and Power: A Preliminary Analysis of Tipu Sultan's Dreams." In *Tall Tales and True: India, Historiography and British Imperial Imaginings*, ed. Kate Brittlebank, 31–41. Melbourne: Monash University Press, 2008.

Brown, Louise. *The Dancing Girls of Lahore: Selling Love and Saving Dreams in Pakistan's Pleasure District*. New York: HarperCollins, 2006.

Brownstein, Rachel M. *Becoming a Heroine: Reading about Women in Novels*. New York: Viking, 1982.

Buehler, Arthur. "The Indo-Pak Qadiriyya," *Journal of the History of Sufism* 1–2 (2000): 339–60.

Buehler, Arthur F. "The Naqshbandiyya in Timurid India: The Central Asian Legacy," *Journal of Islamic Studies* 7.2 (1996): 209–28.

Burke, Peter. *Varieties of Cultural History*. Cambridge: Polity, 1997.

Burton, Antoinette. *Dwelling in the Archive: Women Writing House, Home and History in Late Colonial India*. New York: Oxford University Press, 2003.

Butalia, Urvashi. *The Other Side of Silence: Voices from the Partition of India*. New Delhi: Penguin, 1998.

Butler, Judith. *Bodies That Matter: On the Discursive Limits of "Sex."* New York: Routledge, 1993.

Butler, Judith. *Gender Trouble: Feminism and the Subversion of Identity*. New York: Routledge, 1990.

Chakraborty, Sambudhha. *Andare Antare: Unish Shatake Bangali Bhadramahila*. Calcutta: Stree, 1995.

Chakravarti, Ishita. "Pinjar theke Pinjare: Jautha Itihasher Khoje." In *Naishabda Bhenge: Atmakathane Bharatiya Nari*, ed. Ishita Chakravarti et al. Calcutta: Khoj Ekhon Parishad and Stree, 2005.

Chakravarti, Uma. *Rewriting History: The Life and Times of Pandita Ramabai*. Delhi: Kali for Women, 1998.

Chambers, Samuel A., and Terrell Carver. *Judith Butler and Political Theory: Troubling Politics*. London: Routledge, 2008.

Chandra, Moti. *The World of Courtesans*. Delhi: Vikas, 1973.

Chandramani, "Gunijan khana," in Jai Narayan Asopa, ed. *Cultural Heritage of Jaipur*. Jodhpur: United Book Traders, 1982, 95–103.

Chatterjee, Partha. "The Nationalist Resolution of Women's Question." In *Recasting Women: Essays in Colonial History*, ed. Kumkum Sangari and Sudesh Vaid, 233–53. New Delhi: Kali for Women, 1989.

Chatterjee, Partha. *The Nation and Its Fragments: Colonial and Postcolonial Histories*. Princeton, NJ: Princeton University Press, 1993.

Chatterjee, Partha. *The Partha Chatterjee Omnibus*. New Delhi: Oxford University Press, 1999.

The Chronology of Modern Hyderabad (1720–1890). Hyderabad: Central Records Office, 1954.

Cole, Juan R. *Roots of North Indian Shi'ism in Iran and Iraq: Religion and State in Awadh 1722–1856*. Los Angeles: University of California Press, 1988.

Conway, Jill Ker. *When Memory Speaks: Exploring the Art of Autobiography*. New York: Vintage, 1998.

Courtright, Paul B. "The Iconographies of Sati." In *Sati: The Blessing and the Curse; The Burning of Wives in India*, ed. John Stratton Hawley, 27–54. New York: Oxford University Press, 1994.

Dale, Stephen F. "The Legacy of the Timurids," *Journal of the Royal Asiatic Society*, 3rd series, 8.1 (1998): 43–58.

Dale, Stephen Frederic. "Steppe Humanism: The Autobiographical Writings of Zahir al-Din Muhammad Babur, 1483–1530." *International Journal of Middle East Studies* 22 (1990): 37–58.

Dalmia, Vasudha. "*Orienting India: European Knowledge Formation in the Eighteenth and Nineteenth Centuries*. Gurgaon: Three Essays Collective, 2007.

Dalrymple, William. *White Mughals: Love and Betrayal in Eighteenth-Century India*. London: HarperCollins, 2002.

Das, Sant Vijendra. *Sant Kavyitri Ma Piro*. Panchkula: Satluj Prakashan, 2011.

Das, Veena. *Critical Events: An Anthropological Perspective on Contemporary India*. Delhi: Oxford University Press, 1996.

Deb, Chitra. *Antahpurer Atmakatha*. Kolkata: Ananda Publishers, 1984.

Debi, Ashapurna. *Subarnalata*. Kolkata: Mitra and Ghosh Publishers, 1967.

Dehlavi, Khwaja Hakim Ghulam Hussain Khan Zaman Khan. *Tarikh-i-Asafjahyiyan (Gulzar-i-Asafiya)*, ed. M. Mehdi Tavassoli. Islamabad: Iran-Pakistan Institute of Persian Studies, 1999.

Dehlavi, Mir Insha Allah Khan "Insha." *Kahani Rani Ketaki aur Kanwar Aude Bhan Ki*. Karachi: Anjuman Taraqi Urdu Pakistan, 1993.

de Man, Paul. "Autobiography as De-facement." *Modern Language Notes* 94.5 (December 1979): 919–30.

de Man, Paul. *Rhetoric of Romanticism*. New York: Columbia University Press, 1984.
Dev Sen, Nabaneeta. "The Wind Beneath My Wings." *Indian Journal of Gender Studies* 6.1 (January–June 1999): 221–39.
Devji, Faisal Fatehali. "Gender and the Politics of Space: The Movement for Women's Reform in Muslim India, 1857–1900." *South Asia* 14 (1991): 141–53.
Durgaprasad "Nadir." *Tazkirat-al-Nisa*. Delhi: n.p., 1878.
Dyson, Ketaki Kushari. *A Various Universe: A Study of the Journals and Memoirs of British Men and Women in the Indian Subcontinent 1765–1856*. Delhi: Oxford University Press, 2002.
Eakin, Paul John. *Fictions in Autobiography: Studies in the Art of Self-Invention*. Princeton, NJ: Princeton University Press, 1985.
Engineer, Asghar Ali. *The Bohras*. New Delhi: Vikas, 1980.
Erdman, Joan L. *Patrons and Performers in Rajasthan: The Subtle Tradition*. Delhi: Chanakya, 1985.
Fallon, S. W. *A New English-Hindustani Dictionary*. London: Trübner, 1883.
Faruqi, Shamsur Rahman. "The Poet in the Poem or, Veiling the Utterance." In *A Wilderness of Possibilities: Urdu Studies in Transnational Perspective*, ed. Kathryn Hansen and David Lelyveld, 173–91. Delhi: Oxford University Press, 2005.
Faruqui, Munis D. *The Princes of the Mughal Empire, 1504–1719*. Cambridge: Cambridge University Press, 2012.
Fasih-al-Din "Ranj." *Baharistan-i-Naz*. Meerut: n.p., 1882.
Felski, Rita. "On Confession." In *Women, Autobiography, Theory: A Reader*, ed. Sidonie Smith and Julia Watson, 83–95. Madison: University of Wisconsin Press, 1998.
Findly, Ellison Banks. *Nur Jahan: Empress of Mughal India*. New York: Oxford University Press, 1993.
Findly, Ellison Banks. "Women's Wealth and Styles of Giving: Perspectives from Buddhist, Jain, and Mughal Sites." In *Women, Patronage and Self-Representation in Islamic Societies*, ed. D. Fairchild Ruggles, 91–122. New York: State University of New York Press, 2000.
Folkenflik, Robert, ed. *The Culture of Autobiography: Constructions of Self-Representation*. Stanford, CA: Stanford University Press, 1993.
Friedman, Susan Stanford. "Women's Autobiographical Selves: Theory and Practice." In *Women, Autobiography, Theory: A Reader*, ed. Sidonie Smith and Julia Watson, 72–82. Madison: University of Wisconsin Press, 1998.
Fyzee, Asaf A.A., ed. *The Autobiography of Tyabji Bhoymeeah: Merchant Prince of Bombay 1803–1863*. Bombay: The Government Central Press, 1964.
Fyzee, Atiya. *Zamana-i-tahsil*. Agra: Matba' Mufid-i-'Am, 1921.
Gaborieau, Marc, Alexandre Popovic, and Thierry Zarcone, eds. *Naqshbandis: Historical Developments and Present Situation of a Muslim Mystical Order*. Istanbul: Institut Francais d'Etudes Anatoliennes d'Istanbul, 1990.
Gauhar, Ghulam Samdani. *Gulzar-i-Mah Laqa*. Hyderabad: Nizams Press, 1906.
Ghosh, Anindita. *Power in Print: Popular Publishing and the Politics of Language and Culture in a Colonial Society*. Delhi: Oxford University Press, 2006.

Ghosh, Saurindra Kumar. *Peary Chand Mitra O Samakalin Bangla*. Calcutta: Anandadhara, 1985.
Ghosh, Srabashi. "'Birds in a Cage': Changes in Bengali Social Life as Recorded in Autobiographies by Women." *Economic and Political Weekly* 21.43 (October 25, 1986): ws88–ws96.
Ghouse, Zakira. "Baquir Agah's Contribution to Arabic, Persian and Urdu Literatures." MLitt thesis, Madras University, 1973.
Ghouse, Zakira. "Hamāra Daur-i Hayāt." Unpublished ms., 1953–60.
Ghouse, Zakira. *Hayāt-i Haq: 'Abdul Haq kī Zindagī kī Cand Jhalkīyan*. Madras: Model Art Press, 1975.
Ghouse, Zakira. "Khawātīn-i Khānwāda-i Badr-ud Daula kī Adabī, Tālimī aur Mazhabī Khidmāt." PhD diss., Madras University, 1994.
Ghouse, Zakira. *Maulānā Bāqir Āgā Velūrī: Shakhsiyat aur Fan*. Madras: Tamilnadu Urdu Publications, 1995.
Gibbs, Hamilton A. R. "Islamic Biographical Literature." In *Historians of the Middle East*, ed. B. Lewis, 54–58. London: Oxford University Press, 1962.
Grace, Sherrill. "Theatre and the Autobiographical Pact: An Introduction." In *Theatre and Autobiography: Writing and Performing Lives in Theory and Practice*, ed. Sherrill Grace and Jerry Wasserman. Vancouver: Talonbooks, 2006.
Greenblatt, Stephen. *Renaissance Self-Fashioning: From More to Shakespeare*. Chicago: University of Chicago Press, 1980.
Grewal, J. S. *The Sikhs of the Punjab*. 1994. New Delhi: Cambridge University Press, 2002.
Guénon, René. *Studies in Hinduism*. Translated by Henry D. Fohr. Hillsdale, NY: Sophia Perennis, 2001.
Gusdorf, Georges. "Conditions and Limits of Autobiography." In *Autobiography: Essays Theoretical and Critical*, ed. and trans. James Olney, 28–48. Princeton, NJ: Princeton University Press, 1980.
Hansen, Kathryn. "Making Women Visible: Gender and Race Cross-Dressing in the Parsi Theatre." *Theatre Journal* 51.2 (1999): 127–47.
Hansen, Kathryn. *Stages of Life: Indian Theatre Autobiographies*. Ranikhet: Permanent Black, 2011.
Hansen, Kathryn. "Staging Composite Culture: Nautanki and Parsi Theatre in Recent Revivals." *South Asia Research* 29.2 (2009): 151–68.
Hansen, Kathryn. "Who Wants to Be a Cosmopolitan? Readings from the Composite Culture." *Indian Economic and Social History Review* 47.3 (July–September 2010): 291–308.
Hasan, Farhat. "Presenting the Self: Norms and Emotions in Ardhakathanaka." In *Biography as History: Indian Perspectives*, ed. Vijaya Ramaswamy and Yogesh Sharma, 105–22. Hyderabad: Orient Blackswan, 2009.
Hasan, Z. A. *Guide to Nizam-ud Din, Memoirs of the Archaeological Survey of India Office*. Issue 10. Calcutta: Archaeological Survey of India, 1922.
Hawley, J. S., and M. Juergensmeyer, eds. *Songs of the Saints of India*. Delhi: Oxford University Press, 2008.

Hawley, John Stratton. *Three Bhakti Voices: Mirabai, Surdas and Kabir in Their Time and Ours*. New York: Oxford University Press, 2005.
Heddon, Deirdre. *Autobiography and Performance*. Basingstoke, UK: Palgrave Macmillan, 2008.
Heilbrun, Carolyn G. *Writing a Woman's Life*. New York: Ballantine, 1988.
Hina, Zaheda. *Na Junoon Raha*. Delhi: Zubaan, 2011.
Hjira, Nawab Begam. "Ser-e Europe." *Ismat*, August 1908, 23–38.
Hodges, Sheila. *Gollancz: The Story of a Publishing House 1928–1978*. London: Victor Gollancz, 1978.
Hosain, Attia. Sunlight on a Broken Column. London: Virago, 1988.
Husain, Ali Akbar. *Scent in the Islamic Garden: A Study of Deccani Urdu Literary Sources*. Karachi: Oxford University Press, 2000.
Hussain, Syed Liyaqat. *The Chishti Shrine of Ajmer: Pirs, Pilgrims, Practices*. Jaipur: Publication Scheme, 2004.
Hyder, Nazr S. *Guzashta Barson Ki Baraf*, ed. Qurratulain Hyder. Delhi: Educational Publishing House, 2007.
Hyder, Qurratulain. *Kar-e Jahan Daraz Hai*. Delhi: Educational Publishing House, 2003.
Ibbetson, D. C. J. *Panjab Castes*. 1883. Patiala: Languages Department Punjab, 2000.
Ikramullah, Shaista S. *From Purdah to Parliament*. Karachi: Oxford University Press, 1998.
Jaffrey, Nausheen. "Jahanara Begam: A Biographical Study 1614–81 A.D." MPhil diss., Jamia Millia Islamia University, 1997.
Jahangir, Nuruddin Muhammad. *Tuzuk-i Jahangiri*. Vols. 1–2. Translated by H. Beveridge. Delhi, n.p., 1989.
Jana, Naresh Chandra, et al. *Atmakatha*. Vol. 2. Calcutta: Ananya Prakashan, 1982.
Jarrett, H. S., trans. *'Ain-i- Akbari of Abul Fazl-i-'Allami*. Vol. 3. Calcutta: Asiatic Society of Bengal, 1948.
Jelinek, Estelle C. *Women's Autobiography: Essays in Criticism*. New York: Twayne, 1980.
Jit, Hasrat Bikrama. *Dārā Shikūh: Life and Works*. New Delhi: Munshiram Manoharlal, 1982.
Joseph, Ammu, et al., eds. "Nabaneeta Dev Sen." In *Storylines: Conversations with Women Writers*. New Delhi and Hyderabad: Women's WORLD (India) and Asmita Resource Centre for Women, 2003.
Kabir, Ananya Jahanara. "Gender, Memory, Trauma: Women's Novels on the Partition of India." *Comparative Studies of South Asia, Africa and the Middle-East* 25.1 (2005): 177–90.
Kandiyoti, Deniz. "Bargaining with Patriarchy." *Gender and Society* 2 (1988): 274–98.
Karlekar, Malavika. "Constructions of Femininity in Nineteenth Century Bengal: Readings from *Janaika Grihabadhur Diary*." *Samya Shakti: A Journal of Women's Studies* 4–5 (1989–90): 11–29.

Karlekar, Malavika. "Education of a Civil Servant's Daughter: Readings from Monica Chanda's Memoirs." In "Reconstructing Femininities: Colonial Intersections of Gender, Race, Religion and Class," special issue of *Feminist Review*, no. 65 (summer 2000): 127–44.

Karlekar, Malavika. "Showcasing the Family." In *Visualizing Indian Women, 1875–1947*, ed. Malavika Karlekar, 1–38. Delhi: Oxford University Press, 2006.

Karlekar, Malavika. *Voices from Within: Early Personal Narratives of Bengali Women*. Delhi: Oxford University Press, 1993.

Karlitzky, Marlen. "The Tyabji Clan—Urdu as a Symbol of Group Identity." *Annual of Urdu Studies* 17 (2002): 187–207.

Kaviraj, Sudipto, "The Invention of Private Life: A Reading of Sibnath Sastri's *Autobiography*." In *Telling Lives in India: Biography, Autobiography and Life History*, ed. David Arnold and Stuart Blackburn, 83–115. Ranikhet: Permanent Black, 2004.

Khambata, Jahangir Pestanji. *Mahro Nataki Anubhav*. Bombay: Parsi Ltd. Press, 1914.

Khan, Dargah Quli. *Muraqqa-e-Dehli*. Translated and edited by Chandra Shekhar and Shama Mitra Chenoy. Delhi: Deputy, 1989.

Khan, Dominique-Sila. *Crossing the Threshold: Understanding Religious Identities in South Asia*. London: I. B. Tauris, 2004.

Khan, Iqtidar Ali. "The Nobility under Akbar and the Development of His Religious Policy 1560–1580." *Journal of the Royal Asiatic Society* 1 (1968): 29–36.

Khan, Raza Ali. *Hyderabad: A City in History*. Hyderabad: n.p., 1986.

Khan, Sabir. "The Enunciation of Space in Autobiography: Two South Asian Accounts." In 87th ACSA Annual Meeting Proceedings, n.d., 360–67.

Khan, Saiyid Ahmad. *Sir Saiyid ka Safarnama: Musaferan London*. Edited by Asghar Abbas. Aligarh: Educational Book House, 2009.

Kidwai, Saleem, and Ruth Vanita, eds. *Same-Sex Love in India: Readings from Literature and History*. London: Palgrave Macmillan, 2000.

Kinsley, David. *Hindu Goddesses: Visions of the Divine Feminine in the Hindu Religious Tradition*. Berkeley: University of California Press, 1988.

Koch, Ebba. "The Baluster Column: A European Motif in Mughal Architecture and Its Meaning." *Journal of the Warburg and Courtauld Institutes* 45 (1982): 251–62.

Koch, Ebba. *Mughal Architecture: An Outline of Its History and Development (1526–1858)*. Munich: Prestal Verlag, 1991.

Koch, Ebba. *Mughal Art and Imperial Ideology: Collected Essays*. New Delhi: Oxford University Press, 2001.

Kosambi, Meera. *Feminist Vision or "Treason against Men"? Kashibai Kanitkar and the Engendering of Marathi Literature*. Ranikhet: Permanent Black, 2008.

Krynicki, Annie Krieger. *Captive Princess: Zebunissa, Daughter of Emperor Aurangzeb*. Karachi: Oxford University Press, 2005.

Kugle, Scott. "Mah Laqa Bai and Gender: The Language, Poetry and Performance of a Courtesan in Hyderabad." *Comparative Studies of South Asia, Africa and the Middle East* 30.3 (2010): 365–85.

Kugle, Scott. *Sufis and Saints' Bodies: Mysticism, Corporeality, and Sacred Power in Islam*. Delhi: Munshiram Manoharlal, 2009.

Kumar, Krishna. *The Battle for Peace*. Delhi: Penguin, 2007.
Kumar, Radha. *The History of Doing: An Illustrated Account of Movements for Women's Rights and Feminism in India 1800–1990*. New Delhi: Kali for Women, 1993.
Kumar, Raj. *Dalit Personal Narratives: Reading Caste, Nation and Identity*. New Delhi: Orient Blackswan, 2010.
Kumar, Udaya. "Autobiography as a Way of Writing History: Personal Narratives from Kerala and the Inhabitation of Modernity." In *History in the Vernacular*, ed. Raziuddin Aqil and Partha Chatterjee, 418–48. Delhi: Permanent Black, 2008.
Lahawri, 'Abd al-Hamid. *The Badshah Namah*, vol. 1. Edited by Kabir al-Din Ahmad and 'Abd al-Rahim. Calcutta: Bibliotheca Indica, 1867–68.
Lal, Ruby. *Domesticity and Power in the Early Mughal World*. Cambridge: Cambridge University Press, 2005.
Lambert-Hurley, Siobhan. "The Heart of a Gopi: Raihana Tyabji's Bhakti Devotionalism as Self-Representation." *Modern Asian Studies* 48.3 (May 2014): 569–95.
Lambert-Hurley, Siobhan. "Life/History/Archive: Identifying Autobiographical Writing by Muslim Women in South Asia." *Journal of Women's History* 25.2 (summer 2013): 61–84.
Lambert-Hurley, Siobhan. *Muslim Women, Reform and Princely Patronage: Nawab Sultan Jahan Begam of Bhopal*. London: Routledge, 2007.
Lambert-Hurley, Siobhan. "To Write of the Conjugal Act: Intimacy and Sexuality in Muslim Women's Autobiographical Writing in South Asia." *Journal of the History of Sexuality* 23.2 (May 2014): 155–81.
Lambert-Hurley, Siobhan, and Sunil Sharma. *Atiya's Journeys: A Muslim Woman from Colonial Bombay to Edwardian Britain*. Delhi: Oxford University Press, 2010.
Lambton, Ann K. "Persian Biographical Literature." In *Historians of the Middle East*, ed. B. Lewis and P. M. Holt, 54–58. London: Oxford University Press, 1988.
Lambton, Ann K. S. *Theory and Practice in Medieval Persian Government*. London: Variorum, 1980.
Lapidus, Ira M. *A History of Islamic Societies*. 2nd ed. Cambridge: Cambridge University Press, 2002.
Latif, Muhammad. *Agra: Historical and Descriptive*. Calcutta: Oriental Publishers, 1896.
Lawrence, Bruce. "The Sant Movement and North Indian Sufis." In *The Sants: Studies in a Devotional Tradition of India*, ed. Karine Schomer and W. H. McLeod, 359–73. Delhi: Motilal Banarsidass, 1987.
Lejeune, Philippe. *L'autobiographie en France*. Paris: Colin, 1971.
Lejeune, Philippe. *On Autobiography*. Edited and foreword by Paul John Eakin. Translated by Katherine Leary. Minneapolis: University of Minnesota Press, 1989.
Lelyveld, David. *Aligarh's First Generation: Muslim Solidarity in British India*. Princeton, NJ: Princeton University Press, 1978.
Leonard, Karen. "The Hyderabad Political System and Its Participants," *Journal of Asian Studies* 30.3 (May 1971): 569–82.
Lopez Jr., Daniel S., ed. *Religions of India in Practice*. Princeton, NJ: Princeton University Press, 1995.

Losty, J. P., and Malini Roy. *Mughal India, Art, Culture and Empire*. London: British Library, 2012.

Ludtke, Alf, ed. *The History of Everyday Life: Reconstructing Historical Experiences and Ways of Life*. Translated by William Templer. Princeton, NJ: Princeton University Press, 1995.

Lukmani, Yasmin. "The Role Played by the Tyabji Women in the National Movement." In *Women in India's Freedom Struggle*, ed. Nawaz B. Mody, 219–36. Mumbai: Allied, 2000.

Majumder, Indubala. *Ek Aparachita Briddhar Dinlipi*. Calcutta: Ananda, 2000.

Malhotra, Anshu. "Bhakti and the Gendered Self: A Courtesan and a Consort in Mid Nineteenth Century Punjab." *Modern Asian Studies* 46.2 (2012): 1506–39.

Malhotra, Anshu. *Gender, Caste and Religious Identities: Restructuring Class in Colonial Punjab*. Delhi: Oxford University Press, 2002.

Malhotra, Anshu. "The Importance of Being Piro in Punjab." *Tribune* (Chandigarh), December 6, 2012, 11.

Malhotra, Anshu. "Miracles for the Marginal? Gender and Agency in a Nineteenth-Century Autobiographical Fragment." *Journal of Women's History* 25.2 (summer 2013), 15–35.

Malhotra, Anshu. "Telling Her Tale? Unravelling a Life in Conflict in Peero's *Ik Sau Saṭh Kāfiaṅ (One Hundred and Sixty Kafis)*." *Indian Economic and Social History Review* 46.4 (2009): 541–78.

Malik, Fateh Muhammad. "Kar-e Jahan Daraz Hai." In *Qurratulain Hyder: Aik Mutala'ah*, ed. Irtiza Karim, 350–61. Delhi: Educational Publishing House, 1992.

Manz, Beatrice Forbes. "Temür and the Problem of a Conqueror's Legacy." *Journal of the Royal Asiatic Society* 8.1 (April 1998): 21–41.

Martin, John. "Inventing Sincerity, Refashioning Prudence: The Discovery of the Individual in Renaissance Europe." In *The Renaissance in Europe*, ed. Keith Whitlock, 11–30. New Haven, CT: Yale University Press, 2000.

Mastur, Khadija. *Aangan*. Lahore: Simorgh Publications Centre, 2000.

Matringe, Denis. "Krsnaite and Nath Elements in the Poetry of the Eighteenth-Century Panjabi Sufi Bulhe Sah." In *Devotional Literature in South Asia*, ed. R. S. McGregor, 190–206. Cambridge: Cambridge University Press, 1992.

Mayaram, Shail. *Resisting Regimes: Myth, Memory and the Shaping of a Muslim Identity*. New York: Oxford University Press, 1997.

Mehta, Ved. *Mahatma Gandhi and His Apostles*. Harmondsworth, UK: Penguin, 1976.

Menon, Ritu, and Kamala Bhasin. *Borders and Boundaries: Women in India's Partition*. Delhi: Kali for Women, 1998.

Metcalf, B. D. "The Past in the Present: Instruction, Pleasure, and Blessing in Maulana Muhammad Zakariyya's Aap Biitii." In *Telling Lives in India: Biography, Autobiography and Life History*, ed. David Arnold and Stuart Blackburn, 116–43. Delhi: Permanent Black, 2004.

Metcalf, Barbara D. *Perfecting Women: Maulana Ashraf 'Ali Thanawi's Bihishti Zewar*. Berkeley: University of California Press, 1991.

Metcalf, Barbara D. "What Happened in Mecca: Mumtaz Mufti's 'Labbaik.'" In *The Culture of Autobiography: Constructions of Self-Representation*, ed. Robert Folkenflik, 149–67. Stanford CA: Stanford University Press, 1993.

Middlebrook, Diane Wood. "Postmodernism and the Biographer." In *Revealing Lives: Autobiography, Biography, and Gender*, ed. S. G. Bell and M. Yalom, 155–66. Albany: State University of New York Press, 1990.

Milani, Farzaneh. *Veiling and Words: The Emerging Voices of Iranian Women Writers*. Syracuse, NY: Syracuse University Press, 1992.

Milani, Farzaneh. *Words, Not Swords: Iran Women Writers and the Freedom of Movement*. Syracuse, NY: Syracuse University Press, 2011.

Minault, Gail. *Gender, Language and Learning: Essays in Indo-Muslim Cultural History*. Ranikhet: Permanent Black, 2009.

Minault, Gail. "'*Ismat*: Rashid ul-Khairi's Novels and Urdu Literary Journalism for Women." In *Urdu and Muslim South Asia*, ed. Christopher Shackle. London: School of Oriental and African Studies, 1989, 129–38.

Minault, Gail. *Secluded Scholars: Women's Education and Muslim Social Reform in Colonial India*. Delhi: Oxford University Press, 1998.

Minault, Gail. "Urdu Women's Magazines in the Early Twentieth Century." *Manushi* 48 (1988): 2–9.

Minault, Gail. "Women's Magazines in Urdu as Sources for Muslim Social History." *Indian Journal of Gender Studies* 5 (1998): 201–13.

Mir, Farina. *The Social Space of Language in Punjab: Vernacular Culture in British Colonial Punjab*. Ranikhet: Permanent Black, 2010.

Mukhopadhayay, Bhaskar. "Writing Home, Writing Travel: The Poetics and Politics of Dwelling in Bengali Modernity," *Comparative Studies in Society and History* 44.2 (April 2002): 293–318.

Naim, C. M. "How Bibi Ashraf Learned to Read and Write." *Annual of Urdu Studies* 6 (1987): 99–115.

Naim, C. M. "Prize-Winning *Adab*: A Study of Five Urdu Books Written in Response to the Allahabad Government Gazette Notification." In *Moral Conduct and Authority: The Place of* Adab *in South Asian Islam*, ed. B. D. Metcalf, 290–314. Berkeley: University of California Press, 1984.

Naim, C. M. "Transvestic Words? The Rekhti in Urdu," *Annual of Urdu Studies* 16 (2001): 3–26.

Naim, C. M., ed. *Zikr-i-Mir: The Autobiography of the Eighteenth Century Mughal Poet: Mir Muhammad Taqi "Mir."* Delhi: Oxford University Press, 1999.

Najmabadi, Afsaneh. *Women's Autobiographies in Contemporary Iran*. Cambridge, MA: Harvard University Press, 1990.

Nawaz, Mumtaz Shah. *The Heart Divided*. Lahore: ASR Publications, 1990.

Nazli Rafia Sultan Nawab Begam Sahiba. *Sair-i-Yurop*. Lahore: Union Steam Press, n.d.

Nevile, Pran. *Nautch Girls of India: Dancers, Singers, Playmates*. New York: Ravi Kumar, 1996.

Nizami, K. A. "Naqshbandi Influence on Mughal Rulers and Politics," *Islamic Culture* 39 (1965): 41–52.

Nomani, Muhammad Shibli. *Safarnama-e Rome, Misr, Sham.* Lahore: Bisat-e Adab, 1992.
Oberoi, Harjot. *The Construction of Religious Boundaries: Diversity in Sikh Tradition.* Delhi: Oxford University Press, 1994.
Ochs, Elinor, and Lisa Capps. "Narrating the Self." *Annual Review of Anthropology* 25 (1996): 19–43.
Oldenburg, Veena Talwar. "Lifestyle as Resistance: The Case of the Courtesans of Lucknow, India," *Feminist Studies* 16.2 (summer 1990): 259–87.
Olney, James. *Memory and Narrative: The Weave of Life Writing.* Chicago: University of Chicago Press, 1999.
Orr, Leslie. *Donors, Devotees and Daughters of God: Temple Women in Medieval Tamil Nadu.* New York: Oxford University Press, 2000.
Orsini, Francesca. *The Hindi Public Sphere, 1920–40: Language and Literature in the Age of Nationalism.* Delhi: Oxford University Press, 2002.
Panchotia, Bhailal Bulakhidas. *Jayashankar Sundari and Abhinayakala.* Bombay: Bharatiya Vidya Bhavan, 1987.
Pandit, Vijaya Lakshmi. *The Scope of Happiness: A Personal Memoir.* New York: Crown, 1979.
Pascal, Roy. *Design and Truth in Autobiography.* Cambridge, MA: Harvard University Press, 1960.
Patel, Dhanjibhai Nasarvanji. *Parsi Natak Takhtani Tavarikh.* Bombay: Kaiser-I Hind Press, 1931.
Peacock, J. L., and D. C. Holland. "The Narrated Self: Life Stories in Process." *Ethos* 21 (1993): 367–83.
Pemberton, Kelly. "Muslim Women Mystics and Female Spiritual Authority in South Asian Sufism." In *Contesting Rituals: Islam and Practices of Identity-Making*, ed. Pamela J. Stewart and Andrew Strathern, 3–39. Durham, NC: Carolina Academic Press, 2005.
Pernau, Margrit. *The Delhi College, Traditional Elites, the Colonial State and Education before 1837.* New Delhi: Oxford University Press, 2006.
Perti, R. K., ed. *Acquired Documents*, vol. 3, *1356–1790 AD*. Delhi: NAI, 1992.
Peterson, Linda H. "Institutionalizing Women's Autobiography: Nineteenth-Century Editors and the Shaping of an Autobiographical Tradition." In *The Culture of Autobiography: Constructions of Self-Representation*, ed. Robert Folkenflik, 80–103. Stanford, CA: Stanford University Press, 1993.
Petievich, Carla. "Feminine Authorship and Urdu Poetic Tradition." In *A Wilderness of Possibilities: Urdu Studies in Transnational Perspective*, ed. Kathryn Hansen and David Lelyveld, 223–50. Delhi: Oxford University Press, 2005.
Petievich, Carla. *When Men Speak as Women: Vocal Masquerade in Indo-Muslim Poetry.* New Delhi: Oxford University Press, 2007.
Platts, John T. *A Dictionary of Urdu, Classical Hindi, and English.* London: W. H. Allen, 1884.
Pollock, Sheldon. "Ramayana and Political Imagination in India." In *Religious Movements in South Asia 600–1800*, ed. David N. Lorenzen, 153–208. New Delhi: Oxford University Press, 2004.

Poole, Stanley Lane. *The Coins of the Moghul Emperors of Hindustan in the British Museum*. New Delhi: Inter-India Publications, 1983.

Portelli, Alessandro. *The Death of Luigi Trastulli and Other Stories: Form and Meaning in Oral History*. Albany: State University of New York Press, 1991.

Porter, Roy, ed. *Rewriting the Self: Histories from the Renaissance to the Present*. London: Routledge, 1997.

Pritchett, Frances W. "A Long History of Urdu Literary Culture, Part 1: Histories, Performances, and Masters." In *Literary Cultures in History: Reconstructions from South Asia*, ed. Sheldon Pollock, 864–911. Los Angeles: University of California Press, 2003.

Puri, Jyoti. "Reading Romance Novels in Post-colonial India." *Gender and Society* 11.4 (1997): 434–52.

Quinn, Sholeh A. "Through the Looking Glass: Kingly Virtues in Safavid and Mughal Historiography." *Journal of Persianate Studies* 3.2 (2010): 143–55.

Qureshi, Ghulam Sarvar. *Tarikh Makhzane Punjab*. Lahore: Dost Associates, 1996.

Qureshi, Regula Burckhart. "The Indian Sarangi: Sound of Affect, Site of Contest," *Yearbook of Traditional Music* 29 (1997): 1–38.

Radway, Janice. *Reading the Romance: Women, Patriarchy, and Popular Literature*. Chapel Hill: University of North Carolina Press, 1984.

Rafiq, Zakaria. *100 Glorious Years: Indian National Congress, 1885–1985*. Bombay: Reception Committee, Congress Centenary Session, 1985.

Raheja, Gloria, and Ann Gold. *Listen to the Heron's Words: Reimagining Gender and Kinship in North India*. Berkeley: University of California Press, 1994.

Raj, Sheela. *Mediaevalism to Modernism: Socio-economic and Cultural History of Hyderabad, 1869–1911*. Bombay: Popular Prakashan, 1987.

Rak, Julie. *Negotiated Memory: Doukhobor Autobiographical Discourse*. Vancouver: University of British Columbia Press, 2004.

Ramanujan, A. K. "The Ring of Memory: Remembering and Forgetting in Indian Literatures." In *A. K. Ramanujan: Uncollected Poems and Prose*, ed. Molly Daniels-Ramanujan and Keith Harrison, 83–100. New Delhi: Oxford University Press, 2001.

Ramanujan, A. K. "Towards a Counter-system: Women's Tales." In *The Collected Essays of A. K. Ramanujan*, ed. Vinay Dharwadker, 429–47. Delhi: Oxford University Press, 1999.

Ramanujan, A. K. "Where Mirrors Are Windows: Toward an Anthology of Reflections." In *The Collected Essays of A. K. Ramanujan*, ed. Vinay Dharwadker, 6–33. New Delhi: Oxford University Press, 1999.

Ramaswamy, Vijaya. "Muffled Narratives: The Life and Times of Neelambakai Ammaiyar." In *Biography as History: Indian Perspectives*, ed. Vijaya Ramaswamy and Yogesh Sharma, 123–51. Hyderabad: Orient Blackswan, 2009.

Rao, Velcheru N. "A Ramayan of Their Own: Women's Oral Tradition in Telegu." In *Many Ramayanas: The Diversity of a Tradition in South Asia*, ed. Paula Richman, 114–36. Berkeley: University of California Press, 1991.

Rashid-ul Khairi. *Jauhar-i Qadāmat*. Karachi: 'Allamah Rashid-ul Khairi Akaidami, 1971.

Rasul, Begam Qudsia Aizaz. *From Purdah to Parliament*. Delhi: Ajanta Publications, 2001.

Ravikant, and Tarun K. Saint. *Translating Partition*. Delhi: Katha, 2001.
Ray, Bharati. *Daughters: A Story of Five Generations*. New Delhi: Penguin, 2011.
Ray, Bharati, comp. and ed. *Nari O Paribar: Bamabodhini Patrika 1270–1329*. Kolkata: Ananda Publishers, 2002.
Raychaudhuri, Tapan. "Love in a Colonial Climate: Marriage, Sex and Romance in Nineteenth-Century Bengal." *Modern Asian Studies* 34.2 (May 2000): 349–78.
Rege, Sharmila. *Writing Caste/Writing Gender: Narrating Dalit Women's Testimonios*. New Delhi: Zubaan, 2006.
Rehman, Samina. "Birjees: The Daastan Go." In *Locating the Self*, ed. N. S. Khan et al., 179–90. Lahore: ASR Publications, 1994.
Reynolds, Dwight F., ed. *Interpreting the Self: Autobiography in the Arabic Literary Tradition*. Berkeley: University of California Press, 2001.
Richards, J. F., ed. *Kingship and Authority in South Asia*. Delhi: Oxford University Press, 1988.
Richards, John F. *The Mughal Empire*. Cambridge: Cambridge University Press, 1993.
Rizvi, Kishwar. "Gendered Patronage: Women and Benevolence during the Early Safavid Empire." In *Women, Patronage, and Self-Representation in Islamic Societies*, ed. D. Fairchild Ruggles, 123–76. Albany: State University of New York Press, 2000.
Rizvi, S. A. A. "Sixteenth Century Naqshbandiyya Leadership in India." In *Naqshbandis: Historical Development and Present Situation of a Muslim Mystical Order*, ed. Marc Gaborieau, Alexandre Popovic, and Thierry Zarcone, 153–65. Istanbul: Institut Francais d'Etudes Anatoliennes d'Istanbul, 1990.
Rizvi, Shafqat, ed. *Urdu Ka Classiki Adab Diwan Mah Laqa Bai Chanda*. Lahore: Majlis Taraqqi-e-Adab, 1990.
Robinson, Francis. *Islam and Muslim History in South Asia*. Delhi: Oxford University Press, 2000.
Rose, H. A. *A Glossary of the Tribes and Castes of the Punjab and the North-West Frontier Province*. 1911. Patiala: Languages Department Punjab, 1970.
Rowbotham, Sheila. *Woman's Consciousness, Man's World*. London: Penguin, 1973.
Roy, Manisha. *Bengali Women*. Chicago: University of Chicago Press, 1972.
Ruggles, D. Fairchild, ed. *Women, Patronage, and Self-Representation in Islamic Societies*. Albany: State University of New York Press, 2000.
Russell, Ralph. *The Pursuit of Urdu Literature*. London: Zed, 1992.
Ruswa, Mirza Muhammad Hadi. *Umrao Jan Ada*. Translated by David Matthews. Delhi: Rupa, 1996.
Sachdeva, Shweta. "In Search of the Tawa'if in History: Courtesans, *Nautch Girls* and Celebrity Entertainers in India (1720s–1920s)." PhD diss., SOAS, 2008.
Sahgal, Nayantara. *From Fear Set Free*. New York, W. W. Norton, 1962.
Sahgal, Nayantara. *Prison and Chocolate Cake*. Delhi: HarperCollins, 2007.
Sahgal, Nayantara, and E. N. Mangat Rai. *Relationship: Extracts from a Correspondence*. Delhi: HarperCollins, 2008.
Saksena, S. P. *Indian Autobiographies*. Calcutta: Oxford University Press, 1949.
Sangari, Kumkum. "Mirabai and the Spiritual Economy of Bhakti." *Economic and Political Weekly*, July 7, 1990, 1464–75.

Sangari, Kumkum, and Sudesh Vaid, eds. *Recasting Women: Essays in Colonial History*. New Delhi: Kali for Women, 1989.

Sangster, Joan. "Telling Our Stories: Feminist Debates and the Use of Oral History." In *The Oral History Reader*, ed. Robert Perks and Alistair Thomson, 85–100. London: Routledge, 1998.

Sarkar, Sumit. "Kaliyuga, Chakri and Bhakti: Ramakrishna and His Times." *Economic and Political Weekly* 27.29 (July 1992): 1543–66.

Sarkar, Sumit. *Writing Social History*. Delhi: Oxford University Press, 1997.

Sarkar, Tanika. "A Book of Her Own. A Life of Her Own: Autobiography of a Nineteenth-Century Woman." In *From Myths to Markets: Essays on Gender*, ed. Kumkum Sangari and Uma Chakravarti, 85–124. New Delhi: Manohar, 2001.

Sarkar, Tanika. *Hindu Wife, Hindu Nation: Community, Religion and Cultural Nationalism*. Delhi: Permanent Black, 2005.

Sarkar, Tanika. *Words to Win: The Making of* Amar Jiban; *A Modern Autobiography*. Delhi: Kali for Women, 1999.

Saunders, L. S. *Report on Revised Land Revenue Settlement of the Lahore District 1865–69*. Lahore: Central Jail Press, 1873.

Schimmel, Anne-Marie. *The Empire of the Great Mughals: History, Art and Culture*. Translated by C. Attwood. New Delhi: Oxford University Press, 2005.

Schofield, Katherine Butler. "The Courtesan Tale: Female Musicians and Dancers in Mughal Historical Chronicles, c.1556–1748." *Gender and History* 24.1 (April 2012): 150–71.

Scott, Joan W. "Experience." In *Women, Autobiography, Theory: A Reader*, ed. Sidonie Smith and Julia Watson, 57–71. Madison: University of Wisconsin Press, 1998.

Seizer, Susan. *Stigmas of the Tamil Stage*. Durham, NC: Duke University Press, 2005.

Sen, Haimabati. *"Because I Am a Woman": A Child Widow's Memoirs from Colonial India*. Translated by Tapan Raychaudhari. Edited by Geraldine Forbes and Tapan Raychaudhari. Introduction by Geraldine Forbes. New Delhi: Chronicle Books, 2011.

Sen, Indrani. "Resisting Patriarchy: Complexities and Conflicts in the Memoir of Haimabati Sen." *Economic and Political Weekly* 47.12 (March 24, 2012): 55–62.

Sen, Nabaneeta D. "Chandravati Ramayana: Feminising the Rama Tale." In *Faces of the Feminine in Ancient, Medieval, and Modern India*, ed. Mandakranta Bose, 183–91. Delhi: Oxford University Press, 2000.

Sewak, G. I. "Gulab Dasi Sampradaye: Rachna Ate Vichar," PhD diss., Guru Nanak Dev University, 1984.

Shaharyar, "Kalaam Mata Piro Ka," *Hun* (January–April 2009).

Shahnawaz, Jahan Ara. *Father and Daughter: A Political Autobiography*. Karachi: Oxford University Press, 2002.

Sharar, Abdul Halim. *Lucknow: The Last Phase of an Oriental Culture*. Translated and edited by E. S. Harcourt and Fakhir Hussain. Boulder, CO: Westview, 1975.

Sharma, Kumud, and C. P. Sujaya, eds. *Towards Equality: Report of the Committee on the Status of Women in India*. Delhi: Ministry of Education and Social Welfare, 1974.

Sharma, Sunil. "Celebrating Writing and Books in Safavid and Mughal Court Poetry." In *Écrit et culture en Asie centrale et dans le monde turco-iranien*, XIVe–XIXe siècles, ed. Francis Richard and Maria Szuppe. Paris: Association pour l'Avancement des Etudes Iraniennes, 2008.

Sharma, Sunil. "Delight and Disgust: Gendered Encounters in the Travelogues of the Fyzee Sisters." In *On the Wonders of Land and Sea: Persianate Travel Writing*, ed. Roberta Micallef and Sunil Sharma, 114–31. Boston: Ilex Foundation, 2013.

Shulman, David. "Cowherd or King? The Sanskrit Biography of Ananda Ranga Pillai." In *Telling Lives in India: Biography, Autobiography and Life History*, ed. David Arnold and Stuart Blackburn, 175–202. Delhi: Permanent Black, 2004.

Sibghatullah, Muhammad. *Riyāz-un Niswān: Misāil-i Fiqh Shāfa'i*. Hyderabad: Matbu'a Ibrahīmiya Mashīn Parais, 1937–38.

Sikand, Yoginder. *Shared Spaces: Exploring Traditions of Shared Faith in India*. Delhi: Penguin, 2003.

Singh, Ganesha. *Bharat Mat Darpan*. Amritsar: Vaidak Bhandar, 1926.

Singh, Giani Amar Singh. *Jiwan Chariter Singh Sabha Lehar de Ughe Sanchalak Giani Ditt Singh Ji*. Amritsar: Gulab Singh Malak Firm, 1962.

Singh, Giani Gian. *Sri Guru Panth Prakash*. Patiala: Bhasha Vibhag, 1970.

Singh, Namwar, ed. *Bulleh Shah ki Kafian*. Delhi: National Institute of Punjab Studies, 2003.

Sivaraman, Mythily. *Fragments of a Life: A Family Archive*. New Delhi: Zubaan, 2006.

Smith, Sidonie. "Performativity, Autobiographical Practice, Resistance." In *Women, Autobiography, Theory: A Reader*, ed. Sidonie Smith and Julia Watson, 108–15. Madison: University of Wisconsin Press, 1998.

Smith, Sidonie. *Subjectivity, Identity, and the Body: Women's Autobiographical Practices in the Twentieth Century*. Bloomington: Indiana University Press, 1993.

Smith, Sidonie, and Julia Watson. "Introduction: Situating Subjectivity in Women's Autobiographical Practices." In *Women, Autobiography, Theory: A Reader*, ed. Sidonie Smith and Julia Watson, 3–52. Madison: University of Wisconsin Press, 1998.

Smith, Sidonie, and Julia Watson. *Reading Autobiography: A Guide for Interpreting Life Narratives*. 1st ed. Minneapolis: University of Minnesota Press, 2001.

Smith, Sidonie, and Julia Watson. *Reading Autobiography: A Guide for Interpreting Life Narratives*. 2nd ed. Minneapolis: University of Minnesota Press, 2010.

Snell, Rupert. "Raskhān the Neophyte: Hindu Perspectives on a Muslim Vaishnava." In *Urdu and Muslim South Asia: Studies in Honour of Ralph Russell*, ed. Christopher Shackle, 29–37. Delhi: Oxford University Press, 1991.

Snitow, Ann, and Rachel Blau Du Plessis. *The Feminist Memoir Project: Voices from Women's Liberation*. New York: Three Rivers Press, 1998.

Spivak, Gayatri. "Subaltern Studies: Deconstructing Historiography." In *Subaltern Studies: Writings on South Asian History and Society IV*, ed. Ranajit Guha, 330–63. Delhi: Oxford University Press, 1985.

Sreenivasan, Ramya. "Drudges, Dancing-Girls, Concubines: Female Slaves in Rajput Polity, 1500–1850." In *Slavery and South Asian History*, ed. Indrani Chatterjee and Richard Eaton, 136–61. Bloomington: Indiana University Press, 2006.

Stewart, P., and A. Strathern, eds. *Contesting Rituals: Islam and Practices of Identity-Making*. Durham, NC: Carolina Academic Press, 2005.

Stien, Karen F., "Monsters and Madwomen: Changing Female Gothic." In *The Female Gothic*, ed. Julian E. Fleenor, 123–37. Montreal: Eden, 1983.

Streusand, D. E. *The Formation of the Mughal Empire*. Delhi: Oxford University Press, 1989.

Suhrawardy, Shaista Akhtar Banu. *A Critical Survey of the Development of the Urdu Novel and Short Story*. London: Longmans, Green, 1945.

Sultaan, Abida. *Memoirs of a Rebel Princess*. Karachi: Oxford University Press, 2004.

Sundari, Jayshankar. *Thodan Ansu: Thodan Phul: Jayshankar "Sundari" ni Atmakatha*. 1st ed., compiled by Dinkar Bhojak and Somabhai Patel. Ahmedabad: Gandhi Sombarsa, 1978. 2nd ed., compiled by Somabhai Patel and dinkar Bhojak. Unjha: Asait Sahitya Sabha, 1989.

Tagore, Rabindranath. "Khata." *Galpaguchha*. Calcutta: Viswabharati Granthalay, 1957.

Talbot, Cynthia. "Inscribing the Other, Inscribing the Self: Hindu-Muslim Identities in Pre-Colonial India." *Comparative Studies in Society and History* 37.4 (1995): 692–721.

Thackston, Wheeler. "The Poetry of Abú-Tálib Kalim: Persian Poet-Laureate of Shahjahan, Mughal Emperor of India." PhD diss., Harvard University, 1974.

Thackston, Wheeler M., trans., ed., and annotator. *The Baburnama: Memoirs of Babur, Prince and Emperor*. New York: Modern Library, 2002.

Thakkar, Usha, and Jayshree Mehta, eds. *Understanding Gandhi: Gandhians in Conversation with Fred J. Blum*. Delhi: Sage, 2011.

Tharu, Susie, and K. Lalita, eds. *Women Writing in India: 600 B.C. to the Present*. Vol. 1. Delhi: Oxford University Press, 1991.

Thornton, Edward. *A Gazetteer of the Territories under the Government of the East India Company and the Native States of the Continent of India*. Vol. 4. London: W. H. Allen, 1954.

Thys-Senocak, Lucienne. *Ottoman Women Builders: The Architectural Patronage of Hadice Turhan Sultan*. Burlington, VT: Ashgate, 2006.

Trivedi, Madhu. "Female Performing Artistes in North India: A Survey." In *Art and Culture: Painting and Perspective*, ed. Ahsan Jan Qaisar and Som Prakash Verma, 153–64. Delhi: Abhinav, 2002.

Tucker, Judith. "Biography as History: The Exemplary Life of Khayr al-Din-al Ramli." In *Auto/Biography and the Construction of Identity and Community in the Middle East*, ed. Mary Ann Fay, 9–17. New York: Palgrave, 2001.

Tyabji, Badruddin. *Memoirs of an Egoist*. 2 vols. New Delhi: Roli Books, 1988.

Tyabji, Raihana. *L'Ame d'une Gopi*. Translated by Lizelle Reymond. Frameries, Belgium: Union des Imprimeries, 1935.

Tyabji, Raihana. *Das Herz einer Gopi*. Darmstadt: Synergia/Syntropia, 1977.

Tyabji, Raihana. *Het hart van een Gopi*. Rotterdam: Synthese Uitgeverij, 1995.

Tyabji, Raihana. *The Heart of a Gopi*. Bombay: Vora, 1941.

Tyabji, Raihana. *The Heart of a Gopi*. Delhi: East West Publication, 1971.

Tyabji, Raihana. *The Heart of a Gopi*. Poona: Miss R. Tyabji, n.d.

Vahab, Vir, ed. *Piro Kahe Saheliyon*. Jalandhar: R. B. Printing, 2012.
Vaidik, Aparna. *Imperial Andamans: Colonial Encounter and Island History*. New York: Palgrave Macmillan, 2010.
Van der Veer, Peter. *Gods on Earth: The Management of Religious Experience and Identity in a North Indian Pilgrimage Centre*. Delhi: Oxford University Press, 1989.
Vatuk, Sylvia. "The Cultural Construction of Shared Identity: A South Indian Muslim Family History." In "Person, Myth and Society in South Asian Islam," ed. P. Werbner, special issue of *Social Analysis* 28 (1990): 114–31.
Vatuk, Sylvia. "Dr. Zakira Ghouse: A Memoir." In *Muslim Portraits: Everyday Lives in India*, ed. Mukulika Banerjee, 109–27. New Delhi: Yoda Press, 2008.
Vatuk, Sylvia. "Family Biographies as Sources for an Historical Anthropology of Muslim Women's Lives in Nineteenth-Century South India." In *The Resources of History: Tradition, Narration and Nation in South Asia*, ed. J. Assayag, 153–72. Paris: École Française d'Extrême Orient, 1999.
Vatuk, Sylvia. "*Hamara Daur-i Hayat*: An Indian Muslim Woman Writes Her Life." In *Telling Lives in India: Biography, Autobiography and Life History*, ed. David Arnold and Stuart Blackburn, 144–74. Delhi: Permanent Black, 2004.
Vatuk, Sylvia. "Household Form and Formation: Variability and Social Change among South Indian Muslims." In *Society from the Inside Out: Anthropological Perspectives on the South Asian Household*, ed. J. N. Gray and D. J. Mearns, 107–39. New Delhi: Sage, 1989.
Vatuk, Sylvia. "Identity and Difference or Equality and Inequality in South Asian Muslim Society." In *Caste Today*, ed. C. Fuller, 227–62. New Delhi: Oxford University Press, 1996.
Vatuk, Sylvia. "Older Women, Past and Present, in an Indian Muslim Family." In *Thinking Social Science in India: Essays in Honour of Alice Thorner*, ed. S. Patel, J. Bagchi, and K. Raj, 247–63. New Delhi: Sage, 2002.
Vatuk, Sylvia. "Schooling for What? The Cultural and Social Context of Women's Education in a South Indian Muslim Family." In *Women, Education and Family Structure in India*, ed. C. C. Mukhopadhyay and S. Seymour, 135–64. Boulder, CO: Westview, 1994.
Vaudeville, Charlotte, ed. *A Weaver Named Kabir: Selected Verses with a Detailed Biographical and Historical Introduction*. 1993. Delhi: Oxford University Press, 2005.
Venkatachalapathy, A. R. "Making a Modern Self in Colonial Tamil Nadu." In *Biography as History: Indian Perspectives*, ed. Vijaya Ramaswamy and Yogesh Sharma. Hyderabad: Orient Blackswan, 2009.
Viramma, Josiane Racine, and Jean-Luc Racine. *Viramma: Life of an Untouchable*. London: Verso, 1997.
Walida-i Afzal Ali [Akbari Begam]. *Gūdar kā La'l*. Lucknow: Nasim Book Depot, 1967.
Walsh, Judith. *Domesticity in Colonial India: What Women Learnt When Men Gave Them Advice*. Lanham, MD: Rowman and Littlefield, 2004.
Walsh, Judith E. *Growing Up in British India: Indian Autobiographers on Childhood and Education under the Raj*. New York: Holmes and Meier, 1983.

Wierling, Dorothee. "The History of Everyday Life and Gender Relations: On Historical and Historiographical Relationships." In *The History of Everyday Life: Reconstructing Historical Experiences and Ways of Life*, ed. Alf Ludtke, trans. William Templer, 149–68. Princeton, NJ: Princeton University Press, 1995.

Williamson, Captain Thomas. *The East India Vade-Mecum or Complete Guide to Gentlemen Intended for the Civil, Military, or Naval Service of the Hon. East India Company*, 2 vols. London: Black, Parry and Kingsbury, 1810.

Wright, Theodore, Jr. "Muslim Kinship and Modernization: The Tyabji Clan of Bombay." In *Family, Kinship and Marriage among Muslims in India*, ed. Imtiaz Ahmad, 217–38. Delhi: Manohar, 1976.

Zaman, Taymiya R. "Inscribing Empire: Sovereignty and Subjectivity in Mughal Memoirs." PhD diss., University of Michigan, 2007.

Zonis, Marvin. "Autobiography and Biography in the Middle East: A Plea for Psychopolitical Studies." In *Middle Eastern Lives: The Practices of Biography and Self-Narrative*, ed. Martin Kramer, 60–88. Syracuse, NY: Syracuse University Press, 1991.

CONTRIBUTORS

ASIYA ALAM is an assistant professor in the Department of History, Louisiana State University. In 2013–14, she was a postdoctoral scholar at Yale University. Her research focuses on discourses of marriage and family among Urdu-speaking Muslims in colonial India.

AFSHAN BOKHARI has taught art history, women and gender studies, and Islamic studies at Suffolk University, Dartmouth College, and Wellesley College. In 2014–15, she was a fellow at the Institute of Sacred Music and Arts at Yale University. She has published several articles in collections of essays and international journals, including *Marg*, *Journal of Persianate Studies*, and the Routledge Sufi Series. She is the author of *Imperial Women in Mughal India: The Piety and Patronage of Jahanara Begum* (2015).

UMA CHAKRAVARTI is a feminist historian who taught at Miranda House, Delhi University. She is now an independent scholar who lives and works in Delhi. She has written on ancient India, the nineteenth century, and contemporary India on various themes. Her lifelong interest in history has inspired her to undertake filmmaking; her two films—*A Quiet Little Entry* (2010) and *Fragments of a Past* (2012)—deal with questions of history and memory.

KATHRYN HANSEN is professor emerita at the University of Texas at Austin, where she served as director of the Center for Asian Studies and interim director of the South Asia Institute. Her interests include gender and performance, folklore and orality, and early cinema. She is the author of *Grounds for Play: The Nautanki Theatre of North India* (1991), winner of the A. K. Coomaraswamy Book Prize. She coedited with David Lelyveld *A Wilderness of Possibilities: Urdu Studies in Transnational Perspective* (2005) and translated and edited *The Parsi Theatre: Its Origins and Development* (2005). Her most recent book is *Stages of Life: Indian Theatre Autobiographies* (2011).

SIOBHAN LAMBERT-HURLEY is a reader in international history at the University of Sheffield. Her research focuses on women, gender, and Islam in South Asia. She recently led an Arts and Humanities Research Council research network, Women's Autobiography in Islamic Societies (http://www.waiis.org), and, with Marilyn Booth, created the website Accessing Muslim Lives (http://www.accessingmuslimlives.org). Her publications include *Muslim Women, Reform and Princely Patronage: Nawab Sultan Jahan Begam of Bhopal* (2007); *Rhetoric and Reality: Gender and the Colonial Experience in South Asia* (coedited with Avril A. Powell) (2006); and *Atiya's Journeys: A Muslim Woman from Colonial Bombay to Edwardian Britain* (with Sunil Sharma) (2010). She is currently completing a book manuscript, tentatively entitled "The Ultimate Unveiling: Gender, Autobiography and the Self in Muslim South Asia."

SHWETA SACHDEVA JHA teaches English at Miranda House, University of Delhi. Her research has been published in journals and books. Currently she is working on a book manuscript on courtesans and tawa'if performers.

ANSHU MALHOTRA is an associate professor in the Department of History, University of Delhi. Her research focuses on the cultural and gendered histories of Punjab. She is the author of *Gender, Caste and Religious Identities: Restructuring Class in Colonial Punjab* (2002) and has coedited (with Farina Mir) *Punjab Reconsidered: History, Culture and Practice* (2012). She has published widely in international journals and in collections of essays. She is currently coediting (with Tyler Williams and J. S. Hawley) a volume on texts and traditions in early modern India. She is also completing a manuscript tentatively titled "Self, Sect and Society: Religion, Caste and Gender in Punjab from the Nineteenth Century."

RITU MENON is a publisher and writer who cofounded Kali for Women, India's first and oldest feminist press, in 1984. In conjunction with her work on women and the nation, she has written extensively on women and religion; women and violence; women in situations of armed conflict; and the gendering of citizenship. She is the author and editor of numerous books, including *Borders and Boundaries: Women in India's Partition* (with Kamla Bhasin) (1998); *Unequal Citizens: A Study of Muslim Women in India* (with Zoya Hasan) (2004); *From Mathura to Manorama: Resisting Violence against Women in India* (with Kalpana Kannabiran) (2007); and *Making a Difference: Memoirs from the Women's Movement in India* (2011). Her most recent book is *Out of Line: A Literary and Political Biography of Nayantara Sahgal* (2014).

SHUBHRA RAY researches in the areas of autobiographical studies, gender studies, and the nineteenth-century history of Bengal. She teaches in the Department of English in Zakir Husain Delhi College (Evening), University of Delhi. She also translates from Bengali, for which she won the Katha Award for Translation in 2005.

SYLVIA VATUK is professor emerita of anthropology at the University of Illinois at Chicago. For many years she has been conducting ethnographic field research in India, focusing on kinship, marriage, and family systems among both Hindus and Muslims, with particular emphasis on issues of women and gender. She is the author of *Kinship and Urbanization: White Collar Migrants in North India* (1973), and numerous articles in academic journals and edited volumes. For the past decade she has been exploring legal anthropological questions around Muslim family law as it is applied in India and its implications for women.

INDEX

Aangan (Khadija Mastur), 121–22, 126–27, 129, 132, 134–35
Abdullah, Begam Sheikh, 83
Abla Nind, 211
Aboobacker, Sara, 102
Abu'l Fazl, 178–79, 181, 182
activism, 82–84
Agra mosque, 187–89, 196; inscriptions on, 189
Agraval, Pratibha, 259, 261, 270
Ahmad, Nazir, 39
Akbar, 174, 176, 178–79, 181–82; divine kingship, 174, 179. See also *Akbarnama*
Akbari, Begam, 81, 84
Akbarnama, 176, 178–79, 181
Alaler Gharer Dulal, 96
Alam, Nawab Mir, 146, 150–51
Ali, Birjees Dawar, 128
Ali, Fazl Mir, 81
Ali, Hameed, 239
Ali, Hazrat, 152, 156
Ali, Imtiaz, 73–74

Ali, Jabir, 233
Ali, Syed Mumtaz, 83
Ali, Tyab (Tyabji Bhoymeeah), 232, 241, 245
Ali, Walida Afzal, 39
Aligarh movement, 72
All Passion Spent, 127–28
Alu ka Bharta (Chughtai), 44
Amader Katha (Profullamoyi Debi), 99
Ameena, Begam, 232–33, 241
Amis, Kingsley, 63
Ammaiyar, Neelambakai, 10
Anjuman Hami-e Talim-e Niswan, 82–83
Anjuman-i-Islam, 239
Ardhakathanaka, 8
Arif, Kishan Singh, 212
Arnold, David, 5, 8, 246
Ashraf-un-Nissa, 232
ashurkhanas, 156–57
atmacharit, or *Jibancharit*. See auto/biographies
Aurangzeb, Emperor, 168, 195; contestations of, 182; military achievements of, 183

autobiographers, 22, 36, 69, 100–102, 277
autobiographical: acts, 15, 57, 157; articulations, 141–42; narratives, 11, 18, 22, 165, 196; practice, 1, 4, 14–16, 19, 21–22, 246; writings, 12, 35, 99, 238
auto/biographies, 2–11, 99–100, 167–68, 181, 196, 270–71, 274; Aboobacker and, 102; in Bengali, 99; Betab on, 276; of Dalit women, 9; de Man on, 7, 14, 22, 143, 157; feminist reading of, 57; as genre, 10; history of, 2–7; identity of, 7; Joan Scott on, 88; as literary genre, 141; and marginalization, 10; Metcalf on, 12, 246; and Muslims, 240; of performers, 256–57, 259–60, 262; and Radheshyam on, 276; as self-representation, 231, 247; Walsh on, 47; and women, 56, 144; by women, 9, 69, 277; on women, 257
Autobiography of Those Who Do Not Write, The (Philippe Lejeune), 261
Ayyam-e Guzashta [Past days], 74
Azmi, Rahat, 158

Babur, 4, 167, 168, 174, 176
Baburnama, 165, 168, 176
Babu Roshan Lal Company, 275
Badakshi, Shah (pir Mullah), 165, 167, 169, 173, 178, 189–93, 196
Badran, Margot, 13
Bahadur, Mir Alam, 151, 232–33
Bahadur, Sabit Jang, 151
Bai, Burj Kanwar, 148
Bai, Haseen Laqa, 146
Bai, Mehtab Kanwar, 148
Bai, Polan Kanwar, 148
Bai, Raj Kanwar, 148
Bakhle, Janaki, 146
Baksh, Ilahi, 217
Banarsidas, 8
Baqr, Mustafa, 80
Baqr, Nazr-ul, 81, 84
Basu, Rajnarayan (*Atmacharit*), 99
Beg, Tawakkul, 181
Begam, Muhammadi, 39
Begamāt-ke Ānsū [The ladies' tears] (Hasan Nizami), 42
Bengali theaters, 258, 275
bhadramahila, 104

Bhakti, 237–40; devotionalism of, 6, 232, 241, 246; movement, 206, 218, 231, 235, 240; poetry, 207
Bhattacharya, Rimli, 100
Bhave, Vinoba: Bhoodan movement of, 63
Bhojak, Dinkar, 259
Bibi, Nur, 148
Bibi, Polan, 148
Biharilal, Govind, 62
Blackburn, Stuart, 5, 8, 13, 246
Bohras, 238–39, 247
Bokhari, 15
British East India Company, 145–46, 151–52, 159
Brown, Louise, 222
Brownstein, Rachel M., 49–50
Buck, Pearl, 62
Burke, Peter, 16
Burton, Antoinette, 87
Butler, Judith, 21, 262

Carpenter, Mary, 96
caste injunctions, 106–7
Chakravarti, Ishita, 99
Chand, Kishori, 95–96
Chand, Peary (Tek Chand Thakur), 96–97
Chandralekha, 60–61
Chatterjee, Partha, 19–20, 98–99, 107
Chaudhurani, Saratkumari, 110
child marriage, 44
Chishtiyah order, 174, 176, 183. *See also* Khwaja Moinuddin Chishti shrine
Chughtai, Azim Beg, 44; *Anguṭhī* [The ring], 44, 98
collective voice, 9–10
colonialism, 19–20, 77, 240
Compton-Burnett, Ivy, 63
concubines, 133, 147–49, 158; Mida Bibi as, 148
Confessions of St. Augustine, 2, 18
conversion narrative, 16, 220
Conway, Jill Ker, 3
courtesans, 2, 6, 22, 142, 145–47, 149–50, 156, 158–59, 206, 208, 210
Courtier, The (Baldassare Castiglione), 19
courtiers, 19, 145–46, 149, 151, 156, 158–59
Cronin, A. J., 63
Crusoe, Robinson, 97

Dalani, Begam, 176
Dale, Stephen, 4
Das, Krishnabhamini, 106; *Swadhin O Paradhin Nari Jiban*, 110
Dasi, Binodini, 100, 258; *Abhinetrir Atmakatha*, 258
De, Sushil Kumar, 100
de Avitabile, Paolo, 217
Deb, Chitra: *Antahpurer Atmakatha*, 99
Debi, Ashapurna, 101
Debi, Bamasundari, 109
Debi, Kailashbashini, 6, 20, 95–97, 100–103, 105–8, 110–11; *Atmakatha*, 100; diary, 20, 97–102; serializing diary, 100
Debi, Nistarini, 99, 108
Debi, Prasannamayi, 19; *Adha Adha Bhashini*, 98
Debi, Radharani, 104; *Amar Jiban*, 98
Debi, Rassundari, 19; *Amar Jiban*, 99
Debi, Sarada Sundari, *Atmakatha*, 100
de Certeau, Michel, 262
de Man, Paul, 7, 14, 22, 143, 157
Derozio, Henry Louis Vivian, 96
Dihlawi, Shah Waliullah, 246
Ditta Ram, Sant, 211
Dulles, John Foster, 64
du Maurier, Daphne, 63

Faruqi, Shamsur Rahman, 155
Faruqui, Munis, 187
femininity, 13, 48–49, 152, 267
Fifty Years in the Parsi Theatre (Pratibha Agraval), 259
freedom movement, 57, 62
Fyzee, Atiya, 85, 244

Gandhi, Mohandas Karamchand, 3, 19, 59, 61, 233–38, 243, 245, 247; on Islam, 239; and Raihana, 236; to Sarojini, 235
Gauhar, Ghulam Samdani: *Hayat-i-Mah Laqa*, 157–58
gender, 7–13, 14–18, 132–35; segregation as, 79–80
Ghalib, 155
ghazals, 27, 85, 142, 144, 152–55, 214, 238; as autobiographical, 154
Ghazipur, 86, 88
Ghaziu'd-Din (Delhi College) khanaqahs, 193

Gita Govinda (Anandaghan), 264
gopi tradition, 232, 240–45
Gordimer, Nadine, 63
Grihabadhur, Janaika, 5, 100, 102–11
Gūdar kā La'l, 43, 45
Gulabdas, 6, 205–6, 208–14, 216–17, 220, 225; admitting a prostitute, 210; the Nirmalas, 210
Gulabdasis, 205–6, 208–13, 216, 225
Gupta, Kailashbashini, 98; *Hindu Mahilaganer Heenabastha*, 109
Guzashta Barson ki Baraf (Nazr S. Hyder), 18, 77, 90

Habib, Muhammad, 239
Haidar, Nazr-i Sajjad, 39
Hansen, Kathryn, 7–8, 12, 14, 17, 21, 48
Harrison, George, 230
Hasan, Sadiq, 41
Hayat-i-Mah Laqa, 157
Heart Divided, The, 121–22, 124, 129–30
Heart of a Gopi, The, 16, 230–32, 237, 243–47
Heilbrun, Carolyn G., 56, 69
Hindu Mahilaganer Heenabastha [The woeful plight of Hindu women] (Kailashbashini Gupta), 98
Hindustani Prachar Sabha, 235
Hir, 218, 226–27
history writing, 168
Hossain, Attia, 87; *Sunlight on a Broken Column*, 137
Husain, Fida, 7, 17, 21, 255–62, 270–78; *Fifty Years*, 277; New Alfred Theatrical Company, 271; oral history, 262
Husain, Syed Karamat, 83
Hussain, Ghulam "Jauhar," 157
Hussain, Khwajah, 147
Hussain, Shah, 214, 226
Hyder, Mustafa, 80–81
Hyder, Nazr Sajjad, 5, 18, 72, 74, 86–87; campaigns for social reform, 82; death of her brother, 80; death of her children, 80–82; death of her mother, 79; diary and memoir of, 72, 74, 77–78, 84, 90; family gatherings of, 75, 84, 87, 89–90; *Ismat*, 75, 77, 84; letters, 73–78; and Muslim Ladies Conference, 89; and Muslim

Hyder, Nazr Sajjad (*continued*)
  university in Aligarh, 83; and *qaumi* school, 83; self-narration, 78–82, 89–90; at Syed Karamat Husain Girls School, 83
Hyder, Qurratulain, 18, 72, 74, 77, 90
Hyder, Syed Jawad, 80

Ikramullah, Shaista Suhrawardy, 89
imperial idioms, 167, 169, 188–89, 193
Indar Sabha, 276
Indian Autobiographies (S. P. Saksena), 4
Iqbal, Muhammad, 244
Ismat, 72–78, 81, 84

Jah, Aristu, 146, 149–53
Jah, Asaf, II (Nizam Ali Khan), 145–46, 148, 157–58
Jah, Asaf, III, 158
Jah, Nizam Sikandar Asaf, 151
Jah, Nizam ul-Mulk Asaf, 145
Jahan, Sultan Begam, 83
Jahanara, Begam, 6, 15, 22, 165–69, 173, 176, 178–85, 187–90, 193–97
Jahangir, 167
Jami Masjid, 188
Jayasinghe, Peter, 59
Jelinek, Estelle C., 47, 49
Jugal Jugari (Mulshankar Mulani), 266

Kabir, 224–25, 227
Kaishek, Chiang, 61
Kalelkar, D. B., 235
Kalim, Abu Talib, 193
Kanchan Kachehri, 146
Kanitkar, Kashibai, 20
Karlekar, Malavika, 97
Kathavachak, Radheshyam, 259; *Parivartan*, 272
Khairi, Rashid-ul, 39; *Jauhar-i Qadāmat*, 44
Khairi, Raziq-ul, 75, 77
khalifas, 174, 178–79, 185
Khambata, Jahangir, 258
Khan, Ali Muhammad, 83
Khan, Bahadur "Turki," 148
Khan, Dominique-Sila, 231, 238
Khan, Ilahi, 217
Khan, Inayat, 187
Khan, Muhammad Yar, 148

Khan, Sayyid Ahmed, 72
Khan Ba-Iman, Muhammad, 150
Khwaja Moinuddin Chishti shrine, 176
kingship, 145, 167–68, 173, 179, 182, 184, 196; Akbar's semidivine concept, 178; Shah Jahan's vision, 176
Kirkpatrick, James Achilles, 151
Koch, Ebba, 174
Krishna, 17, 230–32, 238, 240, 242–46, 275
Krishnamurthi, J., 63
Kugle, Scott, 150, 152, 154, 155
Kulinism, 108–9
Kumar, Udaya, 102

L'autobiographie en France (Philippe Lejeune), 3
Lakshmi, Vijaya, 57, 61
Lal, Raja Chandu, 146, 151
Lambert-Hurley, Siobhan, 7, 16, 22
Laqa Bai, Mah "Chanda," 6, 15, 22, 141, 143–59; *ghazals*, 154; life history, 142; as *naubat*, 156; patronage at Khat Mela, 156; as tawa'if, 141, 158; *Urdu Ka Classiki Adab Diwan Mah Laqa Bai Chanda*, 158; in Urdu print culture, 143
Laxman, R. K., 59
Lejeune, Philippe, 3, 22, 261, 270
life narrative, 4, 14, 78, 102, 256, 260–61; theatrical, 258
life stories, 5, 11, 237, 240, 258, 261; Barbara Metcalf on, 12; Parsi theater and, 259
life writing, 2, 7, 4–5, 13–14, 23, 75, 89–90, 98, 138, 232, 240, 242
Lodi, Sultan Sikander, 224
Luce, Henry, 62

Mahal, Mumtaz, 165
Mahmuda Begam, 46
Majumdar, Janaki, 87
Malcolm, John, 151
Mangat Rai, E. N., 64, 68–69
Mansur-al-Hallaj, 224
Mehrunissa, 215
Mehta, Narsi, 17, 262, 275
memoirs, 34–35
memories, 13–18, 34–35; public archive of, 138
Metcalf, Barbara D., 12–13, 237, 246

Milani, Farzaneh, 13, 22
Mir, Mian, 176–77, 217
Mirāt-ul Urūs [The bride's mirror] (Nazir Ahmad), 43
Mitford, Mary, 69
Mitra, Kishori Chand, 95
Mitra, Peary Chand, 96
Moraes, Frank, 59
Mrinalini (Bankimchandra Chatterjee), 97
Mufti, Mumtaz, 237, 246
mullahs, 214–15, 217–18, 221, 223–26, 231
Mumbai Gujarati Natak Mandali, 265
Munis al-arvah (Jahanara), 165, 196
Muslim Hudugi Shale Kalithaddu (Aboobacker), 102
Mustafai Begam, 73, 79

Na Junoon Raha (Zaheda Hina), 121, 127, 129, 135–36
Naidu, Sarojini, 61, 124
Naim, C. M., 8, 155
Nanavati, Sarojini (Saroj), 235
Narayan, R. K., 59
nationalism, 20, 258
Nawaz, Mumtaz Shah (Tazi), 121–22, 124, 130
Nayak, Bapulal, 263, 265, 269
Neelambakai Ammaiyar, 10
Nehru, B. K., 58
Nehru, Indira, 62
Nehru, Jawaharlal, 57–58, 60–61, 63, 65–67
Neumeyer, Sarah, 62
New Alfred Theatrical Company, 270–72
Nirmalas, 209–10, 213, 225
Nizam al-Din Awliya, 194
Norman, Dorothy, 62
Nur Jahan, 167

obituary biography, 10
Ogra, Sohrabji, 271
Oldenburg, Veena Talwar, 148

Pandit, Ranjit Sitaram, 57, 61
Pandit, Vijay Lakshmi, 57, 61
Panth Prakash (Giani Gian Singh), 205
Parivartan, 272
Parsi Theatre, 17, 256, 258–60, 267, 270, 272, 274–76, 277, 278
Partition, 75, 122, 135–37

Pascal, Roy, 3
Patel, Dhanjibhai, 258
Patel, Somabhai, 259
patronage, 15, 142, 144, 155–59, 188–89; of artists, 145, 156; of Asaf Jah II, 148; of courtesans, 146; of history writing, 166; to Husain, 275; of Islamic organizations, 239; of Jahanara, 176; of *Khat Mela*, 156; under Safavids, 193; to Shi'a religious gatherings, 160n5; of *tawa'if*, 150
performance, 13–18, 21–22, 190, 262
performers, 14–15, 22–23, 141–42, 145–49, 156, 258, 260, 264, 277; autobiographies of, 256
personal narratives, 2, 5, 18, 102
Petievich, Carla, 214, 226
Phoenix Fled (Attia Hossain), 137
Piro, 6, 17, 205–27; on daughters, 221–22; evoking Bhakti tradition, 224; *Ik Sau Sath Kafian*, 205; *kanjari*, 210, 217; Malhotra on, 160, 241; as Sita, 218–23
Pitrismriti (Saudamini Debi), 99
poetry: of Bulleh Shah, 225; of Bhakti, 207; during Shah Jahan's reign, 193. *See also* Urdu poetry
polygamy, 44–46, 108
Premanand (*Nalakhyan*), 265
Prison and Chocolate Cake, 20, 57–58, 60–64, 67–68, 70
Pritchett, Frances, 150
prostitutes, 6, 143, 205, 208, 210–11, 218–19, 222
prostitution, 141, 206, 208, 210, 213, 222
Puratoni (Gnadanondini Debi), 99
Purbakatha (Prasannamoyi Debi), 99
purdah, 79–80, 82, 104, 125, 129, 133

Qadiriyah order, 167, 176, 178, 200n30
Qandhari, *Tarik-i Akbari*, 189
Quinn, Sholeh, 179

Radway, Janice, 49–50
Ramakrishna, 19
Ramanujan, A. K., 17, 207
Ramayana, 208, 217–20, 241
Rambha Sahib, Raja Rao, 146
Ranjha, 226; *qissa*, 218
Rao, Maharaja Sayaji, III, 233
Rashid-ul Khairi, 39, 44

Rashsundari: Tanika Sarkar on autobiography of, 277; Vaishnava Bhakti for, 20
Raskhan, 231
Rasul, Begam Aizaz, 89
Rau, Santha Rama, 59
Raushnak Begam [Lady Raushnak] (Mahmuda Begam), 46
Ray, Bharati, 6, 11, 20
Raychaudhuri, Tapan, 109
Red Fort, 130, 189
Rege, Sharmila, 9
religious: conflict, 223–27; identity, 223, 225, 237, 240, 255, 257, 277
remarriages, 69, 98
Reynolds, Dwight F., 3–4
Rich Like Us (Nayantara Sahgal), 57
Risalah-i Sahibiyah (Jahanara), 6, 165, 167, 169, 173, 176, 178–79, 181–85, 196, 197
Rizvi, Shafqat, 158
Robeson, Paul, 62
Robinson, Francis, 240
Rousseau, Jean-Jacques: *Confessions*, 2–4
Rowbotham, Sheila, 48
Roy, Manisha, 51
Ruggles, D. Fairchild, 144
Ruswa, Mirza Muhammad Hadi, 147, 158

Sabavala, Jehangir, 59
Sabavala, Shireen, 59
Sa'di, Mulla Muhammad, 178
Safavids, 182, 193
Safia Ali, 233
Sahgal, Gautam, 58–59, 63, 65–66, 69
Sahgal, Gita, 63
Sahgal, Nayantara (Tara Pandit), 5, 20, 21, 57–70; *From Fear Set Free*, 20, 57, 62–64, 66–68, 70; *Prison and Chocolate Cake*, 20, 57–58, 60–64, 67–68, 70
Sahgal, Nonika, 63
Sahgal, Ranjit, 60–61, 63
Saghal, Rita, 61
Saksena, S. P., 3
Salim, Shaikh, 174
Sarkar, Tanika, 20, 98, 277
Sarvat Ara, 80–82, 84–87
Saubhagya Sundari, 264
Sayers, Dorothy, 63

Schofield, Katherine Butler, 142
Seizer, Susan, 277
self: actor's self, 256, 262; adult self, 5, 241; authorial self, 122, 133, 138, 197; coherent self, 17, 21; constructing of, 9, 260–62; fabricating selves, 22; feminine self, 6, 123, 226, 266; gendered self, 12, 14, 269; imperial self, 166; inner self, 19–20, 230, 247; narrative self, 122, 196; performative self, 17–23, 260–61; self-abnegation, 10, 43; self-absorption, 213, 241, 267; self-articulation, 141, 144; self-censorship, 69; self-control, 272–74; self-effacing, 13, 47, 89; self-expression, 67, 75, 95–96, 159; self-fashioning, 1–2, 6, 23, 73, 142–43, 149–50, 155, 157–58, 207, 222, 231; selfhood, 8, 48, 101–2, 223, 260, 269; self-narration, 73, 77; self-referential narratives, 16; self-representation, 2, 4, 6–13, 22, 144, 156–57, 237–38, 242, 246–47; self-revelation, 14–15
Sen, Keshab Chandra, 100
Sen, Krishna Bihari, 100
Sen, Nabaneeta Dev, 101–2; *The Wind Beneath My Wings*, 104
sexuality, 14, 17, 89, 272
Shaarawi, Huda, 13
Shah, Bulleh, 214, 225–26, 231
Shah, Mullah, 176, 178–79, 181–82, 184–85, 187, 190, 193
Shah Jahan, 147, 165–66, 168, 173, 176, 178–79, 181–82, 184, 187–90, 193, 195–97
Shah Jahan, Nawab Begam, 244
Shah Jahanama, 187
Shahnawaz, Jahan Ara, 89
Shah "Zafar," Bahadur, 155, 238
Sharar, Abdul Halim, 39
Shastri, Shibnath, 99; *Atmacharit*, 99
Shikdar, Radha Nath, 96
Shikoh, Dara, 167, 169, 176, 178, 181–83, 185, 187, 196–97
Shulman, David, 16
Singh, Chatar, 215–17, 219
Singh, Ganesha, 209–10, 213, 217, 222, 225
Singh, Gian, 209–10, 213, 225
Singh, Gulab, 215–16, 219
Singh, Kala, 217
Singh, Mehtab, 148–49

Singh, Ranjit, 217
Singh, Salim, 148
Singhania, Kamlapat, 275
Singhania, Padmapat, 275
Singh Sabha movement, 211–12
Situation in New Delhi, A (Nayantara Sahgal), 57
Smith, Sidonie, 14, 21, 36, 260, 262
Smritikatha (Somendranath Basu), 100
Snell, Rupert, 231
Some Blossoms, Some Tears (Jayshankar Sundari), 259, 270
Sorabji, Cornelia, 87
Sreenivasan, Ramya, 147
Storm in Chandigarh (Nayantara Sahgal), 57
Story of My Experiments with Truth, The (Mohandas K. Gandhi), 3
subjectivities, 166
Sufism, 166, 169, 173, 238, 240; and Mughal relationship, 168, 173; Qadiriyah order, 167, 178; sacral-sexual encounter in, 183–87; sovereign affiliation, 173–78; *tariqahs*, 183
Sundari, Jayshankar, 7, 14, 21, 255–56, 261–72, 278; marriage and, 270; proposals, 268; *Some Blossoms, Some Tears*, 259
Sunni conventions of Islam, 195
Swadeshi movement, 59

Tagore, Debendranath: autobiography of, 99
Tagore, Jyotirindranath, 98
Tagore, Rabindranath: *Khata*, 101
Tahzib-e Niswan, 18, 72–79, 82–84, 90
Tahzib un-Niswan wa Tarbiyat ul-Insan (Nawab Shah Jahan Begam), 244
Taj Mahal, 187, 194
Taqi, Mir Muhammad: *Zikr-i-Mir*, 8
Tarikh-i Akbari (Aref Qandahari), 179
tawa'ifs, 6, 141–43, 145–52, 157–59; as *apsaras* or *devadasis*, 141; as courtesan, 156; in Hyderabad, 146; as *nautch* girls, 150; origin of, 142; performing poetic compositions, 150
Thanthaniya Natak Mandali, 265
Thapar, Raj, 59
Thapar, Romesh, 59

theatrical memoirs, 257–60
Thelly, Tata, 59
Thunthi, Dadabhai, 267
Time to Be Happy, A (Nayantara Sahgal), 57, 64
Timur, Amir, 168, 173, 176, 179
Tucker, Judith, 10
Turaks, 205–6, 209, 214–15, 218, 223
Tyabji, Abbas, 137, 232–33, 235, 239, 241, 243
Tyabji, Ameena, 243
Tyabji, Badruddin, 232
Tyabji, Raihana, 16–17, 22, 230–32, 234–39, 241–47; and Bhakti tradition, 238, 240; devotionalism as self-representation, 247; as disciple of Gandhi, 243; and Gandhi, 233–35; in Gandhi's ashram, 243; personhood of, 232; self-representation of, 244; at Sevagram, 235
Tyabji, Salima, 245
Tyabji, Shamsuddin, 232
Tyabjis, 232, 236, 238–39, 241, 244

Udasis, 209–10, 213, 225
Urdu poetry, 6, 141, 149–50, 155; *rekhta*, 152, 155. *See also* poetry
Urdu women's magazines, 72–73
Urner, Catherine, 230

Villon, François, 77
violence, 11, 75, 122–23, 138

Wagle, Premi, 59
Watson, J., 4, 9, 13, 267, 269
Weinstock, Herbert, 62–63
widowhood, 107, 111
Wilson, Colin, 63
women: agency, 13; autobiography, 9; as companionate wife, 109; and education, 72, 82–84, 86, 95–96, 98, 101, 109; education, among Muslims, 77 (*see also* Anjuman Hami-e Talim-e Niswan); history of, 2, 5, 12, 123; narratives of, 9; performers, 142, 146–47, 158; religious identity of, 225; rights of, 44, 85, 235; as *satitva*, 111; subjectivity of, 101; voices of, 11–12, 226, 241; writing, 9, 98, 122–23

Woolf, Virginia, 56
Wright, Theodore, Jr., 239

Yildirum, Sajjad Hyder, 74, 79–81, 83, 85–87

Zaheda, Hina: *Na Junoon Raha*, 121, 122, 127–29, 138

Zakira, Begam (Zakira Amat-ul Wahid), 5, 15, 33–51, 52n1; extended family, 35, 37; memoir, 35–37; reading books, 39; to study medicine, 42
Zayn al-Din, Sayyid, 195
zenana system, 96
Zonis, Marvin, 4

www.ingramcontent.com/pod-product-compliance
Lightning Source LLC
Chambersburg PA
CBHW051049230426
43666CB00012B/2616